D1241115

Hysterical Men

A volume in the series
CORNELL STUDIES IN THE HISTORY OF PSYCHIATRY
 edited by
Sander L. Gilman
George J. Makari

A full list of titles in the series appears at the end of the book.

Hysterical Men

*War, Psychiatry, and the Politics
of Trauma in Germany, 1890–1930*

Paul Lerner

CORNELL UNIVERSITY PRESS | *Ithaca & London*

First published 2003 by Cornell University Press

Printed in the United States of America

Library of Congress Cataloging-in-Publication Data

Lerner, Paul Frederick.
  Hysterical men : war, psychiatry, and the politics of trauma in Germany, 1890–1930 / Paul Lerner.
      p. cm. — (Cornell studies in the history of psychiatry)
Includes bibliographical references and index.
  ISBN 0-8014-4094-7 (alk. paper)
  1. War neuroses—Social aspects—Germany. 2. Hysteria—Social aspects—Germany. 3. Psychic trauma—Social aspects—Germany.
4. Psychiatry—Germany—History—20th century. 5. Psychiatry—Germany—History—19th century. 6. World War, 1914–1918—Medical care—Germany. 7. Military psychiatry—Germany—History—20th century. I. Title. II. Series.
  RC550.L44 2003
  616.85'212'00943—dc21

2003001169

Cornell University Press strives to use environmentally responsible suppliers and materials to the fullest extent possible in the publishing of its books. Such materials include vegetable-based, low-VOC inks and acid-free papers that are recycled, totally chlorine-free, or partly composed of nonwood fibers. For further information, visit our website at www.cornellpress.cornell.edu.

Cloth printing 10 9 8 7 6 5 4 3 2 1

To the memory of Clara Band Rosen and Baruch (Benny) Lerner

■

But what is hysteria for once and for all? . . . A woman in an unhappy marriage, who after an unpleasant scene, develops paralysis in the leg so that she must lie in bed and can no longer stand or walk. Or a soldier, who, mentally not up to the demands of war service, begins to shake and develop tics. These things we call hysteria.

ERNST KRETSCHMER, "Hysterie"

Nobody dies—it's all made up. Otherwise, we'd all get hysterical.

MEL BROOKS

Contents

Acknowledgments

ONE OF THE many rewards of finishing this book is the chance finally to thank the numerous individuals and institutions whose help made it possible. This project began at Columbia University, and I remain deeply indebted to István Deák for his wisdom, guidance, and humanity. Atina Grossmann also provided invaluable criticism and advice, and she continues to be a cherished colleague and friend. Most of the research was supported by grants from the German Academic Exchange Service (DAAD), Columbia University, the National Endowment for the Humanities, and the Historial de la Grande Guerre. The Wellcome Trust, the James H. Zumberge fund at the University of Southern California, and the BMW Center for German and European Studies at Georgetown University provided crucial financial assistance as I wrote, revised, and reworked the manuscript. I also wish to thank the college deans at USC for providing a generous subvention for the book's publication.

Bill Bynum kindly sponsored my stay as a fellow at the Wellcome Institute for the History of Medicine in London, where I was able to participate in a unique community of historians of medicine and psychiatry. Roy Porter, whose recent, tragic death remains unfathomable, continually inspired me with his brilliance, his energy, and his humor. At that stage, a number of colleagues, including Geoffrey Cocks, Stephen Jacyna, Mark Micale, Katharina Rowold, Andrew Scull, and Elaine Showalter read and commented on early drafts of the book.

I also thank many valued friends and colleagues for years of inspiring conversations on such subjects as trauma, the history of medicine, and German history. These include, in Germany: Gerhard Baader, Michael Hubenstorf, Ragnhild Münch, Thomas Schlich, Wolfgang Schäffner, Heinz-Peter Schmiedebach, and Bernd Ulrich; in Britain: Peter Barham, Natsu Hattori, Molly Sutphen, and Cornelie Usborne; and in this country: Dorothe Brantz, Eric Caplan, Deborah Cohen, Brigid Doherty, Greg Eghigian, Mark Micale, Uta Poiger, Bernhard Rieger, Marc Roudebush, and Julia Sneeringer. Mitchell Ash, Jane Caplan, Alon Confino, Peter Fritzsche, Michael Geyer, Tony Kaes, the late George Mosse, and Jay Winter offered important comments and suggestions at various points and refined my thinking on issues related to the book.

I would also like to acknowledge the assistance of a number of librarians and archivists. Frau Bauer at the archive of the University of Tübingen was enormously helpful, and I thank Dr. Michael Wischnath for granting permission to reproduce many of the images in the book. I am also quite indebted to Ilona Kalb, assistant archivist at the Humboldt University in Berlin. The Knorr Family generously allowed me to work with the Ernst Kretschmer papers in Marburg, and I am grateful to archivists and staff members at a number of other institutions, including the Kriegsarchiv of the Bayerisches Hauptstaatsarchiv in Munich and the National Library of Medicine in Bethesda, Maryland. Rolf Winau and Johanna Bleker provided me with an institutional home at the Institute for the History of Medicine at the Free University in Berlin, and Albrecht Hirschmüller was exceedingly helpful during my stay in Tübingen.

I am also very grateful to Sam Barnes and Greg Flynn for bringing me to the BMW Center at Georgetown University, where I wrote most of the manuscript. Roger Chickering was a particularly gracious host at Georgetown, and Christoph Mauch always made me welcome at the German Historical Institute. Marion Deshmukh included me in the Mid-Atlantic German History Seminar, where I received a great deal of helpful criticism. I also wish to thank Andreas Daum, Jan Lambertz, Amy Leonard, Judd Stitziel, and Richard Wetzell for being such great and generous colleagues during my stay in Washington. Marcia Klotz, Jan Lambertz, Susan McCabe, Kathy Pence, Vanessa Schwartz, Andrew Scull, and Andrew Zimmerman kindly read and critiqued chapters or the entire manuscript as it neared completion.

Working with Cornell University Press has been a great pleasure; my editor, Catherine Rice, handled the manuscript with enthusiasm, efficiency, and skill, and Melissa Oravec and Karen Hwa have also been extremely helpful. I am also most grateful to the series editors, George Makari and Sander Gilman, both of whom have been long-time supporters of this project and my career as a whole, and I thank the two anonymous readers for providing many useful comments. I would also like to thank John Bradshaw for doing the index and helping with proofreading, and Karen Lang and Suzanne Royal for helping me find the cover art. Many thanks also to Claudine Dixon of the Grunwald Center at UCLA's Hammer Museum for all of her assistance.

My colleagues in the history department at USC, especially Elinor Accampo, Marjorie Becker, Charlotte Furth, Jason Glenn, Kyung Moon Hwang, María Elena Martínez, Vanessa Schwartz, Terry Seip, and Carole Shammas, have provided a supportive and stimulating atmosphere, and around USC I have a number of exceptional colleagues—including Amy Binder, Carla Kaplan, Andrea Frisch, Tara McPherson, Viet Nguyen, Kirill Postoutenko and Phiroze Vasunia—and many fabulous students. In general, southern California has been an excellent place to work, due in large part to the other German historians in the area and our ongoing workshops. In particular I would like to thank Frank Biess, Sharon Gillerman, Ann Goldberg, David Luft, and Ulrike Strasser for participating in the workshops and for being simultaneously exacting critics and amiable colleagues. Jane McNamara, Victoria Mendoza, Margaret Rubin, Dan Sherman, Moshe Sluhovsky, and Tamara Zwick have helped transform Los Angeles from a daunting tangle of freeways and stripmalls into an intellectual and emotional home.

I feel very fortunate to have an extraordinary group of friends who have provided many years of camaraderie, support, and stimulation: above all, I would like to thank Maria Benjamin Baader, Amy Binder, Penelope Falk, David Feige, Jason Glenn, Dan Krasnoff, Jordan Orlando, Kathy Pence, Ben Veghte, and Patrick Young. I am also grateful to my family, especially my parents, Jack and Carol Lerner, and my brother, Dan Lerner, for their patience and support. Most of all, I thank Sarah Cohen for the joy, beauty, and intelligence that she has brought to my life.

I dedicate this book to the memory of my grandmother, Clara Band Rosen, and my grandfather, Baruch (Benny) Lerner—may they rest in peace. Both spent their adult lives in Washington, and for me the city is filled with traces of their history. As I was finishing this book, working just blocks from the site of my grandmother's market in Georgetown, I was awash in memories of her and of my frequent childhood and adolescent visits to her and to my grandfather. It was, I believe, their foreignness, their rootedness in the ways of the old world, that first aroused my interest in the European past. Perhaps this book can serve as a small token of appreciation for the hardships they endured for the sake of their descendants.

PAUL LERNER

Los Angeles, California

Hysterical Men

Introduction

AS THE CELEBRATIONS greeting the outbreak of World War I faded and the German army's rapid westward advance ground to a halt, its soldiers began suffering from debilitating shakes, stutters, tics and tremors, and dramatic disorders of sight, hearing, and gait. Although sporadic breakdowns had been known to occur in prior wars, the epidemic appearance of these hysteria-like symptoms caught medical authorities completely unprepared and shattered prevailing assumptions. Hysteria, of course, was generally considered to be a female problem, one more likely to afflict more volatile peoples such as the French; its widespread appearance in German men, military men no less, was unprecedented. And yet their numbers continued to increase. The ranks of the so-called war neurotics soon crowded Germany's reserve hospitals, threatening military medicine's morale, resources, and competence.

But before long doctors mobilized. They rejoined the diagnostic debates of decades past and eventually concluded, with near unanimity, that these bizarrely debilitating disorders were in fact hysteria, that they were based not in the body but in the mind, and that they had less to do with "trauma"—emotionally or physically jarring shock events—than with the fears and stresses of the constitutionally feeble. Soon psychiatrists asserted that the possibility of escaping service and the desire for a pension, and not the material impact of industrial warfare, were to blame for these symptoms. Thereafter, old methods of treatment such as hypnosis, electric current, isolation, and suggestion—once banished by established scientific medicine—were readopted and began making hysterical symptoms disappear with stunning speed and success. Even Sigmund Freud's psychoanalysis, which had been relegated to Germany's social and medical margins, showed its utility to the war effort and made strides toward winning the favor of psychiatric professionals, lay intellectuals, and ultimately officials from the Ministry of War.

These therapeutic breakthroughs, in turn, led to a "war against hysteria," a systematic campaign designed to stop the spread of hysterical symptoms and, significantly, to spare the state vast sums in potential pension payments. Soon research psychiatrists, who had shown little interest in studying or treating neurosis before the war, found themselves presiding over extensive networks of special war hysteria stations that systematically stripped soldiers of their symptoms and sent them to work in factories or on farms. Indeed, parallel to its profound effects on German politics, society, and culture, World War I, with its tens of thousands of psychiatric casualties, revolutionized German mental medicine.

But why was hysteria, with its feminine associations and its enduring stigma, the diagnosis favored for Germany's shell-shocked soldiers? The answer can be found in the social and medical history of Imperial Germany, where economic concerns overlapped with scientific changes. Male hysteria, this book argues, emerged out of a set of developments unique to late-nineteenth-century Germany, as new directions in psychiatric diagnosis intersected with Bismarck's social insurance legislation of the 1880s in the context of the nation's brisk and violent path to modernity.

During debates over psychological trauma in the late nineteenth century, hysteria was diagnosed with increasing frequency for (male) survivors of railroad and factory accidents. Unlike traumatic neurosis, a diagnosis formulated specifically for this type of patient, hysteria attributed nervous and mental symptoms not to an external traumatic event but to the patient's pathological mind. As such, it reflected the psychiatric profession's growing concern with psychopathologies, with describing behavioral abnormalities and defects of character, and with establishing hierarchies of human value. Simultaneously, hysteria ruled out disability compensation for posttraumatic pathologies. The diagnosis, thus, found fervent support in antiwelfare crusaders who condemned the nation's "work-shy" working class, and it resonated in Imperial Germany's socially divisive political climate. Consequently, hysteria began to take on other, class-based associations alongside its traditional gender dimensions, and by the beginning of World War I, a cultural space for male hysteria had been well established.

Thus, in a process that had already begun in the 1890s, male hysteria gave doctors a diagnosis for pathologizing working-class Germans, and it was within this framework that they understood the nervous and psychological casualties of World War I. In peacetime and war, then, male hysteria bespoke the economic and military failings of German masculinity. Perhaps the most striking thing about modern male hysteria is its ever-present political and economic dimensions. In psychiatric discourse, hysterics sought pensions rather than working, broke down rather than serving, and joined the revolutionary cause rather than peacefully returning to their prewar occupations. This book, therefore, traces male hysteria back to the factories and railroads of rapidly industrializing central Europe in the late nineteenth century and tells the story of the disorder and its diagnosis, treatment, administration, and representation, through war, revolution, and republic.

A Psychiatric Special Path?

The history of psychiatry—like so much else in modern German history—has been dominated by the backward shadows cast by the Third Reich. And for good reason. Doctors, as recent studies have abundantly shown, were among Hitler's earliest and most devoted supporters, and their crimes against the mentally ill and disabled rank among the most unspeakable acts of modern history.[1] The transformation of healers into killers poses pressing questions that historians and ethicists will continue to grapple with for some time. Indeed, it would be naïve, even callous, to write of early-twentieth-century developments in German psychiatry without a view toward the 1930s and 1940s, and the connections and continuities between the turn to eugenics in the imperial period and the racially conceived biopolitics of the Nazi state are as palpable as they are tragic.[2]

Nevertheless, psychiatric history, like German social and political history of decades past, has been excessively influenced by an assumed *Sonderweg*, a "special path" from the *Kaiserreich* to the Third Reich resulting from Germany's allegedly flawed modernization, and this assumption obscures many of the historical record's nuances and complexities.[3] Like the more general *Sonderweg*, the psychiatric special path extends from Bismarck to Hitler; it focuses on the failure of the medical profession to break free of the strong state and pursue the more appropriate, liberal agendas of a democratizing middle class.[4]

World War I occupies a prominent place in this trajectory. In fact, the desire to locate the roots of "Nazi psychiatry" informs most historical work on German mental medicine in the war.[5] As a result, psychiatry's role in World War I has often appeared as the prehistory to the sterilization and "euthanasia" programs of the Third Reich; the tens of thousands of starvation deaths in German asylums during the British naval blockade are frequently figured as a rehearsal for *Aktion* T4 (the murder of the mentally ill and disabled) and ultimately genocide.[6] The consequential picture emphasizes the brutality of wartime practice, the zealous collaboration of doctors with the imperial state's expansionist and militarist goals, the ethical dilemmas faced by medicine in war, and the devaluation of individual life amid the war's unprecedented destruction.

While these works have yielded many useful insights and deserve credit for opening up new historical topics and questions, they suffer from a number of historical and historiographical limitations. By treating the German case in isolation, these authors imply that German psychiatry was uniquely brutal in its suppression of war neurosis, an assumption not borne out by comparison with psychiatrists from other belligerent nations.[7] Indeed, French and Italian doctors used essentially the same treatments, often with even greater brusqueness, which is consistent with the more punitive disciplinary practices of their respective armies and which reflects the deep social and regional schisms that colored doctor-patient relationships in those countries.[8] The British case presents a similar picture. The coercive methods Lewis Yealland used in London's Queen's Square hospital rival anything done in Germany or Austria-Hungary for brutality.[9]

The special path approach also assumes that psychiatrists forced shell-shocked soldiers back into combat and that psychiatric treatment functioned as little more than a crude instrument of military complicity with the state. This claim, however, misses the crucial fact that surprisingly few psychiatric cases were returned to the field after treatment. Once treated, the overwhelming majority of these patients were rehabilitated into the war economy. As soon as they were able to work, most were placed in industrial or agricultural jobs, a policy that was overdetermined by economic necessity and psychiatric theory and that frustrates attempts to mount categorical ethical critiques of German military medicine. Rather than simply serving the war-making state, psychiatrists used the challenges of war to pursue their own scientific agendas and to increase their own professional prestige. In short, instead of condemning the militarization of medicine, a more profitable approach might emphasize the medicalization of the military; that is, the ways in which medical professionals benefited from their relationships with the Prussian army and managed to achieve a greater role in the lives of individuals—combatants and civilians alike.

Thus, while there are certainly important medical continuities between the two world wars and wartime treatments were often shockingly brutal, the prevailing emphasis has come at the expense of a deeper historicization of World War I–era psychiatry into its multiple early-twentieth-century contexts. In this book I argue that psychiatry in World War I had less to do with the murderous initiatives of the next generation than with the economic discourses of its own time.[10] My analysis, therefore, posits a different chain of continuity, one that extends from the trauma debates of the later imperial period through the welfare programs of the Weimar years.[11] Its time frame, thus, extends from 1890 through 1930, covering the years typically associated with the advent of modernity, understood here as the rapid material changes that swiftly altered the European economic and demographic landscape, the attendant social and administrative transformations, and the discourses that reflected, embodied, and furthered these changes.

Rationalization

Max Weber's vision of modernity, in which bureaucratic structures and rational science were stripping the world of mystery, resonates powerfully throughout this study. For Weber the passage from "traditional" social systems to "rational" society meant increasing standardization and homogenization, the encroachment of bureaucratic administration into intimate spheres of life, and the establishment of the scientific expert as a source of authority.[12] While these modes of social organization were ideal types, this passage, nevertheless, described tendencies that Weber both bemoaned and understood as unavoidable in the world around him. It also provides a useful framework for the evolution of German science and medicine in the late nineteenth and early twentieth centuries, the period described by historian Detlev Peukert as "classical modernity."[13]

In these years, Peukert writes, scientific experts turned their attention to solving Germany's collective social and medical problems.[14] Emboldened by medical success at isolating disease pathogens, scientific and academic disciplines embraced a new "social-scientific discourse," a kind of utopian planning that they brought to bear on the so-called social question of the late nineteenth century. One outcome of this impulse was the classification of human beings according to their "value" and the prioritizing of the needs of the national community over the rights of the individual, tendencies that eventually slid down the slippery slope from zealous medical utopianism to state-sponsored Nazi racism.

With these observations, Peukert refuted depictions of National Socialism as the culmination of Germany's historical aberrations from modernity and recast Nazism as one possible outcome of modernity's many trajectories. His important insights facilitate keeping in mind psychiatry's repressive tendencies and inhumane outcomes while also viewing it within the modernizing and rationalizing dynamics of the imperial and Weimar years. Indeed, rationalization turns out to be the key to understanding wartime psychiatry. As several historians have shown, rationalization not only dominated German economic thinking—both in World War I and after the Weimar Republic's economic stabilization—but it also became a cultural craze, encompassing everything from industrial production to chorus girl lines to sexual hygiene.[15]

Rationalization also provided a model for psychiatric care and administration during the war, as psychiatrists came to mediate between the realms of industrial destruction and mechanized production. Psychiatric techniques sought to impose order on and objectify the inherently subjective experience of shock and stress. And German medical officials, one historian has argued, approached the war as a giant industrial accident.[16] Even the modern male hysteria diagnosis can be traced back to the experience of factory "accident neuroses" in the 1880s and 1890s.

By 1917 psychiatrists oversaw the construction of networks of special nerve hospitals, which were fed by large observation centers and which, in turn, led directly into industrial or agricultural work. The concerns of speed and efficiency dominated discussions of wartime therapy, and work—industrial work in particular—was increasingly integrated into the core of the therapeutic process; the workplace replaced the hospital as the site of psychic and nervous healing. The therapeutic act and pre- and posttreatment procedures became progressively standardized and centralized, and rationalizing psychiatry came to serve the needs of rationalizing industry, handling patients as resources to be efficiently allocated and exploited. The resulting "worker-patient," the treated, "symptom-free" war hysteric who lived in the hospital and worked in a nearby factory, fulfilled the goals of rationalizing psychiatry. Rather than prefiguring the murderous medicine of the Nazi period or highlighting German aberrations from modernity, rationalized psychiatry set the stage for psychiatric reform in

the Weimar period.[17] German psychiatry was at the forefront of modernization; its role in the war points to the intertwining of health and productivity
characteristic of the modern era, and the dilemmas it faced heralded the central
role of medicine in the modern, industrialized welfare state.[18]

Hysteria, Gender, and Power

But psychiatric rationalization never eradicated hysteria. Indeed, the disease
has remained ever elusive—for the psychiatrists of a century ago and for today's historians.[19] Hysteria's centrality to the Freudian project and more generally to the medical treatment and social position of women has ensured it
continued historical scrutiny and cultural attention. Its changing manifestations
over its multimillennial history raise fundamental questions: Is the malady that
was recorded in Egyptian papyri from 1900 B.C. the same as the condition that
aroused such heated medical attention around A.D. 1900? Is hysteria one timeless disorder or a term used in different ways by successive cultures? Why has
it broken out in epidemic form in certain periods and among particular populations, such as women during the last turn of the century, only to wane afterward? Is it truly an illness or rather an expression of discontent with social or
political conditions? And why has it disappeared?

This book responds to hysteria's methodological challenges by embedding it
in the economic, military, and political contexts of Imperial and Weimar Germany. Rather than judging its validity by today's diagnostic standards—or retrospectively diagnosing past suffering—it treats the disorder as both real and
constructed, as a set of authentic responses to trying circumstances, whose
physical expression was shaped by individual experience, medical expectations,
and indeed German insurance practices.[20] As such, this analysis is deeply indebted to the work of historian Roy Porter, who portrays hysteria as a mind-
body disorder that has revealed itself in historically changing configurations
and has continually belied the materialism and mind-body dualism of western
medical thought.[21]

The men who are the subject of this study therefore can rightfully be called
"hysterical" in terms of their period's diagnostic standards. From the medical
side, the diagnosis was made possible as psychiatrists began to redefine mental
illness in the late nineteenth century, and hysteria was transformed from a distinct illness into a (pathological) mode of reacting to stimuli—in this case the
fear of war or work and the possibility of a pension. The male hysteria diagnosis, then, represented a convergence of changes in psychiatric approaches to
disease, social transformations, and German economic interests.

As a diagnostic choice, hysteria had other advantages. By locating the source
of the pathology within the patient's mind, it implied that these men could be
corrected through psychological interventions, that their debilitating symptoms
could be suggested away. This prospect resonated in a profession whose status

had been challenged by years of therapeutic pessimism, and many psychiatrists viewed the war as an opportunity to prove their field's utility to the national community. Although baffled by the war neuroses for months, by the middle of the war certain psychiatrists and neurologists could point to incredible therapeutic successes by resurrecting old, abandoned treatments. These successes led to the construction of a set of institutions and facilities over which psychiatrists had complete control. Treating war neurotics, thus, gave a generation of doctors the opportunity to leave the laboratory and cast their authority and professional expertise over issues that lay in a gray area between the legal, military, and medical spheres. After the war, psychiatrists continued to exercise this authority, pushing for increased intervention in daily life and participating in the biologically based politics of the Weimar years.[22]

What is often overlooked in accounts of shell shock is that the interests of doctors frequently coincided with those of their patients. Increased psychiatric power and control saved thousands of men—including those suspected of malingering—from both severe military punishment and the dangers of the front, a fact that is obscured by the excessive emphasis on medical brutality and state complicity. Medicalization, an inexorable intertwining of healing and medical control, proves to be a more useful way of conceiving of the power psychiatrists exercised over their (hysterical) patients. Indeed, psychiatric power inhered in wartime treatment methods. Treatment was often conceived of as a battle of wills between doctor and patient, and patients' wills were the object of the therapeutic intervention. As such, treating hysteria created a forum for incorporating medical values directly into therapeutic practice. Curing male hysterics meant medically manufacturing proper German subjects.

These theoretical perspectives can be loosely traced back to Michel Foucault, whose influence on the historiography of psychiatry is pervasive.[23] Foucault's writings on psychiatry laid bare the constructedness of mental illness, the normative function and disciplinary operation of state institutions, and the diffusion of power through professional and technical discourses.[24] Since Foucault's recasting of psychiatry's history and his reconceptualization of power, however, numerous Foucault-inspired studies have addressed issues such as professionalization, gender, and race in the history of psychiatry, and these studies are of greater significance for the analysis that follows. Hysteria, in particular, has been alternately depicted as a form of protofeminist protest by disenfranchised Victorian women, a phase in psychiatry's long history of misogyny and patriarchy, the result of psychiatric professional growth and French Republican secularization, and the ultimate psychosomatic riddle that has continually confounded medicine's materialism and forced it to deal with the mind.[25]

But what about male hysteria? In the hysterical male soldier, Elaine Showalter has found the wartime counterpart of the powerless Victorian woman. World War I, she has argued in a highly influential interpretation, focused psychiatric attention on men's mental health, a unique moment in a profession previously (and subsequently) devoted to suppressing and pathologizing women.[26] For Showalter, the symptoms that debilitated the bodies of tens of thousands of physically healthy soldiers represented a form of resistance both to military authority and prevailing masculine norms. Since it was not culturally acceptable for British men to show their emotions, they converted their fear into psychosomatic symptoms, an analysis that some of Freud's followers would have certainly accepted. In an earlier, equally suggestive interpretation, historian Eric J. Leed was similarly attentive to issues of power. Leed portrayed war neurosis as a desperate attempt to escape war, a response by both soldiers and doctors to the increasing parity between home and front, between industrialized war and an industrial world.[27]

These rich perspectives on psychiatric history, however, have been slow to surface in the German literature, where, for example, historians have yet to bring a gender analysis to bear on the male hysteria problem, a gap that this book seeks to redress.[28] Most striking about psychiatric writings on male hysteria in Germany—particularly when compared to the British case—is the absence of explicit feminization; the diagnosis certainly retained vague feminine associations, yet only a handful of doctors, most of whom were psychoanalysts or sexologists rather than mainstream psychiatrists, addressed the condition's sexual and gendered dimensions. For the great majority of psychiatrists, the operative opposition lay between healthy masculinity and a pathological lack of male behavior, between men who worked and fought and those who broke down and collected disability pensions, and later, between those who supported the state and those who joined the postwar revolutionary movements.[29] Psychiatrists, then, used their new institutional and discursive power to further their notions of healthy German masculinity, a vision centered around patriotism, self-sacrifice, and, most of all, economic productivity.

Memory and the Politics of Trauma

With its nearly ten million dead soldiers and its many more wounded, sick, or otherwise displaced victims, World War I had a profound political, social, and cultural impact on all the belligerent countries. Its legacies and memories have inspired lively historical debate.[30] The first war to bring widespread soldier neurosis, the Great War, particularly the horrifying ordeal of the western front, suggests the ultimate historical example of trauma.[31] The study of trauma and memory, thus, provides a third historiographical context for this book.

Historians have turned to the 1860s and 1870s as the moment when trauma became the subject of medical and psychological scrutiny and the belief spread that a sudden or violent blow could engender long-term mental and nervous consequences. Several scholars have traced trauma through the century that separates "railway spine," an early English term for the symptoms following train accidents, and posttraumatic stress disorder (PTSD), a diagnosis adopted by the American Psychiatric Association in the aftermath of the Vietnam War.[32] Sigmund Freud, of course, emerges as a crucial figure in this trajectory. Traumatic repression lay at the basis of his earliest hysteria theory and deeply influenced his development of psychoanalysis. The connections Freud drew—and then later revised—between sexual abuse and neurotic illness constitute an ever contentious chapter in the history of trauma.[33] Freud and several of his close followers debated about traumatic neurosis during and after the war, and their interventions have generated extensive historical commentary.[34] But Freud was far from the central trauma theorist in late-nineteenth-century Europe. The French physician Pierre Janet was probably more influential at the time and is now recognized as the intellectual precursor of much contemporary thinking about trauma. Janet's association of sexual trauma and multiple personality in the 1890s has inspired new directions in the history and practice of psychiatry.[35]

While Freud remained somewhat on the margins of German medicine—which is why he remains somewhat on the margins of this study—the neurologist Hermann Oppenheim stood at the center of the German trauma debates. Oppenheim's biography intersected with the trauma question in peacetime and war, in ways that illuminate the debate's stakes, its tone, and its outcome. Oppenheim's traumatic neurosis diagnosis, which established a direct connection between traumatic shock and posttraumatic symptoms, led to the acceptance of trauma-induced conditions as worthy of insurance compensation. This provoked a controversy that lasted thirty-seven years, from the legal decision of 1889 until its reversal in 1926, seven years after Oppenheim's death—a controversy that runs through this book. Most German psychiatrists came to oppose Oppenheim's ideas out of a combination of scientific and economic concerns, which drew rhetorical power from the heated backlash against the early welfare measures Bismarck introduced in the 1880s.[36] And out of the opposition to Oppenheim, in a medical crusade laden with subtle anti-Semitism and clamorous nationalism, hysteria became the diagnosis of choice for posttraumatic suffering in peace and war.

From Freud to Oppenheim to the famous French neurologist Jean-Martin Charcot, psychological trauma preoccupied many of the leaders of European mental medicine, and studying trauma triggered a number of their key discoveries and contributions.[37] On one level, then, this book adds a chapter to the growing literature on trauma and its medical and intellectual lineage. However, these connections between late-nineteenth-century trauma theory and today's ideas should not be construed as evidence for the timelessness or irreducibility of traumatic experience.[38] Drawing on the works of philosopher of science Ian Hacking and medical anthropologist Allan Young, this book assumes that trauma—as an idea and an experience—is shaped by historically determined, sociocultural forces such as doctor-patient interactions and prevailing values and assumptions.[39] It therefore resists the temptation to speculate about the "reality" or authenticity of traumatic pathologies and is interested, rather, in the ways individual suffering is constructed by larger social and medical forces. It uses trauma, furthermore, as a window into past historical moments, as a historical object rather than an analytical tool for making sense of the German response to industrialization and war. Particularly instructive in this context are works that focus on narrative, on the ways narratives shape and give meaning to memories and construct discrete sickness stories out of diverse experiences; these works shape my discussion of German veterans and their compensation claims in the 1920s.[40]

Finally, trauma and hysteria necessarily pose questions of individual and, indeed, collective memory. The final chapter of this book follows the disputes between doctors and veterans over individual traumatic memories (and their financial consequences) and maps them onto the broader process of collective memory formation in Weimar Germany.[41] It challenges the view of Weimar as a "culture of trauma" and focuses instead on the struggles between veterans' and psychiatrists' war narratives and the ways they played into broader political and cultural currents.

The idea of trauma—already politically charged in the 1890s and increasingly fraught during war and revolution—reemerged as a highly contentious category in the 1920s. In their steadfast rejection of traumatic pathology, psychiatrists implicitly denied the traumatizing impact of war as a whole and in many cases embraced it as a positive influence on the minds of individuals and the spirit of the nation. This perspective, together with psychiatric diagnoses, treatment, and organization, helped recast the memory of the war and furthered the forces of forgetting. Ernst Jünger's worker-soldier and what I call the psychiatric worker-patient both embodied new notions of a modern, mobilized masculinity, a male body steeled for the shocks of war and mechanized modernity. Ultimately, psychiatric theory came to complement a strand of interwar revisionism that constructed the ordeal of war as a transcendent and invigorating experience and condemned the moral and physical dangers of the Weimar welfare state.

This book is organized thematically, but its themes progress in a roughly chronological manner. Chapter 1 sketches psychiatry's professional and political situation in Wilhelmine Germany. It shows how the male hysteria diagnosis emerged amid the psychiatric backlash against Hermann Oppenheim's traumatic neurosis theory and the application of accident insurance to nervous and mental suffering. Chapter 2 turns to images of war among German doctors and argues that war was celebrated as a cure for the degeneration and decadence that psychiatrists condemned, a construction that was challenged by the onset of the war neurosis crisis in the war's first winter.

In Chapter 3 I trace the wartime diagnostic debate, showing how the military and economic context provoked and informed the repetition of Germany's original trauma controversy and turned the male hysteria diagnosis into a patriotic cause among German doctors. Chapter 4 turns to treatment. It follows the development and dissemination of several therapeutic methods, which in the context of military stagnation and psychiatric impotence came to be celebrated as miracle cures, capable of relieving long-standing conditions in a matter of seconds. Chapter 5 examines the psychiatric organization that was then constructed around these new treatments. It emphasizes the close connections between psychiatric practice and wartime industry and the resulting "worker-patient," the object of rationalized psychiatric treatment.

Chapters 6 and 7 address resistance to rationalized psychiatry. Wartime psychoanalysis is the subject of Chapter 6, which focuses on a group of doctors who were, at least superficially, at odds with the goals of the new treatments and looked more deeply into sex and psyche to explain war hysteria. Chapter 7 views the psychiatrist-patient relationship as a microcosm of social and political tensions. It traces patient opposition and medical responses from military stagnation through defeat and discusses the overt politicization of war hysteria in the Revolution of 1918–1919. Through a collection of pension proceedings, Chapter 8 follows the fate of "nervous veterans" after the war. It then analyzes the formation and contestation of individual and collective memories of war and trauma in Weimar society, psychiatry, and culture. From the moment it entered the political stage in the 1880s, through the interwar struggles over its consequences, male hysteria remained intertwined with broader concerns about the health and future of the German people and the viability of their regimes.

PART I

Imperial Origins
*Psychiatry and
the Politics of Trauma*

CHAPTER 1

Pathological Modernity

And so hysteria—an evanescence, so full of contradictions and problems—a great liar, which nevertheless tells us age-old truths, exciting and
deceptive; seemingly a matter of will and intention and yet so deeply regular; with symptoms in which the last decadence of modern urban civilization appears in the prehistoric forms of our ancestral existence.

ERNST KRETSCHMER, "Hysterie"

The war brought us immense work in Eppendorf . . . after only several
months we saw a syndrome that had before only very rarely been
observed—the condition of Hysteria virilis, "male hysteria." This had
been shown before by Charcot in Paris, and at that time we had said,
"Such a thing only occurs among the French, in Germany there is no
male hysteria."

MAX NONNE, *Anfang und Ziel meines Lebens*

GERMAN PSYCHIATRY in the late nineteenth century was a profession plagued by institutional, intellectual, and political insecurities, a profession that was the world's most advanced, but
which struggled for status at home, a profession that purported to transcend
ideology, but which participated in the divisive class politics of the German Empire, a profession that could do little to treat its own patients, but which sought
to cure the entire nation.[1] The most modern of medical specialties, psychiatry
in Germany was largely preoccupied with studying the deleterious effects of
modernity on the nation's physical and mental fitness. Psychiatry was at once
a product of modernity and a forum for critiquing modernity, a paradox that
mirrored the larger ambiguities of Wilhelmine society and politics.

By the turn of the twentieth century, Germany's ascendance in medical science was beyond dispute.[2] The discoveries and fame of such scientists as Robert
Koch, Rudolf Virchow, and Wilhelm Röntgen signaled that the epicenter of scientific and medical research had shifted from France to German-speaking Central Europe. Indeed, the late nineteenth century witnessed an explosion of new
medical chairs, research facilities, and clinics at Germany's universities, which
had become the world's preeminent institutions of higher learning.[3] Advances
in pathology and new microscope technologies filled German researchers with

an abiding optimism in the powers of medical science to conquer illness and improve life.[4]

Such breakthroughs in scientific knowledge helped drive the professionalization process in German medicine, a process that has typically accompanied nations' paths to industrial and demographic modernity.[5] Historians commonly conceive of *professionalization*—that is, the path by which an occupation constitutes itself as a profession—as the development and enforcement of standardized (and often costly) qualifications for admission and training and the assumption of a high level of responsibility.[6] Professions generally govern themselves through member organizations and publicize current knowledge in professional journals.

By these standards, the German psychiatric profession appeared relatively late, but by the end of the nineteenth century, it was expanding with great speed and dynamism. Psychiatrists, or mad-doctors (*Irrenärzte*) as they were originally called, were still largely employed as asylum administrators and struggling with the churches for control over the mentally ill when their principal professional organ, the *Allgemeine Zeitschrift für Psychiatrie und psychisch-gerichtliche Medizin* (General Journal for Psychiatry and Psychic-forensic Medicine), began publishing in 1844. Two decades later their main professional organization, the *Verein Deutscher Irrenärzte* (Association of German Mad-doctors), officially came into being.[7] Although only thirty-two doctors participated in the *Verein*'s founding meeting in 1864, its numbers grew rapidly in the later nineteenth century, as did the quantity and renown of its publications. By the beginning of the twentieth century, the organization could boast of 300 members, and at the outbreak of World War I, total membership reached 627. But in Imperial Germany the most highly prized marker of a profession's success—and its scholarly or scientific legitimacy—was its presence at the universities, and the locus of psychiatric attention began shifting from the asylums to the universities in the later part of the century. Indeed, the first German university chair in psychiatry was established in 1863, although it took another two decades before psychiatry's university position was secure, as reflected by the proliferation of university psychiatric clinics and the addition of a psychiatric requirement to state medical board exams.[8]

Neurology was even slower to emerge and suffered from even greater professional insecurity in the late nineteenth century. At the turn of the twentieth century, neurologists had only begun to gain autonomous research and clinical facilities, and their professional roles remained caught between psychiatry and internal medicine.[9] Wilhelm Griesinger, Germany's preeminent mid-nineteenth-century psychiatrist, promoted the unity of neurology and psychiatry; that most psychiatric journals and conventions continued to cover more strictly neurological topics well into the twentieth century testifies to Griesinger's enduring influence in this area. On the other hand, many internists were reluctant to allow neurology independence from its original home in internal medicine, which further delayed the establishment of independent neurological clinics. Until the establishment of their professional association in 1907 and even decades afterward, many neurologists participated in psychiatric meetings and published in psychiatric journals.

As the psychiatric profession sought to anchor itself in the universities, many psychiatrists embarked on ambitious research agendas to scientize the study of mentation and behavior. The circle of "brain psychiatrists" around Griesinger, which pioneered biological approaches to the mind in the 1850s and 1860s, devoted itself to localizing the sites of mental functions in the brain's anatomy. Madness, for Griesinger, was mental illness, which in turn could always be traced to somatic disturbances in the brain.[10]

A generation later, Munich professor Emil Kraepelin revolutionized the psychiatric approach to illness by systematizing and standardizing its diagnoses. Kraepelin organized the hundreds of known symptoms and syndromes around a handful of coherent disease types. Furthermore, under Kraepelin's influence, the prevailing medical materialism of Griesinger's era gave way as psychiatrists became interested in the new field of experimental psychology. Soon many researchers began incorporating psychological and statistical approaches to mental illness, studying its prognosis as well as its hereditary and demographic dimensions.[11] Kraepelin also made personality an object of psychiatric scrutiny and thus opened up new areas for research and professional colonization. His influence further sealed Germany's domination in psychiatric science, a position it retained until fascism forced many of the world's leading practitioners into exile in the 1930s.

But even as the psychiatric profession was expanding and its activities flourishing, the field was faced with a central, existential problem: "We know a lot, and can do little," admitted Georg Dobrick, an asylum doctor in Posen.[12] Indeed, among medical specialties, psychiatry was uniquely powerless to treat the very illnesses that fell in its domain, and the steady accumulation of scientific knowledge had made little impact on clinical practice. To be sure, psychiatry had come a long way—late-nineteenth-century practitioners were armed with science, statistics, and taxonomy; their leaders had largely left the asylums for the university clinics and traded in their straitjackets for lab coats. But the nature and cause of chronic mental illness remained ever elusive. In contrast to the conquering optimism that prevailed in many medical branches, psychiatrists languished in a morass of therapeutic pessimism. As Dobrick wrote: "When a future historian describes today's psychiatric era, he will come away with a curious impression. He will find an enormous blossoming of psychiatric literature alongside a low level of practical success."[13]

"The position of the psychiatrist around 1900 was not a particularly happy one," noted the medical historian Erwin Ackerknecht:

> Although he was better able to classify the psychoses and predict their outcome than his predecessors a century before, he still suffered from the same ignorance of the causes of mental illness and he still had to be content with the same miserable methods of treatment . . . although anatomy and physiology had been so

helpful to his medical colleagues, they had failed to teach him anything about the nature of these illnesses. . . . His patients were prisoners and in a way he himself was a prisoner caught up in the difficulties of the field in which he had chosen to work.[14]

The early nineteenth century had been the golden age of the psychiatric asylum. Emboldened by the successes attributed to moral treatment in eighteenth-century England and then later in revolutionary France, European states embarked on a great project of asylum building under the assumption that confinement could cure.[15] But psychiatric optimism faded as the century wore on, and the asylums that had sprung up across Europe and North America evolved into giant warehouses of insanity, presided over by psychiatrists who stood powerless before (and increasingly indifferent to) their patients' suffering. By the century's end, psychiatric leaders were turning their attentions elsewhere, preferring the university environment to the more isolated, lower-status world of the asylum, a world that Kraepelin, among many others, found "distasteful."[16] Simultaneously, patients and their relatives began denouncing asylum conditions vociferously. After a series of highly publicized asylum scandals in Germany in the 1890s, an oppositional movement emerged to agitate for patients' rights and call for national legislation monitoring psychiatric institutions.[17]

Historians and sociologists tend to depict these asylums as sites of medical power and social control and generally see confinement as a way of enforcing social norms and policing deviance.[18] As such, the asylum constructed abnormalities even as it purported to treat them.[19] In general, the asylum experiment, even from a medical point of view, was a grandiose and costly failure, and therapeutic pessimism—together with late-nineteenth-century social change—helped push the profession's attentions elsewhere. Emerging psychological perspectives encouraged medical reflection on character and personality, and medical judgments were increasingly rendered in terms of patients' ability to be reintegrated successfully into society, in short to work and contribute economically. At the same time, concern with the welfare of the chronic, "incurable" mental patient became subsumed to a devotion to the general health and fitness of the nation. Psychiatry in the Wilhelmine period was increasingly preoccupied with collective health; inspired by perceived public health crises in the late nineteenth century, its practitioners were newly receptive to organistic views of the nation and eugenic approaches to disease prevention and hygiene.

The Insanity Boom

While psychiatry was growing into a modern profession, Germany was undergoing a rapid and brutal drive to modernity, an experience that indelibly marked medical ideas. The so-called second industrial revolution—the manufacture of steel, chemicals, and pharmaceuticals that took off in the late 1850s and 1860s and fueled the voracious growth of German industry—was accompanied by widespread economic and demographic change. Between 1871 and 1910 the population of the newly unified state expanded by some 60 percent; at the beginning of that period roughly one-third of Germans lived in cities, but by the end the number of urban dwellers reached 60 percent. Such cities as Hamburg and Munich, still overgrown towns at the start of the nineteenth century, reached populations of 768,000 and 422,000 respectively by the century's end, and Berlin's population soared past two million at the beginning of the twentieth century.[20] Migrating into the cities, more and more Germans gave up agriculture and entered the factories—by the outbreak of World War I, less than half of the nation's workers made their living by farming. As a reflection of these shifting demographic realities, working-class social and political power grew steadily through the trade union movement and the Social Democratic Party (SPD), which by 1912 had the largest bloc of parliamentary deputies in the *Reichstag*.

Many middle-class Germans cheered as industrialization and demographic transformations turned Germany into a world economic and military power, poised to challenge Britain for industrial output and dominance of the seas. But in the eyes of some observers, this apparent progress also had a dark side. A common contemporary assumption, shared by psychiatrists and numerous other medical thinkers, was that the era's vertiginous changes were taking their toll on national health and fitness. Reformist associations advocated returning to a healthier, more "natural" way of life, and alternative movements around such causes as environmentalism, vegetarianism, and even nudism sprang up around the turn of the century.[21] Filthy factories and squalid living conditions within the new metropolises stood as signifiers for modernity's blight and were blamed for rampant increases in alcoholism, suicide, criminal behavior, and mental disease. Concern with the so-called social question—how to peacefully integrate the burgeoning proletariat into the polity—grew with the expansion of the cities and the emergence of the urban underclass, and contemporaneous increases in crime and disease replaced the optimistic reformism of mid-nineteenth-century medicine with the fears of disorder, decline, and degeneration.[22]

These fears were particularly palpable among psychiatrists, and state statisticians recorded staggering increases in admissions to the already crowded mental asylums. In Prussia, for example, between 1880 and 1910, the number of asylum inmates rose 429 percent, from 27,000 to 143,000; during the same period the general population increase was from twenty-seven to forty million, or some 48 percent.[23] That is, out of every 100,000 Prussians, 98 were admitted to asylums in 1880; in 1910 that figure reached 356.[24] Alarmist articles began appearing in the German press warning of the growth in the insane population and the lack of available funds and facilities to house and care for them. Social critics even diagnosed a "boom in insanity" (*Irrenboom*), which many blamed on the increased consumption of alcohol and the corruption of values endemic to big city life.[25] More recently historians have attributed this sharp increase in the asylum population to other factors, including changes in family structure, mistaken diagnoses, and the spread of syphilis, but for contemporaries these numbers represented a pointed warning of modernity's mental and physical dangers.[26]

Turn-of-the-century critics decried the modern city as the source of these dangers. The city's fast rhythms and constant sensory stimulation appeared to overtax the nerves, while its social and cultural anarchy and rampant consumerism threatened traditional values. In a wildly popular 1892 book, the Hungarian-born physician, journalist, and ultimately Zionist leader Max Nordau diagnosed an epidemic of physical and moral decline in the form of hysteria and degeneration, caused by both fatigue—due to the dizzying tempo and nervous overstimulation of modern life—and increased tobacco consumption and reflected in the era's debased art (impressionism), amusement (cross-dressing), and mores (mysticism).[27] Individual degenerates could not be cured; the *fin de siècle* threatened to be the *fin de race*. What distinguishes Nordau from the ranks of the period's many antimodernist polemicists was that his was a thoroughly medical vision of national decline, a vision that managed to attribute cultural tastes and political catastrophes to physical and mental deterioration. Nordau, like many German psychiatrists, was influenced by the theories of the French anthropologist Bénédict-Augustin Morel, who first publicized the idea of degeneration in an 1857 treatise.[28] Morel's ideas caught on for a variety of reasons; historian Richard Wetzell argues that they offered the advantage of combining hereditary and environmental concerns in one theory—a theory that linked psychological illness to physical signs and could be used to explain a whole range of mental and nervous disorders.[29]

At the same time, their turn to psychological observation led many psychiatrists to focus more on patient personality and behavior, and most embraced the idea of psychopathology or mental inferiority to characterize types of behavior deemed deviant. Psychopathic inferiority (*psychopathische Minderwertigkeit*) ultimately replaced degeneration in the psychiatric vocabulary. It served as an effective way of linking insanity, social and sexual deviance, and criminal behavior within one concept; simultaneously it supported the extension of psychiatric authority into new, borderline areas where it competed with nascent fields such as criminology and sexology for professional expansion.[30] The notion that certain individuals possessed a psychopathic, or inferior, constitution, though seldom rigorously defined, sounded scientific and lent the semblance of somaticism to psychiatric conditions; it endured for many decades as an organizing principle in psychiatric and social thought.[31]

These assumptions and concerns dominated Wilhelmine psychiatry and determined the research agendas for many of the profession's emerging leaders. To investigate the relative role of heredity and environment in "psychopaths" and to grasp the causes and consequences of the urban "insanity explosion," several German psychiatrists conducted empirical studies of the issue of mental disease, crime, and deviance among the urban poor. Before he was called to a chair at Berlin in 1912, psychiatry professor Karl Bonhoeffer studied alcoholism, criminality, suicide, and vagabondage at the University of Breslau.[32] Through detailed statistical analysis of Breslau prisoners, he distinguished between the psychological profile of young criminals and those who turned to criminality only later in life. Among the former, Bonhoeffer argued, inborn psychic deficiency played the most significant etiological role; among the latter, the negative influence of the urban milieu had driven congenitally normal individuals into criminal behavior.

An even sharper condemnation of the psychic effects of the cities can be found in the work of psychiatrist Robert Gaupp. Gaupp had started his career at the University of Heidelberg, and then followed Emil Kraepelin to Munich before he was called to a professorship in Tübingen. Perhaps it was this path that inspired him to compare the psychiatric dimensions of the urban environment of Munich to those of the predominantly rural areas surrounding Heidelberg. In the resulting study, Gaupp ascertained a clear statistical difference in rates of mental and nervous illness between the inhabitants of urban areas and those in the countryside. In the former, he wrote, there were disproportionately high numbers of paralytics, alcoholics, epileptics, psychopaths, and suicides, and he noted the "extraordinary fruitfulness of the big city in producing mental illnesses."[33]

Willy Hellpach was a pioneer in the field of social psychology, who endeavored to combine his psychiatric training with social criticism and political action. Hellpach pinpointed the "great turning point" in German society as the late 1870s, a time that brought catastrophe to German liberalism as represented by Bismarck's suppression of the Social Democratic Party, the end of his anti-Catholic campaigns (the *Kulturkampf*), the turn to economic protectionism, the splintering of the German liberals, and the first signs of political anti-Semitism.[34] These events, according to the Karlsruhe psychiatrist and liberal politician, represented the victory of irrationality in German public life and hastened the nation's "nervous collapse." Hellpach blamed the onset of modernity, unchecked capitalism, and mechanized production in particular for the nation's steep decline. While mechanization rendered the individual essentially superfluous, he argued, speed, technology, and the prodigious excitements and stresses of modern life were the source of rampant nervous illness.

Many groups, including social reformers, criminologists, anthropologists, and psychiatrists bemoaned these conditions. Joining the debates among middle-class professionals on the social problem, they turned increasing attention toward preventive and eugenic measures in the years before World War I.[35] As historian Paul Weindling has suggested, the transition in German medicine from the emancipatory reformism of the 1850s and 1860s to the "state-oriented expertise" of the late nineteenth century was most evident among psychiatric professionals.[36] Indeed, leading psychiatrists, such as Kraepelin and Ernst Rüdin, count among the early, adamant adherents to the eugenics or race hygiene movement, which sought to promote national health and fitness through direct state intervention in hygiene, marriage, and reproduction.[37] In 1908 Rüdin became a coeditor of the *Archiv für Rassenhygiene,* the Racial Hygiene Association's official publication, and Kraepelin advocated an extensive research program concerning the heredity of nervous and mental illnesses, which he finally succeeded in establishing in the middle of World War I.[38]

Robert Sommer, a psychiatry professor at the University of Giessen, was particularly active in this research agenda and contributed to the field of heredity research and mental hygiene with his work on the family and the inheritance of mental disease. His 1907 treatise on *Familienforschung* (Family Research)[39] resonated not only with physicians but also with jurists, teachers, clergy, and philologists, as seen by the attendance at his 1908 course on the subject.[40] The Racial Hygiene Association appointed a commission consisting of Sommer, his Giessen colleague Heinrich Adolf Dannemann, and Alfred Ploetz, one of the founders of the German race hygiene movement, to pursue scientific research into genealogy, heredity, and racial regeneration. Sommer's approach could be summarized as "recognize, cure, prevent"; this became the slogan for the Fourth International Congress on Caring for the Mentally Ill, which was held in Berlin in 1910.[41]

Alarmed by the fluctuating birth rate and increases in infant mortality, German thinkers began to probe the idea of state supervision and regulation of marriages to prevent the inheritance of mental illness and to protect the "race" from further decline. In 1899 the psychiatrist Paul Näcke was the first to advocate the sterilization of "inferiors" as a way of combating degeneration. However, few of Näcke's colleagues were prepared to endorse such drastic measures, and the German eugenics movement refrained from supporting sterilization until after World War I.[42]

While an earlier generation of historians saw in eugenics the kernel of National Socialism's racialist worldview and the seeds of its genocidal programs, newer works have represented it as a broad and international coalition of groups, ranging from Marxists and Social Democrats on the left through *völkisch* nationalists on the right.[43] Indeed, eugenic ideas were equally influential in Britain, Scandinavia, the Soviet Union, and the United States, which pioneered the (involuntary) sterilization of the mentally and physically disabled. Therefore, direct continuities between late-nineteenth-century eugenicists and Nazi race zealots do not stand up to scrutiny. Furthermore, it was not until the later 1920s that the movement fragmented into competing splinter groups, and the racist and anti-Semitic eugenicists did not take control of the concept in Germany until the 1930s.[44] What united these groups in the Wilhelmine period was not race but class. Eugenics enthusiasts in Germany and abroad were generally members of the bourgeoisie driven by a concern with the expansion of the uneducated urban underclass and its impact on the nation's strength, fitness, and genetic future.[45]

Psychiatry certainly internalized the class prejudices of turn-of-the-century medicine. The new emphasis on behavior and personality, and the acceptance of "inferiority" as a medical category, facilitated the judgment of the moral (and ultimately economic) value of psychiatric patients. The effect of these emerging perspectives, together with changing demographic circumstances, was to alter the relationship of individual patients and psychiatric practitioners. Standing further removed from their patients than their midcentury predecessors, late-nineteenth-century psychiatrists were more likely to see the mentally ill in abstract terms and to judge them based on their economic potential and social normality.[46] Mental medicine, increasingly, involved submitting patients to a kind of cost-benefit analysis, innocuous enough perhaps when times were good, but the source of flagrant abuse in trying economic moments, such as the difficult winters of World War I and the aftermath of the 1929 crash.

Traumatic Hysteria

Within the generalized anxiety over modernity and the medical dimensions of the social question, a particular concern about Germany's men arose in the 1880s. This concern centered on psychological trauma, a medical concept with very visible economic repercussions. *Trauma* is an age-old idea that comes from the Greek word for wound; it had a long history in surgical medicine before entering the neurological and psychiatric vocabulary in the 1860s and 1870s. As a concept in medical psychology, trauma emerged with the railroads of Britain and North America before making its way to the neurological clinics of the French and German capitals in the 1880s and 1890s. This trajectory had a profound impact on the history of psychiatry, specifically on the hysteria diagnosis, on emerging psychological perspectives, and on the class and gender dimensions of disease. In fact, it was the convergence of Imperial Germany's industrial growth and its new social insurance legislation that turned male hysteria into a cultural phenomenon.

The rapid expansion of the rail networks over the mid-nineteenth century dramatically altered European life, and the railroad forcefully entered the European imagination, becoming a symbol of both modernity's possibilities and its dangers. Life on the railroads was indeed dangerous. In the United States in 1889, one out of every 117 train workers was killed, and for every twelve trainmen, one was injured.[47] Passengers and bystanders were not immune to the railroad's risks, and train collisions and derailings were frequent occurrences in the late nineteenth century. Alongside the common and predictable accident effects, many individuals showed unique symptoms that defied simple categorization: mental and nervous maladies such as headaches, dizziness, paralysis, and general ennui with no apparent somatic basis. A British legislative act of 1864 that made railway companies financially accountable for the health of their passengers focused intensive medical and legal attention on these conditions.

Two years later the English physician John Eric Erichsen published seven cases of this condition, which he dubbed "railway spine," an early theorization of what came to be called posttraumatic neurosis and a diagnostic ancestor of posttraumatic stress disorder (PTSD).[48] Erichsen viewed railway spine as an organically induced neurosis, which derived from anatomical lesions of the spinal cord suffered in accidents.[49] Although he could find no anatomical or pathological evidence for the occurrence of a spinal lesion, he noted the preponderance of the same sets of symptoms in the overwhelming majority of these patients. Among the most common were memory loss, confusion, diminished business aptitude, ill temper, sleep disorders, sensory impairment, attitude changes, loss of motor power, numbness, and sexual impotence.[50] Although other jarring experiences could potentially induce this syndrome, Erichsen linked this curious condition to the particularities of rail travel:

> It must . . . be obvious that in no ordinary accident can the shock be so great as in those that occur on Railways. The rapidity of the movement, the momentum of the persons injured, the suddenness of its arrest, the helplessness of the sufferers, and the natural perturbation of the mind that must disturb the bravest, are all circumstances that of necessity greatly increase the severity resulting to the nervous system, and that justly cause these cases to be considered as somewhat exceptional from ordinary accidents.[51]

Railway spine was thus a somatic diagnosis, a physical injury to the nervous system brought on by the unique horrors of the train accident. Significantly, if he had explained these symptoms as psychological, Erichsen would have been calling these patients hysterical. But hysteria, at this time, was regarded as an almost exclusively female illness. For centuries it had been explained with recourse to female anatomy. The term itself derives from the Greek word *hystera* (womb), and for most of its three-thousand-year history, the illness was linked to the female reproductive system.[52] As a French doctor exclaimed earlier in the century: "A man cannot be hysterical; he has no uterus."[53] Coughing, for example, one of the earliest and most consistently documented symptoms of this mysterious illness, was explained in classical medicine as the result of the uterus wandering to the throat. Even though anatomical explanations of hysteria no longer held sway by the mid-nineteenth century, the vague identification of hysteria with women—and indeed female sexuality—continued to dominate psychiatric thought, and connections between the illness and allegedly female characteristics were assumed by a great many physicians into the twentieth century.[54]

Erichsen's railway spine patients, however, were predominantly men. This reflected the fact that men were more likely than women to travel by train, but it also highlighted the possibility of the same sorts of symptoms in both sexes.

Although the symptoms paralleled those of hysteria, rather than labeling them hysterical, Erichsen created a gender-neutral category for them.[55] "Is it reasonable," he asked, "to say that such a man has suddenly become 'hysterical,' like a lovesick girl? Or is this term not rather employed merely to cloak a want of precise knowledge as to the real pathological state that is perceptible to the most casual observer in the mental state and bodily condition of the patient?"[56]

Erichsen's views sparked debate across Europe and North America. His diagnosis enraged the railway companies who feared having to bear financial responsibility for these mysterious conditions. As one German commentator acerbically asked his colleagues: Why go through the trouble of studying and practicing medicine when one could make a perfectly decent living just riding the rails and waiting for accidents? Estimating the compensation for railway spine to be some one to two thousand pounds annually, he added that such a sum could guarantee a rather comfortable life.[57] Unsurprisingly, then, the biggest medical challenge to railway spine came from a surgeon who worked for the London and Western Railway Company, Herbert W. Page. In opposition to Erichsen's somatic diagnosis, Page focused on the psychological aspects of the accident, namely psychic shock and its emotional consequences. Influenced by the British surgeon James Paget and his theories of nervous mimicry—according to which psychic disorders could take a form that imitated previous physical illnesses—Page argued that the emotional consequences of railway accidents were strong enough to induce prolonged physical disabilities. With this argument, Page psychologized railway spine, opening up the floodgates for psychological interpretations of nervous and neurotic illness.[58]

Such was the state of the debate when Continental neurologists took up the trauma issue. Around 1879 Jean-Martin Charcot first turned his attention to trauma, which instantly elevated its importance. Charcot was a towering figure in nineteenth-century medicine, and he occupied a central place in the intellectual life of the Third Republic.[59] His Salpêtrière Hospital on the outskirts of Paris became the site for some of the most important developments in the history of hysteria, hypnosis, and traumatic neurosis. In 1882, at Charcot's behest, the Salpêtrière added a section for men, where as the historian Mark Micale has written, cases of male hysteria became a daily diagnostic reality.[60] There Charcot observed numerous cases of motor and sensory disturbances in individuals who had endured traumatic experiences, including railroad accidents, workplace mishaps, and even service in the Franco-Prussian war.[61] Among the symptoms Charcot saw in these men were fatigue, headaches, back pain, heart palpitations, chest pain, irregular pulse rate, constipation, dizziness, fainting spells, and trembling of the hands and neck. He also recorded cases of emotional and sleep disorders, mental disorientation, and intellectual diminishment.[62]

Charcot believed that an environmental *agent provocateur,* a traumatic stimulus, could trigger these conditions in individuals with an inherited, constitutional disposition, or *diathèse*. Etiologically, he attributed posttraumatic neurosis to a combination of causes, but he gave primacy to the pathogenic effects of the emotions unleashed by trauma, in particular, fear.[63] But both organic and psychological factors played a role, and Charcot posited that traumatic experiences often became superimposed atop physical injuries or irregularities. His diagnosis was *hystérie traumatique* (traumatic hysteria).

For many neurologists and psychiatrists, hysteria, the "great neurosis," presented the ultimate challenge; its study triggered some of the most enduring innovations in the history of psychiatry, including, of course, the birth of psychoanalysis. As Gaupp noted in a 1911 article, "The literature on hysteria has expanded so over the last decades that it could now fill an entire library, and every day brings new publications."[64] This medical obsession reflected contemporary concern with hysteria's epidemic appearances, as doctors' offices from Paris to Vienna and as far away as New York and Buenos Aires were flooded with women suffering from such symptoms as sudden loss of speech, narrowing of the visual field, tics, tremors, and partial paralysis in the legs and arms.[65] From the renowned "historical hysterics" such as Joseph Breuer's Anna O. and Charcot's Blanche Wittmann to the anonymous ranks of the countless "inarticulate" sufferers, these women engaged the vigorous interest of psychological medicine's leading lights.[66]

Charcot was no exception. The fascination he continues to hold for historians derives in no small part from his investigations into the disease and his (ultimately failed) attempts to force its elusive and mysterious manifestations into his positivistic paradigm.[67] Using his formidable powers of observation and aided by the camera, over the 1870s and 1880s, the so-called "Napoleon of the neuroses" sought to document the disease's stages and states, clinging to the conviction that hysteria was a real, timeless disorder with objective clinical symptoms. In that vein—and reflective of his anticlerical positions—his students conducted historical investigations that attributed outbreaks of witchcraft and other mysterious past phenomena to misidentified hysteria. Starting in the late 1870s, Charcot incorporated hypnosis into his investigations and used it to have his female patients reproduce and perform hysterical symptoms before large crowds of curious onlookers.[68] Most intriguing were the women who suffered from *grande hystérie,* a severe seizure that passed through four stages, from a kind of epileptic trance, through clonic tremors and tics, to a highly theatrical reenactment of the patient's prehysteria life, and ending in a state of withdrawn detachment.[69]

The traumatic hysteria diagnosis challenged hysteria's status as a specifically female illness. The disease's male manifestations, however, were linked to jarring physical experiences—a blacksmith who burned his arm, a ditch digger whose shovel struck him in the face, and so on—in clear contrast to female hysteria, which was commonly brought on by the emotions or passions, suggesting that this radical move notwithstanding, Charcot retained gender stereotypes in his differential diagnoses. In fact, he posited that hysteria was some twenty times more common in women than men. Nevertheless, Charcot rejected theories that attributed the malady to female anatomy. Traumatic hysteria, furthermore, seemed most common in workers and artisans, not men easily dismissed as effete or effeminate.[70]

Charcot's influence on international medicine was extensive, and traumatic hysteria soon spread far beyond the Salpêtrière. His German reception was certainly not limited to his most famous disciple, Sigmund Freud.[71] Max Nonne was another Central European neurologist who journeyed to Paris to study with the famous doctor.[72] But Nonne stayed at the Salpêtrière for only six weeks; although impressed by Charcot's charisma, he remained skeptical of the authenticity of his therapeutic demonstrations and had little sympathy with the Frenchman's arrogance. Decades later, Nonne recalled his 1889 visit: "As a German—it was only eighteen years after the peace of Versailles—I could not expect more affability from Charcot with his strongly chauvinistic attitude, nor did I."[73]

But it was at the Salpêtrière that Nonne saw male hysteria for the first time. For years he believed that the condition only arose in French men, reflecting a common German tendency to ridicule and diagnose the shortcomings of French masculinity.[74] That Nonne became a vocal proponent of the hysteria diagnosis for Germany's war neurotics twenty-five years later was probably a consequence of his Paris sojourn. Freud also left Paris a believer in male hysteria, and he lectured about it to his Vienna colleagues shortly after he returned home.[75] Freud's contemporary and sometime rival, Hermann Oppenheim, was likewise influenced by his exchanges with Charcot. Oppenheim, however, took a different diagnostic route.

Hermann Oppenheim and the Theory of Traumatic Neurosis

Hermann Oppenheim was arguably Germany's leading neurologist in the late nineteenth and early twentieth centuries and was certainly its most prominent theorist of trauma. His traumatic neurosis diagnosis, a response to Charcot's notion of traumatic hysteria, triggered years of intense debate and controversy in German medical circles before, during, and after World War I. Oppenheim as an individual—and indeed his identity as a Jew and as an outsider in university medicine—became deeply entwined with the reception of traumatic neurosis, and his career trajectory reflected important changes in German medicine and society, which influenced the course and outcome of the German trauma debate.[76]

The medical profession that Oppenheim entered in the 1870s transformed itself rapidly over the next decades. Indeed, its reputation as a tolerant profession and a reliable means of social ascent—the very reasons why Oppenheim's father encouraged him to study medicine—was already becoming an anachronism when the young neurologist sought promotion within the university. Oppenheim was steeped in the mid-nineteenth-century medical traditions established by Wilhelm Griesinger, which stressed the unity of neurology and psychiatry, the somatic basis of mental illness, and a humane and sympathetic approach to psychiatric patients. His Berlin mentor, Carl Westphal, had been a student of Griesinger and a prominent member of the latter's circle of brain psychiatrists, and as a young assistant doctor at the Charité, the training hospital attached to the University of Berlin, Oppenheim participated in the cerebral localization research that brought German mental medicine great renown.

Around 1884 Oppenheim first dedicated himself to the study of neurosis, began a correspondence with Charcot, and was swept up into the ongoing controversies over traumatic shock and its neuropsychiatric consequences. These controversies had reached German medicine around the time of national unification, when an imperial law held railway companies responsible for injuries sustained during rail travel.[77] Oppenheim's first lecture on the topic, delivered in Berlin in 1884, aroused heated opposition.[78] His habilitation thesis concerned the "Significance of Shock for Diseases of the Nervous System" and appeared in 1886, two decades after the publication of Erichsen's railway spine lectures. And in 1889 he published the results of five years of research on patients in the Charité (1883–1888) and presented forty-one cases of postaccident nervous and mental suffering, most of which he diagnosed with traumatic neurosis.[79]

The patients Oppenheim observed displayed the same kinds of symptoms that were reported by Charcot, Erichsen, and Page; that is, shaking, stuttering, tics, tremors, paralyses, and disturbances of sight, hearing, and movement. Significantly, nearly all of these patients, all but two of whom were men, came from Berlin's growing working class; most were either railroad employees or workers in factories or on construction sites. And in most of the forty-one cases, the nervous symptoms occurred after accidents at factories or workshops, terrifying moments in which workers' arms or legs were caught in machinery, heavy objects fell on them, or they were thrown in some kind of explosion or mishap.[80]

Oppenheim posited two explanations for these symptoms. In many cases, he shared Erichsen's conclusions: The physically jarring experience of an accident could directly lead to minute lesions in the brain or central nervous system, which, because of their size, were undetectable and hence untreatable. Their prognosis, he added, was "sad." Such lesions disrupted the functioning of the nervous system and caused pain, loss of feeling, and temporary paralysis in accident survivors. But these consequences made up only half of Oppenheim's etiological picture. What continually eluded the attention of his critics, many of whom relentlessly cast him as a rigid somaticist in the debates to come, was Oppenheim's simultaneous attention to the psychological consequences of fear and shock. He made this particularly clear in his description of such cases as the fireman who was trapped in a burning building or a train conductor who saw another train rapidly approaching head on and only averted a catastrophe at the last possible minute.[81] Both men suffered from serious posttraumatic symptoms. As Oppenheim wrote in the first and second editions of his traumatic neurosis monograph:

> In the genesis of this illness, physical trauma is only partially responsible. An important—and in many cases the major role—is played by the psyche: terror, emotional shock. Even in cases where there is no external wound, the injury can have direct consequences, which would normally take on no great importance, if the sickly mind did not create a lasting illness on the basis of its abnormal way of reacting to the physical symptoms.[82]

Oppenheim's fundamental contribution, then, was to view traumatic neurosis as a discrete diagnostic entity, a particular pathological state, which was broader than railway spine, and which, importantly, could not just be attributed to hysteria. As such, Oppenheim put forward an explicit critique of Charcot's traumatic hysteria diagnosis.[83] He theorized that traumatic neuroses had their own rules and prognoses, and he traced their symptoms to the direct results of traumatic events, even if those effects were sometimes psychological. Charcot's diagnosis of traumatic hysteria, Oppenheim feared, placed too great an emphasis on the subject's emotions, ideas, and thoughts and thus blurred the distinction between sickness and simulation. To be sure, traumatic neurosis and traumatic hysteria overlapped, a fact that Oppenheim readily acknowledged, but ultimately the difference was one of emphasis: Oppenheim stressed the primary pathogenic effect of traumatic events rather than the wishes, fears, and secondary mental processes associated with hysteria.[84]

Oppenheim's interventions in the trauma debate brought him some renown, and, by all accounts, he seemed headed for a distinguished academic career. Indeed, when Westphal became ill in 1886, he designated Oppenheim to take over his lectures, suggesting that the young neurologist was likely to succeed him in the prestigious Berlin chair. But the events of the next several years shattered Oppenheim's academic aspirations and propelled him from the rarified realm of university medicine into the less glamorous world of the private clinic. In these years he also experienced bitter opposition to his trauma theory.

Westphal was replaced not by Oppenheim, but by the Freiburg psychiatrist Friedrich Jolly. In 1889, encouraged by friends, Oppenheim applied for a professorship in Berlin.[85] His chances seemed promising, as he enjoyed the respect and support of such prestigious and influential faculty members as Rudolf Virchow, and his candidacy was unanimously backed by the medical faculty. Nevertheless, Oppenheim's application was rejected by the Minister of Culture, Friedrich Althoff.[86] Several accounts of the proceedings attribute the minister's objections to anti-Semitism, which, starting in the early 1880s, increasingly colored Germany's political and social landscape.[87] The appearance of shrill political anti-Semitism and heightened, xenophobic nationalism had begun to transform the universities, once the well-traveled midcentury path of Jewish ascent and acculturation. By the 1880s there were far fewer coveted academic positions than qualified applicants, and with the contraction of the academic job market and university overcrowding, Jews, because of their extremely conspicuous presence, became an easy target. The medical profession also reflected these changes, and the liberalism that had made medicine such an appealing path for Jewish students in the middle of the century was on the wane. Simultaneously, the high status world of academic medicine, like the universities as a whole, fell increasingly prey to the radical and nationalist sentiments stirring in Germany's political sphere.[88]

Although reticent to address the issue publicly, in private circles Oppenheim confided his belief that he was rejected because he was Jewish. The Minister of Culture allegedly suggested that Oppenheim either convert or marry a non-Jewish woman to aid his professional ascent.[89] Whether or not the putative anti-Semitism of one official is actually to blame, what is clear is that Oppenheim's university career ran into the "glass ceiling" faced by numerous Jewish academicians, and the neurologist perceived his Jewishness to be his primary professional obstacle.

Embittered with the academic establishment, Oppenheim set out on his own and established a private practice in northern Berlin. His reputation in the medical world continued to grow steadily, and his book *Textbook of Nervous Diseases*, referred to by his students as a "neurological Bible," went through seven editions and a number of translations between 1894 and 1923.[90] Oppenheim's trajectory from academia into private practice was typical of Jewish doctors of the time and resembles the path of Sigmund Freud, who, one year older than Oppenheim, was likewise trained in brain anatomy and was also acutely attuned to the limitations his Jewish background placed on his professional ascent—Freud had to wait seventeen years before his professorship came through.[91]

The medical profession in Wilhelmine Germany was deeply stratified, and psychiatrists' precarious status led to a kind of obsession with their national and social standing. Such concerns, historian Michael Kater has argued, helped foster an aristocratic, even military ethos among doctors, an ethos that was not out of place in the imperial middle class.[92] But unlike other professional groups with historical ties to the state and bureaucracy, doctors, as relative newcomers, pursued these ends more aggressively and created rigid intraprofessional hierarchies, in which university professors stood at the top. This certainly characterized the psychiatric community. Indeed, Berlin's large population of psychiatrists and neurologists can be roughly divided into two groups, university researchers and private clinicians; the groups differed in terms of status, patient pools, and often ethnicity.

Oppenheim's rejection, thus, brought a precipitous loss of status. He descended from the peak of the medical profession to the ordinary world of the clinic, a world that was largely inhabited by Jewish doctors.[93] The city of Berlin, the site of some sixty clinics for nervous disease, had never had a Jewish professor of psychiatry despite the large number of Jewish doctors practicing mental medicine. Few Jews were to be found in psychiatry chairs around Germany.[94]

Furthermore, university psychiatrists, who supervised training hospitals and clinics, treated different kinds of patients from their counterparts in private clinics.[95] While the former were well compensated and thus free to engage in extensive research programs, private clinicians were forced to compete in a crowded medical marketplace.[96] In contrast to university clinics and training hospitals, private clinics for nervous illness were often visited by the kind of affluent patients whose neuroses and obsessions were immortalized in Freud's case histories. Oppenheim came to treat a similar patient population when he opened his clinic, and the clinic's reputation became particularly well established among Eastern European Jews, large numbers of whom traveled to Berlin, appealing to the neurologist to cure their "nervous" suffering.[97]

Thus, while Oppenheim's 1889 study was conducted on working-class patients, nearly all of whom were men, in a later case compendium, his 1906 *Letters on Psychotherapy,* he described a group of patients, both men and women, who were predominately affluent and educated.[98] Among the eleven cases he included in the *Letters* were an army general, a high-ranking civil servant, and a well-known female author; although the details of the cases are not always possible to infer, they did not involve the consequences of workplace accidents but rather the nervous complaints of the privileged classes.

The decades around the turn of the century were often described as a "nervous era," and numerous elites and intellectuals routinely complained of their weak and overtaxed nerves.[99] Nerves, in this period, became a metaphor for expressing personal and social discontent, and in contrast to the stigmatized working-class degenerates and hysterics, bourgeois nervousness connoted an aristocratic temperament and refinement and often carried other, generally positive associations.

Neurasthenia, a nervous illness originally described by the New York City doctor George Miller Beard, made its way to the European continent in the early 1880s.[100] According to Beard's mechanistic conception of the nervous system, modern civilization drained the individual's finite reserve of "nerve force." As a result neurasthenic symptoms such as fatigue, headaches, sleeplessness, dizziness, digestive problems, irregular heart beat, and impotence were appearing with increasing frequency. Beard conceived of neurasthenia as a purely American phenomenon that he attributed to the country's peculiar social and economic relations, but when his writings were translated into German in the 1880s, the illness he described was rapidly subsumed into the cultural and medical landscape of Imperial Germany. Neurasthenia and nervous weakness quickly became major medical concerns, to which German doctors attributed a wide range of symptoms.[101] As of 1902, the state of Prussia recorded statistics on the admission of neurasthenics into its asylums, and eight years later it registered an increase from 12,492 to 15,490.[102] During this same period, private facilities for the nervous complaints of the bourgeoisie sprouted up in cities throughout Germany, and the era saw the birth of new cultural archetypes such as the nervous housewife, the nervous poet, and the nervous Jew.[103]

This, then, was Oppenheim's new world. He soon found himself competing to treat nervous patients in Berlin's increasingly competitive medical marketplace. Competition had a great impact on clinical practice and, significantly, diagnostic choice, and doctors in private practice were more likely to diagnose somatic disorders, even as psychological approaches were waxing among their university counterparts around the turn of the century. Somaticism sounded better and such diagnoses lacked the stigma of mental disease—nerves were acceptable, even fashionable for members of the bourgeoisie; mental illness, on the other hand, carried a dreaded stigma.[104] The cases Oppenheim published in his *Letters on Psychotherapy* illustrate this well. They show how he carefully used somatic language to avoid agitating or offending his sensitive patients; even as he diagnosed their nervous disturbances, he affirmed their sound mental health.[105]

But the economic needs of private clinicians provide only a partial explanation of the often distinct behaviors and pathological signs of this type of patient. Historian Edward Shorter has asked whether Eastern European Jewish patients showed somatic symptoms to conform to medical theories or, conversely, if nerve doctors published somatic theories to appeal to such patients, who found nervous disease far less troubling than mental disease.[106] Shorter poses an unanswerable question; of primary importance is the fact that Oppenheim's new environment, the largely Jewish world of private neurological clinics, clung to somatic language and diagnoses in an age when the leaders of German mental medicine were moving further and further into the psychological camp.

From Traumatic Neurosis to Male Hysteria

Oppenheim's trauma theories were inauspiciously timed. Their publication coincided with the implementation of a thoroughgoing insurance scheme in Germany, which Bismarck instituted in a series of measures over the 1880s, in a politically shrewd, though ultimately failed attempt to defuse the revolutionary potential of the growing Social Democratic Party and trade union movement.[107] Five years after Bismarck's accident insurance plan of July 1884, the Imperial Insurance Office granted posttraumatic neuroses the status of actionable conditions.[108] This decision ignited a class-based controversy over trauma. It meant that workers were entitled to compensation if an accident rendered them nervously or mentally incapable of returning to their jobs. Before long the 1889 act was held responsible for the epidemic appearance of "pension neurosis" (*Rentenneurose*), a widespread addiction to compensation that seemed to sap the productive potential of the German workforce.

Amid the heightened concern with Germany's economic (and military) competitiveness that marked the Wilhelmine period, concern over pension neurosis led to an enormous medicopolitical backlash, much of which, as Oppenheim recalled in 1915, "was directed not only at the issue [traumatic neurosis], but also to a great extent against me personally."[109] "After the appearance of the first edition of Oppenheim's traumatic neurosis diagnosis," wrote the neurologist's friend and colleague Ludwig Bruns, "in Germany a veritable flood of opinions flowed forth and soon this question divided authors into two hostile camps, which attacked each other so bitterly that it became a matter of personal honor."[110] Personal honor, of course, was a fundamental bourgeois value, and Oppenheim's conspicuous dueling scars suggest that he too was a participant in the rituals of honor that marked German medical culture and Wilhelmine masculinity.[111]

In real economic terms, traumatic neurosis was essentially inconsequential; the numbers of posttraumatic pension applications composed a mere 1 to 2 percent of all accident insurance claims.[112] But that did not prevent the phenomenon from becoming a highly politicized, propagandistic cause for a number of psychiatrists and physicians. Indeed, the medical profession in these years saw itself as under siege by the insurance system; as a response German doctors came together in 1900 to found the *Hartmannbund*, the Association of German Doctors for the Protection of Economic Interests, an organization that sought to combat the influence of state welfare legislation and the insurance societies to preserve doctors' autonomy, status, and economic position.[113]

Medical politics throughout the later imperial period were dominated by the struggle with the insurance societies. In 1910 the *Hartmannbund*, whose organization had grown to include more than three-fourths of all German doctors, threatened massive strikes, which only the intervention of the Reich's government was able to deter.[114] Though the organization was officially politically neutral, and many German doctors saw themselves as the apolitical (or suprapolitical) promoters of the value-free science of hygiene, the struggle against the insurance associations belied that neutrality and propelled the organized medical profession toward a vehement opposition to anything smacking of Social Democracy.[115] Indeed, for many opponents, worker health insurance was an ominous sign of socialist strength, even a plot perpetrated by Jews.[116]

This general medical backlash against social insurance colored the reception of Oppenheim's ideas. Soon traumatic neurosis was depicted as a disaster with grave consequences for Germany's treasury, its public health, and its national strength, particularly during the nearly quarter-century-long depression that began in 1873. Building on long-standing cultural associations that extolled the healthful benefits of work, pension collecting (i.e., not working) was construed as a dangerous, deviant behavior. On the one hand, receiving a pension was a sign of psychopathology; on the other hand, not returning to work eliminated any chance these accident victims had of recovering. In either case, not working represented a failure to inhabit the proper masculine role.

"The spread of this pension addiction," warned psychiatrist Robert Wollenberg some years later, "has developed into a true epidemic, which must be fought by doctors without prejudice or severity, but with a manly firmness."[117] The link between pensions and pathology was so strong that for many doctors even the idea of a pension was dangerous, and hence a new class of neuroses was born, the "pension struggle neuroses" (*Rentenkampfneurosen*), which were believed to derive merely from the pension application process and from dealing with the labyrinthine social insurance bureaucracy.[118]

Among psychiatrists Alfred Hoche was one of the sharpest and most outspoken critics of the traumatic neurosis diagnosis. In his 1910 rector's address at the University of Freiburg, Hoche held the recognition of traumatic neurosis—and implicitly the insurance doctors who awarded pensions—responsible for an epidemic of nervous weakness:

> Still an unknown concept thirty years ago, today an illness, a cancer on the organism of our whole working class . . . This peoples' epidemic [*Volksseuche*] arose not only chronologically after the enactment of the accident insurance legislation, but also in a direct causal relationship. The law has, there is no doubt about it, produced the illness. . . . The by now well-known pattern is that after accidents, no matter how small or trivial, all kinds of nervous symptoms arise, which combined with a general hypochondriac disorientation, then make the person in question unable to work and at the same time secure for him the right to draw a pension in accordance with his condition. It is not the case, as was assumed at the beginning, that it is a matter of simulation, of intentional faking of symptoms that are not there. The individuals are in fact sick, but they would be well, strangely enough, if the law did not exist.[119]

Hoche's objections drew from the ideas of neurologist Adolf Strümpell, who in 1895 coined the term *Begehrungsvorstellung* (imaginative desire), a kind of powerful, semiconscious wish that lay at the basis of such neuroses.[120] For Hoche, then, the traumatic event itself had no pathological significance; what made these men sick—and he did not doubt that they were sick—were pathological ideas, such as the desire to avoid working or to collect a pension. These ideas also operated on a collective level. Awareness of the pension laws created this illness and made German workers prone to breaking down after inconsequential "traumatic" events. The more the pension laws were publicized, Hoche feared, the more this cancer would spread through the German working class.

Other objections to traumatic neurosis tended to focus on the problem of simulation. Arguing that the symptoms Oppenheim had identified were easy to fake, doctors feared that the system was rife for abuse. Neurologists Friedrich Schultze and Adolf Seeligmüller led the attack. Schultze recognized the existence of the condition, but raised many practical problems, such as the risk of erroneously rewarding simulated suffering.[121] Seeligmüller heightened the debate's stakes by pointing to the opposite problem, the possibility of discounting authentic suffering as simulated, and went on to challenge the existence of traumatic neurosis as a whole and to hold Oppenheim personally accountable for the havoc his diagnosis was wreaking.

Schultze and Seeligmüller stepped up their attacks at a medical congress in Berlin in August 1890. Schultze began by critiquing the term *traumatic neurosis* as too general, arguing that it described conditions that were actually hysteria, neurasthenia, or hypochondria.[122] Trauma alone, Schultze claimed, was not sufficient to bring about a neurosis. After Schultze's presentation the congress turned to the question of simulation, and several doctors repeated the critique that Oppenheim's conception made it too easy to fake symptoms to achieve an undeserved pension. Seeligmüller charged that some 25 percent of traumatic neurosis cases were simulators, a number that was more than five times higher than Oppenheim's estimate. The participants ultimately split into two camps around the simulation question. As Oppenheim later recalled:

> The bitterest and most vigorous opposition came to the fore with the question
> of simulation and pension hysteria. Two currents distinguished themselves here.
> A great number of the insurance doctors, who were not trained in neurology or
> psychiatry, saw simulation everywhere they looked when confronted with symp-
> toms that could not be explained by a lesion of the nerves, brain or spinal re-
> gion. It was especially the psychic and psychogenic disorders which they were
> completely helpless against. And since it mostly involved patients who de-
> manded that the doctors recognize their suffering, they had to impose the suspi-
> cion of simulation.[123]

Thus, for Oppenheim, physicians without clinical experience in psychiatry or neurology, those unfamiliar with the mysterious interplay of mind and body, tended to exaggerate the suspicion of simulation. Psychiatrists, however, committed a different but equally dangerous mistake. When they turned their attention to trauma, he argued, they emphasized the psychological dimensions to the complete exclusion of somatic effects. And the new psychological turn, Oppenheim feared, was accompanied by an increasing emphasis on the pension question. That is, as German psychiatrists paid greater attention to the psychic roots of mental disorders, they focused not on the traumatic event itself but on the subsequent desire for compensation and the pathological effects of pensions. Oppenheim saw danger in this new, ideogenic approach, "And the next step was that the cause of the malady was viewed not as the psychic or emotional consequences of the accident, but rather in the emotionality of the pension struggle."[124] Reflecting back on the status of his theories, years later

Oppenheim recalled, "The term traumatic neurosis [was] everywhere expunged and tabooed, the conception of traumatic hysteria was acknowledged, but tainted by the fact that no sharp boundary between it and simulation was recognized. The trauma was understood as shaped not by the accident, but by the imaginative desires."[125]

Between the 1890 congress and the beginning of World War I, traumatic neurosis fell into ever increasing disfavor with German doctors and social critics. Berlin political scientist Ludwig Bernhard, for example, used pension neurosis to launch an attack on Germany's social insurance system, which, many noted, encouraged sickness and "placed a premium on whining."[126]

Significant changes in the hysteria diagnosis, in its social associations, and in its etiology helped make hysteria an attractive diagnostic alternative to traumatic neurosis. Because it located the pathology's source in the subject's constitution (rather than exogenously in an accident event), hysteria offered the possibility of undoing the economic damage of traumatic neurosis. It complicated the connection between the accident event and postaccident symptoms, thus potentially releasing the state or railway companies from financial accountability. And importantly, it highlighted the will. Hysteria could be seen as a willed, goal-oriented behavior, a so-called *Zweckneurose;* that is, a neurosis that arose as a means to a specific (economic) end. Hysteria's emergence at this time was possible because it had begun to shed its gendered associations, as the process that Charcot began in France took root in German medicine. Indeed, in the late nineteenth century, doctors began to refashion the unwieldy, catch-all diagnosis that hysteria had become into an entity compatible with modern psychiatric currents.[127] At the same time, its persistent gender associations were, to some extent, replaced with the class prejudices of contemporary medicine. "Hysterical" was becoming a description for pathological reactions to stimuli, and its usage as a distinct kind of illness was occurring with less and less frequency. This change reflected a broader transformation in the way psychiatrists viewed mental disease.

Central to this transformation was Emil Kraepelin's taxonomic system, which the psychiatrist publicized in his extremely influential *Textbook of Psychiatric Diseases,* which appeared in many editions between 1883 and 1916.[128] While psychiatric disorders had traditionally been viewed descriptively, that is, defined through common symptoms, Kraepelin reconceptualized mental illnesses by observing their development over time. He recognized common patterns of onset and development and devised the crucial distinction between dementia praecox—later renamed schizophrenia by Eugen Bleuler, an early onset psychosis that deteriorated over time—and manic depressive psychosis, which approximates today's bipolar disorder. With the advent of Kraepelin's nosology, hysteria began to wane from the German psychiatrist's diagnostic arsenal. This does not mean that it disappeared. First, this change was incremental and was never fully completed, and many doctors continued to diagnose hysteria deep into the twentieth century. Second, hysteria survived in its new form as a description or addendum, giving rise to such diagnoses as hystero-neurasthenia, hystero-epilepsy, and hysterical psychopathology, or simply hysterical reaction, hysterical paralysis, or hysterical character. Above all, *hysteria* denoted an abnormal, or psychopathic, mode of reaction, most likely to occur in the constitutionally feeble.[129] The ultimate psychiatric condition was being reduced to an adjective.

What historian Mark Micale calls the "clinical deconstruction" of hysteria began occurring around the turn of the century. Alfred Hoche and Willy Hellpach had made similar arguments in the first years of the twentieth century, but two important articles on the topic which appeared in 1911 suggest that by that year the change was well underway. Robert Gaupp, one of Kraepelin's most influential followers, declared: "Hysteria is not an autonomous illness, not an *entité morbide,*' if by that we mean a disease with a distinct temporality and pattern . . . Rather hysteria is an abnormal way of reacting in the individual. . . . The ranks of those who still hold on to the idea of hysteria as a unified illness are getting smaller every day."[130]

In the same year Karl Bonhoeffer also criticized the old idea of hysteria as a discrete disease. Bonhoeffer did not go so far as several of his colleagues; namely, Karl Wilmanns, who rejected hysteria as a diagnosis, Hoche, who once suggested doing away with the word, and Robert Sommer who proposed the term "psychogenesis" (*Psychogenie*) as a replacement.[131] Hysteria was more than a psychological reaction, argued Bonhoeffer, it also represented a mental constitution or disposition and should thus be retained in the diagnostic arsenal. The key to hysteria, he noted, was the role played by the will. Thus neurotic responses to traumatic experience could occur in perfectly normal people, but in a hysterically disposed subject, the combination of traumatic stimuli and the "will to sickness" would lead to a long-term neurotic condition.

The concept of will, primarily a philosophical idea with strong Nietzschean overtones, took on increasing importance for psychiatry in the late nineteenth century. Despite its significance and widespread usage, *will* was conceived of differently by different neurologists and psychiatrists; originally a nonscientific concept, it was seldom subjected to rigorous scientific scrutiny or given a precise and consistent definition. Its first appearances in psychiatry concerned questions of accountability; a common psychiatric task in the nineteenth century was to judge whether an individual who committed a crime acted out of his own will and intent—that is, to determine whether he deserved punishment or psychiatric confinement—and forensic rulings constituted a major part of psychiatry's midcentury professional activities. Yet, it was beyond dispute that the will played a central role in mental and nervous illness. Gaupp theorized, for example, that the will acted as a "mechanism of inhibition" with which the healthy individual could overcome mental stimuli and control his psychological condition. Willpower, he wrote, protected individuals from illness and "represents the highest achievement of health and strength."[132]

For Gaupp, strength of will was not only a medical characteristic but also a sublime moral virtue. The will connoted self-control, discipline, and stoic calmness, in short, the qualities that contemporaries associated with the masculine ideal.[133] Conversely, Gaupp claimed that individuals lacking a firm "mechanism of inhibition"—in particular, women, effeminate men, children, the uneducated, and those outside the cultural world of Western Europe—were most likely to lose self-control and react to stimuli by "fleeing into" hysterical symptoms. The very vagueness of the will as a psychiatric concept made it a powerful and elastic metaphor that could easily be appropriated for military, economic, and political purposes.

In their 1911 articles, both Gaupp and Bonhoeffer effectively blurred the distinction between hysterical and normal individuals. "There are countless gradations between the hysterical and the normal," wrote the former.[134] So both normally disposed people and those with hysterical constitutions could react hysterically to the same stimuli, but only those with premorbid personalities would develop serious neuroses. Yet, Gaupp's theory raised the question of how, in the absence of objective scientific criteria, the doctor could tell who or what is hysterical and what is not. Gaupp was aware of this problem, but could propose no purely scientific way of resolving it. The doctor simply has a feeling for hysteria, he wrote, "Whether pathological or not is not revealed by the clinical symptomology, but rather requires the evaluation of a whole series of factors which normally do not fall in the natural-scientific realm."[135] By this Gaupp meant that psychologically informed character observation, a judgment based on a grasp of the patient's personality, would be necessary to identify a "hysterical character."

The psychiatrists and neurologists who participated most ardently in the deconstruction of hysteria, men such as Bonhoeffer, Gaupp, Hoche, and Sommer, belonged to a generation born in the decade between 1860 and 1870.[136] As a cohort, they were beginning to become influential in the late imperial period and reached full professional maturity and, in many cases, university chairs in the decade before World War I. As such doctors advanced in the profession, they brought psychology and psychological observation firmly into the psychiatric sphere while increasingly attending to the question of psychopathology and the predisposition to mental and nervous illness.

Due in part to the influence of members of this generation, the two decades before the war's outbreak were tumultuous ones for psychiatry and hysteria. Although Oppenheim was only some seven years older than Sommer and eleven years older than Bonhoeffer, his ideas bore the stamp of a different medical era, a period of materialistic medicine and more liberal politics. Oppenheim's detractors, on the other hand, embodied the growing influence of collectivistic and organicist views on national health; these men tended to subordinate ideas of individual health to what they conceived of as the needs of the national community.[137] These generational and diagnostic changes, together with the experience of the alleged epidemic of pension neurosis, in the context of the economic fluctuations and medical and cultural crises of Wilhelmine Germany, colored the reception and rejection of Oppenheim's ideas and determined the diagnostic trajectory from traumatic neurosis to male hysteria.

CHAPTER 2

Mobilizing Minds
German Psychiatry Goes to War

On all fronts, in the field just as at home, German victory sparkles. It is
the victory of strong German nerves, German composure, German will,
and the discipline of German men. The proliferation of psychoses and
neuroses feared by many has by no means occurred. And the war has
brought no significant increase in nervous and mental illness.

A. A. FRIEDLÄNDER, Medicin und Krieg

In the field all neurotic symptoms disappear as by magic, and one's whole
system is charged with energy and vitality.

FRITZ KREISLER, Four Weeks in the
Trenches: The War Story of a Violinist

Hundreds of thousands of times shells explode in the immediate vicinity
of our soldiers, tens of thousands are buried and dug out only with great
effort, but the elastic nature of the healthy man, who accepts the necessity
of endurance in war, pulls him together quickly again and again. Only a
small percentage succumbs and takes flight into sickness.

ROBERT GAUPP, "Kriegsneurosen"

IN 1910 KAISER Wilhelm II addressed an audience of officers and
cadets at the Naval Academy of Flensburg-Mürwick and proclaimed: "[T]he next war and the next battle at sea will demand of
you healthy nerves. It is through nerves that its outcome will be decided."[1] Victory, declared General Paul von Hindenburg at the height of World War I, will
belong to the nation with the strongest nerves.[2] These uses of nerves as a
metaphor for military strength, resolve, and fitness resonated in Germany's
medical and political culture, and nerves and nervousness had become pervasive parts of Wilhelmine discourse, associated with a sense of national decline,
but also used as symbols of masculine resurgence and strength.[3] More specifically, when military and political leaders invoked nerves, they ceded a certain
degree of authority to those doctors who specialized in the nervous system and
its interdependence with the mind. It implied, thus, an influential role for nerve
doctors—psychiatrists and neurologists—in matters of individual as well as na-

tional health. If, as the Kaiser maintained, nerves determined military success, then neurologists and psychiatrists would be indispensable in the wars of the future.

Emboldened by the culturally prevalent use of nerves as a metaphor for vitality and fitness—and indeed the Kaiser's valorization of nervous strength—many psychiatrists and neurologists believed that their discipline played a crucial role in matters of national health, in peace and in war. Kurt Singer, a Berlin neurologist, echoed this view several months after the outbreak of World War I, writing that superior nerves and a well-balanced nervous system were the keys to successful military service.[4] While serving in the neurological section of a hospital station near the western front, Singer foresaw the significance of psychiatry in modern warfare and drew a connection between military discipline, obedience, and mental health:

> Will and obedience are ultimately determined by the intactness of the nervous system. Therefore psychiatry plays a major role in war, next to the main areas of medical activity: surgery, internal medicine and hygiene. It separates out the ill from the healthy. It prevents the will of an individual, when led astray, from contaminating those around it. Its task is important because mental disorders, when they remain unrecognized, are dangers for the many, for those fit for combat, and for the basic principle of military organization, which is discipline.[5]

In this passage Singer assumes that mental illness can be contagious, and consistent with the collectivistic, social hygienic approaches of Wilhelmine medicine, he asserts that psychiatry's role is to stop that contagion to spare the health of "the many." What is perhaps most striking about Singer's statement, however, is his association of military values such as will, discipline, and obedience with the material properties of the nervous system. In such a way, he medicalizes a set of military and political concerns as he imbues psychiatry with great national and military importance. Psychiatrists, then, used the same language as political and military leaders. As Robert Gaupp stated in a 1917 lecture: "Neither numbers, nor technology, but strength of nerves, that is, mental strength will decide the fate of Europe and the whole world."[6] And in the words of Willy Hellpach, "To restore an endangered life to health is the medical art, but simultaneously to restore the will, to set it back into motion, is the particular art of military medicine."[7]

Indeed, as the events of July and August 1914 unfolded and the European powers slid into war, some of the loudest cheers came from doctors, psychiatrists and neurologists conspicuous among them. Recent scholarship has cast doubt on the assumption that Germans erupted in celebration with a shared prowar enthusiasm and has revealed the shallowness of the *Burgfrieden* (the social truce, or literally palace peace, that the Kaiser declared on the eve of war), showing the subsequent political constructions and appropriations of these national myths.[8] Attitudes toward war clearly varied along such lines as class and region, and the Kaiser's words did little to overcome German society's deep divisions, and while these were temporarily suppressed in the fall of 1914, they forcefully reemerged several years later. Nonetheless, contemporary medical writings consistently celebrated the war's arrival. Although they cannot be taken as representative of a broader war enthusiasm, German doctors' views valorized the idea of national unity, and those heady August days remained a powerful medical reference point for years to come. Doctors, it seems, played a substantial role in establishing and perpetuating the myth of "the spirit of 1914," and medical assumptions throughout the war were shaped by the perception that war overcame social divisions, forged a healthful national unity, and reinvigorated a languishing people.

World War I was what historians call a "total war," a prolonged conflict that embraced nearly all sectors of society and that ultimately required a fully mobilized home front.[9] Doctors were, of course, integral to Germany's encompassing war effort. Many reported for duty immediately after the war's declaration, seeing it as their responsibility to set an example for other members of the populace.[10] Between 1914 and 1918 some 26,300 doctors served in the war (out of the 33,000 who then lived within the borders of the German Empire); approximately two-thirds saw duty in the field, and one-third remained within Germany.[11] These doctors tended the nearly 6 million cases of wounded soldiers and 21.5 million cases of illness that the war produced.[12]

University medical professors, a great many of whom had become reserve officers after fulfilling their compulsory military service, were particularly outspoken in their support of the German cause. These, the most prestigious and influential members of the profession, signed numerous academic petitions and declarations that expressed national solidarity and justified the war as the defensive struggle of a "surrounded" nation, reflecting the rather paranoid fear of "encirclement" that ran through the German imaginary. One such petition, the Reply of the Cultural Federation of German Scholars and Artists to the Declaration of the Professors of Great Britain and the English Academic Circle, bore the signatures of at least fourteen doctors, including psychiatrists Karl Bonhoeffer of Berlin and the Swiss-born Otto Binswanger of Jena. Like numerous other contemporary petitions, this declaration harshly condemned Britain for disrupting the peaceful existence of the German Empire, adding that England had never been threatened by Germany and even denying claims that Belgian neutrality had been violated.[13]

Binswanger expanded on these themes in a lecture he held several months later. Abruptly dismissing accusations that German actions had precipitated the war, he countered that the nation's attention had been devoted to enjoying its newly won national unification and economic prosperity. He rejected the charge that Germany aimed to expand through the acquisition of eastern territories; Germans were aware, the psychiatrist added, that incorporating peoples of different cultural and linguistic identities would threaten their precious and delicate unity.[14]

Other academic declarations cited the need to protect German culture from a perceived threat from abroad and represented armed conflict in abstract cultural, even metaphysical terms. Social theorist Werner Sombart's 1915 polemic, for example, devised a heuristic opposition between "heroes" and "traders" to characterize the differences between German and English archetypes.[15] Praising the generous spirit and dedicated heroism of German culture, Sombart disparaged the English who, he wrote, were motivated solely by profit and individual gain. Though Sombart's view is perhaps an extreme example, similar formulations were found throughout the academic world, and most university scholars shared historian Ulrich Wilcken's readiness to serve the Fatherland with the "weapons of the mind."[16]

As members of Germany's *Bildungsbürgertum,* its educated, affluent bourgeoisie, most doctors had come to embrace the distinct combination of cultural pride and uncompromising patriotism peculiar to their class.[17] Antiwar sentiment among German doctors was scarce in August 1914, even among the small contingent of leftist doctors. None other than the noted left-wing eugenicist Alfred Grotjahn wrote of his "war-fever," a state of intense excitement he experienced at the war's outbreak.[18] In short, medical support for the war effort—even when it meant nothing more than a crude embrace of national stereotypes—transcended political differences and found expression in the terms of an allegedly value-free and suprapolitical science.[19]

The Great Experiment

While their attitudes in August 1914 certainly overlapped with broader European notions, German doctors conceived of war in distinct ways and articulated their support in terms that were unique to their nation and profession. Some welcomed World War I, as many had prior wars, for opportunities to advance medical knowledge, that is, for the chance to analyze the outbreak and development of various diseases in new conditions. In effect, the war promised medical scientists a vast field of human experimentation that would have been unthinkable under normal circumstances, and since all military recruits were screened, the army seemed to provide a perfect experimental sample, a homogeneous, healthy population that could be studied, categorized, and analyzed indefinitely. War conditions, furthermore, seemed ideal for evaluating the relative role of environment and disposition in disease development, a subject of intense interest in many medical fields.[20]

Many medical scientists hoped for a testing ground for the recent breakthroughs in hygiene and pathology, a source of resurgent national pride and scientific optimism; Robert Koch's bacteriological discoveries and late-nineteenth-century microscope technology gave German doctors confidence that they could meet whatever medical challenges the war had in store.[21] Such ambitions were, to a great extent, vindicated: German doctors had unprecedented success in checking disease epidemics, which, in prior wars, had devastated armies and caused far more deaths than combat wounds, and they made significant advances in the areas of blood transfusions, surgical techniques, the treatment of head wounds, and, most notably, orthopedic medicine and the rehabilitation of amputees.[22]

Psychiatrists and neurologists, for their part, looked forward to the "stimulating task" of analyzing the war's effect on the prognosis of mental and nervous illness.[23] During the wars of the 1860s, psychiatry had only recently entered the German university scene, but by 1914 the field was firmly entrenched in the universities, and psychiatrists could mobilize as a profession and vigorously pursue their own research agendas. Furthermore, only at the beginning of the twentieth century had psychiatry become a topic of instruction at the Kaiser Wilhelm Academy for Military Medicine, and it was around that time when the first scientific works on the prevention and treatment of mental illness in the army began to appear.[24]

The steady and prodigious output of neurological and psychiatric studies in both the general medical press and in specialized psychiatric journals during the war attests to the immense professional and intellectual interest these doctors brought to war and its associated conditions. For many, war was "a great teacher," and many psychiatrists and neurologists looked forward to the results of this "massive experiment." Robert Gaupp, director of the psychiatric clinic at the University of Tübingen and Army General Doctor, quoted Heraclitis and extolled war as "the master of all things"; Robert Sommer, head of Giessen's university clinic for nervous disorders, was one of many doctors who described war as an ideal laboratory for studying human nature and the workings of the mind.[25]

In 1915 Sommer characterized war as "a kind of world-historical experiment in the area of national psychology" and termed it "a massive experiment in the functioning of affect and in the activation of mental characteristics."[26] Sommer theorized that the war environment freed people from social inhibitions and unleashed a whole range of sensations that were seldom experienced during normal peacetime existence. The individual in war, he wrote, was subjected to severe physical strain and wild emotionality, but these extraordinary demands were counteracted by the healing influences of patriotism, the desire to be victorious, and "heightened cleverness." Measuring how individuals balanced and processed these powerful sensations provided Sommer with an exciting research agenda. "In a psycho-physiological sense," he wrote, "the war constitutes an enormous stimulant to which individuals react in keeping with their pre-disposed natures, so that their natures, as in a psychological experiment, are clearly illuminated in total sharpness. The war is a great experimenter which brings to light the essence of the individual psyche."[27]

Sommer also saw war as an opportunity to advance psychological and psychiatric treatment. "Since war has as its consequence an endless series of injuries in the physical and psychological sense, the art of healing makes the effort to do away with them and limit them where possible. In this effort it is not just a question of using long familiar methods, rather the art of healing has in many respects achieved great advances through meeting the demands of war."[28] Sommer, who, in addition to his medical degree, had earned a doctorate in philosophy and written a thesis on John Locke's political and legal theory, was particularly interested in the relationship between war and the creative capacity of the human mind.[29] An amateur inventor himself, having designed a machine to enable walking on water, with intended military applications, Sommer linked war with great inventions and human progress in an unpublished treatise on war and creativity. "There is no doubt," he asserted, "that through the experience of the current war in many respects, intellectual ability and inventiveness, by which human knowledge reaches new heights, have been spurred on to extraordinary achievements."[30]

The writings of psychiatrists and neurologists in the summer and fall of 1914 reflected an eagerness to prove their therapeutic proficiency and their indispensability to the nation, goals that betray their prewar professional insecurities. Positing connections between mental health and national strength served to bolster the importance of a science that was threatened by its practical ineffectiveness. Both psychiatrists and preachers, according to Binswanger, were responsible for the mental and moral health of the nation, and both had to provide leadership in moments of national emergency.[31] Dr. Emil Roth, outlining the importance of psychiatry and neurology for the nation and the war effort, wrote, "Just as every other organ, the nerves must be exercised and trained; mental and physical discipline are necessary in order to achieve and preserve the highest possible degree of competitiveness, of nervous discipline and of the hardening [*Stählung*] of the will . . . to constantly increase and improve our capital of nervous strength must be seen as one of the most important tasks of civil—as well as military hygiene."[32]

But beyond the idea that war was good for medicine, many doctors believed that war was good for the men who fought in it. In a nation beset by "nervous crisis," plagued by fears of degeneration, epidemics of neurasthenia, and unchecked traumatic neurosis, war emerged as a kind of nervous cure-all, a collective "nerve corrective."[33] Like the naïve poet sons of the European bourgeoisie, doctors and social critics alike expressed longing for what Franz Marc called "war's purifying fire."[34] Psychiatrists valorized "the mighty healing power of the iron bath [*Stahlbad*] for nerves dried up and languishing in the dust from years of peace and monotonous vocational activity."[35] Indeed, many doctors glorified the wartime environment as a natural and pleasingly bucolic antidote to the deteriorating conditions of Germany's expanding cities and the perceived effects of technology and industrial growth on the mental and moral health of the nation.[36] "The most urgent task of our time," Binswanger proclaimed, "consists without a doubt in freeing the national mind from the damaging effects of modern developments . . . and this task is the common responsibility of doctors and teachers."[37]

Such prescriptions implicitly feminized peace and construed warfare as masculine medicine to revitalize a nervous and sickly populace. "Hardness" had become the new masculine ideal in the later nineteenth century.[38] Masculinity was defensively defined in late-nineteenth-century Germany as a bulwark against the chaos and upheaval associated with the growth of the feminist and labor movements as well as the spread of new technologies and rapid social change. Perceived threats to masculinity and male norms, such as homosexuality and other forms of deviant behavior, were commonly conceived of in medical terms and became increasingly the domain of medical professionals.[39] Nerves, and in particular the allegedly weak nerves of the modern man, writes historian George Mosse, became the locus for fears of degeneration, decadence, and demographic decline.[40] Similar processes were at work in Britain and France too, but in Wilhelmine Germany, with its military values and persistent cultural crises, they took on particular urgency.[41] War, thus, could make things right again by curing the nervous crisis and restoring men to their rightful role.

The celebration of war as the antithesis of a weak and degenerate civilization, indeed as an antidote to the confusions and complexities of modern urban life, can be found in a multitude of medical as well as lay writings, even before 1914.[42] According to the military doctor Walter Fuchs, war was "the only means by which we, as a nation, can be saved from the physical and psychological lethargy and emasculation which are relentlessly threatening."[43] A number of medical scientists theorized that the war created a healthier psychological atmosphere than conditions at home because it provided a simplified existence. Furthermore, doctors celebrated the military environment and the community of comrades at the front, which, they hoped, would further seal the salubrious civil peace.[44] The front experience, according to psychologist Erich Everth, directed the individual's attention to one single goal, thus releasing him from the emotionally damaging dissonance of the modern metropolis.[45] And consistent with the critique of conditions in the cities, a handful of studies concluded that urban professionals, especially intellectuals, and businessmen were more susceptible than country dwellers and agricultural workers to nervous breakdowns in the field.[46]

In light of the realities of World War I, with its appalling trench conditions, its horrifying battlefield carnage, and its formidable new technologies of destruction, this celebration of the war environment appears rather naïve, even absurd. Most of these authors, of course, imagined that the war would be quick and that Germany's soldiers would soon return victorious. But such views endured, even long after the illusion of a short war had been dispelled. Indeed, the belief that war made men healthy was scarcely challenged by reports from the first months of fighting.[47] In fact, observations from the field seemed to confirm the widely held view that war improved the health and uplifted the spirit of its participants. In a 1915 study Alfred Goldscheider, a Berlin neurophysiologist, affirmed that the first winter of fighting had significantly bettered the health of Germany's men. Goldscheider claimed that many individuals who had complained of nervousness before the war had been transformed into healthy and fit soldiers, and he attributed such reversals to, among other causes, the lack of the "damaging influences of civilization" on the front; the success of German hygienic medicine in creating a clean, disease-free environment; and the value of medical screening of recruits, so that those who easily fell ill and spread contagious diseases were not present at the front.[48]

Sommer agreed. Months after the war's outbreak, he noted that war service increased fitness levels. He referred to a "sharpening of the senses," commonly observed among combatants, such that soldiers could hear a railroad approaching from many miles away or distinguish the sound of distant French artillery from that of their own weaponry.[49] As late as September 1915, a colleague at the western front informed Sommer, who remained in Giessen throughout the war, that the health and morale of the troops was holding out remarkably well "It is miraculous how well individuals have adapted to conditions here. They take everything with a degree of indifference; with stoic calmness they read their mail or continue to eat their food quietly in the midst of the strongest shelling. Their state of health is astonishingly good, especially the spirit of the troops, in view of the conditions at hand."[50] Sommer saved a satirical article from a Frankfurt newspaper that reported that the German soldiers had been performing so well that the Russians believed German science had actually developed a "fighting pill" that made soldiers healthier and more effective in battle.[51] The psychiatrist did note, however, that a war of movement was psychologically healthier than stationary, trench warfare; the excitement and exhilaration from advancing effectively counterbalanced any remorse soldiers may feel at having killed—German expansionism, then, was conducive to mental health.[52]

Even sexologists extolled the war's positive impact, reporting that sexual neuroses and impotence improved when men were plunged into the "iron bath" of combat.[53] Given the prevailing concern with degeneration, the crisis of nervousness, and the spread of traumatic neurosis, and in light of the scale and scope of the war that was unfolding and the power of modern weaponry, these early results came as a great surprise to some observers. In the words of Budapest neurologist Julius Donath, "Nothing seemed more likely than that the children of our nervous epoch would lack the necessary resistance to be able to hold off the huge demands of a war of armies of millions with its fronts of hundreds of kilometers in distance; its monotonous, filthy and wet trenches; the astoundingly effective frightful instruments of destruction; combat in water, on land, underwater, in the air; as well as the battles which last for weeks."[54]

However, as Donath reported, "our nervous system . . . has proved to be more durable than was expected."[55] What accounted for the continued nervous health and strength of the Central Powers' troops? What explained the lack of traumatic neuroses and hysterical conditions that Donath and others reported?

The answer, for many doctors, lay in the salutary effects of communal and patriotic feelings. Others valorized the nervous and psychic benefits of fear and danger as opposed to the complacence and idleness of peacetime.

Medical writers also reported that the war was improving the mental and nervous health of the civilian population.[56] In these accounts war fostered feelings of communal solidarity that, many hoped, could overcome decades of division, continuing the Bismarckian strategy of using external conflict to forge domestic unity. As a German nationalist wrote in 1913, "Let us regard war as holy, like the purifying force of fate, for it will awaken in our people all that is great and ready for self-sacrifice, while it cleanses our soul of the mire of petty egotistical concerns."[57] Psychiatric writings endowed national unity and devotion to community with great medicopsychological significance and claimed that the urgency of the war had swiftly resuscitated Germany's sickly, self-absorbed middle classes and reinvigorated its lazy, underproductive workers. Neurotic illness, implied Freiburg psychiatrist Alfred Hoche, among others, was a kind of privilege for the wealthy, a self-serving luxury that was sacrificed amid the national emergency at hand. And traumatic neuroses, the working-class counterpart to bourgeois nervousness, appeared, like worker discontent as a whole, to be suppressed by the salutary effects of mobilization and combat.

Hoche theorized that war conditions, indeed the hardships active soldiers were undergoing, had shamed such people into abandoning their mostly "hypochondriacal" complaints. "[It] is especially noteworthy," he wrote in a 1914 tract, "how frequently functional nervousness has been cured; how, exactly as I prophesied years ago, the luxury-sanitariums have emptied out; how we witness surprising battle achievements from neurasthenic individuals who were relatively useless during peacetime."[58] Goldscheider also observed that since the war's beginning, "the clientele of the nerve doctors has dwindled."[59] In Strasbourg, psychiatrist Robert Wollenberg reported that the hospitals and neurological clinics were quickly deserted. Only the most inveterate of hypochondriacs, he noted, could dwell on their own petty concerns at a time of national urgency.[60] And Bonhoeffer claimed that increasing community feelings caused civilians to disregard the types of minor complaints that usually sent them to the doctor. The Berlin psychiatrist added that people were seeking medical advice less frequently, not only in "luxury sanitariums," but even in prisons.[61]

Even Gaupp, who had so recently decried the state of mental health in Germany's cities, joined in the optimistic chorus, proclaiming: "The nervous health of our people has proved itself to be better than many expected. [Internist Wilhelm] His's statement that 'when it's a matter of life and death, the nervousness ceases,' has often held true. . . . All in all the nervous system of our people in war has shown itself to be strong and good."[62] And writing from the western front in November 1914, the Berlin neurologist Kurt Mendel, noting that the war had lasted far longer than he or anyone else had expected, praised the nervous strength of German men. "Above all," he observed, "it is conspicuous just how few cases of psychoses have arisen in the current war in view of the almost superhuman hardships, excitation and emotional strain which our troops have had to endure . . . in any case, the special facilities for mental illness which were considered in the medical ordinances have proven to be unnecessary."[63]

Otto Binswanger found grounds for optimism in his clinical experiences. After nine months of war, he mused, "despite the aforementioned damaging influences there is still a huge reserve of psychological willpower in the German people."[64] The Jena psychiatry professor celebrated war as the great purifier and described its positive effects on the health of the nervously ill:

> I had a whole series of weak-nerved youths in treatment over the course of the last year and up to the time of the war's outbreak: anxious, cowardly, irresolute, weak-willed little creatures, whose consciousness and feelings were determined only be their own egos and who amounted to nothing more than whiners, complaining of physical and mental pain. Then came the war. The illnesses fell away in an instant. They reported to their divisions and—what seems even more remarkable to me—every single one of them, with only one exception, has held up to this day . . . Thus, even among those with sickly dispositions the great purifier war has done its work.[65]

Others interpreted these results as proof that the Wilhelmine nervous crisis had been greatly exaggerated. "For a long time now," Hoche averred in 1914, "alarmists have been claiming that the mental and nervous health of our people is in dire shape; they have spoken about the morbid countenance of our time, of our decaying culture, of this degenerate nervous epoch . . . I declared war against this opinion in another place a few years ago and made it known that I believed in the future of this people."[66]

Whether German nervous health was holding up better than expected, or if the war deserved credit for restoring it, prevailing psychiatric opinion was optimistic. Alfred Sänger, a Hamburg neurologist, pointed out the positive influence the war was having on the nervous system of psychopaths, many of whom turned out to be effective, even decorated soldiers.[67] Hoche also noted that men with "psychopathic tendencies" often prospered in war. War service, he argued, removed them from unfavorable circumstances and appealed to their sense of adventure.[68] In a widely cited study, the social hygienist Adolf Gottstein observed a decline in suicide rates in Berlin during the first six months of the war, and many doctors, most notably Karl Bonhoeffer, reported with satisfaction that rates of alcoholism had dropped in response to the war, attributing this too to the positive effects of the new unity and communality among the German people (and not to the more obvious antecedent of the alcohol bans and rationing that were enacted during mobilization.)[69] A study by the city of Berlin's welfare office showed that many alcoholics often performed well in the army, becoming "new men"; others, however, had to be quickly rushed back home.[70] Finally, doctors and criminologists noted that the war's advent brought a decrease in civilian delinquency, which could not be entirely explained through the enlistment of criminals; some theorized that this decline owed to the fact that war created a natural and healthy outlet for pathologically pent-up aggression.[71]

In addition to praising the physical benefits of the war's material conditions, its "fresh air" and "disease-free" front circumstances, numerous psychiatrists put forth political-psychological explanations for the health and good performance of the German troops. Beyond the argument that war discouraged selfishness and individualism and cultivated more exalted feelings of national community, medical commentators credited the *Burgfrieden* and the new sense of national unity for exerting a positive influence on individual and collective mental health. The key concept in these formulations was the will; Germany's health and strength depended on the union of individual wills behind the national cause.

Goldscheider was one of many doctors who extolled the *Burgfrieden* as the retreat of the self behind a collective, unified will: "The experience of war causes things that concern the individual ego to appear less significant, the attention is devoted to the body populace [*Volkskörper*], the individual feels no longer in the center of things, rather as a member of the whole nation."[72] By submerging himself to the collective, Goldscheider continued, the individual becomes a stronger, healthier being. "The activity of the will is raised to the highest conceivable level through love of Fatherland, through mutual example and not least through camaraderie, which melds superiors and subordinates into a single mass of will. The emanations from this heightening of will benefit individual hygiene in many different ways."[73]

Because hysteria was understood as an illness of will, resulting from a lack of self-control or willpower, national unity emerged as hysteria's corrective, as a guarantor of national nervous health; individual weakness of will, that is, could be counteracted and strengthened by the collective will of the national community. For Goldscheider, then, the strengthening of the will, achieved through feelings of patriotic unity, also supported the natural healing process, strengthened the body's resistance to illness, and enabled individuals to overcome tremendous physical adversity. Just as a strong will was seen as keeping the individual's personality in a balanced state, the will of the Fatherland was supposed to impose healthful order on all of its members, encourage them to place their own needs behind the general good, and in such a way greatly improve their military effectiveness. Goldscheider saw no contradiction between individual willpower and obedience to the "national will"; the individual was made strong and healthy through subservience to the national community.

Testaments to the salutary effects of national unity run throughout these early wartime medical writings. "This whirlwind war," wrote Binswanger, "and especially the communal ideal, the ideal of the Fatherland, has purified and fortified our minds, raising them to a new, more sublime level."[74] And in a vividly organistic passage, Hoche also praised the feelings of national unity and simultaneously extolled the healthful consequences of the unity of will:

> Our subjective, individual claim on everything has dwindled away; there is no more right to individual joy, no right to mourn as an individual; the entire *Volk* has been transformed into a single, unified, closed organism of a higher order, not only in a political-military sense, but also for the consciousness of each individual. The telegraph lines are the nerve endings of this great new body, through which identical feelings, identical strivings of the will oscillate at the same moment without regard for time and space.[75]

The psychiatrist Ernst Meyer, writing from a hospital station in Königsberg, proclaimed: "The interest of the single individual retreats behind the greater goals of the collective [*Gesamtheit*], and in such a way the individual, as a component of the whole, takes on the strength [to overcome] extraordinary psychological and physical demands."[76] And for Sommer, "the training of the will is the most important task of military education—on it depends the war preparedness of the individual as well as of the whole *Volk*."[77] The goal of military training, Sommer elaborated, was to train the individual recruit so that his will completely dominated his body. And concerning the psychological reasons for "Germany's enormous military strength," he later wrote: "It is a matter of the training of recruits—psychologically expressed—of the completion of the individual will through the collective; the individual will finds firm ground in the collective will, which breathes life into millions of comrades in the same manner."[78]

In these examples, doctors were merely articulating a medical version of widely held beliefs, and organistic, even mystical depictions of national unity ran through Germany in the summer of 1914. Gertrude Bäumer, for example, leader of the League of German Women's Associations, recalled that during those August days, "The limitations of our egos broke down, our blood flowed to the blood of the other, we felt ourselves one body in a mystical unification."[79] To be sure, these evocations of national and spiritual unity were themselves propagandistic and did not reflect deeply held, long-term values. They did show, however, a widespread tendency to sanctify war and to use an external cause to diffuse internal conflict and division. Their organicism, furthermore, can be seen as a response to the social question, an appeal to the peoples' biological unity as an organizing principle for a socially, regionally, and religiously fragmented country. Indeed, these assumptions strongly influenced medical perceptions and approaches—for many doctors a lasting association had been forged between national unity, military success, and mental health, and reestablishing these conditions became a central medical goal through the Great War and beyond.

The valorization of the positive effects of the unified will also had a negative side. Sufferers of wartime psychopathology, that is, those viewed as mentally or nervously unfit for the demands of war, came to be seen as not only weak-willed individuals, unable to control their own bodies, but also as men who were antithetical and threatening to national unity, communal health, and the collective well-being of the German nation. With the duration of the war and the onset of epidemic war neurosis, strength of will became increasingly synonymous with military obedience and ultimately with economic productiveness and German patriotism.[80] The notion of the will, which united medical, psychological, and philosophical concepts, was laden with political meanings in 1914 as Germans celebrated mobilization, in 1916–1917 when they once again succumbed to fractious social struggle, and in 1918 and beyond as they sought explanations and scapegoats for military defeat and political upheaval.

The Pathologies of Mobilization

Despite these panegyrics to war and its physical and psychological benefits, several doctors did find cause for concern in the appearance of so-called mobilization psychoses, the pathological delusions and obsessions that were widely observed among the population during the days leading up to the war.[81] The intense upheaval and excitement of national mobilization seemed overwhelming for many civilians and mobilizing soldiers, a phenomenon that captured the attention of a number of psychiatrists and neurologists. Freud, for example, wrote of the sense of bewilderment and the "mental distress" suffered by many civilians at the outbreak of war.[82] The Strasbourg psychiatrist Robert Wollenberg noted that from the very beginning of mobilization, "a veritable flood of excited patients flowed over the psychiatric clinic."[83] The situation seemed even more serious in East Prussian towns, where doctors reported outbreaks of mass hysteria, especially among women terrified by the Russian army's rapid approach.[84]

In its portrayal of the heightened suggestibility of the crowd, psychiatric concern with mobilization psychosis betrays an intellectual debt to Gustav LeBon, the French founder of mass psychology. Writing at the end of the nineteenth century, LeBon warned of the dangerous influence of the irrational, debased crowd on the Third Republic's cultural and political life.[85] Like LeBon, German commentators portrayed the crowd as an organism, an irrational, fickle entity that rushed to the lowest common denominator of its constituent members. Being part of the crowd made people prone to rash, short-sighted judgments and to the seductive entreaties of demagogues—it represented a kind of lower evolutionary state, the exact antithesis of the health-giving properties of the unified national will.

Chroniclers of mobilization psychosis invoked this kind of critique in describing the reactions to national mobilization. They claimed that the civilian population quickly fell prey to a series of rumors, from an obsession with espionage, to fear of starvation, to anxiety over bank collapse.[86] Most at risk were urban populations because mobs could easily form in the cities, where communication was rapid, and city dwellers were seen as less stable than their rural counterparts. Yet, many diagnosticians of mobilization psychosis reached optimistic conclusions. For Helenefriderike Stelzner, a psychiatrist and school medical officer in Charlottenburg, and one of the few women who wrote on wartime psychiatry or neurology, the phenomenon's prompt disappearance proved the enduring mental health of the German people. Mobilization psychosis was nothing compared to the hysteria that gripped British women around suffrage, and the fact that these "egoistic" reactions to the outbreak of war faded and "flowed together into a stream of communal altruism" reaffirmed Stelzner's faith in the power of national unity.[87]

Nevertheless, the fear that German society was gripped by mobilization psychosis did inspire attention in psychiatric circles. Apparently, the idea that the German people suffered from a mass psychosis during the mobilization phase was first proposed by a French psychiatrist.[88] Germany's nerve doctors generally conceded that the populace had reacted somewhat pathologically, but they commonly dismissed this as a short-term disturbance rather than an ominous sign of troubles to come. For many doctors, the pathologies of mobilization resulted from a temporary discrepancy between intellect and affect; that is, the mind was overwhelmed and unable to smoothly process the sudden emotions of fear, excitement, and anxiety. Significantly, according to Bonhoeffer and others, only those predisposed to psychic illness were affected.[89] More seriously, however, mobilization psychosis seemed to affect many recently called-up soldiers. But again, the individuals in question were most often deemed predisposed to mental illness; as such, mobilization provided a way to screen recruits for psychopathology. "It is instructive," wrote Wollenberg, "to see with what certainty and speed the organism of the army immediately discharged these, its least fit members."[90]

In a 1915 article Walter Fuchs contradicted the positive conclusions of many of his colleagues. Fuchs observed that "even before the first shots were fired, the mental institutions filled up with astonishing suddenness."[91] Significantly, Fuchs noted that such psychoses arose only in the predisposed, in those who lacked willpower and possessed a degenerate constitution; their self-absorption and preoccupation with their own lives then turned into somatic symptoms. Like Stelzner, however, Fuchs concluded that the prognosis was good. And mobilization psychosis could certainly be seen in a positive light; it did the army a service by quickly removing these "inferior" men from its ranks. "All in all," Hoche added, "one could say that mobilization has served as a fine, very useful filter for weeding out militarily unfit elements."[92]

Albert Moll, a sexologist, noted that such "mass psychoses" appeared with decreasing frequency as one approached the front, showing that the common assumption of the front's salubrious environment—and indeed civil society's pathogenic influence—remained dominant despite the mobilization experience.[93] And finally, the psychiatrist Konrad Alt, acknowledging the occurrence of this so-called epidemic, argued that it should not be viewed as a source of shame. Alt asserted that mobilization psychosis was short-lived; soon the positive mental effects of war would outweigh the pathology of overexcitation, he reassured. He even used this occurrence as evidence of Germany's peaceful intentions: "Is it not unmistakable proof that the German people were living in complete peace, never even entertaining the possibility of war?"[94]

The War Neurosis Crisis

While the assumptions behind them remained firmly intact, the vociferous celebrations of war's miraculous healing powers faded amid the unforeseen horrors of prolonged, industrial warfare. Although many German doctors continued to rhapsodize on the superior nervous and mental health of their nation's troops and the purported healthful benefits of the military environment, by Christmas 1914 alarming reports of widespread psychological breakdown among soldiers in the field had begun to appear, and the increasingly frequent occurrence of nervous disorders could no longer be overlooked.[95] "Certainly we are a nervously strong people," wrote Hermann Oppenheim, "but that does not change the fact that we observe severe and very serious forms of nervousness (in the broadest sense of the term, including hysteria, etc.) even in sturdy peasant boys, workers, active officers and NCOs [noncommissioned officers] from all parts of the land."[96]

Robert Gaupp, who had rejoiced that the war was bringing an end to the "crisis of nervousness," saw his Tübingen university clinic converted into a hospital for nervously ill soldiers in September 1914. Like Oppenheim and numerous others, Gaupp considered December 1914 the starting point after which numbers of nervous casualties sharply rose. He blamed that month's French counteroffensives for producing "pathological states of agitation and nervous breakdowns . . . in those persons in whose vicinity shells have exploded."[97]

Thus, the events of late fall and winter 1914, the transition from a war of advancement to one of stagnation, indeed the entrenchment along an essentially stagnant front that soon stretched some four hundred miles—from the Swiss border in the south all the way up to the English Channel—was held responsible for a severe outbreak of psychological breakdown among German troops in the field. In particular, heavy artillery, with its powerfully reverberating and frightening, repetitious firing, appeared to pose unforeseen dangers to men's nervous and mental health. The symptoms shown by this new class of casualties—the stuttering, persistent shaking, nervous tics, and sudden loss of speech, hearing, and sight—expressed the fragility of the body against the mysterious and terrible powers of the war's massive new weapons and the hardships of life in the damp, disease-ridden trenches. These conditions—soon labeled war neuroses—became the central preoccupation of many neurologists and psychiatrists for the next four years, and the number of men affected reached well into the tens of thousands, ultimately approaching as many as two hundred thousand.[98]

Early reports of mounting nervous casualties caught Germany's medical corps completely unprepared. The negligible numbers of recorded cases from earlier wars, mainly the Franco-Prussian and Russo-Japanese conflicts and Germany's colonial campaigns in southwest Africa, had yielded little therapeutic insight. Despite the warnings of several prescient psychiatrists, special military psychiatric facilities were scarce, field hospitals did not contain psychiatric wards, and most medical officers in the field had little or no training in how to recognize these disorders and handle psychiatric patients. Furthermore, in light of the generally favorable findings about the mental and nervous health of German troops early in the conflict, the sudden and dramatic increase in nervous disorders at the end of 1914 came as an even greater surprise and forced some (but by no means all) doctors to reevaluate their faith in the healing powers of war.[99]

At first, psychiatrists concentrated on prophylaxis, and early wartime studies seldom even entertained the possibility of treating these vexing disorders. This emphasis reflected the profession's prewar activities and attentions, and few psychiatrists possessed significant practical, clinical insight. Nor had very many psychiatrists shown interest in neurosis, a subject that was dominated by neurologists and general practitioners in the late nineteenth and early twentieth centuries. The therapeutic pessimism of the prewar years was conspicuous in psychiatrists' early confrontations with the psychological casualties of war.

In place of therapy, and reflecting the influence of the prewar mental hygiene movement, several doctors stressed the necessity of separating so-called war neurotics from their units, to protect healthy men from the dangers of "psychic contagion."[100] In an essay written on the eve of the war's outbreak, Bonhoeffer singled out prophylactic measures—to avoid epidemics of what he called "war psychosis"—as the most important task of wartime psychiatry. The goal, for Bonhoeffer, was to weed out those likely to succumb to mental illness in the face of combat. Soldiers who were "not up to the demands which discipline, the physical and mental exhaustion of military service place upon them, and are thus disposed, as a consequence of their mental instability, to be thrown off kilter," were to be kept far from their units and discharged as quickly as possible.[101] Significantly, Bonhoeffer assumed that these conditions were contagious and that keeping infectious men away from their healthier comrades was a psychiatric responsibility.

Yet, in determining which soldiers were most susceptible to developing nervous disorders, that is, screening out recruits predisposed to breaking down, doctors had little to go on. The German Ministry of War had appointed a commission under the direction of psychiatrist Theodor Ziehen in 1905 to develop methods for identifying the so-called feebleminded (*Schwachsinnig*) and mentally ill in its ranks.[102] But it was not until December 1917 that psychological testing was first instituted, and those tests focused on measuring intelligence, not on seeking evidence for predisposition to neurosis or psychosis, an endeavor that the Americans pioneered when they entered the war in 1917.[103] Indeed, the signs of predisposition remained frustratingly elusive, and later studies refuted any simple correlation between physical health, intelligence, and mental stability. If anything, the heightened manpower needs of the middle of the war lowered the recruitment standards and brought in greater numbers of individuals who would have been considered prone to mental or nervous breakdown by existing criteria.[104] There was also some discussion of how to prevent breakdowns in the field, by, for example, restricting mobilized soldiers' use of tobacco, a stimulant that at least since Max Nordau was often linked to nervous weakness and neurasthenia.[105] These various initiatives and the warnings of psychiatrists such as Bonhoeffer, however, generally concerned chronic states of mental illness and disorientation rather than functional neuroses and nervous breakdowns. Even the most vocal prognosticators of degeneration had no idea of the challenges awaiting wartime psychiatry.

Doctors in the field were perplexed by these conditions. Believing that such patients suffered from treatable organic afflictions, simply puzzled by their symptoms, or acting to prevent much feared "psychic epidemics" in their units, they generally sent neurotics back to German territory to be treated in the large reserve hospitals.[106] The field doctor's task, then, was to keep neurotics calm as they were prepared for transport, which was often accomplished through the injection of morphine or various anesthetics and the use of restraining mechanisms, isolation, and baths where the appropriate facilities existed.[107]

Once transferred to reserve hospitals, such patients generally faced a series of ineffectual treatments. Because these conditions seemed to have an organic basis in the nervous system, many doctors used remedies that worked on the nerves somatically. These early attempts at therapy sought above all to calm the patients. Early therapeutic interventions generally aimed to soothe soldiers through warm baths, massages, and nutrient-rich diets, often with the addition of sedatives and painkillers such as morphine or veronal.[108] Others strove to recharge their subjects' depleted nervous systems with bed rest, hydrotherapy, or mild doses of electric current.[109]

These regimens represented a peculiar adaptation of the "rest cure," a treatment program developed by the Philadelphia physician Silas Weir Mitchell and used to treat neurasthenic women of the upper classes around the turn of the century.[110] Based on the premise that the strains of modern life could dangerously deplete the nervous system's energy, Mitchell's treatments—derived from his experiences as a doctor in the Civil War—involved enforced bed rest in a soothing pastoral setting, cessation of all stimulating activities, and occasional bursts of electrotherapy to recharge the weakened nerves. Sharing Mitchell's materialist model of the nervous system, many German doctors assumed that mobilization and combat could overtax the body's finite supply of nerve energy; consequently, therapy aimed to reinvigorate the nerves and refresh the body. Yet, such techniques, with their emphasis on creating a relaxing, calming environment, did little to cure the ranks of suffering soldiers, and few German doctors reported much if any success in treating the first waves of war neurotics who arrived at their hospitals.

Treatments that involved work soon became more popular than those that stressed relaxation. In southwestern Germany, a form of work or "occupational therapy" (*Beschäftigungstherapie*) was implemented in 1915. War neurotics were put to work on farms and in forests in the hope that these activities would distract them from their symptoms and encourage them to recover naturally.[111] But the program met with little success, and most of the patients were returned to hospitals for several months until they were discharged uncured and with pensions "with the expectation that the cessation of military service would exert a healing influence on their maladies."[112] That was, however, seldom the result. Once discharged, according to most psychiatrists, these men had no reason to get better and could become "addicted" to their pensions. A Baden study followed up on a sample of these uncured patients after discharge and ascertained that only 11 percent had recovered. Of the others, roughly one-third had reentered their prior occupations in a limited capacity, and two-thirds were "severely economically diminished." A discouraging 38 percent of the sample "lived completely idly off their military pensions and the charity of their fellow-men."[113]

With few exceptions, through 1915 the growing ranks of war neurotics were either discharged as unable to serve or, having been quickly evacuated to German territory, remained in army reserve hospitals where they occupied precious space and taxed limited military-medical resources. Gaupp's fear that "in the end hysteria has revealed itself [to be] stronger than the doctor" seemed incontrovertible.[114] Indeed, the enormous casualties produced by the massive battles of 1916 further exacerbated the problem of overcrowding in army hospitals. Furthermore, doctors deemed the presence of large numbers of neurotics "idly lying about" (*herumliegen*) medical facilities a detriment to the morale and discipline of convalescent soldiers that could encourage otherwise healthy men to simulate nervous disorders.[115] This judgment, amplified through the rhetorical use of "idly lying about"—and the occupational therapy regime itself—reflected the medical assumption of the healing power of work and by extension the pathological and even pathogenic nature of idleness.

Eventually, the gentle and "mild" approach to war neurotics began to draw fire. For some critics its pleasantness made neurosis too attractive an option for terrified soldiers and encouraged further outbreaks.[116] "In roughly the first year of the war," psychiatrist Karl Pönitz recalled, the war hysterics were treated with extraordinary mildness, they were allowed to lie about the hospitals, so that they might enjoy their peace, with the result that virtually nothing was achieved, the symptoms either remained, or suddenly reappeared when they were to be returned to their troops, and the number of hysterics who lay around in the hospital stations at the beginning increased more and more.[117]

Pity and charity were increasingly decried as soft, feminine, and, as Pönitz implied, pathogenic; newer approaches placed patients in an all-male world, away from the "damaging pity" of sympathetic relatives and welfare workers.[118] The war hysteric, like the peacetime accident hysteric, was becoming an object of opprobrium for whom traditional medical standards were deemed inappropriate. To rehabilitate hysterical men, many doctors came to believe, required abandoning passive, "soft," and soothing cures and adopting active, "harder," and more aggressive interventions that offered no relief from the conditions and hierarchies of war.[119] Rather than condemning war for its apparently destructive powers over mind and body, many psychiatrists continued to uphold it as a healthy antidote to civilian conditions. These enduring assumptions were reflected in the diagnosis, treatment, and rehabilitation of the war's countless nervous casualties.

PART II

War Hysteria

Diagnosis, Treatment,
Rehabilitation

CHAPTER 3

Long Live Hysteria!
The Wartime Trauma Debate and
the Fall of Hermann Oppenheim

The great fight against traumatic neurosis ended, and it was dethroned.
And now the phrase of choice is "Down with traumatic neurosis, long
live hysteria!"

ARTHUR VON SARBO,
"Granatfernwirkungsfolgen und Kriegshysterie"

Hysteria has now overflowed all banks, and nothing is safe from it.

HERMANN OPPENHEIM

FIRST FACED WITH the shaking, stuttering, tremors and tics,
muteness, deafness, and paralysis in the many men who arrived
at their war hospitals, Germany's doctors tried out a number of
theories and diagnoses. In the absence of diagnostic uniformity, doctors often
gave these symptom sets descriptive designations, such as nerve shock (*Ner-venshock*) or shell concussion (*Granatkontusion*);[1] other typical terms included
exploding-shell paralysis (*Granatexplosionslähmung*) or the distant impact of
shell explosions (*Granatfernwirkung*).[2] These early designations emphasized
the direct connection between a combat-related shock, such as a mine or gre-
nade explosion, and the subject's subsequent nervous symptoms. Such somatic
sounding diagnoses resemble the English term *shell shock*, which proved to be
an enduring expression and remains part of standard English parlance, reflecting, in the terms of one scholar, the tremendous influence of World War I
on the modern imagination.[3] *Shell shock*, however, was banned by the British
War Office in 1917 because it implied a somatic connection between the shell
and the shock, which, British doctors came to believe, was not only misleading
but also discouraged men from getting better; the term was replaced with "Not
Yet Diagnosed Nervous" or NYDN.[4]

Like shell shock, early German diagnoses were less a reflection of sustained
medical inquiry than of the awe inspired by the war's powerful weapons. As
was the case with the nineteenth-century's new technologies of transportation

and production, the war's modern methods of destruction were associated with new and mysterious pathologies. The bizarre, involuntary contortions of the war neurotic's body bespoke, it seemed, the hidden dangers of modern, mechanized warfare. The unprecedented power and range of modern artillery, for example, seemed especially damaging to the mind and nerves. Indeed, persistent shaking, perhaps the paradigmatic war neurosis symptom, seemed to be the inscription of the resounding, repetitious blasts on the fragile body—patients' nervous twitching mirrored the rhythm of the ceaseless, distant drum of enemy fire.

Most German doctors had never seen anything resembling these peculiar symptoms, but they looked familiar to one group of practitioners, those who had dealt with the so-called accident neurotics or pension hysterics before the war, and this group quickly asserted its authority over the war neurosis issue. Hence, it was not long before diagnostic disunity gave way and the great majority of German psychiatrists reached a consensus that these conditions—like the accident cases of the 1890s—were best labeled hysteria. "War hysteria," a direct parallel to "pension hysteria," became the diagnosis of choice.

As such, psychiatrists chose a diagnosis with a powerful negative stigma and enduring feminine associations. The male hysteria diagnosis, once a taboo, was not only acceptable by the middle of the war but was turned into a rallying cry, a patriotic crusade inflected with nationalistic and military language. This passage, the trajectory from a state of diagnostic disunity to the new hysteria consensus involved, in many respects, a repetition of the traumatic neurosis debate of the 1880s and 1890s, but at a time when concern over economic productivity and male health reached new levels of urgency. It offers a striking example of the ways in which the surrounding political, economic, and social context influence diagnostic change in the history of psychiatry and how scientific ideas can resonate with broader cultural patterns. Indeed, even the idea of objective science, as the trauma debate shows, became a highly politicized weapon, which was closely tied to, and often indistinguishable from, concern with the national cause.

History repeated itself, for once again the debate centered around Hermann Oppenheim, and once again, Oppenheim found himself at odds with the leaders of the profession and with larger social and cultural forces. In the debate's second round, the stakes were higher and the results more consequential for Oppenheim, for his profession, and for the German state.

The War and Traumatic Neurosis

In the war's early months, as wounded men began streaming into Germany from the front, Berlin's Museum of Applied Arts, like numerous other civilian facilities, was converted into a reserve hospital. Alerted to the rapidly growing numbers of nervously ill combatants, military-medical authorities set aside some two hundred beds in the makeshift museum hospital for neurological and psychiatric casualties. The director of this wing was the neurologist Hermann Oppenheim.[5]

As the first waves of nervous casualties came into the museum hospital station in 1914, Oppenheim saw hysteria. He subscribed, at first, to the view that these disorders were strictly functional, that is, that they had no basis in anatomical or physiological change and could be explained as purely psychological reactions. Oppenheim also believed, initially, that such disturbances occurred chiefly in predisposed individuals, that is, that traumatic combat events themselves were not inherently pathogenic and played only a secondary role to the patient's internal constitution. As he later recalled, "When this or that soldier suffered a nervous breakdown, he was so disposed, nervously weak or psychopathic. The psychological trauma of the war seemed only to bring to fruition that which was already latent. I too had this impression at the outset."[6]

Yet, after prolonged exposure to these cases, Oppenheim changed his mind. He became convinced that the symptoms were genuine and that they did not require some sort of constitutional deficiency. His detailed neurological investigations, furthermore, unearthed a range of neurophysiological abnormalities that were difficult to dismiss as hysteria. Indeed, coming from private practice, his inclination was to take patient complaints seriously and to look closely for somatic, physiological irregularities. This meant that Oppenheim found himself moving in the opposite direction from most of his colleagues; as he turned away from the hysteria diagnosis, they were embracing it with a new zealousness. "In terms of the symptoms . . . which fit under the label of traumatic neurosis," he asserted in 1915, "the war has confirmed our earlier experiences, deepened our knowledge and supplied our theories with a more solid basis."[7] "The war has given me the opportunity," he stated in a lecture at Berlin's Charité clinic:

> to make a great number of observations which exactly conform to those that I made twenty-five to thirty years ago here at the Charité—especially those in connection with severe railroad accidents—these are the observations which led me to put forward the highly contentious doctrine of traumatic neurosis. I said nothing on this topic for a long time, particularly because other scientific questions and interests increasingly occupied my attention. But it gives me great satisfaction to see it all again and to see every single one of my characterizations and conceptions confirmed.[8]

In war neurotics, thus, Oppenheim saw further evidence for traumatic neurosis, leading him to revive his earlier theories at a time when, for most German psychiatrists and neurologists, the trauma debate had been long resolved. Traumatic neurosis, firmly rejected by the majority of the profession already in the 1890s and closely associated with alleged epidemics of "pension hysteria," had been constructed as a threat to the *Volk*'s collective health and economic productivity. And the precedent of the Wilhelmine pension neurosis scare left its mark on wartime practice. It meant that military-medical authorities strove to avoid epidemics of pension hysteria among soldiers and veterans. The course and tenor of the diagnostic debate reflected the depth of this abiding concern.

This prehistory helps explain the particularities of the war neurosis issue in Germany. Histories of British psychiatry have recounted the vigorous debate between somatic theories, with their more dignified, manly connotations, and psychological explanations, which tended to chastise, even effeminize soldiers.[9] In Germany, on the other hand, since the late nineteenth century, the hysteria diagnosis had become entangled with notions of work and productivity, and thus its class-specific characteristics emerged as stronger than its gender associations.[10] Unlike their British and French counterparts, who showed great concern with the sexuality of neurotic soldiers, German psychiatrists saw war neurosis within the narrower framework of work and rehabilitation.[11] Hysteria still retained the stigma of femininity—neurologist Max Nonne, for one, noted the disease's "feminine and ignoble connotations" in the middle of the war[12]—but the late-nineteenth-century precedent helps explain why the taboos against diagnosing hysteria proved far less durable in German medicine, why few German doctors called attention to the improbability of male hysteria, and why male hysterics were not frequently effeminized or castigated as homosexuals.[13]

Economic concerns, which were heightened by the tremendous costs of waging total war, and in particular the fear of "renewed" epidemics of pension hysteria, sharpened the trauma controversy and turned opposing traumatic neurosis into a matter of national urgency. Less than a year after the war's outbreak, in fact, Gaupp declared it "the most important duty of the neurologist and the psychiatrist to protect the *Reich* from a proliferation of mental invalids and war pension recipients."[14] Around the same time, Hoche, no less strident an opponent of traumatic neurosis than before, was already concerned with the consequences of demobilization, when millions of working-class men would return home from the war. "Then a grave and thankless task will await the German medical profession," he warned, "since all kinds of physical and nervous disorders, which will have arisen without any external causes, will be traced back to the demands of battle."[15] Hoche, among others, feared the coming crisis of postwar invalid pensions; the psychiatric contribution to the war effort thus involved, above all, refuting traumatic neurosis and trying to root it out of medical and popular discourse.[16]

Doctors such as Hoche believed that Germans should be more concerned with the dangers of diagnostic and pension policies than with the direct nervous and mental consequences of war conditions. In the words of the Altona psychiatrist Walter Cimbal:

> I have no fear that after the war countless pension hysterics will interrupt the continued production of the people—that is, unless we artificially create an epidemic of war neurosis. It is simply a matter of avoiding the false doctrine of the

accident neuroses, through which influential circles of our colleagues have imposed upon the German *Volk* the heavy burden of thousands of work-shy individuals. I am referring to the accident hysterics, whose epidemic appearance was
made possible solely by the introduction of an elusive and uncontrollable concept.[17]

Cimbal's statement centers on an opposition between "influential circles of
our colleagues" and the German *Volk*. His contemporaries would have understood that the "influential circles" referred to Oppenheim, whom he not only
separates from the German people but whose ideas he blames for creating the
pension hysteria epidemic, which in turn burdened the hard-working *Volk*.[18]
The task for good, patriotic doctors, then, was to combat Oppenheim's nefarious influence over the profession and the German people. This opposition—
and indeed the construction of traumatic neurosis as a threat imposed from outside—evoked the ways in which the medical world was divided. Oppenheim,
as a private clinician with a bourgeois, partly Jewish, and often foreign patient
base, belonged to a medical subculture that was vulnerable to being construed
as antithetical and alien to the "hard-working German people." Oppenheim's
home, Berlin, was represented as a bastion of his influence, a depiction that
drew from the capital's liberal medical tradition, its history of oppositional politics, and its high concentration of Jewish doctors.[19] Thus, Cimbal's words were
part of a larger discourse that evoked Oppenheim's status on the margins of
university psychiatry and neurology. Such formulations helped lay the ground-
work for the wholesale rejection of Oppenheim's ideas and the casting of the
wartime trauma debate in explicitly nationalist terms.

Oppenheim understood the hostile reaction to his theories. He admitted that
accident disability cases had become a tremendous time drain on psychiatrists
and neurologists and that such patients had begun to crowd hospitals and clinics in the years before the war, earning the resentment of the medical profession, particularly of those doctors who worked in universities and public
hospital settings and who shouldered the burden of the numerous pension applications.[20] He further acknowledged that dealing with trauma cases and assessing pensions was an unappealing responsibility, but, he cautioned, "We
have to admit that the aversion with which many of us approach this activity
is not exactly suited to keeping our judgments free, pure and just."[21]

Oppenheim was also keenly aware of the economic implications of the debate. It was clear that traumatic neurosis was a more expensive diagnosis because
it meant that, in theory, every war neurotic was untreatable and pension-eligi-
ble, an extremely unpopular proposition in the context of wartime economic
concerns. In the words of a charitable chronicler of the debate, "I have no doubt
that [Oppenheim's] theory of traumatic neurosis will experience a more favorable reception in the world to come than it has been given amid the passions of
the war mood of our world."[22]

With the hysteria diagnosis, on the other hand, the pension question became subjective and malleable, which made it attractive for economic reasons and which also resonated with newer currents in psychiatric classification. Since hysteria denoted an abnormal way of reacting to an event, it meant that the pathology was not unleashed by the event itself but lay rather in the patient's constitution or could be attributed to ideas that had been planted in the subject's mind. Such reactions were not necessarily actionable, and if a pathological predisposition could be established, then a pension was ruled out because only conditions *caused* by war service qualified for military compensation.[23] The diagnostic debate was not about economics per se, but economic considerations shaped the reception, misrepresentation, and rejection of the traumatic neurosis theory. "In view of the enormous economic damage to the state," wrote the Hamburg neurologist Alfred Sänger, "[traumatic neurosis] should be jettisoned not only for scientific but also for practical reasons."[24]

The diagnostic debate flared up many times during the early part of the war, and Oppenheim's confrontations with his opponents were consistently described (by both sides) with militaristic metaphors. Referring to the first wartime meeting of the Berlin Society for Psychiatry and Nervous Illness, Oppenheim noted that the differences "were nearly as great as those between the belligerent countries."[25] That meeting was held at the Charité on December 14, 1914, not long after the first reports of war neurosis made it back to home territory.[26] Karl Bonhoeffer began the proceedings by presenting several patients who showed typical symptoms, such as inability to walk or stand (abasia), voice and speech disorders, functional tremors and trembling, gross contractions, and irregular heart beat and blood pressure. These symptoms, he asserted, were hysterical in character.

Bonhoeffer drew a crucial distinction between the cause of the neurotic symptoms, or their "moment," and the symptoms' subsequent "fixation." He distinguished between the fear, terror, or shock at the root of a hysterical reaction and the ideas or desires that could cause these reactions to develop into full-blown, persistent neuroses. Under normal circumstances, Bonhoeffer added, these cases presented no great therapeutic difficulty; the symptoms could be easily removed when the diagnosis had been made accurately and promptly. But when these psychogenic cases were "misdiagnosed" by untrained army medics and erroneously labeled organic they could become "fixed" and often proved tenacious. Thus, leading a soldier to believe that his malady was real (i.e., rooted in an organic cause) was catastrophic for his prognosis. And therein lay the danger of the traumatic neurosis diagnosis. The diagnosis itself was a pathogenic idea; it misled patients and made them much harder to treat.[27]

Oppenheim was the second doctor to comment on Bonhoeffer's presentation. The neurologist noted that posttraumatic conditions often arose in the immediate aftermath of a traumatic event, long before pathogenic wishes or desires would have time to form. This he put forward as proof that the direct, mechanical effects of trauma, rather than subsequent psychological processes, underlay war neuroses. But Bonhoeffer contested Oppenheim's clinical observation, claiming that wishes and other secondary mental processes could develop instantly, which he supported with an example drawn from his own experience as a child: "Once I fell down when a buddy lobbed a stone that struck me on the head, and it has remained clear in my memory that as I was falling and experiencing slight disorientation the thought came momentarily that I should remain lying down in order to frighten my buddies. A similar psychological process was innocuously reported to me by an individual who fell during an artillery barrage."[28]

Oppenheim refrained from challenging the comparison of a childhood accident to an artillery barrage, but he did criticize Bonhoeffer's view of neurosis as the result of wishes. It meant ignoring or at least downplaying the legitimacy of the suffering, which, he asserted, was thoroughly authentic. Oppenheim concluded: "The war has taught us and will continue to teach us (1) that just as before there are traumatic neuroses; (2) that they are not always covered by the concept of hysteria; and (3) that they are really the product of trauma and not goal-oriented, well cultivated pseudo illness."[29] (Several months later, Oppenheim did acknowledge the power of wishes to influence physical conditions, but, as he claimed to observe at the museum hospital station in Berlin, most of his patients wished to get better quickly so that they could return to the field.)[30]

Diagnostic Debate: Hysteria versus Traumatic Neurosis

Over the next two years—before the debate reached its dramatic and bitter climax at a 1916 congress—most German psychiatrists and neurologists weighed in on the traumatic neurosis issue. As the dispute took shape, it became increasingly clear that Oppenheim stood nearly alone. Few doctors came out in favor of the traumatic neurosis diagnosis. Most of Oppenheim's friends and students remained silent, although several did try to stake out middle ground to salvage the neurologist's dignity. More vexing to Oppenheim, however, was that his position was constantly misrepresented by his opponents. His belief in the direct pathogenic effects of trauma was consistently cast as pure somaticism, and his interlocutors repeatedly attacked a somatic straw man with evidence of the psychogenic nature of war neurosis.

As the trauma debate developed over the course of 1915 and 1916, several types of evidence were frequently used to refute Oppenheim's diagnosis: (1) the apparent absence of war neurosis among prisoners of war and the physically wounded; (2) the lack of neurotic symptoms among soldiers with serious injuries or illnesses; (3) the frequent occurrence of neuroses behind the lines and away from the fighting; and (4) the success of treatments based on psychological and suggestive interventions.

The case of POWs, who showed neurotic symptoms only very rarely, seemed to prove the functional nature of neuroses and their basis in wishes and desires.

As Bonhoeffer later recalled, hysterical symptoms served regular soldiers by saving them from the threat of the front (and giving them cause for compensation), but they would do prisoners no good whatsoever:

> My observations at the Verdun front supplied, I believe, a fundamental contribution to my conception that hysterical reactions are the result of the more or less conscious wish for self-preservation. The difference in behavior between the Germans who came directly from the line of fire into the hospital station and the French prisoners was striking. Among the Germans the familiar forms of hysterical reactions could be found with great frequency, while among the French, who had come from the same front circumstances, no trace of hysteria was to be seen. For them, the danger had disappeared. "Ma guerre est fini," was the common turn of phrase. There was, hence, no longer any reason for an illness to develop.[31]

Such claims were reinforced by several systematic studies, first appearing late in 1915, that presented striking statistical evidence. A Koblenz doctor, Fritz Mohr, observed a sample of twelve thousand prisoners of war—two thousand of whom had experienced shocks and burials from heavy artillery fire—and did not find a single case of neurosis; Karl Wilmanns reported only five cases in some eighty thousand enemy prisoners, and not one among twenty thousand Germans interned in Switzerland; and a study of French prisoners in Baden ascertained only one war neurotic out of eighty thousand men.[32] The Wiesbaden psychiatrist Friedrich Mörchen, who conducted several surveys of French POWs, found a total of only eight cases among the more than sixty thousand men he had seen in his capacity as a prison camp doctor.[33]

These extraordinary results, Mörchen explained, reflected the relative security of the prison environment.[34] Having escaped the dangers of the front, prisoners of war no longer feared for their lives. "They are in safety," he reported at a meeting of the German Neurological Society, "the war is over for them; they have saved their own lives, and everything else is irrelevant to them."[35] Above all, a neurosis served no purpose in the prison environment. Gaupp presented the absence of hysterical symptoms among prisoners as conclusive proof that war neuroses resulted from neither physiological disturbances nor from such somatic causes as exhaustion and overexertion. Like Bonhoeffer, Gaupp conceived of war neuroses as hysterical reactions in terrified, weak-willed individuals, motivated by fear of the front or pure pension greed. A prisoner, therefore, would not be likely to become hysterical "since in prison there is no insurance money, [there are] no pensions, and none of the other advantages of being sick."[36] Taking the argument a step further in another context, Gaupp noted that prison circumstances would actually militate against the development of neuroses "because the prisoner must hold up so that he may return home healthy."[37]

These studies confounded Oppenheim. His first response was to question their accuracy, suspicious that prisoners with nervous symptoms had somehow

been separated out from the sample groups. But after conducting his own investigations of POW populations, he arrived at the same results as his opponents, which he vaguely attributed to "unknown factors."[38] One doctor did
offer a defense of Oppenheim's theories, however. In an article published in
1917, Arthur von Sarbo, a Budapest neurologist, put forth an alternate explanation that focused on the way prisoners were selected and taken. Those soldiers most likely to develop neuroses, that is, those shaken up by surprise
attacks or buried in the rubble of explosions, would not be taken prisoner because they were probably lying unconscious on the battlefield. Sarbo's explanation for the absence of neurosis in POW camps, however, had no apparent
effect on the course of the debate.

A second set of observations cited by the opponents of traumatic neurosis
was the astounding lack of neurotic symptoms among soldiers with serious injuries or illnesses. In fact, it appeared that the severity of a man's wounds was
inversely proportional to the likelihood that he would show hysterical symptoms. While perhaps counterintuitive on the surface, this argument followed
the same logic that Gaupp asserted in the case of POWs. Seriously injured
patients were ensured of discharge and pensions and thus would have little reason to develop hysterical symptoms. Although it seems likely that such symptoms would accompany severe wounds; indeed one might expect a soldier,
having been through the horrifying experience of a combat wound to react hysterically, most psychiatrists assumed the opposite. "Hysterical symptoms only
arise where they are a means to a specific goal, when they seem to be of practical use to the subject," argued Karl Pönitz. "[F]or people who are organically
sick, hysterical symptoms have, of course, no purpose."[39] This included, then,
only cases where the illness or wound was serious enough to rule out further
service, assumptions that a number of psychiatrists confirmed with empirical
studies.[40]

These results posed yet another formidable challenge to the traumatic neurosis concept. If war neuroses truly resulted from the direct effects of shocks
and explosions, then the wounded would be among the most likely candidates.
Further, as the Freiburg physician Alfred Hauptmann pointed out, if ammuni-
tion explosions did directly cause neurosis, then soldiers would occasionally
suffer these symptoms from firing their own weapons, a phenomenon that had
never been recorded. Moreover, Hauptmann argued, the observation that individuals who happened to be asleep at the time of explosions did not develop
neurotic symptoms further testified to the inaccuracy of Oppenheim's ideas.[41]

A third argument against traumatic neurosis derived from the surprisingly
common occurrence of neurotic disorders behind the lines and in men who had
never been exposed to combat conditions. By some accounts, these numbers ultimately outweighed the numbers of neurotic soldiers who had actually been at
the front. As Gaupp wrote in the middle of the war: "The cause [of neurotic
symptoms] is sometimes shock and agitation after shell or mine explosions in

the field, after being buried or wounded. More often the symptoms arise not directly at the front, but rather afterwards as an expression of the fear of returning to the front. Lately we see it very often in soldiers who were *never* in the field, rather have been ordered to head to the front for the first time."[42] The presence of neurotic conditions behind the lines—and even among civilians far from the dangers of the front—represented another serious setback to Oppenheim and offered solid support for purely psychological explanations. In light of such findings, it appeared that war neuroses were only vaguely, if at all, related to any particular combat events.

This observation reflected the common psychiatric view that, as the war dragged on, the "quality" of the war neurotics was declining; that is, the early cases—as in Bonhoeffer's examples from 1914—showed how weak-willed men became "neurotically fixated" after a traumatic event and that their desire to escape service or to collect a pension prevented their recovery. Later cases, however, often involved men who had never even seen action and broke down at the mere thought of front duty. These subjects, most psychiatrists believed, had pronounced psychopathic tendencies and easily succumbed to suggestion and "psychic contagion" from their peers.[43]

A fourth line of argument used for the hysteria diagnosis derived from the seemingly miraculous treatment successes with suggestive, psychic therapies that many doctors began to report. Max Nonne, who toured Germany and Austria demonstrating his method of hypnotic suggestion, was emerging as Oppenheim's most formidable opponent and as the most visible and vocal advocate of the hysteria diagnosis. Imploring doctors to reject traumatic neurosis, Nonne rehearsed a familiar argument when he maintained that the diagnosis implied incurability, which was not only misleading but also had a destructive effect on patients' prognoses. That these conditions could be "cured" quickly and reliably with hypnosis or suggestion was for Nonne proof enough of their hysterical character and of the absence of organic damage.[44]

Indeed, in contrast to the therapeutic pessimism that accompanied traumatic neurosis—Oppenheim had admitted that its prognosis was "sad"—the hysteria diagnosis facilitated the introduction of a whole range of suggestion-based "miracle treatments" with which doctors could boast of remarkably high curing percentages. Oppenheim had also tried treating war neurosis with hypnosis and verbal, suggestive therapy—techniques he had experimented with in his clinic before the war—and did report modest successes.[45] He believed that these interventions helped dispose the patient to recovery by improving his attitude and strengthening his will, but he did not regard them as therapeutically sufficient.[46] He was, furthermore, skeptical about the duration of the "quick cures," which were effective at bringing soldiers into the workplace and removing their visible symptoms, but failed to address the problems at their core.[47] For those conditions that did have an organic basis, Oppenheim warned, hypnotizing symptoms away could have devastating consequences. However, Op-

penheim's cautions had little impact; the apparent success of hypnosis and suggestion at clearing out the neurosis stations and supplying Germany with much-
needed workers—together with the empirical evidence from POWs and the
wounded—was too much to counter and kept him continually on the defensive.

Taken together, these studies seemed to offer irrefutable evidence that fear,
the desire for pensions, and other psychological, emotional, and intellectual
forces, rather than the direct effects of actual battlefield experiences, accounted
for the overwhelming majority of nervous casualties. While POWs and the
wounded were large samples of soldiers who had been exposed to battle conditions but showed no neurotic conditions, studies on civilians safely distanced
from the field seemed to confirm that debilitating neuroses could develop in the
absence of shocks and explosions.[48] Gaupp took the argument one step further
when he presented evidence that war neuroses occurred more commonly behind the front lines than among front soldiers. These views ultimately led to a
reversal of Oppenheim's position—and a return to prewar ideas—according to
which war and war service were construed as healthier alternatives to civilian
society. Pre-1914 society had been condemned as degenerate and pathogenic;
now, with most of the healthy men mobilized, civil society was seen as even
more rife with bad influences. In short, after an initial period of uncertainty,
most German psychiatrists and neurologists concluded that the "war neuroses"
had little to do with war. On the contrary, they were essentially identical to the
peacetime accident neuroses and could be explained as psychological—that is,
hysterical—reactions in terrified, weak-willed, or lazy men, those who, in most
cases, probably would have broken down anyway.

With such views, Oppenheim feared, his colleagues had drastically underestimated the manifold effects of modern warfare on the brain and nervous system. "What gives us the right," he asked in his 1916 monograph on war
neuroses, "to attribute such minimal significance to physical trauma?"[49] "Certainly, there are neuroses of a purely psychic origin," Oppenheim continued,
"but whether all the symptoms and complexes which I and others have portrayed as the consequences of trauma could come about through a psychic
mechanism has yet to be proven."[50]

In his 1916 book Oppenheim set out to clarify his position in the face of the
growing opposition. In a theoretical appendix, he made three strong claims:
(1) that he too recognized the existence of psychic trauma and included it within
his concept of traumatic neurosis;(2) that the wartime advocates of so-called
terror neurosis (*Schreckneurose*) had added nothing to what he had asserted already in 1889; and (3) that "terror neurosis" often includes a physical element
along with the psychological component.[51]

Oppenheim then distinguished between traumatic neurosis (*traumatische
Neurose*) as a specific diagnostic entity and the plural posttraumatic neuroses
(*traumatische Neurosen*), a collective term that encompassed all forms of neu-

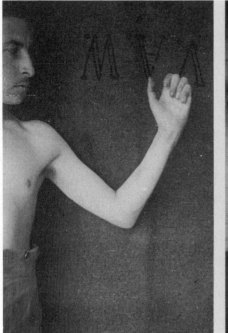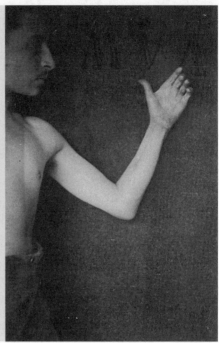

Functional (hysterical) paralysis of the hand in a war neurosis patient. By permission of the archive of the University of Tübingen.

roses that followed traumatic experiences, regardless of their etiological connection. The latter category included "pure" hysteria, neurasthenia, hysteroneurasthenia, various combinations of organic and functional conditions, and traumatic neurosis in the narrow sense. In the etiology of the posttraumatic neuroses, Oppenheim recognized three factors: ideogenesis, psychic trauma, and mechanical trauma. The first, *ideogenesis*, corresponded to Bonhoeffer's descriptions of hysteria and included those cases in which a wish or set of ideas underlay the neurotic condition. Oppenheim asserted that he had recognized the existence of such conditions as early as 1890 and implored those who failed to credit him to reread his earlier writings on the subject. The second type, *psychic trauma*, was a more common occurrence, in which the symptoms arose out of the strong emotions that accompanied traumatic experiences. And the third, *mechanical trauma*, represented the direct physical effects of traumatic experiences on the nerves and muscles, effects that manifested themselves in a range of physiological signs, including changed blood pressure, body temperature, and motility.

In these conditions, he argued, disturbances of movement were not simply the result of the patient's will; the bent toes, the partially paralyzed arms, and

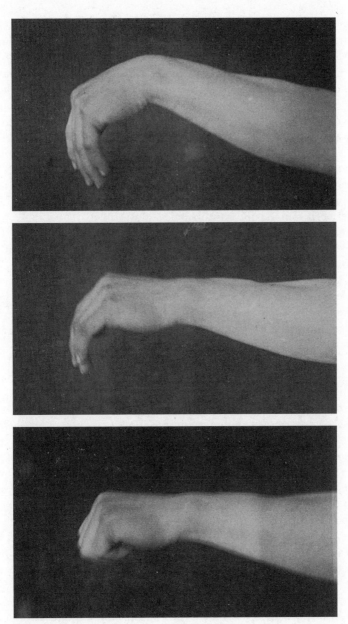

Functional (hysterical) paralysis of the wrist and hand in a war neurosis patient. By permission of the archive of the University of Tübingen.

the quivering hands he had observed stood beyond the working of the subjects' wishes and desires. "Are they nervous, hysterical individuals from birth?" he asked, "Has the war made them nervous through its effects on body and mind?"[52] Acknowledging that both of these factors—predisposition and the war's general impact—potentially played a role and that pain weakened the psyche's resistance to injury, Oppenheim nonetheless stressed a different mechanism. He theorized that a powerful sensory stimulus catalyzed a kind of wave through the nervous system which, in turn, caused subtle, essentially undetectable damage to the nerves. In these cases, Oppenheim included detailed investigations of the subjects' physiological and anatomical states. He also introduced the concept of "amnestica askina," a trauma-induced lapse in bodily memory, whereby muscles "forgot" how to act, a condition that lay somewhere between somatic and psychogenic states.[53]

Above all, this compilation of clinical material aimed to illustrate that mind and body are interrelated in complex ways and that hysteria was insufficient as a diagnostic and etiological label for all of the war neuroses. Indeed, in Oppenheim's experience, disturbances that appeared to be purely functional often had hidden organic bases. Nevertheless, despite the care with which he articulated his position, Oppenheim's opponents continued to seize on his belief in mechanical trauma as representing his entire theory. Neither the misrepresentations nor the attacks waned in the year to come.

The Munich Congress and the Fall of Hermann Oppenheim

The immense battles of 1916, with their unprecedented casualty levels, intensified the concern over (military and economic) manpower and helped turn the war neurosis problem into an issue of great national urgency. By this time, military officials were beginning to take an interest in war psychiatry, and psychiatrists themselves approached their responsibilities with increasing zeal. Military language continued to seep into psychiatric discourse, and psychiatrists and neurologists launched a series of "campaigns" throughout the war and beyond. The first and most enduring was the fight against traumatic neurosis.

As the Battle of the Somme neared the end of its third month and the German lines continued to hold off the Allies' massive offensive, the largest and most significant wartime meeting of psychiatrists and neurologists was convened in Munich. Dozens of psychiatrists from Germany and Austria-Hungary, along with observers from several Saxon and Bavarian Army Corps and the Prussian Ministry of War, assembled for a special War Congress of the German Association for Psychiatry, which was timed to coincide with the annual meeting of the German Neurological Association. On the morning of September 21, 1916, the venerable Berlin psychiatrist Karl Moeli, chair of the Association's governing board, called the proceedings to order in the lecture hall of the university psychiatric clinic. The purpose of the gathering, Moeli announced, was to encourage doctors to share their wartime experiences and observations and to achieve psychiatric consensus on matters that affected military policy.[54] Raising the stakes of the already fraught debates, Moeli added that psychiatric unity on pressing wartime issues would be of immense benefit to the entire nation.

The first day's presentations, which were devoted to strictly psychiatric issues, proceeded uneventfully. Bonhoeffer lectured on the classification and prognosis of the mental and nervous illnesses he had observed in the soldiers sent to his Berlin clinic; Karl Wilmanns, professor of psychiatry from the University of Heidelberg, discussed pension matters and the military fitness of the mentally ill; and the Königsberg psychiatrist Ernst Meyer addressed the effect of military service on the prognosis of preexisting psychoses.

The day's deliberations ended with discussion of a resolution proposed by Alfred Hoche to reform pensioning practices for war neurotics. Hoche's resolution urged the replacement of continuous pension payments with capital settlements, so that men eligible for compensation would be paid off in one single payment. The justification was based on old assumptions that the process of collecting pensions was itself pathogenic and disruptive to the subject's return to work. Hoche explained, revealing the power of the prewar experience in shaping wartime approaches: "Numbers of nervous war disabilities, if we can deduce from the thousand-fold experience with the nervous consequences of accidents in peace-time, will multiply in their significance by fusing with the psychological effects of the compensation process. In particular we can count on a great number of neurosis cases whose rehabilitation to work will be delayed or completely prevented by the form of compensation in a continuous pension."[55] In Hoche's formulation, then, the pension, once considered just compensation for injuries suffered while serving the state, appears as a threat both to individual health and national well-being. The resolution passed unanimously, and Moeli brought the proceedings to a close promptly at five o'clock.

On September 22 and 23, the second and final days of the congress, the psychiatrists were joined by the leaders of German neurology, and some three hundred doctors crowded into a lecture hall at the university medical clinic. On these two days the discussion concentrated on issues that lay at the intersection of neurology and psychiatry, in particular the neuroses and psychoses of war, and most of all, the contentious topic of traumatic neurosis. The second day's discussions brought an abrupt end to the businesslike mood of the day before, and the debate over traumatic neurosis, having been revived in the first years of the war, finally reached its climax.

Oppenheim was the first to speak on the morning of September 22. In his concise lecture he summarized many of the views he had represented all along—including the idea that trauma operates through both physical and psychic mechanisms—with one significant change. In a statement that came to haunt him, Oppenheim conceded that he had underestimated the presence of hysteria among the war neuroses. He also noted the importance of the "will to recover"

(*Wille zur Genesung*) for the prognosis of hysteria and neurasthenia and emphasized that in such cases pensions should be as low as possible. Rather than smoothing over differences, Oppenheim's concessions to the other side inflamed the debate and emboldened his opponents to step up their attacks. Despite having firmly acknowledged the role of psychological factors, Oppenheim was continually associated with strict somaticism, for which he was repeatedly criticized. Discussant after discussant marshaled evidence against the somatic explanation and aimed to refute traumatic neurosis and isolate its author.

Max Nonne was the day's second keynote speaker and took the opportunity to reiterate his critique of traumatic neurosis. Not only did he object to it on scientific grounds, he also warned of its practical consequences both "for the economic well-being of the state and the health of the individual."[56] Nonne ascribed most of the cases of posttraumatic nervous disorders to hysteria, neurasthenia, and various combinations of neuroses, but parting from the majority position, he asserted that hysteria and neurasthenia could arise in individuals with no "constitutional inferiority." Then, in a performance that sent shock waves through German mental medicine, Nonne demonstrated his hypnotic technique on a number of soldier-patients, providing powerful visual support for his assumption of purely psychological causation and helping launch the therapeutic revolution, which profoundly altered approaches to the war neurosis question.[57]

Robert Gaupp, in the third and final formal lecture, parted from Nonne and called the individual's internal disposition or constitution the most important element in the development of war neurosis. But like Nonne, Gaupp devoted most of his time and energy to challenging traumatic neurosis by refuting somatic mechanisms. He rehearsed two of the standard arguments in favor of psychogenesis: the scarcity of war neurosis among both POWs and seriously wounded or sick soldiers.[58]

After Gaupp's presentation, Hoche reintroduced his capital settlement resolution before the neurological society, which also passed it easily. Following a break, a vigorous discussion of the morning's presentations ensued, in which some thirty-six doctors spoke.[59] Nearly every discussant attacked traumatic neurosis: Several impugned its utility as a diagnosis; a handful brought up new POW studies and data from wounded soldiers who showed no neurotic symptoms; and others introduced evidence of civilians showing no trace of neurosis even after periods of heavy shelling.[60] As the critiques mounted, a new bitterness entered the discussion, and even doctors who were somewhat sympathetic to Oppenheim's position and shared his neurological approach took great care to distance themselves from traumatic neurosis.

Discussion on the following morning followed the same pattern, and Oppenheim quickly found himself aggressively opposed from all sides and defended by no one.[61] Dr. Alfred Sänger, referring to Oppenheim's comments of the previous day, noted with pleasure that the neurologist had backed away from his prior point of view. In a comment that one observer singled out for its bluntness, Sänger attributed the purported inaccuracy of Oppenheim's theory to his lack of attention to the traumatic neurosis issue since leaving it in the 1890s.[62] Implying that Oppenheim was "out of touch" and his theories out of date, Sänger hoped that, "persuaded by the constantly mounting factual evidence, [Oppenheim] will give up his position."[63]

Much of the final afternoon was spent on matters of treatment and more technical, neurological issues. Late that afternoon, after enduring two days of intense opposition, Oppenheim rose to deliver his concluding statement.

> In the introduction to my lecture I said that the most difficult task fell to me. Indeed, I never imagined how difficult it would be. And it takes a great deal of strength to defend the convictions which I have acquired through serious work against this onslaught of arguments and evidence. I have always had the principle, "Use the stone, which they would use to smash your house, to build your house." I will try this again, but I fear that I won't be able to get past the concessions I made in my lecture.[64]

Indeed, his comment of the preceding day, that he had underestimated the presence of hysteria, had been widely interpreted as an admission of defeat in the pressure of tremendous opposition. Oppenheim took umbrage at this assumption. Responding to Sänger's comments, he asserted: "I do not bow down before the decisions of the majority. And it is a thoroughly incorrect account of my words, when Sänger presents it as though I had conceded somewhat in the essential points. All that I said was that I had underestimated the presence of hysteria among the war disabilities. That hysteria comes about often, I noted already in my first work."[65] Repeating the term *Ansturm* (onslaught) to describe Sänger's criticism, Oppenheim continued to decry his treatment at the hands of his colleagues. To defend his position, he read a favorable letter from the prestigious neurologist Ludwig Bruns, a supportive colleague, who was unable to attend the congress.[66]

Oppenheim then responded to the main points of Nonne's and Gaupp's lectures. That Nonne, Gaupp, and the majority of the discussants attributed war neurosis to wishes represented a severe underestimation of trauma in his opinion. First, his opponents seemed unwilling to acknowledge that he too accepted psychological explanations, and second, they conflated psychological causes with wish complexes and pension greed. Once again, Oppenheim expressed his frustration that his colleagues failed to heed his cautions; as such, they had deeply underestimated the effects of modern warfare on the fragile nervous system. "[I]t would shock the impartial observer that in a gathering of competent neurologists and psychiatrists the enormous damage of war has been so little appreciated, that it is credited—when not causing organic injuries—with no more than a passing influence on the body and mind."[67]

Oppenheim also addressed the question of predisposition to war neurosis and challenged fundamental psychiatric assumptions. Ascertaining whether a patient's condition owed to the presence of an internal, psychopathic constitution, Oppenheim argued, was scientifically impossible and ethically questionable. If such a constitution could be established, then what would its implications be? Should doctors treat these patients with a different set of standards? Furthermore, given the shifting, even arbitrary criteria for establishing such a constitution, he asked, "how many individuals remain non-psychopaths before the judgment of these stern men?"[68] "Gentlemen!" Oppenheim continued:

> There are two great evils to avoid: the overestimation and the underestimation of the conditions which we are dealing with. The first danger, thanks to the convictions of the majority, as it is here represented, has clearly been avoided. But with great concern I see the other obstacle coming in the near future. Hysteria—*Begehrungsvorstellungen*—simulation, that has become the comfortable route for every practitioner. And if only it were the old, harmless hysteria, as we knew it before.

Oppenheim then sought the moral high ground, concluding his remarks with the following plea for posterity:

> Do you understand, gentlemen, that I view the consequences of our discussion today with very serious reservations, and that in concluding I am forced to make one more warning. If I still harbor the view that one day my doctrine will become an accepted truth, then that may well take a while. I thus ask that the gentlemen who previously gave some credence to my ideas, especially my students, hold in their memory that I have raised an objection against the majority of the views which have been expressed at this annual gathering, indeed in all modesty, but also with the utter certainty of my inner convictions.[69]

Following Oppenheim's conclusion, the day's other keynote speakers, Nonne and Gaupp, also had the opportunity for a final word. Nonne repeated his view that the concept of traumatic neurosis should be discarded. The war showed, he claimed, that trauma operates in a psychological manner and clearly disproved Oppenheim's theories with their somaticist associations. What was unique about "modern war," he concluded, was not the physical impact of its advanced weaponry, but rather its ability to provoke such abundant and powerful wish complexes.

In his concluding statement, Gaupp protested that Oppenheim had misrepresented his position. He denied that he diagnosed hysteria excessively and added that he had not even used the word *Begehrungsvorstellung* in his lecture. He condescendingly addressed the personal tone that the debate had acquired and characterized his concerns—as opposed to Oppenheim's—as purely scientific. Gaupp concluded by stressing the strong connection between diagnostic decisions and the public good:

> I would ask Oppenheim that he study my lecture one more time when it appears in print, in the solitude of his home. Then he will concede to me. And I deny the

accusation that I threw stones at him. Personal thoughts are far from my mind (it is dreadful that one has to even say such a thing); it only has to do with the issue, and I would consider it petty and low if I were to let personal interests or moods be expressed during the fight to clarify questions important for science and the public welfare.[70]

Munich's Aftermath

Witnesses described the Munich Congress as a singular event in the history of psychiatry, a moment that reverberated powerfully in German medical history. Munich essentially marked the end of the diagnostic debate; thereafter, despite lingering, minor disagreements, Germany's leading psychiatrists and neurologists faced war (and accident) hysteria with a uniform diagnostic approach. But beyond that, Munich stood out in the recollections of many as a uniquely fierce confrontation, a scientific discussion made memorable by the bitterness of its tone and marred by a series of ad hominem attacks and subtle political allegations. Participants, furthermore, linked Munich not only with the resounding defeat of traumatic neurosis but also with the demise of its author, with Oppenheim's professional withdrawal and even with his death in 1919. "[Oppenheim] had fought for years for his concept, the traumatic neurosis," recalled Nonne, "and the topic was 'loaded with affect.' A year later [after the Munich Congress] he had a heart attack for which he, a long time sufferer from hypertension, was predisposed."[71] Nonne's description, not unlike other contemporary accounts, suggests the multiple ironies that Germany's most famous theorist of trauma himself died from the traumatic effects of the trauma debate.

Although few doctors actually changed their minds during the Munich Congress, the proceedings certainly strengthened and publicized the conviction that war neuroses were hysterical reactions. Most participants believed, furthermore, that Oppenheim's traumatic neurosis theory was not only inaccurate but also damaging to individual prognosis and dangerous to the national economy. Henceforth, numerous entries in the German medical press referred to Munich as the turning point in wartime psychiatry and as Oppenheim's downfall, which they equated with the unanimous rejection of traumatic neurosis.

After this denunciation, even humiliation in front of the majority of his colleagues, Oppenheim's original impulse was to withdraw from the subject of traumatic neurosis and move on to safer, less controversial areas of research. However, his resolve faded as the attacks—and misrepresentations—of traumatic neurosis continued beyond Munich, and just months after the debacle, he found himself swept up again in the debate.[72] Significantly, these late writings reflect his profound frustration, his growing sense of hopelessness about the possibility of a reasoned discussion of traumatic neurosis. In one passage, for example, eerily written less than two years before his death, Oppenheim likened his theory to a corpse: "Many will be amazed that I even dare to address this issue [traumatic neurosis] again, as if one could make a corpse come back to life."[73] Referring to a new book on accident neurosis by the Tübingen nerve doctor Otto Nägeli—which claimed that Munich had exposed the bankruptcy of Oppenheim's ideas—the neurologist continued with his morbid metaphors, "This pronouncement by a respected university teacher, which amounts to a death sentence, has been calculated to create confusion in the heads of those who will read [my] work without having had their own experience and unable to form their own judgment."[74]

Not long after the Munich Congress, the neurologist Alfred Goldscheider summarized the traumatic neurosis issue in a manner that sought to preserve Oppenheim's dignity.[75] Goldscheider acknowledged the validity of much of Oppenheim's theory. With Oppenheim, he challenged the notion of a pathological predisposition, noted the overuse of hysteria and neurasthenia as diagnoses, and observed that somatic cases were indeed plausible.[76] Nevertheless, Goldscheider asserted that Oppenheim generally underestimated the importance of the psyche. The development or fixation of neurotic symptoms, whether those symptoms originated in the psyche or the soma, owed primarily to emotions, thoughts, and wishes. The patient's will and wishes, concluded Goldscheider, could have both pathological and curative effects, but it was these factors and not the original traumatic moment that determined the course of a neurosis.

But Oppenheim found the conciliatory efforts of his Berlin colleague unsatisfactory. Weeks later in the same journal he addressed Goldscheider's article as well as another essay by Gaupp.[77] Goldscheider misunderstood his work, Oppenheim charged, and characterized it as though he did not acknowledge the role of the psyche at all. Though Goldscheider actually portrayed the debate in an accurate and fair manner, Oppenheim stubbornly charged, "It is inconceivable to me how wrongly Goldscheider sees the state of affairs and how incorrectly he misrepresents it."[78] Oppenheim emphasized that in the 1892 edition of his traumatic neurosis monograph, in his war neurosis monograph of 1916, and in his opening remarks in Munich, he had noted that psychic trauma could be the primary cause of a patient's posttraumatic symptoms. He railed that despite the constant reiteration of this position, he was continuously represented as a strict somaticist. While elsewhere Oppenheim justly claimed that his opponents often mischaracterized his positions, in this essay he failed to grasp their critique of him.

Turning to Gaupp's 1916 article, Oppenheim once again addressed the personal tone of the traumatic neurosis debate. He and Gaupp continually accused each other of professional improprieties in the debate, each attempting to portray his opponent as nonscientific. Oppenheim noted that Gaupp had accused him of a lack objectivity, and criticized the latter for overstepping the boundaries appropriate to scientific discussion. He added, "Everyone who took part in the Munich congress knows which side failed to maintain calm objectivity. I only regret that Gaupp has forgotten that so quickly."[79] Oppenheim continued with more militaristic language: "But especially Gaupp had no right to use this weapon against me, since he himself did not refrain from the emotional prejudices of his position, not only in the discussion, but also in his newest publications, in which he raises this accusation against me. I need but recall the misunderstanding concerning his throwing of stones."[80]

Finally, Oppenheim returned to the crucial issue of predisposition one last time. He pointed out that the major source of disagreement between him and his opponents concerned the relative weight given to the traumatic experience on the one hand and the individual's personality or character on the other. He protested that Gaupp, Bonhoeffer, and the psychiatrist Ewald Stier emphasized the latter factor—that is, the predisposed personality—to the near exclusion of the pathological effects of the trauma. In their view, he charged, "the trauma . . . has only the limited effect of bringing about reactions rooted in a morbid disposition, which disappear quickly unless inhibited by secondary processes, independent of the trauma (wishes, desires)."[81] This meant, therefore, that his opponents did not see war neurosis as *caused* by the conditions or circumstances of the war, a view that had obvious implications not just for diagnosis but also for treatment and most importantly pension policies.

At its core, the idea of a pathological constitution aimed to solve one vexatious dilemma, a problem that has continued to puzzle psychiatrists: Why did some men break down and others remain healthy when they had been exposed to identical conditions and shocks? For most of Oppenheim's opponents, the answer was straightforward: Those with a pathological constitution were predisposed to breaking down, while healthier, mentally sturdier men had the will and self-control to withstand wartime shocks and indeed the temptations of escaping service or the seductions of a pension. While Oppenheim's earlier arguments had stressed the pathogenic effects of shocks rather than the subject's internal state, in his post-Munich writings he proposed a more nuanced alternative.

Here Oppenheim distinguished between a subject's susceptibility to illness, his *Krankheitsbereitschaft*, and a predisposition, or *Veranlagung*.[82] He illustrated this idea with an example drawn from more familiar types of sickness. Since the pathogens that caused diseases such as syphilis, typhus, and diphtheria had different effects on different individuals—some survived unscathed, while others showed lifelong nervous after-effects—trauma could be assumed to act in an analogous way. Thus, persistent posttraumatic symptoms should not be interpreted as evidence of a psychopathic constitution but rather pointed to different degrees of susceptibility among different individuals. Furthermore, as Oppenheim had already implied in Munich, the assumption of innate psychopathy was fraught with ethical and scientific problems. It established different standards for patients of different constitutional "values" and brought notions of inferiority and superiority directly into medical discourse, an ethically dubious step that adherents to eugenics, including some leading psychiatrists, had already taken before the war. And in scientific terms, such a disposition could never be ascertained or measured in any empirical way. Rather, doctors reasoned deductively that if individuals showed certain symptoms they must have preexisting dispositions. Oppenheim concluded, "I fully dispute the justification of concluding that an individual has a pre-morbid personality from the fact that he develops a stubborn neurosis as a consequence of psychological or mechanical injury. This separates me from Herrs Bonhoeffer, Stier, and Gaupp, whom the majority of our colleagues seem to follow."[83]

As a result of the debate's outcome and keenly aware of his isolation, Oppenheim stepped down from his position as president of the German Neurological Association, the organization that he had helped found in 1907. His replacement was Max Nonne, a change that signaled the rise of a new generation and may have reflected Nonne's role in toppling traumatic neurosis.[84] At the same time, Oppenheim resigned from the Berlin museum hospital station and withdrew from the treatment of war neuroses altogether. He justified this step by claiming that he could not conform to the diagnostic standards and compensation practices adopted by the rest of the profession. "I would come into conflict with my conscience if I made judgments that conformed to the majority opinion. I have expressed my support for small pensions and especially for capital settlements for psycho-pedagogical reasons, and in this sense I can stand by my previous decisions, but I cannot take the further step of ruling out war neuroses—as psychopathic reactions—from the beneficence of the war disability laws."[85] If his opponents were correct, Oppenheim concluded, noting that their position would be better for the state, then his practices would be needlessly draining the Imperial Treasury at this crucial time. Picking up on this sentiment, Otto Martineck, a consulting physician for the Prussian War Ministry, who had been a guest at the Munich Congress, criticized the neurologist for stepping down. Martineck claimed that only "scientific" factors should motivate a doctor's actions, rather than the political and economic concerns that led to Oppenheim's resignation.[86] Martineck, like Gaupp, used the idea of "objective science"—and Oppenheim's alleged departures from it—as part of a personal attack against the neurologist.

His humiliation in Munich and the defeat of his theories were, in the eyes of many contemporaries, closely linked to Oppenheim's death at the age of 61 in May 1919.[87] Reflecting on the life and career of his mentor years later, his student and friend Arthur Stern recalled: "Oppenheim did not survive the defeat he suffered at the neurology conference in Munich in 1916, where the renowned neurologist Nonne demonstrated the curing of shakers through hypnosis, and he died at work from a steno-cardiac attack—today you would say from psychosomatic causes—withdrawn and wounded."[88] And as Nonne recalled in the obituary he wrote of his senior colleague: "'Traumatic neurosis' comprised a unique chapter in [Oppenheim's] scientific activities and, one would have to add, his life. The fight over his neurological problem child [*Schmerzenskind*] went on for more than thirty years. Seldom has a topic been treated with so much emotion, and seldom has emotion persisted for so long in a scientific area . . . That he who was used to victory did not remain the victor in this battle caused him deep psychological . . . pain."[89]

That the traumatic neurosis debate became intensely personal and frequently descended into ad hominem attacks made it conspicuous in German medical science, and it remained a memorable event in the minds of its participants. Falsely cast as somaticism's last stand, the Munich Congress took on nearly mythic status in German mental medicine. The Düsseldorf psychiatrist Philipp Jolly, for example, noted in 1930: "For those who experienced this dramatic scene, the image of the *Altmeister* Oppenheim trying to defend the theories he had asserted decades before—but which had become untenable with the war experience—against all kinds of attacks will remain unforgettable."[90] And several years later Ewald Stier, the Berlin doctor who became one of the foremost authorities on military psychiatry and pension questions in interwar Germany, celebrated Oppenheim's downfall and described his defeat in nearly epic terms. In 1936, in the first edition of Nazi Germany's new military-medical journal, he recalled: "At the memorable *War Conference of German Psychiatrists* in Munich in September 1916 the two opposing positions crashed into each other with a bitterness that had not been seen before."[91]

More careful scrutiny, however, reveals that characterizations such as Stier's reinforced the misunderstandings and miscommunications that marked the entire debate and that continue to influence historical accounts. "One approaches any discussion of [traumatic neurosis] with a certain inner resistance, since the operative concepts are so slippery," wrote Freiburg physician Alfred Hauptmann, who had sought to resolve the issue in a balanced, scientific way. "Seldom have I had so strongly the feeling that authors are talking past each other as when I read the wartime literature on traumatic neurosis."[92] Hauptmann accurately observed that the two sides were waging different debates. Most of Oppenheim's opponents argued again and again for the psychogenic explanation of neurosis in contrast to the somaticism that they attributed to him. But, as he explained in the 1916 text and in so many other places, somaticism itself was not central to Oppenheim's theory of traumatic neurosis. What was essential to the theory, rather, was the assumption of a direct, causal relationship between actual traumas and posttraumatic symptoms.

Undeniably, Oppenheim's ideas were burdened by the inaccuracy and implausibility of those somatic explanations he did continue to promote. He failed to respond satisfactorily to several serious critiques, and his stubborn, often indignant behavior did little to help his position. But the precedent of the pension neurosis scare in the prewar period—itself purely propagandistic—prevented any reasoned discussion of the trauma issue during the war. The mere thought of hordes of pension-collecting workers and soldiers sapping Germany's precarious reserves made the discussion impossibly fraught with political implications. And because his opponents believed Germany's economic and military strength hung in the balance, they approached the debate as a patriotic battle, frequently invoking military metaphors and death imagery. Just as in the prewar period, as Oppenheim observed, "the fight was directed not only against the idea, but often against me as a person."[93] In the end Oppenheim lost both his "fight for traumatic neurosis" and his life.

More broadly, the controversy over traumatic neurosis revived an ancient split in German medicine between materialists and spiritualists.[94] As a latter day materialist and a trained neuropathologist, Oppenheim began with the assumption that the peculiar symptoms of war neurosis had a material basis in the brain or nervous system. His approach hearkened back to an earlier, liberal age in German medicine, which followed in the political and medical traditions of 1848, which were perhaps best united in the figure of Wilhelm Griesinger. By treating psychiatric illness as somatic brain disease (and striving to bring neurology and psychiatry together) Griesinger sought to raise the status of mental patients, guaranteeing them, in theory, the kind of care and sympathy previously reserved for the physically ill.[95] Oppenheim, of course, did not conclude that somatic mechanisms were at work in all or even most of these cases, but by starting from that assumption, taking patient complaints seriously and carefully examining individual patients' states, he fell firmly within those nineteenth-century traditions.

Oppenheim's opponents, on the other hand, belonged to a different medical camp, which carried the concerns of a new generation of physicians and social critics. Bonhoeffer, Gaupp, Hoche, Nonne, and the other leaders in the fight against traumatic neurosis came of age in a profession that was dominated by concern with the "social question" and fears of a decline in Germany's collective national health and in a society that saw the growth of mass politics and experienced the social fallout of rapid modernization. These psychiatrists were more likely to embrace collectivistic, eugenic solutions to social problems and spurned the materialism of Griesinger and the individualism of the traditional physician, tendencies that only intensified during the war. The experience of total war, furthermore, greatly magnified Germans' concern with collective, national health. And answering the call to minister to national health was this new generation, whose concern with the collective dictated submerging the interests of the individual patient to the welfare of the national community. Indeed, in contrast to Oppenheim, most of these psychiatrists did not come out of private practice, and their approach to medicine was not shaped by dealing with patients on an individual basis. As university researchers, they were more likely to pose abstract theories and general solutions, further removed from individual experience and suffering.[96]

Finally, the question of anti-Semitism loomed behind Oppenheim's entire career, from his early setbacks through his ultimate downfall. Although anti-Semitism was not an explicit part of the trauma debate, Oppenheim's identity as a Jewish doctor heightened his association with the somaticism of Berlin's private clinics as well as the liberal, individualistic medicine of an earlier era. It also facilitated attempts to construct Oppenheim and his theories as alien and unpatriotic. Indeed, many Jews inhabited a distinct urban medical subculture and were largely barred from becoming university professors or military medical officers. Furthermore, traumatic neurosis, from its beginnings, was associated with anti-German values, which were often conceived of as socialistic, Jewish, or both. Finally, during the war many Germans became preoccupied with assessing Jews' loyalty to the "national cause," and rumors circulated—particularly in Bavaria—that Jews were shirking their duty. The Munich Congress occurred at the same time as the notorious "Jew count," the census ordered by the Prussian War Ministry to measure Jewish participation in the German war effort.[97] The point here is not to accuse any particular doctors of harboring anti-Semitic motives—to be sure, ethnic background and scientific belief did not neatly coincide, and several of Oppenheim's opponents were Jews—but rather to stress that Oppenheim's Jewish background was lurking behind the conflict. Jewishness carried strong associations in the culture of German medicine and in Munich in 1916, and these associations made it easier to marginalize Oppenheim and to turn opposing traumatic neurosis into a national crusade.

The wartime diagnostic debate in Germany was unique. Only in Germany did the debate center on the ideas and career of one individual. And only in Germany did it mean a repetition—albeit a more charged, acrimonious repetition—of a conflict that had already occurred. This context, rooted in the unique circumstances of German social legislation and amplified by wartime conditions, meant that the German debate—and more generally, German concepts of masculinity and mental health—were particularly freighted with economic concerns. Indeed, the economic dimensions of the trauma issue, clearly visible in the prewar period and so much a part of the wartime discussion, also informed the treatment, administration, and, of course, the compensation of war neurotics. The psychiatric unity that Karl Moeli had called for when he opened the Munich Congress was achieved. The victor was the hysteria diagnosis, and the casualties were Oppenheim's career and his trauma theories. For the rest of the war and most of the interwar period, Gaupp, Nonne, Bonhoeffer, and a handful of others remained the unchallenged authorities on war neurosis and hysteria. Ewald Stier, who was about to enter those ranks, recalled that after Munich, "for psychiatric judgment and treatment . . . thus began a new era."[98]

CHAPTER 4

The Powers of Suggestion
Science, Magic, and Modernity in the Therapeutic Arsenal

A miraculous current. It arose out of a method of treatment and helped drive the mill of the war, operated by millers in white coats.

ALFRED POLGAR, "Faradische Ströme"

The doctor cures with his personality, not his method.

ROBERT GAUPP, "Über die Neurosen und Psychosen des Krieges"

"WE EXPERIENCED TWO surprises with the war neuroses," recalled Max Nonne, "first that they appeared with unimaginable frequency, and second that after initial, absolute failure in treating them, we learned to master them with astonishing quickness."[1] In 1916, the same year as the Munich Congress, Nonne produced a short training film on the treatment of war hysteria, in which he showcased the enormous therapeutic success he had begun to claim.[2] The film features fourteen soldiers, each of whom exhibit typical war neurosis symptoms, including partial paralyses, dramatic muscular contractions, loss of speech, or some combination; the two most striking cases scurry around the set with clonic muscle spasms and convulsions reminiscent of Jean-Martin Charcot's famous hysterical women.

In the film, Nonne, a tall, imposing doctor clad in a long white coat, presents the first patient, a much smaller man, who stands trembling and wears only underpants. The intertitle explains that this man had developed a severe stutter after a shell explosion. Placing his hands around the patient's mouth, Nonne demonstrates his difficulty articulating. After a cut, the titles announce that we are to see the patient after successful treatment with hypnosis. Once again, we see the doctor and the patient. Now, as if by magic, the young soldier is fully cured; the doctor demonstrates that the patient's jaws move up and down smoothly, enabling him to articulate fluently. The film's remaining thirteen cases follow the same pattern. First a title announces the symptoms, which Nonne proceeds to demonstrate on the patient's body. Then the screen goes black and the words "after the cure" (*nach der Heilung*) appear, after which each man is

presented in a "symptom-free" (or nearly symptom-free) state, which the doctor confidently demonstrates. All have been cured, the viewer is left to infer,
through hypnosis or one of the other methods of suggestive therapy introduced
to treat war neurosis around 1916.[3]

Beyond its portrayal of Nonne's hypnotic cure—or at least its results—the
film vividly documents other crucial elements of the doctor-patient relationship
during the war. It depicts the power of the mind over the body; that is, it dramatizes the odd and powerfully debilitating physical conditions that, as Nonne
argued, were brought on by hysterical reactions or intense wishes and fears. Significantly, the film also portrays the power of the doctor over the (hysterical)
patient, by showing that a rapid medical intervention could make hysterical
symptoms quickly disappear. By extension, then, the hysteria treatments that
the film promotes show how medical power could intervene to counteract pathogenic wishes and fears in order to produce healthy, symptom-free bodies.

The power doctors had over their hysterical soldier-patients drew from their
superiority in social class, education, and military rank. This power could be
wielded gently or with violence, subtly or with theatrical fanfare, but regardless of the doctor's intentions or style, the exercise of medical power was crucial to the therapeutic process. The therapeutic encounters that doctors staged
were often conceived of as "battles of will" between doctor and patient—between the healthy, patriotic values that doctors represented and their patients'
sickly selfishness. And they served as forums into which doctors injected ideas
of national service, sacrifice, and productivity.[4] "Curing" hysterical soldiers
thus can be seen as a way of constructing healthy German men, who embodied
the virtues of self-sacrifice and service. And while the earliest therapies attempted to counter the conditions of modern war—through soothing rest cures,
massages, rich diets—the "active treatments" that soon replaced them extended
the war's (and the state's) grip over the individual combatant by subjecting him
to medically administered shocks, pain, and fearsome subordination.

But the new hysteria treatments reflected more than just the exercise of medical and political power. By not showing or even describing the therapeutic sessions, Nonne's film shrouds his treatment in mystery, imparting the impression
that these peculiar, debilitating conditions were cured instantaneously, effortlessly, and indeed magically. The mysterious, even miraculous elements of
Nonne's cure are conspicuous in light of the strict scientism that characterized
early-twentieth-century German psychiatry and neurology. Equally noteworthy
is Nonne's use of film—a modern, technologically advanced medium—to
record and promote hypnosis, an old technique historically at odds with the
modernity of scientific, university medicine.[5] In a sense, the film, produced for
the benefit of military officials and army medics, publicizes the introduction of
magic into the therapeutic realm and marks the incorporation of crass sideshow
antics into scientific mental medicine. Hypnosis and the other methods of "active treatment"—a collection of quick, efficient medical interventions that

sought to suggest away hysterical symptoms—embodied this tension between the scientific and the magical, between the quantifying impulses of psychiatric science and the rapturous results of the quick cure. By the middle of the war, German psychiatry was emerging from its decades-long therapeutic crisis. The treatments that accomplished this highlight the profession's precarious position between medical science and mental healing and point to the broader ambiguities of psychiatric modernity.

Therapeutic Breakthrough: The Magical Healer and the Rediscovery of Hypnosis

Looking back on the state of psychiatric treatment at the beginning of the war, Nonne recalled, "At that time [1915] one labored essentially under the impression that only nature and time could cure, that is to say, improve [motoric nervous disorders]."[6] And in his postwar account of the therapeutic lessons of the war years, he noted: "[T]hrough the war's first year, a great deal of work was conducted in vain. The healing powers of spas, with all their complicated apparatus, were needlessly studied and many millions were wasted. . . ."[7] Nonne's comments reflected the general sense that the war, and early encounters with war neuroses, only magnified psychiatry's prewar therapeutic pessimism.

Medical impotence and psychiatric pessimism continued to grow with the steady increases in the numbers of war neurotics. What was needed, many doctors began to believe, were more active treatments that made hospital stays less appealing, shored up medical morale, and reversed the prevailing tides. Within what was taking shape as a war of unprecedented scale and scope—and amid the insatiable manpower needs of army and industry—Germany's psychiatrists launched their own war, a crusade against hysteria, which lasted through 1918 and even beyond. As with the diagnostic war, the "fight against traumatic neurosis," therapeutic efforts were also portrayed in military terms and with metaphors drawn from combat. Frustrated by months of therapeutic failure and facing overcrowded hospitals and limited medical resources, in 1915 Gaupp issued a "call to arms" against hysteria.[8] And as Nonne recounted, after months without success, it soon became "high time to annihilate the war neuroses."[9]

By most accounts it was Nonne himself who made the first strides toward annihilating the neuroses. His therapeutic breakthroughs quickly reverberated through Central European psychiatry and neurology, abruptly ending the pessimistic era and turning him into a reluctant neurological celebrity. Nonne accomplished this by remembering what he had seen in his travels through France and Switzerland as a young assistant. From his own, possibly apocryphal account, the idea of treating war neurosis with hypnosis simply came to him, as a sort of epiphany, when he faced his first neurotic patient several weeks after the war's outbreak. The patient, a young lieutenant, who had been evacuated from the front as the Germans advanced through Belgium, had lost his ability to speak. As a neurologist who apparently had no experience with the so-called accident neuroses, Nonne was baffled by what he saw and searched in vain for an organic disturbance underlying the man's condition. Finding nothing organically wrong, he concluded that this was a case of hysterical muteness, and "Then I remembered what I had witnessed with [August] Forel in Zurich and what I had practiced as an assistant to [Karl] Eisenlohr at Eppendorf. The hypnosis succeeded easily in this case and the lieutenant was 'cured suddenly.'"[10]

Before long this therapeutic act became known around Eppendorf, the Hamburg hospital where Nonne worked. "I gained confidence in my method and in my ability to practice it. The clinic became convinced of my special abilities and 'calling.' . . . From that point on I treated an extraordinarily great number of neurotics and hysterics with hypnosis and freed them from their symptoms."[11] With these early cases, Nonne accomplished the first recorded "rapid cures" (*Schnellheilungen*) and began to develop the first method of active treatment. By the war's end, Nonne had treated approximately 1,600 patients with his hypnotic technique. He later recalled the therapeutic successes that he and his assistant Dr. Wachsner had toward the beginning of the war: "Our reputation grew and with it grew the stream of patients who were sent to us from other hospital stations, where no one had any idea what to do with these people. Eventually it came to the point that several of the soldiers, who had had hysterical paralyses, etc. for quite some time lost their symptoms on the way from the hospital entrance to the 'nerve treatment pavilion.'"[12]

Henceforth, Nonne embarked on a series of lectures and demonstrations, in which he publicized his striking therapeutic successes. He initially claimed to cure some 80 percent of his patients, but by the end of the war he was reporting success rates as high as 95 percent.[13] Nonne concluded a 1916 Hamburg demonstration, in which he hypnotized five soldiers with stubborn neurotic conditions, causing their symptoms to disappear within moments, by praising the many advantages of his hypnotic treatment. It worked quickly and reliably, even on patients with long-standing, recalcitrant symptoms, many of whom had been shuttled back and forth between different treatment facilities; it was effective against tremors and tics as well as severe motor disorders; and its success in restoring the ability to work would save the state a fortune in pension payments.[14] What must have made Nonne's presentation all the more striking was the context in which he reported these results. Germany's psychiatrists were still deeply mired in the "therapeutic crisis" of the war's beginning and were, on the whole, utterly baffled by the mysterious and multiform symptoms of war neurosis. Nonne seemed to be offering a magic bullet against conditions that had thrust neurologists and psychiatrists into a state of deepening frustration and hopelessness.

Nonne later laid out the three necessary conditions for successful hypnotherapy: (1) the doctor had to act from a position of absolute self-confidence, (2) the patient must feel complete obedience toward the doctor, and (3) the environment must be one of healing, where all staff members assume that each patient will be cured.[15] In other words, the therapeutic relationship and the environment in which it took place had fully to reinforce medical domination, patient obedience, and an atmosphere of suggestion. (To amplify patients' subordination and to "increase their feelings of dependence," Nonne required that they be naked.)[16] His hypnotic treatment, thus, recapitulated and reinforced the hierarchical relationships of the military milieu. But beyond these fixed criteria and relationships lay other, less tangible factors that also influenced the outcome of the hypnotic sessions.

Among these factors were the doctor's personality, beliefs, and disposition. For Nonne, it was crucial that doctors had faith in the hypnotic method and in the psychological underpinnings of the war neuroses. Any residual somaticism—including, of course, belief in Oppenheim's traumatic neurosis diagnosis—endangered the therapeutic results.[17] Even a vague suspicion that organic damage underlay the condition risked implanting such a suggestion in the patient's mind, which might make him cling to his symptoms all the more tenaciously. Moreover, the relationship between a doctor and his patient played a significant role: "A perceptive doctor—and nerve doctors must be perceptive—can tell very soon if there is a 'fluid' between him and the patient. If the fluid is not there, then all efforts are in vain."[18] While Nonne's use of the word *fluid*—which hearkens back to Franz Anton Mesmer's theories of animal magnetism—was certainly metaphorical, it implies that he was not completely free of the parapsychological assumptions of his eighteenth- and early-nineteenth-century predecessors in the hypnotic arts.

Even for doctors skilled in hypnosis, results could not always be reproduced. On good days, when the news from the front was positive, Nonne could "put the man into the desired hypnotic sleep almost effortlessly with the first stroke; on gray, unhappy days on the front, my ability to get started was lacking or completely absent."[19] Some cases, it seems, succeeded almost instantaneously, but with others "I had to slave away for hours, with the result that the patient stopped his shaking, but I began to shake from the physical and mental exertion and the need to concentrate. Then the old head nurse Lonny, who had worked for me for twenty-one years at the 'men's nerve pavilion' would bring me a hot cup of coffee to revitalize my spent spirit."[20] Curiously, treating these difficult cases was so strenuous that Nonne himself began to show the hysterical symptoms of his patients.

Fortunately for Nonne and other practitioners of hypnosis during the war, soldiers seemed to be especially easy to hypnotize because they were accustomed to absolute obedience to their superiors. (The method was not meant for officers.) Perhaps this was especially true of German men, whom one historian has described as "subject soldiers" and who were arguably trained to be more subservient and self-sacrificing than their British and French counterparts.[21] Indeed, Nonne reported success at placing 80 to 90 percent of his soldier-patients into the hypnotic state.[22] He did not believe that variables such as race, age, or physical constitution affected an individual's suggestibility, but he did stress the importance of placing patients in the proper environment before commencing with hypnosis. Hence, Nonne had rather tepid success at demonstrations in Metz and Koblenz in 1917, where he was able to hypnotize only a fraction of the cases put before him. However, at his regular location, the Eppendorf Hospital in Hamburg, patients resided in the ward for several days, where they watched their comrades be cured and soaked up the suggestive atmosphere of the therapeutic milieu. With such cases, Nonne's success was usually quick and complete.[23]

During the hypnotic session, Nonne tried to exploit the patient's altered state of consciousness in order to instill in him the "positive willpower" to overcome his symptoms.[24] Unlike earlier practitioners of hypnosis, who often created mystical conditions in their treatment rooms by keeping out all external sound, dimming the lights, or using colored candles and visual effects, Nonne was not terribly concerned with ambiance. He did nothing, however, to reduce the mystery associated with the method; he did not explain the procedure to his patients and used their ignorance to subordinate them more deeply. In his descriptions of the therapeutic sessions, Nonne continually stressed that the doctor had to cultivate the image of a stern and superior healer, an image that would be compromised by dealing with patients so openly and sympathetically. Such explanations, furthermore, would give the impression that the doctor was seeking his patients' permission and could subvert the power relationship.[25] Instead, Nonne simply instructed the patients in a matter-of-fact manner that they would be cured to reinforce the notion that their recovery was a foregone conclusion.[26]

To place a patient into the hypnotic state, Nonne exerted light pressure on his eyelids, gently stroked his body and spoke in a soothing manner. When the patient's muscles had fully relaxed, Nonne knew he had entered the hypnotic trance. Once successfully placed in this state, the patient heeded verbal commands, and various muscles movements could be easily induced. Only then, after he had established that his subject was "in *Rapport*," did Nonne begin his curative suggestion (*Heilsuggestion*), the core of the therapeutic procedure.

Suggestion, in fact, was the key to Nonne's hypnotic method. The method worked by placing patients into a state in which they were more obedient to the doctor, more susceptible to the doctor's commands. "We use hypnosis," he explained, "so that through the altered state of consciousness we can gain influence over that positive strength of will which enables that the symptoms be overcome."[27] In such a way, Nonne sought to replace the dictates of the patient's will with his own commands, overturning the "sickly" will to remain debilitated with the positive will to become and remain healthy. More broadly, then, suggestive hypnosis, as Nonne practiced it, sought to counteract unhealthy wishes—the wish to avoid service, escape dangerous situations, or collect pensions—with the "healthier," more patriotic values of self-sacrifice and loyalty.

Suggestive hypnosis contrasts conspicuously with the more familiar, cathartic method that several doctors, influenced by Freud and Breuer's 1895 *Studies on Hysteria*, practiced during the war. In theory, cathartic hypnosis aids the patient in recovering repressed memories (or fantasies) so that he or she can be cured through abreaction. For Freud, neurotic symptoms carried symbolic significance; his early use of hypnosis sought to decode this symbolism by following a chain of associations, and these associations were easier to gain access to when the patient was placed in the hypnotic state.[28] Nonne's hypnosis, on the other hand, recast the technique as a disciplinary strategy suited to military relationships and the conditions of war. In cathartic hypnosis, as one historian has written, the patient participates actively in the therapeutic process, while with suggestive hypnosis the patient's subjectivity is neglected, and he is treated as the object or recipient of therapy.[29] In the latter method the doctor retains full control of the procedure, as would a surgeon, and the results occur more quickly and reliably.[30] Cathartic hypnosis, finally, aims to understand the meaning and basis of neurosis. Hypnotic suggestion, on the other hand, seeks to persuade patients and implant correct behaviors.

Suggestive hypnosis was not a science. Often it worked with great ease and speed; in some cases, Nonne reported that a single "*suggestion d'emblée*" (immediate suggestion) caused the entire complex of symptoms to vanish suddenly.[31] Even the phenomenon of the *Blitzheilung,* or lightening cure, in which the symptoms disappeared in a split-second, occasionally occurred.[32] In some cases, symptoms remained after the initial session but usually could be removed in a second attempt. Yet, at other times, the hypnotic cure demanded a great deal of sustained effort. In those cases, Nonne proceeded slowly and deliberately, working through the limbs one section at a time, stroking, rubbing, and kneading the affected muscles and joints to show the hypnotized patient that his muscles did work and would obey his own impulses.[33] In treating cases of functional muteness, for example, a category with which he had particularly favorable success rates, Nonne first worked on the muscles necessary for speaking: the lips, tongue, and larynx. Then he instructed the patient to repeat single sounds and build up to whole words, sentences, and eventually even songs.

At the end of the hypnotic session, instead of waking patients abruptly, Nonne preferred to suggest them gradually into the conscious state. Immediately after his patients awoke, he demonstrated the treatment's success to them and to other patients by showing what the formerly paralyzed body parts could now do.[34] After the treatment, Nonne generally kept the patient in bed for several days, in accordance with the intensity of the hypnotic session, and then put him to work around the hospital for a week. When he had completed a week of light work without relapse, the patient was usually declared ready to enter the hospital's workshops, where he could resume the practice of his peacetime occupation in preparation for the "return to real life."[35]

After Nonne exhibited his technique with both live demonstrations and pictures at well-attended meetings—most notably the 1916 Munich Congress—his method gained national, and soon international, attention.[36] In these appearances, he typically hypnotized a series of soldiers before enraptured audiences, using his striking and dramatic results as evidence against traumatic neurosis and in support of the hysteria diagnosis. The neurologist made a deep impression on his Munich audience not only by suddenly curing stuttering, paralyses, and tics but also by placing his subjects back into a hypnotic state through suggestion and having them reproduce their prior symptoms with "photographic fidelity."[37] Nonne's role in the debate with Oppenheim contributed considerably to his reputation and visibility, and his therapeutic demonstrations before so many of his neurological and psychiatric colleagues sealed his association with hypnotic treatment. In his own words, Nonne's appearance at Munich had a "revolutionizing effect" not only for his role in the defeat of traumatic neurosis but also in convincing his audience that war neuroses could be cured and thus in paving the way for the development and promotion of the methods of active treatment.[38]

The Munich Congress was a turning point in Nonne's career. Afterward, he was embraced by military-medical authorities, and later that year, he was called by the medical section of the Prussian War Ministry to demonstrate his method before a group of high-ranking deputy corps medical officers and garrison doctors.[39] From this point on doctors were sent to Hamburg to learn the method from him and to take suggestive hypnosis back to their own hospital stations. By his own account in 1917, Nonne had trained doctors from hospitals in at least a dozen German cities and towns.[40]

Nonne also began to travel, lecturing and performing hypnosis demonstrations before private circles, psychological associations, and groups of military doctors in such cities as Munich, Constance, Koblenz, Berlin, and Metz. He brought eight recovered patients, two noncommissioned officers, and his assistant, Dr. Wachsner, with him to a Dresden performance, where he was led into a hall in which more than seventy neurotics waited. In his first attempt, he met with only limited success because he was so nervous in front of the large, skeptical audience. "However I received such applause to my utter amazement that I gained self confidence and could go after the patients who were brought to me full speed ahead. Then I succeeded smoothly with the next three cases, and Dr. Wachsner too was able to free two cases of their symptoms in the mean time."[41] After three days of solid work, Nonne and Wachsner had successfully treated eighteen men.

That event and a second performance in Dresden attracted much attention among military and political officials, and both Nonne and Wachsner were awarded Saxon medals.[42] These demonstrations continued even after the war, and Nonne traveled around Europe and as far as South America, where his "magical" reputation packed auditoriums in Rio de Janeiro, Montevideo, and Buenos Aires. Yet, it troubled Nonne that these demonstrations, and not his neuroscientific research, were the basis of his growing fame. As he recalled: " . . . I became quite well known and—without justification—'famous' as 'the magic healer' [*Zauberheiler*], and unfortunately my reputation, which has spread through Germany and Europe as a 'great nerve doctor' is based far more on these war-time episodes than on my clinical anatomical works."[43]

Nonne's success against war neuroses must indeed have appeared magical. At a time when most psychiatrists and neurologists stood powerless against vast numbers of nervous casualties, Nonne was dazzling audiences with quick, efficient, and apparently reliable cures, which must have seemed supernatural to uneducated, frightened patients. But this account of Nonne's rise to fame through his promotion of hypnosis raises a number of questions. Why was Nonne the only doctor who practiced hypnosis? After all, hypnosis would not have been unfamiliar to doctors and laypeople in this period, so it would follow that other practitioners must have experimented with it as well. Yet, wartime discussions consistently referred to hypnosis as "Nonne's method," which strongly suggests that when other doctors did take it up, it resulted from Nonne's influence rather than their own, independent choices. And finally, why Nonne? Why was it a doctor whose solid, albeit unspectacular reputation came from his role as a neurologist—not a psychologist or even psychiatrist—who had spent most of his professional life conducting research on paralysis and organic damage to the nervous system, who became the "magical healer," the champion of hypnosis during the war? Clues to these questions lie in Nonne's career trajectory—which took him through the center of the hypnosis debate in late-nineteenth-century France—and the state of psychiatry on the eve of the war.

After studying physiology in Berlin, Freiburg, and Heidelberg, young Max Nonne began working at Hamburg's Eppendorf Hospital as an assistant in internal medicine in 1887. By 1896 he had become director of the hospital's new section for nerves (*Nervenabteilung*), which he ultimately turned into a neurological clinic.[44] Nonne was among the earliest doctors to bring neurology out of internal medicine and help establish its unique research agendas and distinct clinical facilities. He was the youngest founding member of the German Neurological Society and sat on the governing board with, among others, Hermann Oppenheim, whom he replaced as its president after the Munich Congress.[45] Like Germany's other leading authorities on war neurosis, Nonne belonged to the generation born in the 1860s. He had reached professional maturity and the height of his productivity by the beginning of the twentieth century and, as symbolized by his participation in an elite team of German and Swedish doctors selected to attend to Lenin on his sickbed in 1922, he achieved international stature during and after the war.[46]

When Nonne was a young assistant doctor, Jean-Martin Charcot was perhaps the world's most renowned and influential neurologist. Doctors came from near and far to pay homage to Charcot and to observe the demonstrations he conducted at the Salpêtrière Hospital. It was there that Nonne saw hypnosis—and the treatment of hysteria—if not for the first time then in a way that left a lasting impression on him. In fact, his trip to Paris coincided with the emergence of hypnosis as a subject of medical and political controversy.

Charcot had turned to hypnotism in the late 1870s as part of his ongoing investigations into the causes and course of hysteria. Uniquely straddling the worlds of respected scientific medicine and marginal occultist practices, he embraced the practice and dignified it as a research tool, if not as a therapeutic technique.[47] For Charcot, suggestibility—that is, susceptibility to the powers of hypnotism—was itself a pathological sign that pointed to the presence of latent hysteria or the existence of a hysterical constitution. Such subjects, then, could be hypnotized in order to analyze hysteria, which, Charcot theorized, was a fixed disease that followed certain immutable laws and progressed through a succession of stages or "passes."[48]

Nonne cut short his stay at the Salpêtrière. He left after six weeks, viewing the neurologist's legendary therapeutic demonstrations with skepticism and having little tolerance for the theatricality of the Salpêtrière atmosphere. However, despite this antipathy, Nonne's use of hypnosis during the war unmistakably reflects Charcot's influence. His vocabulary for describing hypnosis—*Rapport, suggestion d'emblée, suggestion à échéance*—betrays its French origins. More significantly, Nonne reproduced the "circus like" showmanship with which Charcot approached hysterical patients.[49] His wartime demonstrations even bear a striking resemblance to Charcot's performances, in which the Parisian neurologist routinely hypnotized a row of patients who sat illuminated in a spotlight before a captivated audience. The mood in Nonne's clinic, where, he reported, patients would recover instantly under the influence of the "suggestive atmosphere," evokes the environment of the Salpêtrière, which has been described as a hotbed of suggestion, in which dozens of female patients stood under the sway of the master's hypnotic charisma and contorted their bodies to conform to Charcot's hysteria theories. Nonne's use of film, furthermore, mirrors Charcot's concern with visually representing the hysteric and hence learning to detect hysteria through bodily signs—a concern more in step with the descriptive approach to disease of nineteenth-century French psychiatry than the developmental perspective of mental medicine in twentieth-century Germany.[50]

The French neurological world of the 1880s and early 1890s was riven by schism. Hippolyte Bernheim, once a student of Charcot's, rebelled against the master's teachings, challenged his theories of hypnosis and hysteria, and established a rival school in Nancy, which was the next stop on Nonne's itinerary. If Charcot influenced Nonne in subtle, unacknowledged ways, his Nancy rival had a far more direct impact on the Hamburg neurologist.

In contrast to Charcot, Bernheim and his followers emphasized the therapeutic applications of hypnosis. In their view, the charismatic Charcot, oblivious to the power of suggestion, had influenced his patients to conform to his well-known conception of hysteria and hence physically to recapitulate the hysterical states that he had so influentially documented.[51] Thus, his results with hypnosis could not be reproduced away from his own hospital, and his studies of hysteria proved nothing. Bernheim and the other members of the Nancy school also disputed that suggestibility was a sign of mental pathology. Indeed, their work showed that ordinary persons accustomed to obedience, such as soldiers, were easily suggestible.[52]

Nonne found Bernheim far more persuasive than Charcot.[53] Importantly, in Nancy, he witnessed Bernheim hypnotizing soldiers and saw hypnotic suggestion used for therapeutic ends. Nonne's stay in Nancy along with his brief visit to August Forel, director of Zurich's Burghölzi Sanitarium, led him to accept Bernheim's position that suggestibility was not a sign of pathology—a view that influenced his conception of hysteria decades later, when he parted from such colleagues as Gaupp and Bonhoeffer over precisely this question.

On returning to Hamburg, however, Nonne turned away from what he had seen in France and moved on to other research agendas and professional interests. Other than one article on hypnosis that he published in 1889 and some experiments hypnotizing soldiers while doing his military service that year, Nonne wrote on neither hysteria nor hypnosis in the years immediately after 1889, and his research interests over the next two decades chiefly involved organic diseases of the nervous system, including syphilis and multiple sclerosis.[54]

When Nonne turned his back on hypnosis, he was part of a larger movement in German medical circles. Having always occupied the fringes of acceptable medical practice, hypnosis fell out of favor in late-nineteenth-century Germany and was largely rejected by its psychiatric and neurological establishments.[55] As the neurologist Friedrich Schultze stated in an 1892 lecture:

> Hypnotherapy is in the first place superfluous, because other and better methods
> are at our disposal: furthermore, its consequences are most unsafe and can occasionally cause damage. And it has the after-taste of the theatrical and comic . . .
> it is time-consuming, and ultimately in "favorable" cases and particularly when
> many repetitions are necessary, it leads to a kind of stupefaction and dulling
> [*Versimpelung*] in many patients.[56]

What may have further detracted from its legitimacy was the appearance of hypnosis far from the halls of university medicine and the offices of respectable doctors. Indeed, street-level hypnosis, demonstrated by flamboyant itinerant practitioners, attracted eager audiences in German cities, towns, and villages, as people gathered to see the wonders of the mysterious art performed on volunteers.[57] These shows quickly became a cause for concern among state and local authorities, who were adverse to crowds and feared the impact of dubious performers like the "engineer and physicist Radecki," "Streidl," and "experimental psychologist Nama" on the highly suggestible masses. Newspapers in the 1890s reverberated with rumors of volunteers being left permanently in a hypnotic trance, and tales of murders committed under hypnosis kicked up controversies in Germany and abroad.[58] While hypnosis—along with occultist practices such as magnetic healing, telekinesis, and séances—flourished briefly, even in elite circles, in the later nineteenth century, by century's end such practices were arousing significant political, cultural, and medical resistance, although there was a resurgence during and after the war among aggrieved relatives who sought some sort of contact with their fallen loved ones.[59] Medical opposition culminated in the unsuccessful attempt to pass legislation prohibiting unlicensed hypnotherapy as well as all other mystical methods of treatment.[60] (This campaign, along with a movement to ban the cinematic representation of hypnosis, began again amid revived interest in public hypnosis demonstrations during the war's last months and in its aftermath. This renewed interest may have been the result of Nonne's use of the method in the war.)[61]

More broadly, turn-of-the-century German psychiatry devoted little attention to issues of therapy. Busy observing and classifying chronic mental disorders, for which little could be done therapeutically, psychiatrists were scarcely involved in studying or treating neuroses. Patients with such complaints were more likely to pay a visit to a neurologist or even an internist; it was neurologists such as Freud and Oppenheim, rather than psychiatrists, who pioneered the practice of psychotherapy in German-speaking Europe.[62] While Freud had experimented with hypnosis in the early years of his clinical practice, he abandoned it in the later 1890s, even though, as he later confessed, he had enjoyed being seen as a "miracle worker."[63] Freud argued that hypnosis concealed patients' resistance; indeed, the turn to resistance as the key therapeutic and analytical object was perhaps the crucial step in the development of psychoanalysis. Nevertheless, despite Freud's rejection of hypnosis, it remained associated with him and his controversial theories, which further tarnished its reputation in many medical minds.[64] While some private clinicians continued to use hypnosis before the war, the practice was taboo among medical leaders in Germany, where there was no equivalent to Charcot to lend it his prestige. Its association with private nerve clinics and disreputable street performers only strengthened this stigma.

Shortly after the war, Nonne reflected on the conflict between suggestion-based therapies such as hypnosis and the more strict "scientism" that dominated his professional world: "The move toward suggestive-therapy, which was inspired by the war, runs counter to the new tendency in internal medicine. Out of the narrow straight-jacket of exact science it achieved a freer method of observation which paid equal attention to the biological, mental, social, and personal characteristics of the patient."[65] But the domination of "narrow exact science," the area to which Nonne returned after the war, presented a serious obstacle to the practice and propagation of hypnosis and to the development of any effective treatment for war neurosis. This may explain why it took so many months for Nonne to come forward with the method; only amid the urgency of the war and the desperation bred by therapeutic powerlessness did hypnosis become an acceptable weapon in the emerging "fight against hysteria." Even so it required audacity to be associated with the discredited method. "Here in Baden-Baden," as Nonne recounted in May 1915, "I first had the courage to recommend the usage of hypnosis, which was considered by many as obsolete, that is to say, unscientific."[66]

The urgency of dealing with war hysteria shattered most of the taboos that prevented respectable university physicians from hypnotizing German men. Because he had witnessed hypnosis with Charcot, Bernheim, and Forel in the late 1880s, Nonne was in an ideal position to revive the method during the war. His well-regarded work on organic disorders also solidified his reputation as a respectable doctor. While other doctors who had been using hypnosis before the war also practiced it on war neurotics, it took a prestigious academic neurologist like Nonne to make the controversial technique an acceptable, even vaunted treatment. "At that time," he later recalled, referring to his French sojourn of 1889, "I had no idea that I would give hypnosis honor and fame through the treatment of war neuroses."[67]

The Hypnosis Controversy

Although Nonne may have brought "honor and fame" to hypnosis, his celebrated triumphs did not quell all medical unease with the method. And hypnosis alone did not solve the war neurosis problem. Despite its ostensible therapeutic advantages, it was taken up by a limited number of doctors; more seriously, it generated skepticism and even strong opposition among many. As Nonne showed, hypnotic suggestion could be quick, reliable, painless, and essentially safe, and it required neither equipment nor a special setting. Yet few doctors were able to reproduce the tremendous success Nonne reported, which led many to cast doubt on the veracity of the neurologist's claims.[68]

Nonne conceded that his method placed inordinate demands on the practitioner. Like the other types of active treatment, hypnosis operated through the doctor's personality, which meant that doctors could not rely on their assistants to carry it out.[69] Hypnosis, indeed, was strenuous work; the sessions could last long and could require what Nonne called "wrestling with the patient." "Hypnosis is the most elegant method," he wrote, "but one should not imagine that it is easier on the doctor, since the demand of extreme attention and the necessity of absolute concentration strain the practitioner greatly."[70] In addition to tremendous reserves of energy, successful hypnosis also required experience and perspicacity, in short, the "zealousness of youth [united with] the judiciousness and experience of age."[71] Nonne added: "He who has at his disposal a great deal of physical endurance and patience will favor [hypnosis]. To practice hypnosis demands an exceptional ability to judge the whole personality correctly, I would almost say artistic blood, the ability to take note of the slightest movements of the object, to interpret them, and to judge them in a split-second."[72]

A further obstacle to the method's widespread diffusion was the rarity of the necessary hypnotic charisma, an innate gift shared by few and impossible to teach.[73] This charisma was, for Nonne, even more important than advanced medical training.[74] The neurologist and future Gestalt theorist Kurt Goldstein agreed. Referring to Nonne's demonstration at the Munich Congress, Goldstein wrote: "The doctors who had the opportunity to witness the hypnoses, which Nonne demonstrated at the last Munich meeting, certainly admired the results, but they also saw the great significance of the factor of personality, which came across so clearly in these demonstrations and seems to prohibit the general spread of hypnosis."[75]

The character of the patient, too, determined the treatment's effectiveness. Certain individuals were resistant to the technique; in such cases, it seemed, no amount of medical skill could succeed in achieving the hypnotic state.

Indeed, concern for the patients was the source of Oppenheim's critique of Nonne's method. Oppenheim, who also practiced hypnotherapy in his Berlin hospital station and had used the method on hysterical conditions in his private clinic before the war, attributed Nonne's success to the coincidence that the latter's patients were primarily "pure," monosymptomatic hysterics, whereas the patients he treated more often suffered from combinations of localized hysterical and organically determined symptoms and thus could not be cured by such simple psychic interventions.[76] In addition, Oppenheim doubted the duration of Nonne's results, and from his clinical work on trauma cases, he was generally skeptical about the possibility of the "rapid cure."[77] Oppenheim remarked: "We have also attained some rapid cures through hypnosis and suggestion, but in the greater part of our trials hypnotic treatment failed, even in those cases where the patient could be placed into deep hypnotic sleep. I myself and three of my assistants and colleagues have devoted ourselves to hypnotic treatment in this hospital station, and none of us is a novice."[78] And even when it was apparently successful, hypnosis could have destructive results. Oppenheim among others pointed out that it addressed the neurotic symptoms and not their underlying causes, and could thus allow conditions to return or even deteriorate over time.

Various practical considerations further limited the spread of hypnosis. Fritz Kaufmann, who pioneered electrotherapeutic cures of war neurosis, observed that when unsuccessful, hypnotic treatment could strengthen a patient's resolve not to be cured.[79] Hypnosis was also ineffective, of course, on the large number of patients who suffered from hysterical deafness.[80] And as the Vienna psychiatrist Julius von Wagner-Jauregg pointed out, it only worked on men who spoke German. This ruled it out for many soldier-patients from the further reaches of the Habsburg realm—hypnosis through an interpreter was extremely difficult because the relationship between doctor and patient had to be intense and unmediated.[81] These obstacles, however, did not deter Wilhelm Stekel, who also worked in Vienna during the war. Stekel found that he could overcome the linguistic gap with creativity; in the following passage, which vividly demonstrates the discourse of the miraculous, Stekel describes treating a Hungarian soldier with a rudimentary form of hypnotic suggestion:

> Among my patients there was a man who had lost his speech following a persis-
> tent artillery barrage. I promised to cure him in a few minutes. All the doctors
> of the hospital together with the chief surgeon and the head-nurse gathered to-
> gether to witness this demonstration. I used a different method—fascination.
> The patient, a simple Hungarian peasant (I could not communicate with him as
> I do not speak Hungarian), was sitting opposite me in a chair. I looked persis-
> tently into his eyes for two minutes and then I intoned 'A-a-a.' Like an automa-
> ton he repeated the 'A.' Then I used other vowels, progressed to syllables, and
> finally he repeated a few Hungarian words I had learned at the hospital. At last
> the expected miracle occurred: he was cured. A stream of tears broke from his
> eyes.[82]

An early adherent of psychoanalysis, Stekel would have preferred to analyze many of his wartime patients, but time constraints dictated the need for more efficient measures. Since he was responsible for all of the patients in the 140-bed neuropsychiatric ward of a Viennese hospital, it was not possible for Stekel to analyze each patient. Through hypnosis he could treat his patients rapidly, even en masse, in a manner reminiscent of the public hypnosis demonstrations that incurred the wrath of his profession.[83] The following description reveals, once again, the magical elements at work; it also shows the introduction of deception and theatricality into the therapeutic procedure and betrays medical contempt for and power over an uneducated, unrefined class of patients:

> These simple people believed I was working with magic. As is known, it is diffi-
> cult to hypnotize individual neurotics in the office, but it is easy to hypnotize a
> group of people simultaneously. Each is impressed by seeing the others. There-
> fore, men working with hypnosis often have several particularly submissive pa-
> tients on whom they perform their miracles before starting with the new
> patients. . . . Public hypnotists generally have one or two bogus 'mediums' (as-
> sistants) to implant the suggestion upon others. . . . Sometimes while making my
> rounds I would achieve a general sedative effect by commanding, 'Sleep one
> hour!' while pointing with the index finger at the individual patient, and one af-
> ter the other would fall asleep and remain quiet for the required time.[84]

Fully exploiting the power of suggestion, Stekel created a latter-day Salpêtrière for men, a hotbed of suggestion around a charismatic medical figure.

It was precisely this sort of deception and theatricality that aroused opposition among a handful of doctors. The psychiatrist Ernst Kretschmer confessed that he was uneasy with "magical" effects such as blue lighting that many of his colleagues used, but he conceded that they created an atmosphere more conducive to suggestive treatment.[85] And when Nonne presented his findings before the Medical Association of Hamburg in November and December of 1915, he was sharply criticized by Kurt Böttiger, who charged that the practice of hypnosis degraded both doctors and patients.[86] Böttiger argued that in hypnosis the doctor suppresses the patient's feelings and imagination and at the same time degrades himself by pretending to believe in "medieval nonsense" in order to achieve the illusion of superiority and hence the full suggestive effect. He preferred to appeal to the patient's sense of reason, in short, to heal the patient by enlightening him about the virtues of serving the Fatherland, rather than forcing or tricking his symptoms away.

A small but vocal contingent opposed hypnosis on ethical grounds, viewing the manipulation of the unconscious mind as an intrusion on a patient's right of privacy and condemning the method as a "step back to the dark times of Charcot."[87] Others focused on the subjugation, even violation, of patients' subjectivity that the method entailed. Ernst Simmel, who used hypnosis as part of a modified form of "brief psychoanalysis" in the war, condemned hypnotic suggestion as a "rape of the psyche" that provided only the temporary illusion of healing by forcing patients to further repress their symptoms and act cured, a criticism that Oppenheim had also made.[88] These symptoms, Simmel warned in a 1918 monograph, would inevitably return once the patient was reintroduced to unpleasant or demanding conditions.

Another severe remonstrance was voiced by the Leipzig neurologist, Erwin Niessl von Maiendorf who condoned hypnosis under certain conditions but protested Nonne's method of hypnotic suggestion. Niessl cast doubt on the authenticity of Nonne's public appearances and charged that when abused, hypnotism could actually worsen neurotic conditions. Nonne's much-touted quick cures, he cautioned, were "a matter of successful theater for the self-aggrandizement of the performing doctor, but never really a cure."[89] Furthermore, these so-called cures only served to clear patients out of the clinics; close follow-up studies, Niessl argued, would show that these men were not cured at all and that *"hysteria is never cured through suggestion."*[90] Several of Nonne's detractors, then, shared the basic objection that healing should not be equated with the removal of symptoms and assumed that Nonne's claims would be undermined by further scrutiny and deeper examination.

In response to such accusations and to test the duration of his cures, Nonne performed a follow-up study on a group of patients whom he had discharged from the Eppendorf Hospital over a six-month period.[91] Of the forty-six men who responded to his questionnaire, twenty-six had resumed their prewar occupations in full capacity as agricultural workers, artisans, bank officials, and office workers; sixteen reported that they were working at a reduced pace, for lower wages, and with occasional interruptions for relaxation; and four had suffered relapses and were once again in military hospitals. Significantly, none of the respondents had returned to the field.

The critiques of doctors such as Niessl and Böttiger were also an expression of medical ambivalence toward Nonne's contrived, theatrical displays, which drew on the activities of charlatans and other nonreputable performers rather than the fruits of advanced scientific psychiatry. In so doing, however, Nonne was acting firmly within psychiatric tradition, a tradition that traces back to modern psychiatry's roots in revolutionary France. Philippe Pinel, considered a pioneer of "moral treatment" and a major psychiatric patriarch, borrowed heavily from nonmedical methods, and the therapeutic breakthroughs he publicized involved often elaborately staged deceptions that aimed to trick or persuade patients to abandon their delusions.[92] Suggestive hypnosis, like all the methods of wartime active treatment, also involved stepping out of what Nonne called the "narrow straightjacket of exact science" and incorporating lay techniques that were often theatrical, magical, and at times quite kitschy. Ever defiant of psychiatric positivism, hysterical neurosis seemed to require such radical medical measures. For most doctors, the therapeutic and professional rewards were sufficient to justify any medical indignities they incurred.

Fritz Kaufmann and the Miraculous Current

Following Nonne's "rediscovery" and promotion of hypnosis came a second method that had an equally pronounced influence on the treatment of war hysteria. Just as Nonne's name was intertwined with the practice of hypnotic suggestion, Fritz Kaufmann, an Austrian-Jewish neurologist who practiced in Mannheim, became closely associated with the therapeutic use of electric current.[93] Indeed, Kaufmann's *Überrumpelungsmethode* (surprise attack method) was generally known as the "Kaufmann cure," and near the war's end the name Kaufmann—and the new adjective *Kaufmannisch*—became virtually synonymous with the aggressive, even brutal handling of hysterical patients.[94]

Kaufmann spent the war years at a reserve hospital in Ludwigshafen, a town outside Mannheim. There he shared the widespread frustration with the early, largely ineffective neurosis treatments and grew restless as his patients remained unaffected by a treatment regimen of restorative "relaxation and exercise" (*Schonung und Übung*). Soon Kaufmann concluded that to be effective treatment had to be more active and aggressive.[95] Rather than dealing with the symptoms individually, he urged doctors to treat the "whole patient" and to create an environment that, in effect, coerced hysterical patients into being cured. "When these patients are forced into a cure," he noted, ". . . then at the very least they will be able to practice their peace-time occupations again, and the pension matter is done away with too."[96] Kaufmann was inspired by Nonne's success at curing neurotic patients in a single session, but he eschewed the practice of hypnosis for reasons that remain not entirely clear.[97] While the core of both treatments involved suggestion, Kaufmann's technique borrowed— both discursively and strategically—from the military in order to do battle against this tenacious malady. The modern image of the Kaufmann method made it seem more in keeping with the spirit of scientific medicine; its martial form fit the military environment, and its speed and assembly-line appearance suited it to the enormous numbers of psychiatric casualties that arose around 1916 and beyond.

Like Nonne, Kaufmann reached back to a technique he had observed years before the war and adapted it to the military context. In 1903 Kaufmann had worked as an assistant at Wilhelm Erb's nerve clinic in Heidelberg, where he most likely met both Nonne and Gaupp. The Erb clinic was Germany's leading center for the use of electricity in the study of the nervous system, and there Kaufmann witnessed Erb's attempts to treat hysteria through electricity and suggestion.[98] One case in particular made a lasting impression on the neurologist. A young woman who suffered from a hysterical paralysis stayed in the clinic for four days. The first three days were spent preparing her for her cure. Then on day four she was subjected to a ten-minute burst of relentless electric current with continuous verbal suggestion. The healing occurred promptly, Kaufmann recalled. By his own account, the memory of this experience motivated him to try a similar technique on his hysterical soldier-patients in late 1915.

The resulting method, as publicized in a series of lectures and demonstrations and in Kaufmann's widely cited article of July 1916, consisted of four basic elements.[99] Kaufmann called the first element "suggestive preparation." During this crucial stage, the patient was to be convinced that the impending treatment would be absolutely successful. The doctor and the entire hospital staff must continually stress this idea through all their words and actions, which was Kaufmann's way of achieving what Nonne called the suggestive atmosphere. In fact, suggestion was the key to the entire Kaufmann method: Before treatment the patient was instructed that the treatment would cure him; during the actual session, he was informed that the treatment was working; and afterward, it was stressed that the treatment had worked.

The second element involved the "application of strong, alternating current with the aid of a great deal of verbal suggestion."[100] Kaufmann instructed that, where possible, the current should be directly applied to the appropriate part of the body; that is, a patient whose arm was functionally paralyzed generally received the electric shock on the arm. This was not due to any curative effects the electricity had on disabled limbs; rather it was a ruse that aimed to deceive the patient into thinking that his malady was physical and therefore fully curable by the somatic treatment being applied. The certainty patients feel when routine organic procedures are performed was deemed a necessary precondition for Kaufmann's method to succeed—a strategy that strangely inverted the ascendant position in the traumatic neurosis debate, reversed one of Nonne's therapeutic postulates, and contradicted later psychiatric efforts to enlighten the lay public about the psychic basis of the war neuroses. There was, then, an element of deliberate deception in the Kaufmann cure. Most doctors knew that it worked through suggestion, but they told their patients otherwise to build confidence in the treatment.[101]

Kaufmann administered the sinusoidal current in "bursts" of two to five minutes. Between these bursts, he ordered his patients to perform physical exercises, emphasizing their ability to overcome their handicaps. It was of vital importance, Kaufmann noted, that throughout the entire second step the doctor continue his barrage of verbal suggestion and constantly affirm the treatment's success and the inevitability of a positive outcome. The duration of the cycle of electricity and exercises depended on the patient's progress—some sessions could last as long as two and a half hours.

Kaufmann's third condition was the maintenance of strict military discipline during the entire process. The verbal suggestion as well as the exercises were to be carried out with crisp military commands, "like at the barracks." Furthermore, the patient's subordinate military rank had to be emphasized. As in Nonne's method, therapy required hierarchy.

Finally, as a fourth element, Kaufmann specified that once undertaken, the session could not be terminated before the cure was complete. The premature interruption of the treatment had potentially serious consequences. It risked planting the illusion in the patient's mind that his condition was incurable, which could lead to long-term "fixation." The doctor's determination not to quit until the condition was cured was intended to impart the impression that recovery was inevitable.[102] Thus, the Kaufmann method—analogous to the war itself—was conceived of as a battle of wills. The doctor waged a kind of warfare against the patient, and the latter had to understand that he could not win and holding on to his symptoms would only prolong his pain and suffering.

And it worked. Kaufmann claimed in the 1916 article that with this procedure he had cured forty cases, each in a single session. Later in the war, Kaufmann and several other doctors began to report astonishing rates of success with the method, which they used primarily on "fixed" or "stubborn" cases, men who had been resistant to other forms of treatment and remained in the hospitals or had been discharged as uncured.

The questions posed above about Nonne and hypnosis could certainly also be asked about Kaufmann and electric current. What, then, was new about Kaufmann's method, and why was he the pioneer of wartime electrotherapy? After all, the use of electricity in medicine has a long history that purportedly stretches back to classical antiquity, when Galen used the shocks from electric eels to treat gout.[103] Around the beginning of the nineteenth century electric current was applied in the treatment of hysterical disorders, and by the century's end it had become a common therapeutic method among psychiatrists.[104] However, in the years before the war, the use of electricity began to wane as doctors lost faith in its unique curative powers and saw that ordinary suggestion could achieve equivalent results without the pain and risk.[105] Indeed, one doctor noted in 1906: "Gone is the era when the common practice was to treat those with post-accident nervous conditions—whether voluntarily or involuntarily—with the electrifying machine . . ."[106] Freud also briefly practiced electrotherapy and followed Erb's prescriptions, but he too put his machine aside and concluded that what he had thought was science turned out to be pure fantasy.[107]

Like Nonne, then, Kaufmann reached back to a method that had fallen out of favor with leading neurologists and psychiatrists. Originally, Kaufmann intended the method to deliver a shock to undo or reverse the pathological effects of a somatic trauma. In a sense, the goal of treatment was simply to knock a soldier back on track after a combat event had thrown him psychically off-kilter. Thus, the treatment session was conceived of as a kind of "counter-trauma" for which Kaufmann brought the conditions of battle—strict martial discipline in the face of powerful and jarring shocks—into the hospital to serve therapeutic ends.

But before long, Kaufmann noticed that the method worked in a manner different from his original intentions, that it was not the physical properties of the electricity, but rather the suggestive, psychological impact of the whole procedure that was at work.[108] The pain the procedure caused, once accepted as an undesirable but unavoidable side effect of the healing powers of electricity, became, for Kaufmann, the primary therapeutic agent. Pain added force to Kaufmann's suggestive work and strengthened the illusion that something somatic was happening, making the method all the more effective. "In electro-suggestive sessions," wrote one doctor, "current is only used as a temporary expedient. It is simply a means to an end. Even here the primary factor is the personal effect of the doctor on the patient, to bring about a change in the sickly will, and to force him [the patient] ultimately to overcome the impulses of his own will . . ."[109]

For Nonne, the hypnotic state made patients more susceptible to suggestion, whereas in the Kaufmann method, electricity rendered the suggestion more powerful: The former weakened the patient's resistance, and the latter strengthened the doctor's hand, but both approached the therapeutic act as a battle of wills. The electric current thus functioned as a prop, an aid that allowed practitioners less skilled in the arts of persuasion, suggestion, or hypnosis to accomplish the same therapeutic goals. And with its modern, technological trappings, the technique gave the impression that it could be regulated and controlled, facilitating the incorporation of the thoroughly subjective therapeutic act of suggestion into a standardized system of psychiatric administration.

A further source of originality lay in Kaufmann's use of alternating current instead of direct current, which was conventionally applied in electrotherapy.[110] Not satisfied with its mild effects, Kaufmann modified his electrotherapeutic apparatus to produce a more powerful and intense shock that could cause potentially serious damage to the internal organs.[111]

Kaufmann also emphasized military rank as a way of achieving more suggestive leverage. Even the method's name, *Überrumpelungsbehandlung,* combined a military concept (*Überrumpelung*), the surprise attack or ambush, with the medical concept of treatment (*Behandlung*) into one compound word. In a sense, the Kaufmann method reproduced the experience of modern warfare in the treatment room. Not only did it supply the shocks and terror that characterized the mechanized battlefield, but it also extended military discipline and the need to conform to strict codes of honor and masculinity into the therapeutic realm. It thus represented the complete negation of the earliest forms of wartime therapy, the soothing and relaxing cures, which were later condemned as too passive and coddling. For Kaufmann it was absolutely essential that the treatment room be more unpleasant than the field, that it undo the temptations of the "flight into illness."

Kaufmann's first article and his demonstrations at several medical meetings in 1915 and 1916 had a tremendous impact on the profession. Word of his noteworthy therapeutic success spread rapidly, and forms of electrotherapy were quickly adopted by many doctors. However, some practitioners took umbrage at Kaufmann's 1916 publication. The method struck several of his colleagues as unacceptably brusque. To some it constituted an ethically suspect "militarization of medicine." As Kurt Mendel later recounted: "I must openly confess that I was completely outraged when I read the article . . . ; the exposition struck me as so inhumane, so devoid of human-medical considerations . . . in my review of the article at the time, I concluded 'doctors are not sergeants; hospitals are not military bases.'"[112] Unwittingly foreshadowing the popular outrage that the method eventually provoked, Mendel noted that he had refrained from a more detailed discussion of it for fear of "endangering the *Burgfrieden.*"[113]

Other critics objected to the painfulness of treatment with electric current. Doctor Max Liebers reported that for this reason he applied current only with a patient's permission.[114] Kurt Goldstein, despite using the method himself, thought it unjust to treat men who had risked their lives for the nation with so little compassion.[115] Far more incriminating were the incidents of death and serious injury that occurred during application of the Kaufmann method, two of which were reported at the Munich Congress.[116] These were attributed to heart attacks in men with congenitally weak hearts. Officials ultimately recorded at least ten deaths, and it is quite possible that many more occurred. Yet, with the exception of the Berlin neurologist Max Lewandowsky, who proposed banning the procedure after one of his patients dropped dead, practitioners of the Kaufmann method blamed not the method itself but its incorrect administration or improper patient screening for these accidents.[117] The Prussian War Ministry did ban electrotherapy with strong sinusoidal current at the end of 1917, and the Austrians banned it in 1918, but only in the war's final weeks, when the Kaufmann method became the subject of patient resistance and even popular protest, did military-medical authorities restrict its application and explicitly endorse hypnosis as an alternative.[118]

Strikingly, neurologists and psychiatrists often seemed more concerned with the welfare of the administering doctor than with the patients who were treated with the painful and dangerous procedure. The neurologist Max Rothmann wrote that he preferred other methods to the Kaufmann technique because two hours of electrotherapy could be tremendously grueling for a doctor.[119] Kaufmann acknowledged that the method was exhausting and had its own health hazards. Hypnosis made Nonne shake, and electrotherapy, it seems, taxed Kaufmann's nerves.[120]

Treatment became more difficult and wearisome when patients did not want to be cured. Those patients whom Gaupp labeled "mentally and morally inferior," men lacking the will to recover, often resisted medical intervention. As Gaupp reported to the medical department of the Ministry of War in April 1917, "The number of these inferiors has increased more and more and with it the defamation and denigration of doctors, for whom treatment with electric current constitutes a *very great* personal strain. That it represents an 'abuse' of the soldier is not correct."[121] Gaupp, thus, turned the tables on patients and cast doctors in the role of the victims, forced to carry out strenuous and exhausting procedures on ungrateful, recalcitrant men. This perspective forcefully appeared late in the war and during the Revolution of 1918–19.

Gaupp spoke for most of his colleagues in his emphatic defense of the Kaufmann method. Most doctors, operating from a collectivistic approach to the nervous health of Germany's men, believed that the ends justified the means. They dismissed the critics and argued that the method's miraculous benefits clearly outweighed any possible dangers to isolated individuals. This logic was reflected in a 1918 article, in which one doctor calculated that electric current had been used more than a million times, based on the assumption that one hundred doctors in Germany and Austria-Hungary treated five men per day for three hundred days a year.[122] In view of the presumed one million successful applications of the treatment, the twelve fatalities could be written off as statistically negligible in the practice of this medically indispensable procedure.

In a written defense of the method, Gaupp even praised Kaufmann for his humanity, for developing such a successful treatment that brought so many men if not back into the army then at least into the work force.[123] And in a 1917 address, he conceded that the method did cause pain, but he also celebrated its contribution: "[W]hat is the significance of enduring several seconds or minutes of somewhat painful electric current when through it a sick man condemned to idleness in a hospital station can in just a few minutes be made healthy, able to work and useful to the Fatherland?"[124] Doctors did not enjoy the procedure either, but the demands of duty outweighed their reservations; they were compelled "out of love for the Fatherland and warm concern for [the patients] to do anything which could bring the sick will, which has strayed from the path, back on track."[125] Or, in another doctor's formulation, "One should not only cure patients, but should cure them as quickly as possible, and if in this case that occurs only with a certain degree of ruthlessness, then ruthlessness is the greatest compassion."[126]

Elsewhere Gaupp called any method that could quickly rehabilitate hysterical men permissible, if carried out by a trained doctor. He downplayed the unpleasantness of the Kaufmann method, in view of the soldier's overall experience in the war:

> In the hands of a nerve doctor familiar with the whole procedure, electric treatment is harmless, if momentarily painful. . . . In view of the frightful dangers, exertions, and pains which our soldiers in the field have to endure, with death before their eyes hourly, it takes a pitiful character for a soldier to complain when, to cure his excruciating condition the doctor sends a painful electric current through his body for several seconds or minutes, which cures him of symptoms which had lingered often as long as a year.[127]

Complaints, then, were taken as a sign of a patient's deficient character, psychopathology, or selfish disposition rather than a reflection of the painfulness of the procedure or any brusqueness on the doctor's part. As another doctor pointed out, given the seriousness of the problem, "It is not appropriate to make the choice of methods dependent on aesthetic sensibility or pseudo-moralizing concerns."[128]

Kaufmann himself addressed several of these criticisms at the Munich Congress. There he described his method in somewhat milder terms and modified his earlier presentation and conception. First, the neurologist noted that electrotherapy was an age-old medical treatment. While in his previous description he had written that sessions could last for more than two hours, in Munich he stressed that they seldom exceeded fifteen minutes, and he revised his formulation to emphasize that the therapeutic significance lay in verbal suggestion, rather than the electric current. Kaufmann also underscored what he had maintained from the start, that his method should be used only on "hardened" cases; for soldiers with "fresh" neuroses he relied on more conservative treatments.[129] The notion of knocking the traumatized mind back on track through a countertrauma disappeared from Kaufmann's revised presentation, and the physical exercises that patients performed during the procedure took on greater significance. He further claimed that he kept the current at the lowest levels possible, so that it was "certainly tolerable."[130]

Already in his earlier article, Kaufmann had listed two advantages of his method over Nonne's hypnosis, the only other method of treating war neurosis at the time that had met with widespread and highly publicized success. Kaufmann argued that when attempted by untrained practitioners unfamiliar with the intricacies of hysteria, hypnosis could cause far more damage then his own method. Echoing the concerns of prewar health officials and a scandalized populace, he wrote that some patients never returned from their hypnotic states, while others were permanently altered by the procedure.[131] However, doctors lacking extensive neurological and psychiatric training could perform electrotherapy with little or no danger. In contrast to hypnosis, an unmistakably subjective procedure that could easily backfire and even strengthen a patient's resolve not to let himself be cured, Kaufmann's method, its creator avowed, seldom misfired. In other words, the Kaufmann cure did not depend on such subjective variables as a doctor's charisma or a patient's suggestibility. Since the results could be reproduced in almost any situation on nearly all patients, the method seemed more like a powerful new therapeutic science.

In his second article on electrotherapy, published in 1917, Kaufmann added, "The method is only brutal and rough when it is carried out by a brutal doctor in a rough manner."[132] In this article Kaufmann assured his colleagues that the technique sounded more painful than it actually was and noted that several of his erstwhile critics, including the psychiatrists Ernst Meyer and Karl Wilmanns and the neurologist Kurt Mendel, had become converts to the method. Significantly, the term *Überrumpelung* appeared neither in his Munich presentation nor in this new written exposition. Kaufmann also stressed that he used mild current and emphasized that the current was never applied to vital organs. Only in cases of functional aphonia did Kaufmann augment the mild current with the more painful galvanic type. In such cases, he reported placing a large electrode on the right upper arm and delivering the charge to the biceps. The average application lasted only about one minute. With this speedy and efficient method, Kaufmann noted that he routinely cured six consecutive patients in a day's work.

Finally, Kaufmann resorted to a defense that resembled Gaupp's argumentation: The benefits to both the individual patient and society as a whole far outweighed the several moments of pain that patients had to endure. "Personally I consider every method justified," Kaufmann wrote, "when it serves our ultimate aim, that is to help the patient quickly and to make him once again a useful member of the national community."[133] Furthermore, Kaufmann claimed, a fast, albeit painful cure was certainly better for the patient than letting him remain disabled for months on end.

After Kaufmann adjusted his method and, more important, made the tone of his presentation gentler, the treatment met with even greater approval in Germany's medical community.[134] Suggestive electrotherapy emerged as the most common and visible method of treating war neurotics. It became the cornerstone of active treatment and quickly revolutionized the organization of wartime psychiatric services. The success of both Kaufmann's method and Nonne's suggestive hypnosis came to the attention of military-medical authorities, particularly after the Munich Congress, and army health officials encouraged the widespread dissemination of both techniques. At a meeting of army medical advisors from throughout Germany, held two months after the Congress, partic-

ipants agreed unanimously that "a more vigorous method of treating war neurotics than what has generally been practiced is required, now that numerous
examples have proven that a series of effective—and not dangerous—treatments exist which promise a good chance at substantial success on a great many
patients."[135]

Long frustrated by their therapeutic powerlessness in the face of rising numbers of neurotics, many doctors were deeply impressed by the speed of electrotherapeutic cures and their high rates of success even against long-standing
hysterical symptoms. At last, in the context of a stagnating war, a strained economy, and unimaginable bloodshed, Germany's doctors had something to cele-
brate. Psychiatrists seemed to revel in the success of the Kaufmann cure,
heralding its revolutionary healing powers and dazzled by their own success.
Adjectives such as "miraculous" and "magical" commonly accompanied descriptions of the method, as in this account by Heidelberg psychiatrist Karl
Wilmanns, an erstwhile critic of Kaufmann:

> Its success was magnificent. Patients who had been bed-ridden for months and
> years on end with paralyzed limbs, who had been ordered into wheelchairs and
> who depended on the help of those around them to move, were—within several
> minutes—freed from all of these disorders through this powerful procedure. . . .
> By a supreme effort the doctors and their assistants, the nurses, devote all their
> strength to influencing the patients with the result that, one can say without ex-
> aggerating, that all of the patients are cured or substantially improved and that
> the nerve stations have acquired a reputation as miracle sanitariums [*Wunder-
> heilstätten*].[136]

Numerous other doctors reported astounding success with electrotherapy,
characterizing it as magical science and celebrating Kaufmann's demonstrations
as a watershed that moved psychiatry from pessimistic therapeutic passivity toward a new, optimistic future. The method's nearly perfect results made what
was essentially just another form of suggestive treatment seem like a predictable
and reliable scientific procedure. Gaupp, for example, wrote of an unnamed
doctor who declared that he cured 270 cases of hysteria, each in a single electrotherapeutic session.[137] A 1917 survey showed that several doctors, including Kaufmann himself, claimed success rates as high as 97 percent.[138] And by
June 1918, Kaufmann reported that he had treated approximately 1,500 neurotics in two years and had "freed" more than 95 percent from their symptoms.[139] Max Raether, who boasted of similar rates of success in a Bonn
psychiatric clinic, credited Kaufmann's innovations with transforming the
army's approach to war hysteria. Raether noted that the method had become a
"therapeutic necessity." It was in use in every German corps district, and neurotics were no longer discharged without being treated by Kaufmann's method
or one of the other types of active treatment.[140]

Likewise Goldstein attributed a veritable therapeutic revolution to Kaufmann's method. He cast Kaufmann's 1916 article as a turning point that ush-

ered in the era of quick cures and drastic pension reductions. "True," Goldstein admitted, "[Kaufmann] is not the first who achieved real cures in great numbers of war neurotics, rather Nonne had great success with hypnosis before him. But . . . Nonne's recommendation of hypnosis was not taken up universally; thus it was in fact Kaufmann's report which first eradicated the pessimism of the other doctors."[141]

Goldstein explained that Kaufmann's method had a greater impact than Nonne's work with hypnosis because it was substantially more practical. Nonne's "gift" for hypnotizing was a rare talent, but the use of electrotherapy could substitute for doctors' lack of charisma and augment their suggestive skills. Many psychiatrists and neurologists, including Nonne himself, tried hypnosis first and reserved the less pleasant electrotherapy for those patients who could not be hypnotized or whose symptoms persisted after the hypnotic session.[142] It was against these "stubborn" cases that electrotherapy seemed to work miracles. Finally, electrotherapy must have been less vexing to medical professionals than hypnosis. Despite the fact that the electric current acted only as a psychological agent, the Kaufmann cure nonetheless contained the trappings of science and technology. At least the method looked scientific, and its modern appearance exempted it from the nonscientific, "medieval" taint of hypnosis. The "miracle cures" it effected seemed to involve a more modern, technological magic, a predictable process that could nearly be quantified. Its appearance and effects disguised the fact that the same results could be achieved with any number of other suggestive methods.

Because the key to the Kaufmann method lay not in the nature of the electric treatment but rather in its suggestive force, many practitioners began to part from Kaufmann's prescriptions and tailor the method to suit their own preferences and styles. Some varied the kind of current and its strength; others changed the placement of the electrodes or modified the instrument that delivered the charge; and several doctors anaesthetized their patients with ether before applying the current.[143]

The Bonn nerve doctor Heinrich Bickel, for example, developed a method characterized by "increasing doses of painful current."[144] Bickel put his patients through a series of sessions in which they were exposed to faradic or galvanofaradic current for increasing lengths of time, so that by the sixth session, the pain lasted as long as twenty minutes. Raether described the variation he used in his Bonn clinic in this passage, a striking portrayal of medical power and patient subjugation:

> [T]heir clothes are removed . . . and they are placed lying down on the electrifying bench. A man holds the feet, two men hold the arms, which are laid next to the head, and one man operates the equipment. No one speaks except the doctor. On a short command the machine begins to hum. I usually wait for a while with a timer in my hand. The patient's expectation reaches its peak. I apply the faradic brush [*Pinsel*] suddenly, and only in cases of high analgesics does it take

longer than 1/2–1 minute for tetanus build-up to develop on the whole body. Then I reduce the current substantially, begin with forceful verbal suggestion, faradize more or less the whole body with the exception of the head, neck, palms, and soles with the weaker current, and have the once paralyzed limbs move on command, have those who were voiceless or with other speech disorders repeat words.[145]

Perhaps to make his method more palatable, Raether added that during the "preparatory period" the patients literally begged for their turn in the treatment room. Also, he assured, the cries of pain were only slight, and treatment sessions averaged only about five minutes. Furthermore, he claimed that he had tested the current on his own hand, "and can confidently assert that moderate faradic current is completely tolerable and its application can in no way be criticized as rough and unsuitable as a treatment for defenders of the Fatherland."[146] Raether continued, praising the method's effect on patients: "Already during the exercises a grateful euphoria grips the patients, which occasionally rises to exuberant expressions of gratitude. . . . In the post-treatment stage the cured patients are joyful and happy, obedient and imbued with only a good will, while before the treatment they were moody, idle, contrary, quarrelsome with each other and caused trouble at every chance."[147]

Dr. Gustav Oppenheim devised another variation of electrotherapy especially suited to soldiers suffering from neurotic shaking (*Zitterneurose*). The idea behind this rather Pavlovian technique was that the shaker had to remain still to avoid being shocked. According to Oppenheim, these patients' tremors were the physical expression of unresolved affect, usually fear. But through the patients' wishes (i.e., the desire to escape the front or receive a pension), these symptoms became "fixed." In order to override fixed symptoms, an opposing idea or counterforce of greater magnitude was required. According to Oppenheim's peculiar ingenuity this counterforce was pain, and the goal was to make the patient's shaking so unpleasant that the mechanism of fixation would be "paralyzed."[148]

Oppenheim carried this out by fastening an electrode to the patient's back or shoulder, far enough from the site of the shaking that it would not interfere with physical exercises. Also attached to the induction coil was an "interrupter," which consisted of a small metal tube with a clapper inside. When the small clapper swung, the current flowed through, but when it remained still the current stopped. "The interrupter is placed in the patient's hands, or it is hung on his jacket, pants, or cap, in accordance with the location of the shaking. Through his shaking the patient sets the interrupter in motion, and with every shake he receives a faradic jolt at the site of the electrode, whereas when he holds still he does not feel anything."[149]

The usual outcome, Oppenheim reported, was that patients at first became agitated and shook even more pronouncedly, all the while receiving ever increasing voltages, until they ultimately grasped the connection and learned to keep still to avoid further shock. "He has to remain still for some time, and then the current is turned off and it is demonstrated to him that he has control over his limbs again."[150] Then the patient had to remain in the hospital for several days and undergo the whole procedure again to ensure the results and prevent relapse. The chief advantage of the method, according to Oppenheim, was that it actively involved the patient in the curing process. That is, Oppenheim's method forced the patient to cure himself, and thus, allegedly, created more lasting and certain results. While patients cured with the Kaufmann method were known to suffer relapses once they were reexposed to the conditions of combat, Oppenheim's patients, he claimed, learned to overcome their fears and calmly discharge their affect.

Finally, the Koblenz doctor Fritz Mohr developed a variation in which patients controlled the level of electric current. Mohr instructed them to increase the current's strength gradually until they could no longer bear the pain—this made the treatment into a kind of game.[151] By making the patient do the therapeutic work himself, Mohr's and Oppenheim's methods took the Kaufmann cure a step further and fostered a starker form of behavioral modification. But like Kaufmann's method, these techniques reflected the tenuous balance between science and magic—and the attempts to quantify and standardize an inherently subjective therapeutic act—that marked electrotherapy, hypnosis, and all the methods of active treatment.

Active Treatment and the Powers of Suggestion

The techniques developed by Kaufmann and Nonne ushered in a new era of therapeutic confidence. Once the "most thankless task of the nerve doctor," treating neurotics became a source of pride, a tangible contribution psychiatrists could make to the war effort and the nation as a whole.[152] When treatment success rates reached levels of 80 to 90 percent, the key question for leading neurologists and psychiatrists was transformed from whether they could treat war hysteria to how quickly they could cure it. Speed, efficiency, and reliability then became the decisive therapeutic issues, as Nonne's and Kaufmann's "miracle methods" were used to clear the reserve hospitals of the thousands of neurotics already sent back to German territory. These successes inspired one doctor to rhapsodize in 1917: "The expectation is well-founded that the goal to which we are striving will be reached yet, so that we will be able to say, there are no more shakers [*Zitterer*]."[153] These new (or newly implemented) therapies were so successful that, starting in 1917, war neurotics who had been discharged with pensions were reenlisted and treated again despite the fact that the original pensioning policy had established a five-year period before reexamination.[154] Before long, news of these therapeutic advances led to the construction of new facilities specially suited for active treatment and to the army's campaign to coordinate and standardize the care of the nation's neurotics.

As a whole, these new, aggressive methods fell under the rubric of "active treatment." Although a formal definition of the term appears in neither military nor medical sources, *active treatment* referred to those techniques that operated through the mechanism of suggestion and that depended on an active, and often rapid, therapeutic intervention. It included, in addition to hypnosis and electric current, a number of diverse and often peculiar methods, which ranged from the familiar (isolation, bath-cures) to the obscure (fake operations, X-rays). Significantly, the confidence inspired by these therapeutic successes, together with the observation that suggestion and the doctor's personality or will were the active therapeutic agents, opened the floodgates for a whole range of new, creative methods of suggestive treatment. For the greater part of the war, neither military-medical authorities nor leading psychiatrists sought to regulate the treatments that doctors used. It remained strictly a medical matter, left to "the particular experiences and skills of the doctors and the characteristics of the individual cases."[155] Nonne affirmed his belief that "Each should use the method which he has mastered, in which he has talent and faith and with which he has had success, and each method is successful when it is practiced by the right doctor in the correct manner."[156] If, as Gaupp and others asserted, "the doctor cures through his personality, not his method," then the particular treatment a doctor used was nearly incidental.[157]

Inspired by Kaufmann's stunning successes, many doctors became instant converts to electrotherapy, only to discover that they could achieve the same results with little or no electric current. Henceforth, a number of psychiatrists and neurologists developed milder methods that were less painful and dangerous. These were collectively covered by the vague label of *Wachsuggestion* (waking or conscious suggestion), a term that connoted the operation of suggestion without the aid of the hypnotic trance.[158] However, even if these newer alternatives to the Kaufmann cure were milder and less painful, they similarly furthered medical control while operating through persuasion, deceit, or elaborate trickery.

In one contemporary formulation, the extraordinary variety of methods lay on a spectrum from "mystical suggestion" on one pole through "coercion of will" on the other.[159] That is, some doctors developed methods that relied on deception, while others aimed to "enlighten" their patients through techniques that could be loosely called precursors of psychotherapy. Several methods worked through shock or fear, some by means of persuasion, and others through boredom or distraction. They can be grouped into four categories: deception, startling, isolation, and persuasion. Each shows elements that were also at work in hypnosis and the Kaufmann cure: an emphasis on the hierarchical gap between doctor and patient, a concern with therapeutic speed and efficiency, and a curious mixing of science, magic, and modernity.

Deceptive methods were based on a faux therapeutic intervention that was shrouded in mystery. Many variations relied on phony miracle drugs and other such cures to trick patients into thinking they had been successfully treated.[160]

One example is the "wonder drug" technique developed by the Königsberg neurologist Max Rothmann. Rothmann told his patients that a new drug had been developed that was certain to cure them—of course, this was a lie and there was no such drug. Claiming that the drug was painful to ingest, Rothmann further instructed patients that it would be administered with a short-term general anesthetic. After patients awoke from their anesthesia-induced slumber—not having received any medication at all—Rothmann forced them to demonstrate that their symptoms had disappeared. Then he sent them into a private room where they could sleep off the anesthesia.

Kurt Goldstein—who was chiefly known for his work with soldiers' head injuries, which led to his subsequent elaboration of a holistic psychology—reported great success with Rothmann's phony wonder cure method. He found it appealing because, like Rothmann, he experienced it as significantly less strenuous than the use of either electrotherapy or hypnosis.[161] He noted that he could treat three or four patients in approximately an hour each morning and then have plenty of time left over for his hospital rounds. Goldstein described the method as follows: First he explained about the new wonder drug that would cure disabilities. Then he informed patients that because the injection would be painful, he would administer a general anesthetic. He further explained that, on waking, the patient would regain full control of his body. Once the patient succumbed to the effects of the ether, Goldstein innocuously injected saline solution into the arm, and attached a large bandage to the site of the injection. When the patient awoke Goldstein demonstrated through a series of exercises that the disorders had disappeared. He reported that his patients were particularly prone to suggestion while still half-asleep, but in those rare cases where the symptoms remained, he made use of electric current to demonstrate to the patient that his muscles still worked.[162]

Goldstein reported that with this method he cured thirty-nine out of forty-six patients, many of whom had been sent, uncured, from hospital to hospital for months. To the objection that deceiving patients ran counter to proper medical practice, Goldstein replied that the element of deception was crucial to his treatment, and should the patient learn the truth, it could have negative consequences, not least of which would be a relapse.[163] The treatment, then, had to be shrouded in mystery and shielded from lay interventions. Others objected that, according to a ruling of the War Ministry, a treatment deemed a "serious intervention" (*erheblicher Eingriff*) required the permission of the patient in advance; this applied to the use of anesthesia but not to electrotherapy or other painful methods.[164] Asking a patient for his permission, as Nonne had pointed out, meant risking the hierarchical edge that was so necessary for effective suggestive treatment.

A Dr. D. Dub varied the ether method by binding and blindfolding hysterical patients and placing them on an examination table in a darkened room before administering the narcotic.[165] Prior to giving the drug, Dub promised his patients that, on awakening, their symptoms would be gone. While the patients slept, Dub untied them, removed their blindfolds, and placed them on a carpet on the floor. When they awoke, he assured them that the symptoms had been eliminated. However, if the symptoms did persist, then Dub repeated the whole procedure. He added that this method worked only on relatively simple cases.

On difficult patients, such as those with spasms or contractions, Dub augmented the suggestive effect of the ether by means of an X-ray apparatus. When patients awoke, Dub turned on the X-ray machine and shouted, "Aha!" to give the impression that a profound change had occurred. With its use of the frightening, mysterious X-rays, the blindfold, and the faux medication, this method represents an extreme example of contrived medical magic, which exploited (and misapplied) technology to intimidate, subordinate, and fool patients into recovering.

Methods based on startling or shocking were closely related to these deceitful techniques. In many cases, a shock functioned to force patients into confessing or realizing that they could use a nonfunctioning organ or a paralyzed limb, to outsmart them into abandoning handicaps that were neither feigned nor "real" in a somatic sense. Robert Sommer presented a method tailored for the treatment of psychogenic deafness and deaf-muteness at a 1917 conference.[166] The principle behind this technique was that, when caught off guard, these patients could be tricked into responding to a shocking audial stimulus. Then, when confronted with incontrovertible proof that they indeed had heard and reacted to a stimulus, patients were expected to regain their sense of hearing and let go of their functional disturbances.

This peculiar technique utilized a device that analyzed the movement of a patient's fingers and recorded them on a graph.[167] The device resembles a polygraph and also an early psychotechnical tool that was developed by Walter Moede, a psychologist and director of The Berlin Institute for Psychotechnics.[168] Moede's machine measured the "calmness and steadiness of the hand" and was used to test the capacities of job candidates. Since Sommer, a psychologist and psychiatrist, was also engaged in psychotechnical research, it seems likely that he, perhaps through an accidental discovery, adapted Moede's device for the treatment of war neurotics.

At the beginning of the session, Sommer placed the patient's forearm through a strap, and secured his middle and pointer fingers by the machine in a viselike fashion. (Since these patients had lost the capacity to hear, Sommer communicated with them through written instructions.) "The patient is asked in writing to hold completely still the fingers that have been secured on the apparatus. Then the meter is activated. While the man's attention is focused completely on this procedure, suddenly a bell behind his head is loudly rung."[169] Sommer theorized that the patient's concentration on the apparatus would distract him, nullifying his psychic suppression of the ability to hear.[170] The patient's response to the sound of the bell, that is, the sudden movements of his hand, were

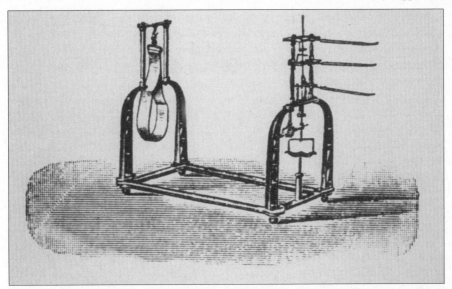

An apparatus designed by psychiatrist Robert Sommer for treating hysterical deafness. From *Schmidts Jahrbücher der in- und ausländischen gesamten Medizin* (1917).

indicated on a graph. Sommer described one successful case as follows: "Immediately there occurred a twitching of the forearm, which brought forth the evidence that the patient must have heard the tone. Then through calm encouragement vis à vis the curve in front of him, the patient's attention was directed to the fact that there could no longer be the slightest doubt that he could hear. From this moment on in point of fact he could hear clearly and reacted correctly to every acoustic-verbal stimulus."[171]

In the several other cases that Sommer presented, the "cures" occurred with equal rapidity, even though the symptoms had persisted for as long as a year. In the third of the five cases he described, a functionally deaf-mute patient reacted to the stimulus with an enormous shock. "Immediately [came] a joyfully surprised utterance: 'I can hear again,' [he] articulated softly but clearly. It was brought to his attention that he also could speak again; he repeated letters and words sporadically with partial phonation."[172] By the end of the speech exercise, as if to finalize his patriotic reeducation, the patient was softly singing along to the national hymn, "Deutschland über Alles." The Sommer method, like all of those techniques based on deception and trickery, highlights the blurry boundary between curing these patients and convincing them that they were not truly ill. Just as the Kaufmann cure used the electric current as a suggestive prop, Sommer, Goldstein, Rothmann, and Dub all used the trappings of science and advanced medical practice—injections, X-rays, psychotechnical graphs—to deceptive, purely suggestive ends. While some methods fostered the illusion of a somatic illness and hence a reliable somatic cure, others functioned in the opposite way, aiming to prove that the symptoms were purely in the mind and hence easily cured.

A similar method that also relied on the shock effect was developed by an Essen otolaryngologist named Otto Muck.[173] In cases that could not be cured through the usual electrotherapeutic method, Muck reasoned that he could induce a scream by blocking up the glottis, the space between the vocal cords at the upper part of the larynx. These men, suffering from functional paralyses of the vocal muscles, had difficulty breathing anyway, and Muck sought to induce a kind of instinctive shriek out of fear of suffocation or choking.

The device Muck employed was a modified tonsil holder. With this tool he held a small metal ball and thrust it into the back of the throat. Guided by a mirror, he then forcefully pressed the ball up against the back of the larynx for several seconds. "The result was that in the moment that the patient was startled, he held his breath for a while, let his tongue go, and let out a shriek. The voice returned immediately."[174] Describing his success, Muck recounted, "The consequence of the psychic shock from the feeling of choking which brought the speech back, was that one patient broke into tears of joy, a second lay for the entire day in a deep sleep."[175]

A year later, in an attempt to enlighten other otolaryngologists about psychogenic speaking disorders, Muck reported that he had successfully cured twenty-one cases with his "ball method." By 1918 this number had risen to 360, and most cures occurred with astonishing speed, in fifteen minutes or less, making Muck's method significantly faster than most of the other types of active treatment.[176] Indeed, one of Muck's medical colleagues praised his technique for being the fastest and "most elegant" of all the therapeutic options and for demanding less of the doctor's time and energy.[177]

But how did patients respond to this treatment? Muck claimed that they were extremely grateful to be cured. "Never have I seen from a patient such spontaneous expressions of gratitude and joy as in the cured mutes. As they heard their voices again, and with it their articulation returned, if at the beginning usually stuttering, they jumped off the chair, squeezed my hand, tried to hug me, and one caressed my face."[178]

Not all of the creative methods used to treat war hysteria involved a swift, sudden intervention. Many doctors experimented with forms of isolation, a third category of treatment, which often involved immersion in long baths. Baths and water cures were among the oldest methods of psychiatric therapy and had been used to treat hysterics for decades, if not centuries. In early times, water was thought to contain unique curative powers; by the second decade of the twentieth century, its attraction lay primarily in its soothing and calming effects. A form of hydrotherapy was adapted to the conditions of war and transformed into active therapy by the psychiatrist Rafael Weichbrodt at the University Psychiatric Clinic in Frankfurt.[179] Weichbrodt had observed that psychotics, when left in a bath for twenty-four hours, often claimed that they were cured and asked to be removed. Hoping to foster a will to be cured, he applied this observation to war hysterics and reported results that he found noteworthy.

As with all of the other methods of active treatment, suggestive preparation before the therapeutic act played an important role in Weichbrodt's technique. "After a thorough examination I explain to the hysteric: 'Your disorders indicate a sickness of the will, thus you must make the effort to regain mastery over yourself, which can succeed within the next few days. If you are not able to accomplish it by yourself, you will certainly be made healthy in the bath, which through its evenly distributed warmth has very healthy effects.'"[180] According to Weichbrodt as many as 25 percent of his patients recovered from the preparation alone and were free of their symptoms by the following morning. This was especially true after his treatment successes became known around the hospital, which further contributed to the suggestive effect.

Most patients, however, even if their symptoms had diminished somewhat overnight, were directed into heated baths (37°C, 99°F) where they had to remain until they were cured. This meant, of course, that patients ate their meals and slept in the baths; their only company were the attendants who adjusted the water temperature.[181] The writer Oskar Maria Graf depicted his miserable experience with a similar treatment in his autobiography:

> We were defenceless, lying stark naked in a bath of hot water at 104 degrees Fahrenheit. The room was full of steam and wet and slippery. Three attendants walked to and fro at the window. If one of us tried to get out of the bath, they simply pushed him in again. So we just had to lie still, to lie and wait. We were given our dinner in the bath, but we were not hungry. We grew weary and then weak, unutterably weak. We heard horrible cries of distress from cell doors on one side: shouts, screams, curses and prayers. It was not till the third day that I was taken out of the bath, utterly exhausted, and put to bed.[182]

Weichbrodt reported that all of his patients had been cured within the first twenty-four hours, with only one exception, a case that lasted some forty hours. When he ascertained that a patient's symptoms had indeed vanished, Weichbrodt praised him, let him have several hours of bed rest, and then sent him straight to work. This method did not work on every patient, and Weichbrodt provided no statistics, nor did he indicate at which point the immersion should be terminated in such cases. What he did say was that if the technique failed in an open environment, then the patient should be sent to a closed asylum. There, if other methods did not work, the individual should be returned to the bath in the section for unruly mentally ill patients.[183]

Otto Binswanger, who eschewed electric current on the grounds that its results were short-term, isolated his soldier-patients into single rooms and de-

prived them of human contact for days on end.[184] This so-called psychic abstinence treatment derived from Silas Weir Mitchell's treatment of neurasthenic
women in late-nineteenth-century America, only Binswanger recast Mitchell's
rest cure as a form of disciplinary therapy. Mitchell's patients were discouraged
from writing or engaging in any stimulating activities and were stuffed full of
fatty foods. Binswanger, however, ordered his patients not to speak and punished them by depriving them of food.[185] While Mitchell's cure had been designed to replenish depleted nerves through prolonged rest and the accumulation
of fat cells, Binswanger conceived of his method in psychological-suggestive
terms. He claimed that he reserved this treatment for severe cases and found
that some two-thirds of his cases were cured after several weeks of isolation.[186]

At a Württemberg hospital station Ernst Kretschmer developed a more severe form of isolation treatment, which he found to work more quickly and reliably than Binswanger's technique. Kretschmer confined patients, alone or
occasionally with one other patient, in a darkened room, where there was just
enough light to see but not enough to read.[187] He only entered the room when
necessary, limiting himself to one daily call on these patients. Patients were told
to remain in bed and that the inactivity would calm their nerves. In typical cases,
after eight to fourteen days, the symptoms usually began to show marked improvement. Based on his preliminary sample of six successful treatments (out
of seven attempts), Kretschmer reported that four to six weeks generally sufficed for the cure to take full effect; in some cases, he relaxed the conditions
once he noticed improvement. The method's advantages were clear to Kretschmer; it saved his own time and energy and could be achieved independently of
the atmosphere of the rest of the station. Finally, he noted that its failure did
not diminish the doctor's authority or preclude the successful application of another form of treatment.

Other doctors conceived of these isolation methods as "boring-to-death" or
not-acknowledging therapy (*Therapie der Nichtbeachtung*). Through enforced
inactivity, the patient's will to be cured would be aroused; he was shielded from
bad influences and was supposed to realize that his neurotic symptoms would
not lead to a more pleasant alternative.[188] To augment the effects of isolation,
Ewald Stier and Rafael Weichbrodt placed their patients into isolation cells in
a psychiatric asylum where they had to endure the howling and wailing of violent or chronically disturbed patients. If they complained that they were not
mentally ill, they were told that people who do not have control over their bodies belong in an asylum.[189] This use of the asylum represents a striking reversal of earlier approaches; while prewar clinicians often used somatic diagnoses
to protect patients from the fear of mental illness, several wartime psychiatrists
exploited this fear to their therapeutic advantage.

Above all, isolation cures tried to force patients not to dwell on or talk about their symptoms. They denied them an audience—whether doctors, nurses, or other patients—and sought to direct their attentions elsewhere. The isolation cell can be seen as a site of unmediated medical power; doctors regulated food and contact with the outside world and used a system of rewards and punishments to coax patients out of their symptoms and modify their behavior.[190]

A final category of suggestive methods functioned simply through direct verbal suggestion or persuasion. Excluding the modified forms of psychoanalysis practiced during the war, the term *psychotherapy,* for wartime nerve doctors, designated attempts to convince a patient to abandon his symptoms. One such method was practiced by Richard Hirschfeld, a Charlottenburg doctor who was commandeered to a "hysteria station" in Aachen in 1916. Hirschfeld had experimented with more coercive methods that involved electricity and narcotics, but abandoned them in favor of less painful techniques when he observed that they aroused mistrust in his patients.[191] Instead he practiced a method that involved deceiving and distracting the patient.

He started this procedure by explaining to his patients that he was about to cure them by restoring their nerve connections. Then he began rubbing the site of the functional disorder.

> For those with shaking of the arm, we sit across from each other. I bend and stretch the arm until I feel that it is totally relaxed. Then I press completely randomly here and there and converse with the patient about his domestic affairs. At the moment that I feel the arm has completely relaxed (after five minutes at most), I quickly interrupt the treatment and say to the patient: 'Take a look, the shaking is gone.' In most cases with that it is taken care of. In a number of patients it begins again slightly. I grab the arm immediately again and explain, if they are still doing it, that it is habitual, but no longer an illness; that now they have to suppress it themselves; that it is in their hands to be completely healthy.[192]

Hirschfeld claimed after using this method (or several variations for other kinds of shaking) on more than one hundred patients, that the cures nearly always worked in a matter of minutes. He continued to fall back on electrotherapy for stubborn cases but discouraged its use as a "wonder cure" for all functional disorders, which in many cases amounted to "shooting a sparrow with a cannon."[193]

In a 1918 article Hirschfeld went one step further and substituted a much more direct and honest technique for his distraction therapy and any other suggestive aids.[194] This method involved explaining the psychogenic nature of a patient's symptoms in a candid and accessible manner. According to Hirschfeld, it only worked on educated patients who sincerely wished to recover; uneducated ones, he noted, fetishized the "miracle cures" that could only come from machines and contraptions. The news that their conditions were actually the physical expression of psychological processes caused a number of his patients to give up their symptoms after one session, although, Hirschfeld noted, this epiphany often led to depression, guilt, and anxiety about being considered a malingerer.

Yet, verbal therapies could also be applied in less honest and humane ways. In his so-called enlightening technique, Edmund Forster, like Hirschfeld, explained to his patients that their maladies had no organic basis.[195] But in contrast to Hirschfeld's method, Forster treated his patients like whiny children and opportunistic malingerers; he instructed his assistants to ignore patients' complaints and demands and rather than appealing to their reason and understanding, he played on their fear and guilt and constantly emphasized their military subordination. Exhibiting functional neuroses, Forster frequently told his patients, did not befit a German soldier and was grounds for punishment. Often that was enough to remove patients' functional paralyses. But when it did not succeed, as was frequently the case with aphonics and aphasics, Forster used more conventional methods such as electric current, cold showers, and ice packs. Unlike most practitioners of these methods, Forster stressed to his patients throughout the procedure that they were not actually sick and that they simply wished to escape their duty. The therapy, he explained, aimed to strengthen their will so that they could overcome their "hysterical habituation" and go back into the field.

Despite the wide variation in the methods of active treatment, most techniques functioned in essentially the same way. Whether it was based on deception, startling, isolation, or persuasion, whether it utilized hypnosis, electric current, or a faux injection, active treatment operated through suggestion. It targeted the patient's will and aimed to convert the will to remain disabled into the will to recover. It sought to restore the patient's control over his own body, but paradoxically, in doing so it demanded that the doctor wield full control and authority over the patient's mind and body. The goal, then, was to create healthier wills through subordination to medical power, which stood in as a representative of the state and the national cause. Indeed, by using these methods, doctors attained a great deal of influence and even control over a whole category of patients and integrated the exercise of medical power into the core of the therapeutic procedure. With the trappings of science and the seductions of magic, medical power operated in the treatment room to forge functioning bodies and patriotic subjects.

Many of these methods involved the introduction of subjective and outmoded psychological notions in a profession whose claims and status had been founded on its scientific status. Even as Emil Kraepelin's 1918 sketch of psychiatry's history celebrated the progressive triumph of science and the downfall of the charlatan, new directions in treatment were belying, or at least complicating, Kraepelin's claims.[196] Psychiatrists' attempts to serve the state and treat hysterical neuroses threw into relief the contradictions that ran through this relatively new medical specialty. Having turned to scientific observation as a means of establishing their field at the university, psychiatrists found that their profession was ill suited to the therapeutic needs of the wartime environment. Psychiatric scientism could not master hysteria. Amid the war neurosis crisis, then, doctors did whatever worked. And the treatments that worked were, in many cases, at odds with prevailing professional tendencies and even offensive to a scientific sensibility.

Thus, alongside the rational, administrative approach best embodied in the assembly-line science of the Kaufmann cure, arose a discourse of the magical and miraculous, a celebration, even fetishization of the machine that runs though the shadow side of German modernity. Indeed, the machine's mysterious power was a theme that resonated in wartime and interwar German culture: hypnosis, electrotherapy, and psychotechnics became lasting symbols of both the wonders and the dangers of scientific power and the vexed status of psychiatric modernity. If Max Nonne's 1916 film promoted the magical powers of medicine, many of the important movies of the Weimar years, from *The Cabinet of Dr. Caligari* to the Dr. Mabuse series, reflected a deep cultural anxiety about psychiatric science and its frightening powers over mind and body.

CHAPTER 5

The Worker-Patient

*The Neurosis Stations and the
Rationalization of Psychiatric Care*

> Effeminate pitying reinforces the patient's self-absorption and hopelessness. In milder cases the best remedy is uninterrupted work.
>
> KARL WILMANNS

> The great majority of the hysterics, with all of their symptoms, can be used much more effectively in war industry, where their energies can be fully exploited.
>
> R. A. E. HOFFMANN, "Über die
Behandlung der Kriegshysterie"

THE TREATMENT OF war hysteria, recalled a doctor from the Fourteenth Army Corps District in Baden, could be divided into three phases.[1] The first phase was characterized by misleading somatic diagnoses and featured mild treatments and rest cures, most of which were ineffective against the "flood" of hysterical patients. The second phase began with the spread of active treatment and most often incorporated the Kaufmann cure—the method of electric current and suggestion that revolutionized wartime treatment. This phase met with great success, but still suffered setbacks. Rates of recidivism remained high, and the most recalcitrant patients often proved resistant to the method's suggestive impact. It was only in the third phase, the period of "systematic mass treatment," that success rates soared.[2] This was achieved when active treatment was integrated into a comprehensive, centralized psychiatric system. The heart of this new system were networks of special neurosis stations, which were closely linked to a systematic program of work therapy and rehabilitation.

Ever increasing numbers of nervous casualties, together with the therapeutic advances brought by active treatment, led to a new campaign to standardize methods for dealing with war hysteria. New military-medical policies—enacted at the level of the corps deputy general commands—aimed to create a "sealed system" or "closed front" for managing hysterical soldiers and systematizing their administration, treatment, and rehabilitation.[3] The task that remained, according to one nerve doctor, was "systematically to construct a net, through whose web no neurotic not rid of his symptoms can slip."[4] To this end, by 1918 at least 5 percent of all base hospital beds in Germany were reserved for hysteria cases.[5] By that time, treating war neurosis had been transformed into "a purposeful, methodical system, founded upon theoretical consideration and practical experience, whose organization and whose effectiveness can no longer be shaken by any variables."[6]

These efforts can be seen as part of the broader process of social and industrial rationalization in Germany. During and after the war, *rationalization* meant restructuring economic organization to function more efficiently through the standardization of parts and equipment and the fullest utilization of human resources. Rationalization and efficiency became Weimar-era credos, values shared across the social-political spectrum, particularly after the German economy stabilized in 1924. Indeed, the principle of rationalization soon transcended industry and was widely adopted as a model for the reform and reorganization of social and household life, medical care, and even marriage and reproduction.[7]

The war itself, several historians have suggested, was conducted in a uniquely rationalized manner: Soldiers fired mass produced weapons, men fought like unskilled workers in "Taylorized" combat spaces, and central high commands made and relayed tactical decisions.[8] And as Germany adjusted to the protracted war, its economy was increasingly centralized and rationalized to compensate for shortages in munitions and matériel.[9] Similarly, wartime health crises prompted the centralization of state power over the country's fragmented and diverse welfare system, and the increasing scale of the war's carnage was accompanied by the growth and increasing centrality of medicine to state and military apparatuses.[10] These new approaches to waging war and to deploying men and resources hastened a transformation in the way soldiering was experienced and represented. Consequently, by the middle of the war, the image of the idealistic volunteer soldier of 1914 was being replaced with a new icon, the modern "soldier-worker," a deindividualized, anonymous participant in massive, faceless battles such as Verdun and the Somme.[11]

Wartime psychiatry was also deeply influenced by new economic and industrial models and new notions of soldiering. As psychiatrists eagerly embraced the methods of active treatment, concerns such as speed and efficiency became reigning medical values. The subsequent organization of psychiatric services further attests to the saturation of psychiatry by the priorities of economy and industry. New methods and facilities rendered psychiatric treatment more efficient, so that increasing numbers of neurotic patients could be handled with limited resources and minimal delays. Rationalization, then, guided the centralization and standardization of psychiatric facilities and the increasing emphasis on therapeutic speed and efficiency. Simultaneously, it led wartime planners to view hysterical patients as potential labor or industrial resources necessary for feeding rationalizing industry. Medical power created a system to serve economic needs.

Reflecting the new emphasis on efficient management, army deputy corps commanders and university doctors worked together to impose order on the chaotic collection of private hospitals, charitable associations, and reserve stations responsible for tending and compensating the war's growing numbers of psychological casualties.[12] They extended these efforts outside German territory as well, endeavoring to detect and treat neuroses as close to the front lines as possible, thereby salvaging much needed manpower for the taxing war of attrition. Yet, there were resistances to rationalization. Psychiatric attention to patient personality and behavior, efforts to treat the "whole patient" worked, in part, against the overall rationalizing dynamic. Nevertheless, in treating a condition associated with the horrifying experience of modern industrialized warfare, Germany's psychiatrists themselves adopted the language and principles of modern industrial organization. Turning hysterical soldier-patients into healthy worker-patients meant subjecting them to the irrepressible logic of rationalization.

Patients into Workers: The Goal of Active Treatment

Max Nonne, Fritz Kaufmann, and many other practitioners of active treatment maintained that their methods brought phenomenal therapeutic success and cited curing rates of 80 to 90 percent. By late 1917, many doctors were claiming success in over 95 percent of their cases. Confidence in active treatment grew so high that in 1918 one psychiatrist asserted, "A doctor whose therapeutic success with war hysterics is much below 100% is really not suited for this sort of activity."[13] But what did it mean to cure hysterical patients? Was removing the subject's symptoms sufficient for a cure, or did these symptoms have deeper sources that treatment was required to address? Military authorities had a clear position on this question, a position that was strikingly similar to the views of most practicing psychiatrists.

The goal of active treatment, as categorically spelled out by military-medical protocols, was to transform idle patients into productive workers. A 1917 War Ministry ordinance defined this task succinctly: "The primary consideration in treating war neurotics is: to help them to the full utilization of their psychically-diminished capacity for work."[14] And in 1918 the function of military psychiatric facilities was described as to "free [patients] as quickly as possible from their functional disorders and to rehabilitate them by reintroducing them into regulated work."[15]

The formulations and goals show how the constellation of health, fitness, and national economic welfare—so visible throughout the diagnostic debate—also determined approaches to treatment. In a passage from 1920, representative of both military and medical assumptions, a Baden doctor observed: "With the war hysterics as with the accident hysterics of peace-time, complete curing is not only the lack of symptoms but also economic rehabilitation," and two doctors wrote in the war's last year that "The goal of treatment can always only be to make the neurotics' capacity for work useful to the community."[16]

These definitions contain two overlapping but distinct notions of work. Psychiatrists and neurologists condemned idleness (i.e., "lying about the hospital") as both a sign and a cause of psychopathology. On the one hand, letting patients remain unoccupied was "a serious moral danger for the individual . . . It also works against the patient's speedy and complete recovery."[17] Thus, work promoted individual health and recovery and prevented the toxic influence of idleness from setting in. On the other hand, notions of individual health were easily blended with collectivistic, communal concerns. Work for the sole sake of occupation or distraction did not suffice; to be truly healthful—particularly in the context of wartime labor shortages—work had to contribute to the national cause.[18] Hence, the healthy man reaped the immediate psychological benefits of work, which prevented self-absorption and hypochondria, while benefiting from the moral righteousness of contributing to the collective good. In such a way, health, morality, and productivity were blended into a normative concept of appropriate masculine behavior.

Wartime conditions thus strengthened tendencies that run deep in the history of psychiatry. Michel Foucault traced the connections between work and mental health—and significantly, the exploitation of psychiatric patients for their labor power—back to psychiatry's roots in the "Great Confinement" of the seventeenth century, when the mad were interned alongside criminals, vagabonds, and other types of social deviants in Europe's vast new institutions.[19] These institutions, Foucault argued, guaranteed a cheap, reliable source of labor when workers were scarce. Alternately, in times of economic crisis, they prevented potential agitators from causing political unrest in the cities. The convergence between Foucault's model and the strategies and principles of wartime psychiatry in Germany is conspicuous. At its core, psychiatric confinement, Foucault asserted, did not derive from a benevolent interest in "curing the sick" but rather was about condemning and overcoming idleness, a concern that reverberated through twentieth-century German mental medicine.

In World War I Germany, idleness represented not only a moral danger for the individual but also a potential economic detriment to the nation. This detriment was personified by the parasitic pensioner, who was constructed as a political, moral, and economic threat. Consequently, military and medical goals essentially conflated the act of treatment with the invalidation of potential pension claims. A 1917 memorandum from General Schultzen of the War Ministry, which stressed the importance of putting war hysterics to work, charged local military-medical authorities with the task of finding jobs for neurotics that were appropriate to their condition, personality, and skills. Hysterics were to understand that the cessation of work would lead to an immediate reenlistment.

"This prospect," concluded Schultzen, "exercises a healthful and encouraging influence in our experience. . . . In such a way it becomes possible to utilize the capacity to work of these unfortunately predisposed natures and at the same time to prevent the breeding of life-long, weak-willed pensioners."[20]

Medical practitioners shared these goals with state and military officials—in fact, the confluence of military and medical goals is striking. In a typical formulation, Otto Muck, inventor of the ball cure for hysterical muteness, defined the doctor's task in treating neurotics as, "saving these war-disabled from unfitness for service and thereby invalidating their claim to a pension."[21] And Max Raether justified the "strenuous job" of treating neurotics with electric current as a way of creating more laborers: "The doctor himself is amply rewarded for his efforts. The state is spared high pensions, and the general labor market is replenished with workers, who without treatment à la Kaufmann, would be lost for years to come."[22]

Perhaps most noteworthy is that doctors strove to send their hysterical patients into the work force rather than returning them to the field.[23] This emphasis was overdetermined by a convergence of psychiatric theory and economic necessity. Most psychiatrists frowned on returning treated neurotics to their units, for fear of causing "psychic epidemics" among active troops. As Kurt Singer wrote, "The bad psychic atmosphere which a single hysteric with seizures, mood swings, depression, is capable of spreading, can have unhealthy effects, and through contagion can be more dangerous than the loss of a dozen healthy soldiers."[24] Furthermore, in the great majority of cases the risk of relapse was seen as too great to justify renewed field duty, and relapses were expensive and wasteful and contributed to hospital overcrowding.[25] For Singer, the nation's labor needs determined that putting a neurotic to work, a duty he could fully carry out, contributed more significantly than sending him into combat, "where he becomes an undesirable comrade, a disastrous soldier, and a burden to the medic and company commander."[26] In fact, in many cases the mere mention of return to the field precluded any therapeutic success. Once they had landed in German territory, neurotics, it was widely believed, would not recover unless they had been assured that they would not have to return to active duty.[27] Thus, after their initial experience, doctors generally agreed that it was wisest to deploy treated neurotics in the war economy at home—which, in a bit of irony that was not lost on the doctors, fulfilled the neurotics' wishes and represented a safer and more pleasant alternative to continued military service.

This medical insight coincided well with Germany's economic needs. There had been labor shortages from the start of the war, but the military situation in 1916 greatly exacerbated this deficiency. The carnage of that year's fighting generated ever growing manpower needs on the front. Simultaneously, shortages in matériel, which resulted from poor industrial planning and the expectation of a short war, created urgent labor needs at home. Hence, a situation arose in which the army and industry were actually competing for men.[28] "The problem," writes historian Richard Bessel, "was how to reconcile the military's insatiable manpower-requirements with industry's desperate need for skilled labor. . . . The only way adequately to supply the soldiers needed at the front was to call them back to Germany!"[29] In this context, war neurotics represented an ideal category of worker. Why send them back into the field, where they were most likely to break down again, when able-bodied workers were in such demand domestically? Putting neurotics to work thus represented the most efficient solution—it rehabilitated them into contributing members of the national community, which simultaneously satisfied medical criteria and mediated military-economic needs.

The success of psychiatric treatment, and all military-medical treatment, was measured according to a scale of fitness that was introduced by the War Ministry's Office of Exemptions (*Abteilung für Zurückstellungswesen*) in June 1915.[30] Fitness levels (of both new recruits and treated soldier-patients) were judged on a twelve-tier scale that measured the level of service an individual was considered capable of performing: war, work, or garrison; the length of time he could serve: long-term or temporarily; and where he could be sent: field, *Etappe* (base) or home. This instrumental scheme left no room for distinctions between the restoration of the full ability to work and complete recovery, and it added a new medical responsibility; namely, determining for which kinds of work individuals were suited.[31] The ability to work was not only the standard for successful treatment but implicitly became a measure of the value of an individual, the marker of his humanity. Active treatment, wrote Otto von Schjerning, the army's Chief Sanitary Inspector, "turned shakers back into human beings and returned to them the ability to work and [to lead] a worthwhile life."[32]

Many doctors freely admitted that their efforts were directed at the symptoms of hysteria and not its root causes and conflicts. Nevertheless, with little exception, Germany's psychiatrists showed far greater concern with the utility of their patients' bodies than the well-being of their minds. Virtually all shared the belief that restoring an individual's ability to work—by removing his hysterical symptoms—was the best a doctor could do for his patients, the army, and the nation as a whole. And this assumption—the equation of work or economic utility with an individual's value—had devastating consequences for those unable to work: As Germans suffered under the British blockade, tens of thousands of chronic asylum inmates starved to death when scarce food supplies were diverted to other, more deserving mouths.[33]

War Psychiatry in Württemberg

The kingdom of Württemberg, home of the Thirteenth Army Corps, offers an instructive case study of the rationalization of psychiatric care and the links between psychiatry and industry. Like Saxony and Bavaria, Württemberg had its own war ministry and was thus responsible for the administration of its psychiatric casualties. Furthermore, military-medical authorities in Württemberg, along with their colleagues in Baden and Alsace—that is, the German districts closest to the Western front—were the first in Germany to systematize the battle against hysteria and had developed the most complete and successful systems by war's end.[34]

At the start of the war, neither Württemberg nor any other corps district had a unified system for dealing with psychiatric casualties. Once sent back to home territory, hysterical soldier-patients were usually placed alongside other kinds of soldiers in civilian hospitals, special army reserve facilities, or charity-operated sanitariums. A War Ministry decree of September 1915 commandeered Tübingen's university medical facilities for wounded students, but it wasn't long before these hospitals became overcrowded and chaotic. Robert Gaupp, the corps' consulting psychiatrist and nerve doctor (*Fachärztlicher Beirat für Nerven- und Geisteskrankheiten*) and arguably the most influential mental health practitioner in Württemberg and one of the leading authorities on war neurosis in Germany, was the director of the clinic for psychiatric and neurological diseases at the University of Tübingen. In January 1916, Gaupp complained that conditions within his clinic had become unmanageable and that he was woefully overburdened.[35] Furthermore, administrative incompetence and general chaos worsened matters, and hospital space was so limited that soldiers often had to be turned away untreated. Gaupp also complained that his forensic duties constituted an enormous time drain, and he bemoaned the presence of increasingly large numbers of "criminal elements"—men he had to examine for military-juridical processes—who negatively influenced the morale of the rest of the patients and whose stays in his clinic were lengthened by frustrating bureaucratic delays.[36]

Gaupp's complaints did not go unheeded. That same month, General Lasser of the Deputy General Command of the Thirteenth Army Corps in Stuttgart, visited the Tübingen clinic on an inspection trip.[37] Lasser's report to the corps district's sanitary inspector reinforced Gaupp's complaints. He wrote that the number of beds in the psychiatric clinic was far from sufficient, but noted that adding more beds would require the construction of new barracks. Thus Lasser, perhaps with Gaupp's prodding, called for the creation of specialized neurosis stations in several locations in Württemberg to relieve the overcrowding. He mentioned the towns of Weingarten, Heilbronn, and Mergentheim as likely candidates. According to Lasser's report, the region also suffered from a shortage of trained doctors to staff these proposed facilities because the majority of medical personnel was away serving in the field. To redress this shortage, authorities in Stuttgart and their superiors in Berlin proposed pulling qualified doctors out of the field and placing them in charge of the new neurosis stations.[38]

Once these changes were implemented, Württemberg became a leader in psychiatric organization. After Gaupp lectured on Württemberg's system before a group of high-ranking officers and health officials at the War Ministry in Berlin at the end of 1916, he reported back to Lasser that the Prussians had acknowledged Württemberg's superiority and that his Berlin audience had hoped to learn from the "more advanced" Thirteenth Corps.[39] Indeed, twelve months after Lasser's report calling for the creation of specialized psychiatric hospitals, the medical section of the Prussian War Ministry urged other districts to follow: "Wherever it has not yet occurred, the creation of special sections for this type of patient is to be set in motion without delay, and it is to be seen to that all eligible patients be directed from unsuitable hospitals into these sections; furthermore, no neurotic may be released as unfit until the vigorous attempt has been made to cure him, or at least to rid him of the symptoms of his illness, under the full guidance of a specialist."[40] Neurotics in corps districts without appropriate facilities were to be transferred to specialized stations in other corps areas for treatment.

The idea of creating specialized military psychiatric facilities had been debated among doctors from the start of the war, and when the German advance came to a standstill in autumn 1914, several such hospitals were added in western Germany.[41] In Strasbourg, for example, as early as September 1914 when a school building was converted into a base hospital, approximately ninety beds were reserved for nervously ill soldiers.[42] Two such facilities were created in Baden at the close of 1914; one was placed in a converted school house, and the second in a rural sanitarium.[43] However, these facilities proved of limited utility and functioned as little more than warehouses for nervously ill soldier-patients. When doctors were still essentially powerless to treat war neuroses, the therapeutic setting mattered little. At that time the argument for psychiatric hospitals invoked the need to separate neurotics from the general patient pool lest they exert a "bad influence" on the morale of the physically wounded. But the alternative, that is, keeping psychiatric patients together, also had serious disadvantages. The presence of so many hysterics, along with alcoholics, epileptics, and sufferers of various other neurological and psychiatric diseases, together in one building was considered a threat to discipline and a cause of "mutual infection."[44] Soon hospital staffs complained that patients were not better separated and screened. One Baden station was described as a "hearth of grand hysteria"—certainly an evocation of Charcot's Salpêtrière.[45]

But active treatment changed everything. The new miracle cures provided a compelling reason for creating specialized treatment facilities. Indeed, when the placement of small psychiatric stations throughout German territory became the stated policy of the War Ministry in 1917, all neurotics still in general reserve hospitals were to be immediately transferred into these special facilities.[46] This policy reflected the prevailing tendency in German military medicine since 1915, which discouraged large, general hospitals in favor of smaller, well-equipped stations that specialized in particular surgical procedures or the treat-

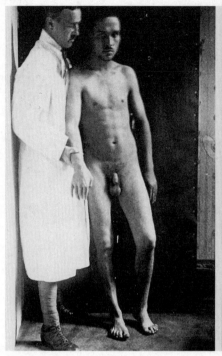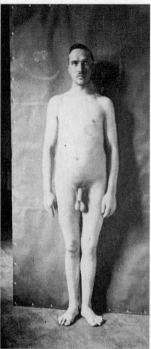

(Here and opposite page) Patients in the Bad Rötenbach neurosis station
(Württemberg) before and after treatment. By permission of the archive of
the University of Tübingen.

ment of specific maladies such as sexually transmitted diseases, head wounds,
or intestinal and kidney disorders.[47] The policy also betrays the continued belief in hysteria's contagiousness.[48]

For its new psychiatric stations, the state commandeered existing facilities
wherever possible, using small mental hospitals, convalescent homes, and even
country inns and hotels. In areas that lacked appropriate buildings, the stations
were to be constructed.[49] General Schultzen, the War Ministry's chief medical
officer wrote in September of 1917:

> The surprising successes in the treatment of so-called war neurotics—80 to 90
> and more cures per hundred in the sense of at least the provisional, full or
> nearly full restoration of the fitness for work and the restoration of a degree of
> usefulness in the war—make it the absolute duty, in view of the pressing need
> for reinforcements for the army and for workers in the war and peace economy,
> as well as for the urgent medical needs of the neurotics themselves, to introduce
> these promising methods of treatment where possible to all suitable neurotics,
> who, through their symptoms, are inhibited in the military or economic utiliza-
> tion of their capacity to work.

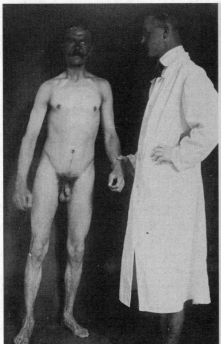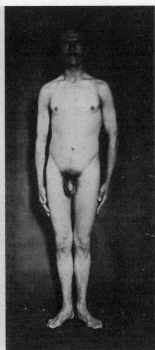

Through the establishment of nerve treatment sections, treatment possibilities are provided in every corps district. Their further expansion and if necessary
their increase will be promoted by all means.[50]

These new nerve treatment facilities differed significantly from the extant
psychiatric "warehouses." From their treatment experiences, most doctors
agreed that maintaining the proper hospital environment was an essential component of an active therapeutic regimen. Effectively carrying out these suggestion-based treatments required small facilities where doctors could exert their
control over the general atmosphere and pay individualized attention to their
patients, tailoring their methods to suit the "entire personality" of each neurotic.[51]

By March 1917 the Württemberg corps district already had five specialized
stations designed for treating neurotics.[52] These included a section of a
Stuttgart hospital, two reserve hospital departments (in Hirsau and Bad Mergentheim), a charitable hospital (*Vereinslazarett*) in Bad Rötenbach, and a base
hospital (*Festungslazarett*) in Ulm. By year's end the number of neurosis stations in the small region reached ten; stations had been adjoined to reserve hospitals in the towns of Ludwigsburg, Gmünd, Heilbronn, Weingarten, and

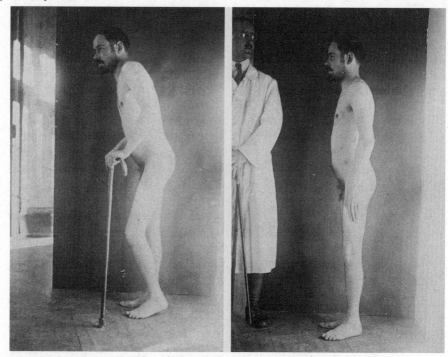

(Here and opposite page) Patients in the Bad Rötenbach neurosis station (Württemberg) before and after treatment. By permission of the archive of the University of Tübingen.

Elisabethenberg.[53] The stated goal of these facilities was to eliminate neurotic symptoms as quickly as possible and swiftly to introduce such patients into the work force or, in rare cases, to return them to the field. The success of active treatment gave military and medical authorities new confidence that this goal could be reached on a large scale, as long as sufficient resources were devoted to it.[54]

When health officials sought models for organizing wartime psychiatry and improving its efficiency, they looked to industry. The use of terms such as "division of labor" and "efficient harnessing of resources" reflected this economic influence. Schultzen's 1917 memorandum reads like an industrial manual: "The continuous and smooth cooperation of all participants is of substantial importance. . . . The particularity of the tasks of the treatment stations requires a strict division of labor among the doctors at these stations."[55]

The corollary to the division and specialization of "medical labor" was the separation of patients according to their maladies and therapeutic needs. Early attempts to treat war neurotics alongside other, physically injured patients were considered fruitless if not downright dangerous due to the risk of "psychic con-

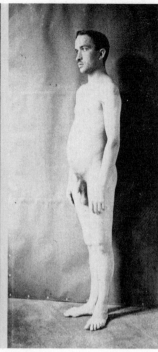

tagion." By the end of 1914, increasing emphasis was placed on separating out psychiatric patients from the general patient pool.[56] Then in a second step, war neurotics were to be weeded out from other psychiatric casualties. In a 1916 meeting, Prussian medical officials suggested that every corps district create six or seven observation stations, each with approximately 150 beds and staffed exclusively by medical specialists.[57] After they were diagnosed in an observation center, neurotics were channeled into specialized stations and prepared for a quick burst of active treatment. In Württemberg the task of separating patients was filled mainly by the region's central observation station, which acted as a sort of psychiatric clearing house for neurological and psychiatric cases in the entire corps district. Gaupp's Tübingen clinic took on this function, and all but three of the local treatment stations had their own, smaller observation sections where regular "polyclinic office hours" were held for evaluating patients received from local garrisons, recruiting commissions, other kinds of military hospitals, and nearby units.[58]

As the director of the central observation station, Gaupp was responsible for coordinating the entire Württemberg operation. His station mediated between

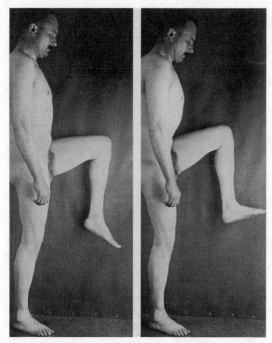

Patient in the Bad Rötenbach neurosis station
(Württemberg) before and after treatment. By permission of the archive of the University of Tübingen.

the medical officers and hospitals in the field and the specialized psychiatric
treatment facilities in home territory. Gaupp was answerable to the Württemberg War Ministry in Stuttgart, and his responsibilities also included supervising
the directors of the smaller psychiatric facilities in the district, "enlightening"
the lay public about wartime psychiatric matters through lectures and pam-
phlets, examining recruits suspected of mental illness sent by the draft board,
and dealing with military courts in forensic matters.[59] His role as director of
the central observation station meant that Gaupp was seldom directly involved
in treatment but rather oversaw the entire system. Significantly, the new system
established separate sites for setting diagnoses, treating patients, and evaluating pension claims, and different doctors were placed in charge of each of the
various phases.[60]

　　Throughout Germany, university towns were the favored locations for regional observation stations. The university setting meant that specialists from
all areas of medicine were nearby and could be conveniently consulted in difficult cases.[61] Thorough physical and mental examination was an absolute prerequisite before individuals were sent on for active psychiatric treatment, and

patients' complete medical histories had to be consulted too.[62] This meant that, for the sake of efficiency, no soldier was to be sent to the observation station without a chart showing his prior medical conditions.[63] The task of the observation center, then, was to evaluate the patient's symptoms and character and to determine which doctor or facility was best suited to treating him.[64] Candidates for active treatment included, above all, sufferers from monosymptomatic types of hysteria; that is, those with a single functional disability such as muteness, deafness, paralysis, or shaking.[65] Such cases were the easiest to treat and were the most likely to be "pure hysterias" without any accompanying somatic disturbances.

In a September 1918 survey of 146 patients treated at the Heilbronn nerve station, the largest share, that is thirty, were described as showing "general nervous disorders."[66] Among the other patients, twenty-six were designated as "shakers," twenty-two lacked the ability to stand, eighteen had aphonia, seventeen suffered from localized paralysis, and thirteen had unspecified seizures or attacks. The remaining twenty suffered from stuttering, deafness, muteness, tics, or nervous bladder problems including bed wetting. After treatment, only four were declared fit for combat, and two of those suffered relapses and were returned to the station. Several were deemed capable of light duties in the Etappe or at garrisons in the field, and the symptoms returned in about a third of those individuals. Seventy-seven were assigned light duties at garrisons in home territory, and the remaining patients ended up working in the war economy or reentering their prewar occupations.

If patients' symptoms did not meet the criteria for active treatment, Gaupp had to determine whether they should be discharged; returned to their troops; sent to state asylums in cases of severe mental illness, disorientation, or extreme agitation; treated in other facilities for organic injuries or diseases; or dealt with as simulators.[67] "Authentic" neurasthenics—that is, patients diagnosed as suffering from the effects of nervous exhaustion, the great majority of whom were officers—were to be sent to rural sanitariums or spas for recuperation.[68] Patients diagnosed as psychotics were also excluded from active treatment. With few exceptions, doctors denied that psychotic conditions (e.g., schizophrenia, chronic alcoholism, and disorientation or stupefaction) could be attributed to war service or cured through suggestion. Most considered the psychoses congenital, untreatable conditions, hence these patients were grouped with the chronically mentally ill.[69] Detecting and dealing with those suspected of simulation posed a more complex set of issues.

Medicalizing Malingering

Simulation was defined by official military-medical protocols as "the conscious imitation of mental or nervous illness."[70] Freud, who had no clinical experience with war neurosis, challenged this simple scheme, remarking that, "all neurotics are malingerers; they simulate without knowing it, and this is their illness."[71] In this statement Freud captured the complexity of the psychiatric problems posed by simulation—because hysteria was seen as a sickness of will, the fulfillment of an unconscious or semiconscious wish, the boundary separating it from conscious simulation was necessarily murky.[72] Most doctors who dealt with these conditions shared Freud's assumption that authentic war hysteria and simulation were divided by differences of degree rather than kind, and many confessed that it was often impossible to distinguish between the two.[73]

Freud's Viennese rival, the psychiatrist Julius von Wagner-Jauregg, also saw the boundaries between hysteria and simulation as subtle and fluid. He located the distinction between the two in a patient's will, contrasting the simulator, who does not want to be able to (do) (*Nichtkönnenwollen*) with the hysteric, who is not able to want to (do) (*Nichtwollenkönnen*).[74] Further compounding the problem was the fact that exaggeration and hypochondria were considered common signs of a hysterical character. But whether the difference was seen as a matter of consciousness or a problem of attitude, hysterics and simulators were believed to share the wish to escape the terrors of war and land safely home. Ultimately, it was left to the individual psychiatrist to judge—or guess—how conscious and calculated the physical expressions of these impulses were. And because simulation and hysteria were both considered a sickness of will, the two conditions were treated similarly.

Ernst Kretschmer was one of the few psychiatrists who sought objective criteria for distinguishing between hysterics and simulators. Writing from the Mergentheim neurosis station in Württemberg, Kretschmer introduced a third category called hysterical habituation (*hysterische Gewöhnung*), which he placed between the poles of simulation and pure hysteria.[75] It was the relative role of the will, Kretschmer theorized, that distinguished an "authentic hysteric" from a habituated one. Habituated hysteria, in other words, showed no direct connection to the activity of the will, while authentic hysterics were motivated by a will to remain sick. Accordingly, Kretschmer defined simulation as the conscious pretense of illness. But both habituated hysterics and simulators suffered from a defect of will, and simulation could easily turn into habitual behavior. Kretschmer concluded:

> The habituated hysteric, who does not want to become healthy, whether out of stubborn weakness of will, or out of other dubious motivations, and the simulator, in whom pretense has become a hysterical habituation, merge so fluidly with each other and are so closely related in their expression of psychological states, that the attempt to draw a useful clinical boundary between them is perpetually hopeless.[76]

Kretschmer saw no use in trying to differentiate hysterics from simulators. Instead he proposed a more practical approach—one useful for evaluating pension claims and forensic cases—based on to what degree the will of an individual hysteric could be held accountable for his hysterical symptoms. For all practical purposes, according to Kretschmer and most of his colleagues who wrestled with the simulation question, simulators (and those suspected of exaggeration) were to be treated no differently from hysterics. "As a matter of principle," wrote the psychiatrist Karl Pönitz, "the simulator, the exaggerator, and the hysteric were all treated in the same way. . . . The therapist was not a judge, rather remained a doctor."[77] Numbers of simulators, most doctors agreed at least as late as 1917, were insignificant—certainly no more than 3 or 4 percent of their patients—and were not recorded in official statistics.[78] The exaggeration of "real" symptoms was considered to be far more frequent, but it too generated little concern and provoked no systematic psychiatric scrutiny.

Rather than sending possible simulators and exaggerators to be tried and punished, in most cases doctors treated them with the same methods they used on more "authentic" war neurotics. In effect, the desire to escape war service was itself seen as a pathology, and even if this desire were conscious, it was treated as a medical problem. Such ideas ensured that simulation fell into the domain of doctors who, by retaining this liminal group, increased the size of their patient pool and their influence over issues that otherwise would have belonged to the military courts.

In such a way doctors were continuing in traditions established already in the later nineteenth century, when psychiatry began incorporating such behaviors as alcoholism, criminality, and homosexuality within its field of expertise. Significantly, by medicalizing the simulation issue psychiatrists were not blindly serving the state, but were using opportunities provided by the war to increase their professional responsibilities and power. But it should also be stressed that in treating so-called simulators, increased medical control coincided with patient interests; that is, patients benefited by being sent on for medical care—however painful and unpleasant—rather than being tried by military courts and subjected to harsh military punishments. Thus, simulation was one area in which increased medicalization represented a humanitarian alternative to purely judicial or military solutions.

All in all, neither military nor medical authorities devoted significant amounts of attention to the simulation issue during the war. It was only after the war, in the context of the pension question, that simulation emerged as an urgent issue, and only then did psychiatrists mount a more concerted campaign to distinguish simulators from hysterics.

Daily Life in the Neurosis Stations

What happened to those soldiers deemed suitable for active treatment and sent to the specialized treatment facilities? Naturally, conditions varied from station to station, but health officials strove to standardize pre- and posttreatment procedures as much as possible, so some generalizations are warranted.

The specialized neurosis station was a space in which the directing doctor had complete power over his patients and staff.[79] Many of these facilities consisted of a number of small, single rooms, an arrangement that facilitated isolation treatments and permitted the strict regulation of the patients' environment. But more important than the physical space of the station was the psychological control that station directors sought to maintain.

According to Nonne, the director of a neurosis station had to seem objective, businesslike, and impartial. He had to give the impression that eliminating patients' symptoms was his only and ultimate aim.[80] Doctors were instructed not to begin the treatment procedure until they had received a patient's prior medical history and had conducted a thorough examination of his physical and mental condition.[81] They were directed to look through the patient's history for evidence of a predisposition to nervousness and read the testimonies of his relatives, teachers, employers, commanding officers, and clergymen. Some—notably Gustav Liebermeister in Ulm—actually lived in their stations; this, Liebermeister claimed was so that "he could get to know [the patients] as thoroughly as possible and find the correct path to curing them."[82] Indeed, only with an acute knowledge of a patient's situation could a doctor draw conclusions about his prognosis and arrive at the appropriate course of treatment. Significantly, this attention to patients' personality and background stood in tension with the tendency to standardize and rationalize psychiatric procedure. Within what was in most respects an assembly-line system, doctors still carved out space for psychological examinations and for tailoring treatment to individual patients.[83] Regardless of external arrangements, active treatment was still an essentially subjective therapeutic act.

The specialized neurosis stations were frequently directed by doctors who had been pulled out of the field and sent to these new facilities in 1916 or 1917. Young medics with some training in psychiatry were considered to have sufficient expertise and were actually favored over more established medical experts who, like Gaupp, usually remained at their university clinics and presided over observation centers.[84] Moreover, younger doctors were thought more likely to have the necessary stamina and energy for performing dozens of active treatment sessions every day and were believed to be more versatile and open to new (or newly resurrected) treatments.[85]

The case of Württemberg provides several examples of this. Kretschmer, who had studied with Gaupp in Tübingen and with Nonne in Hamburg, was to become one of the leaders of German psychiatry in the 1920s and 1930s. Kretschmer was twenty-nine years old and had only completed one year of clinical training in psychiatry, when he was ordered out of the field and charged with single-handedly setting up an eighty-bed neurosis station at the Pax sanitarium in the town of Mergentheim.[86] As director of the station, it was also Kretschmer's responsibility to train his assistants, who were unschooled in neurological and psychiatric matters. Liebermeister, who became the director of a ninety-bed nerve station in Ulm in March 1916, was neither a neurologist nor a psychiatrist, although his father, Carl Liebermeister, was a distinguished late-nineteenth-century psychiatrist who had written extensively on hysteria. The younger Liebermeister was a practitioner of internal medicine, whom Gaupp called out of the field after he had received a bullet wound to the leg.[87]

Daily life in the stations was characterized, above all, by uniformity and monotony. Doctors hoped that through "boring patients to death" they could make health a more appealing option than neurosis.[88] Before the therapeutic intervention, patients were generally ordered to undergo several days of strictly enforced bed rest. During this period they were barred from smoking, game playing, pleasure reading, and receiving visitors and were forced to remain in bed at all times.[89] A patient's contact was limited to visits by the doctor and trained hospital staff members so that his environment could be strictly controlled. Exposure to visitors (and even improperly trained staff) could, it was feared, endanger the suggestive preparation.[90]

Treatment methods varied greatly with doctors' personal preferences and skills as well as the layout and resources of the facilities. At least two of the corps district's nerve station directors, Liebermeister in Ulm and Martin Freund in Bad Rötenbach, and with all likelihood nearly all of the others, used some form of electrotherapy in their treatment sessions but usually only after other, less painful techniques had failed to produce the desired results.[91] At Mergentheim, Kretschmer practiced hypnosis, various forms of protopsychotherapy, and nonhypnotic suggestion such as isolation in a darkened room.[92]

The average, successful stay in a neurosis station lasted up to three weeks. This included at least several days of pre-treatment gymnastics and work therapy to guarantee and "fix" the success of the active therapeutic session.[93] After a successful session (i.e., one in which the symptoms were removed), men who had exhibited severe contractions, tics, and other forms of movement disorders performed calisthenics or gymnastics under the supervision of a trained noncommissioned officer.[94] Once capable, treated neurotics usually carried out light tasks around the hospital station or in its gardens or kitchen, and in some cases they helped alleviate personnel shortages by tending to other patients, although Gaupp considered this inappropriate for his observation center because of the presence of numerous severely mentally ill individuals.[95]

In neurosis stations in agricultural settings, recovering patients worked with crops or tended livestock. (One doctor suggested that the stations aim for economic self-sufficiency in order to foster healthy feelings of community.)[96] During the posttreatment period patients were forbidden from spending their days in bed unless so directed by a doctor for other medical reasons, but in general conditions became less stringent. Station inmates were no longer completely shielded from outside influences; at this stage they were permitted to receive visitors, read, play cards, and even smoke, although alcoholic beverages were strictly prohibited at all times.[97] At some neurosis stations, which were part of larger reserve hospital compounds or in stations near invalid retraining schools, convalescing soldiers could enroll in various adult education courses, such as foreign language instruction and occupational training programs. Elsewhere recovering neurotics could participate in group activities through hospital gaming and singing clubs, pursuits probably intended to strengthen communal feelings and distract men from their solipsistic suffering.[98]

An essential element in these neurosis stations was the prevailing atmosphere or mood. A good atmosphere—one in which patients looked forward to their treatment and watched with envy as their comrades emerged from the treatment room cured—was believed to contribute significantly to therapeutic success and could even lead, in some cases, to spontaneous healing, where patients shed their symptoms immediately after entering the station.[99] Several doctors described this atmosphere as a "Lourdes-mood," reinforcing the sense of wonderment and miracle that active treatment was supposed to convey.[100] The neurosis station, in these depictions, appears as a site of pilgrimage, where curing was dictated by some mysterious divine power and was therefore both desirable and inevitable.

Doctors may have been miracle workers, but they were also officers, and a strict martial atmosphere also characterized the neurosis stations. Special military-medical facilities were favored over charitable hospitals where patients were more likely to be "coddled" and kept longer than necessary.[101] Military discipline, furthermore, was thought to have great therapeutic benefits.[102] While some doctors, like Nonne and Rafael Weichbrodt, wrote that a doctor's personal charisma could easily substitute for the suggestive effect achieved by military hierarchy, most believed that the military subordination of the patient to his doctor was vital to therapy and should be emphasized in the doctor's demeanor and reinforced by his uniform.[103] No one disputed the necessity of military discipline in the neurosis stations: In general, "the neurosis stations stood under extraordinarily strict discipline. No patient was pampered."[104]

It was also important that the stations not be too pleasant lest patients lose their motivation to recover and leave.[105] As Willy Hellpach asserted, in his 1915 article on the healthful effects of military discipline, "The soldier must have the feeling, that all in all nowhere is as nice as in the field, despite all the dangers and stresses, and nowhere is so unpleasant as in the hospital station, in spite of its security and safety."[106] Ewald Stier accomplished this, in part, by forcing patients to sleep in barns when hospital space was limited.[107] In general, the doctor's severe demeanor and the station's unpleasantness were "to make clear to the patients that sickness is not the means for achieving their goals."[108] On the other hand, conditions within the hospital must not be painful or too uncomfortable, warned Hellpach, because relaxation and rejuvenation also played a role in therapy. Nevertheless, he cautioned, "every step past that point involves the danger that life in the hospital, especially for those already convalescing, will become too nice."[109]

Scenes from a neurosis station in Graz, Austria, that show the therapeutic benefits of work. From *Archiv für Psychiatrie und Nervenkrankheiten* (1918).

Patients tending livestock.

Patients tending pigs (above) and enjoying the fresh air (below).

Patients participating in a singing group (above) and taking music lessons (below).

Patients working in the kitchen (above) and in carpentry (below).

The stations' discipline and serious, even unpleasant atmosphere also necessitated the exclusion of women. Only male doctors were believed to possess the strength of will and moral force necessary for carrying out active treatment, an assumption that dates back at least as far as Silas Weir Mitchell's rest cure.[110] Treatment personnel, therefore, were almost exclusively men. Women, whose allegedly sympathetic natures contradicted the spirit of active treatment, were unwelcome on hospital grounds. Because active treatment required firmness and discipline, doctors feared that its results could be threatened by the "numerous expressions of mawkish false pity particular to the female gender."[111] The female nurse, who as an "angel of mercy" (and alternately a scapegoat) was a highly visible part of wartime iconography, had no place in the neurosis station, where her charitable impulses were unwanted and even pathologized.[112]

Just as soldiers often rejected the "pitying" home atmosphere, medical writers continually asserted that hysterical men were best served by the company of other men and by the "hardening" military environment, where they were protected from the false comforts of the increasingly alien and "feminine" civilian world.[113] In psychiatric discourse, pity and discipline were constructed as opposing forces, and their opposition carried explicitly gendered associations. Indeed, the word *pity* often appeared behind the adjectives "feminine," "soft," or even "sick-making." Femininity was also associated with a whole cluster of toxic behaviors, such as charity, idleness—and therefore pension collection— and the prolonging of psychological illness, while such terms as discipline, guidance (*Führung*), recovery, efficiency, and productivity—in short, the goals of rationalization and rationalized care—were coded as masculine.[114] In a passage pregnant with these associations, Ludwig Mann summarized the principles of rationalized psychiatry: "Of particular importance is that the diagnosis be made correctly . . . and that the patients get to a special hospital station right away, without many intermediate stops, where they may find manly guidance instead of feminine pity."[115]

Particularly detrimental to war hysterics were their mothers, wives, and sisters. When possible, therefore, psychiatric patients were sent to stations far from their homes, to keep them safe from these influences.[116] "[The] home," wrote Gaupp, "exercises a detrimental influence on neurotic soldiers."[117] And (female) relatives were to be avoided, since they could easily be "an ally of the hysteria."[118] For this reason officials in Baden sent soldiers from southern Baden to hospitals in the northern half of the land and vice versa.[119] Treatment near the home not only potentially exposed patients to the destructive pity and concern of their family members but also risked giving the impression that their underlying wishes had been fulfilled, that the patient, in other words, had almost made it home.

Like the image of the individual family home as dominated by doting female relatives, the *Heimat* (or home territory as a whole), with its disproportionate numbers of women (and unfit, disabled men), was condemned as a bastion of femininity and thus a hotbed of psychic pathogens. The word *Heimat,* wrote neurologist Kurt Singer, represented a pathological wish and should not even be uttered near convalescing neurosis patients.[120] According to a Baden doctor: "The pity from citizens on the street, contact with relatives and acquaintances as in general the softening and undisciplined influence of the home hospital atmosphere worked against curing, or at least protracted it substantially."[121] A Württemberg health official portrayed this risk in dire terms: "The attempt to arouse sympathy and pity among the civilian population facilitates the persistence of old hysterical symptoms and the creation of new ones."[122]

One way to avoid these bad influences was to keep war hysterics away from the cities; increasingly, as of 1916, rustic locations were considered superior to urban sites for new neurosis stations.[123] This policy also reflected the view that the countryside provided a soothing and more healthful environment than the city and followed in a long tradition of antiurban, antimodernist thinking. It derived from the assumptions of those turn-of-the-century doctors and social critics who condemned Germany's expanding industrial cities as virtual breeding grounds of mental and nervous illness and of degeneration and vice. And a number of studies—building on early wartime investigations—sought to establish that soldiers from urban centers and, in particular, those in quintessentially modern occupations such as civil service and sales jobs were more prone to neurotic breakdown than their "sturdy" rural counterparts. These studies seemed to provide further proof of the degenerative effect of the metropolis and the healthiness and naturalness of rural life.[124]

Medical measures, then, aimed to prevent discharged neurotics—and indeed all types of war wounded—from making their way to cities, where they might beg, grind organs in the streets, or hawk picture postcards rather than working to the benefit of the national community.[125] In the words of the director of the neurosis station in Charlottenburg, outside Berlin: "A walk through the reserve stations in the big city informs [us] that there the war neuroses show a less favorable prognosis than they do here outside [the city]."[126] Likewise psychiatrist Robert Wollenberg recalled that active treatment met with limited success in his Strasbourg clinic. That patients could easily enter the city or receive family members influenced them negatively and disturbed the environment necessary for suggestive treatment.[127]

But the wartime critique of urban life seldom mentioned the deleterious effects that industrial labor was once said to have on mental and nervous health. The healthful influence of work was never challenged, even if that work occurred in the bleakest of factory environments. Shocks and jolts—indeed the various operations of modern technologies on the body—were no longer seen as pathogenic and even, as in the case of the Kaufmann cure, portrayed as beneficial and salutary. Thus, useful, productive work, regardless of its form, was praised for strengthening the subject's self-confidence, discipline, and moral character.[128] Rather than associating the cities with the pathologies of factory life, psychiatric writings condemned the urban environment as the antithesis of work, as a site of idleness, criminality, and (increasingly toward the end of the war) political radicalism. Because they considered neurotic conditions to border on all three attributes, doctors preferred to treat such patients as far as possible from these nefarious influences.[129]

Although the neurosis station was intended to be a "sealed system," removed from bad influences and integrated into a comprehensive program of therapy and rehabilitation, treatment—even when conducted by such masters as Nonne and Kaufmann—was not always effective. In these cases, rather than simply giving up, Württemberg doctors were encouraged either to contact their colleagues and ask that the patient be taken into another station or to come to Gaupp for advice.[130] No patient was to be discharged uncured, War Ministry officials urged, until all conceivable methods had been exhausted.[131]

Since markedly few treated patients were considered fit to return to the field, military and medical authorities concentrated on streamlining the path from the neurosis station to a productive economic position. Symptom-free neurotics received the new fitness designation "capable of work" (*Arbeitsverwendungsfähig* or AV). In 1915 Gaupp proposed that recovered neurotics be put to work where they could be most beneficial to the war effort, that is, in agriculture or munitions factories.[132] He also suggested that these work assignments be made by organizations established in the deputy general command of each army corps. Gaupp's proposals were ahead of their time, and elements of them were implemented nationwide some two years later. Significantly, these suggestions extended psychiatric responsibility from just treating patients to finding the appropriate form of work for them after treatment, an approach that drew from the growing field of psychotechnics or "work science."

In January 1917 the Ministry of War ordered voluntary war-disability associations to work together with deputy commands to help treated neurotics find suitable civilian employment. As of that year no neurotic was to be discharged from the army before an appropriate position in the war economy had been arranged for him.[133] Such patients, once discharged as "symptom-free" from the hospital, were transferred to a reserve battalion at or near the hospital's location. Work assignments were made by regional work exchange or welfare offices (*Arbeitsvermittlungsämter* or *Versorgungsämter*), but soldiers often had to wait around for weeks before an appropriate assignment became available. Indeed, some doctors observed that these periods of idleness and the delays between hospital discharge and the return to work threatened their inherently tenuous therapeutic results, and many treated neurotics were said to undergo relapses even in transport from the neurosis stations to their units.[134] Furthermore, the presence of neurotics in these work battalions was discouraged for reasons of discipline and "psychic contagion," and the suggestion was made that neurotics unable to work be given leave as soon as they were discharged from the hospital rather than risk endangering the morale of their unit comrades.[135]

Military and medical authorities thus turned their attention to eliminating these delays and integrating work more thoroughly into the therapeutic process. Work became a means, not simply the end, of psychiatric treatment.[136] But work merely for the sake of distraction was not sufficient; doctors strove to provide "consequential" work that brought financial compensation and benefited the war effort. Such work was made possible in some cases by adding workshops—for carpentry, wicker work, shoe making, for example—to the neurosis stations, where, in contract with local War Bureaus (*Kriegsämter*), soldier-patients were paid for producing necessary goods.[137] In other cases, new neurosis stations were placed near factories, farms, and forests to facilitate simultaneously the healing powers of work and the full exploitation of this valuable labor source. According to a military-medical directive: "Of the utmost importance is a methodical and sufficiently long post-treatment work therapy, at first under direct medical supervision, later with a certain degree of observation through inquiries made by offices, employers, etc."[138] And treatment was only considered complete, "when the neurotic has provided proof of the return of complete physical and psychic fitness through a long period of continuous occupational activity in hospital workshops and commercial factories."[139] As Otto von Schjerning, the Army's Chief Sanitary Officer, recalled, "Entire villages for the nervously ill were constructed so that, under the direction of nerve doctors, they could be enlisted into all kinds of jobs."[140] Another solution, which eliminated the intermediate stage between the hospital and the return to war work and further streamlined the passage from patient into worker, was pioneered in Baden in 1917 and was henceforth known as the "Baden system."

Psychiatry and Industry: The Baden System

Doctors in Baden began experimenting with work-therapy and "distraction," or occupational therapy, almost from the start of the war. But the limited success they had in sending neurotics to work in 1915 had changed by 1917. The key difference, what changed in those two years, was the implementation of active treatment. Studies showed that work-therapy was effective only when it followed electrotherapy or another method of active, suggestive treatment administered in a neurosis station. What became known as the Baden system grew out of this insight.

The Baden system was first developed in the remote Black Forest town of Hornberg.[141] There, a specialized neurosis station opened in December 1916 in the hope that the "ozone rich" air would help neurasthenics and that the location would provide abundant outdoor work opportunities for hysterics.[142] The Hornberg station quickly acquired a reputation for impressively high curing percentages, and its director, the Freiburg neurologist Ferdinand Kehrer, boasted of the miraculous cures he had effected and the fame he and his station consequently acquired.[143] Once patients had been successfully treated in the

Hornberg neurosis station, they remained there for several weeks, participating in communal exercises and gymnastics under the supervision of an NCO and carrying out light work around the station or in its garden.[144]

As soon as they were considered capable of regular and strenuous work—ideally, according to Kehrer, at the end of the first or beginning of the second week of exercises—Hornberg patients were placed on the assembly line of a nearby clock factory that had been converted into a munitions plant.[145] Baden doctors preferred assigning such patients to factory or agricultural work, in contrast to handicrafts, which they labeled "feminine" and "tasteless"; only work that contributed to the Fatherland would give recovering neurotics the self-confidence and discipline to return to civilian life.[146] Heidelberg psychiatrist Karl Wilmanns, among others, noted that working expedited the convalescence of neurotic patients but observed that without financial incentive, such patients often lacked the motivation, or "will," to devote themselves fully to their work.[147] The military administration was unable to provide the funds necessary to pay patients for working, but the problem was solved by enlisting the cooperation of private enterprise. The director of a nearby factory agreed to hire already treated patients straight out of the local neurosis station.

Once this plan was enacted, the men toiled eight to ten hours a day in the Black Forest plant, and at night they returned to the hospital. Instead of receiving pensions, they were paid wages commensurate with the work they performed. At this stage, the neurotics were no longer subjected to the station's strict rules—working convalescents were permitted to stay out as late as nine o'clock and even to visit local restaurants and taverns.[148] They were also free to spend their wages to support their families. These financial incentives, along with the new freedoms and the cessation of the monotonous hospital routine, were, for one observer, the reason neurotics responded so favorably to work.[149] This arrangement not only seemed to speed up recovery but also, as Wilmanns remarked in 1917, eliminated the pathogenic effects of pensions, lifted morale in the hospitals, and favorably influenced other patients. The heightened morale meant that many men were cured almost as soon as they entered the neurosis stations, and "the goal of training a great number of nervously ill [patients] as capable workers has been reached."[150]

Observers praised the Baden system for streamlining the transition from soldier-patient into civilian worker. It removed bureaucratic delays and the wasted labor power of about-to-be-discharged neurotics by creating the worker-patient, an intermediate stage between the hospital and civil society. To this end, an employment exchange office was annexed to the hospital, so that the entire work assignment procedure could be conducted under close medical supervision and, if medically necessary, individuals could be instantly readmitted for further treatment without time-consuming formalities.[151] A designated officer sought positions that corresponded to the experience, skills, and medical condition of treated neurotics.[152] In such a way, Taylorist principles were integrated directly into the hospital system, where debilitated soldiers were smoothly transformed into productive worker-patients.

Most of the patients who were natives of Baden were, after working for some time without relapse, discharged from the army and automatically retained (without interruption) as full-time civilian workers in the same factory. Farmers were the only major exception; they were directed to return to their prewar occupations where they were desperately needed. Patients from other parts of Germany were transferred directly to appropriate war production jobs in their home districts.[153]

By October 1917 the Hornberg plant employed roughly 250 neurotics, 100 of whom had become quasi-permanent, full-time workers. The success of the Hornberg operation inspired Baden's officials to implement this system elsewhere, and they opened small hospital stations with employment exchanges throughout the industrialized areas of the Black Forest, in the towns of Billingen, Triberg, St. Georgen, Überlingen, and Weinheim.[154] Patients who suffered relapses were to be returned to the same station where they had been treated to create the impression of an impermeable system, where the only options were to work or be returned to the hospital.[155] The Black Forest's large country inns were considered ideal for neurosis stations because of their soothing pastoral settings and their abundance of private rooms, which facilitated active treatment. Furthermore, their use aided the country innkeepers, whose business had sharply declined during the war. The arrangement seemed to suit all parties: the patients, the state, and the factory proprietors who benefited from the work performed.[156]

The Baden system also featured special work units known as "neurotic battalions" for men considered unfit for regular labor. The patients in this category, the "severely psychopathic hysterics," had been rendered symptom-free but were nevertheless considered prone to breakdowns and thus incapable of working without continued close supervision.[157] Rather than discharging them to a life of pension collection and inactivity or allowing them to influence other patients, healthy troops, or the general public, officials put these men to work in a strict military environment. These battalions were described by one doctor as "a troop unit with a nerve station directly attached."[158] The Triberg neurosis station formed a forestry troop in 1917 to gather materials for the coming winter, and several of its neurotic battalions collected hay in the fields.[159] Under these conditions, hysterics were supposed to enjoy the healthful benefits of military discipline and close supervision without the distractions and temptations of the civilian environment. Although they remained in uniform and were placed in military formations, these men were reassured that they would not see any combat duty to keep them from becoming agitated. They lived under constant pressure to stay healthy. Relapses met with renewed electrotherapy and strictly enforced bed rest.

As a whole, the Baden system seemed to be extremely successful; once it was enacted, Baden's neurotics were rehabilitated at a rate well above the national average. Wilmanns reported that out of the 451 men who were released from the 800-bed neurosis stations in Baden in the month of May 1917, only 9—all of whom suffered from some form of organic malady in addition to their neurotic symptoms—were judged to have a diminished earning power; the other 442 neurotics were able to work at full capacity.[160] In a retrospective summary from 1920, a Freiburg doctor claimed that after the introduction of the Baden system, nearly 100 percent of the neurotics treated within the Baden corps region were freed of their symptoms. While some 8 to 10 percent of treated neurotics in the rest of Germany were collecting pensions for their persistent hysterical symptoms, the number of pensioned neurotics in Baden was estimated to be less than half that, or a mere 3.7 percent.[161] The result, according to the report's author, was:

> The hysteria treatment, which was implemented according to these principles, when it was ultimately applied uniformly to all of the nerve hospital stations in Baden, led to an air-tight system; in such a way it comprised a closed front against the war hysterics. This effective organization of treatment enabled the most complete inclusion of the total hysteria material [*Hysterikermaterial*] in the corps district, its cure and its utilization in a manner most useful for the war.[162]

Thus, the Baden system not only streamlined the work assignment procedure for individuals, it facilitated the most efficient economic exploitation of this key category of potential labor. Due to these successes, elements of the Baden system were incorporated in other parts of Germany. Fritz Kaufmann, for example, met with Wilmanns in Triberg in early summer 1917 to learn about Baden's progress in psychiatric organization, and he adopted many of the same principles in his Ludwigshafen hospital.[163] Testimonies suggest that the Baden system was seen as a model to be emulated throughout the nation and even in Austria, where it was called the "German system." It was even praised in the *Reichstag*.[164]

The therapeutic principle behind the Baden system was that patients were (medically) well served by spending their time productively engaged in useful work. The alternative, idly occupying hospital beds, was condemned as literally counterproductive; thus, the act of healing was relocated from the hospital station to the workplace. Significantly, industrial work at this time was losing its gender specificity with the massive influx of women into factory positions and other visible, previously male occupations and roles.[165] Perhaps filling Baden's factories with recovering patients represented a way of displacing women from traditionally male jobs and attempting to right the war's jarring gender inversion by which the men were the hysterics and the women the workers. Simultaneously, it reflected the belief in the healing powers of labor and the common view that neurotics were constitutionally unfit for the rigors of combat. And by giving these men the means to support themselves and their families, the Baden system returned them from their hysterical incapacitation to the traditional male role.

Despite its apparent successes and influence on German and Austrian psychiatry, the Baden system did encounter resistance. The primary obstacle came from local industrialists hesitant to take on convalescing neurotics in their plants. Other skeptics charged that the Baden system ran the risk of appearing to be too pleasant an alternative to further military service for neurotics. As Württemberg officials contemplated adapting the Baden plan to their own situation in the winter of 1918, one doctor protested that the system rewarded those men who simply lacked the will to recover by placing them in well-paying jobs, and that as an attractive alternative to further military service it would prove disastrously tempting to those who were susceptible to hysterical attacks.[166] Another issue specific to Württemberg was the disproportionate need for agricultural laborers. According to a regional health official, placing neurotics in agriculture was less practical than employing them in factory work. In factories they could easily be supervised and "controlled." In the fields, on the other hand, "many prefer to limp about and shake rather than [perform] long and hard work, especially when family members—primarily female—pity them."[167]

Such critiques notwithstanding, Württemberg doctors did look to the Baden system as a model. Gaupp visited Heidelberg in the spring or early summer of 1917 and reported on the organization of Baden's psychiatric services in glowing terms.[168] Consequently, Württemberg officials began to incorporate elements of it into their own corps district, adding, for example, a work exchange office in spring 1918. Patterned after the Baden system, this office sought to smooth the process of discharging neurotics from the army and into the war economy.[169] To alleviate long delays and put neurotics to work as quickly and efficiently as possible (and avoid their pathological addiction to pensions), the Württemberg Deputy General Command created a special "pension unit" to work closely with the region's neurosis stations and channel neurotics into appropriate work positions as efficiently as possible.

Determining the right sort of work for convalescing neurotics was considered a medical responsibility. The doctor who had treated a particular patient was believed to be the only one aware of his needs, abilities, and limitations.[170] Already in 1915 Gaupp had made such a proposal:

> And who should seek out these positions, who should declare which position is the most appropriate? . . . Certainly it is the doctors in the reserve hospitals, chief among whom the nerve doctors, with their good psychological-psychiatric training, who have to concern themselves with this. From them it is to be demanded that they do not simply return the nervous, hysterical soldiers, whom a longer hospital stay will help no more for the reasons sketched above, to their units, rather that they specify how each individual can be used in the greater military organization.[171]

Tübingen, rather than Stuttgart, was chosen as the pension unit's location so that Gaupp, psychiatric consultant for the entire corps, could be easily consulted in difficult cases. The unit was run by a staff of three: a medical director; a Lieutenant Kübler, who had the final say in all work assignments; and a designated NCO who was supposedly knowledgeable about local industry and work conditions and who managed the unit's correspondence. The unit was scheduled to begin operating in mid-June of 1918.[172]

A main advantage of the work exchange procedure was that patients did not have to be present while their work assignments were made. While convalescent patients were undergoing their posttreatment exercises and performing light tasks around the station, a doctor contacted the pension unit in Tübingen to initiate the work assignment process. In such a way a neurotic's work-therapy would not have to be interrupted while officials in the central office sought more permanent arrangements for him.

Liebermeister proposed that Württemberg create special "neurotic battalions" modeled after those in Baden. He also advocated setting up bed-wetter companies, which had apparently been formed in Bavaria.[173] But Dr. Maring, the assistant director of the reserve hospital in Ulm, raised doubts about such battalions. He argued that placing these men too close to the front would trigger fear-induced relapses, while deploying the units near home territory would engender the same risk. Indeed, Maring considered strong military discipline and forced labor necessary to counteract the influence of civilian pity and indulgence.[174] The troop's leader would have to be familiar with war neuroses and see to it that conditions within the company remained less than pleasant. In September 1918 Gaupp opposed forming neurosis battalions on the grounds that they might lead to excessive disciplinary problems. He doubted that an officer could keep a whole company of neurotics orderly and productive and noted that no psychiatrically trained doctors had yet been named company commanders.[175] It appears that the battalions were never formed in Württemberg.

As a rule, neurotics were to be discharged neither as "war disabled" nor as "fit for military duty" but rather as "fit to work in the war economy"—a designation that was used exclusively for this type of patient.[176] Rather than paying them directly, Württemberg employers sent neurotics' salaries to their hospital stations, which held them until patients were released lest these men be tempted to squander their wages on alcohol. Moreover, officials believed that presenting neurotics a large sum of money at discharge helped raise their self-esteem, thus further reducing the likelihood of relapse.[177]

The Therapeutic Front: War Psychiatry in the Field

The efforts made to improve psychiatric treatment and administration within German territory were, however, only part of the army's campaign against war hysteria. Military and medical authorities increasingly concerned themselves with prophylaxis and with trying to detect and treat neuroses in the field before they could become full blown or "fixed," so that mobilized soldiers would not have to be sent back to German soil. Naturally, such efforts would not have been applicable in all cases because some neurotic breakdowns occurred in transport, in the Etappe, and even in hospitals, and very many war neurotics had never even seen action.[178] But for those who did break down in the aftermath of combat events, sending them back to base hospitals, many psychiatrists feared, risked confirming their sense of being sick and thereby strengthening their symptoms.

Once again, the goal was to keep soldiers far away from the pathogenic influences of home territory, where they might be pitied and succored. "Nothing is more detrimental than transporting neurotics back home," Gaupp wrote. "The neurotic who has crossed the Rhine once will in almost no case be fit for serving again, while those who remain with their troop medics or go to a field or war hospital, show a much better prognosis for quick pacification and a return of the ability to serve."[179] Indeed, Gaupp noted, neuroses could be "nipped in the bud" if they were caught in time. Well-trained medical officers knew how to use suggestive therapy near the front to calm frightened soldiers and prevent their early symptoms from becoming fixed.[180] Others believed that military discipline and the rigors of life on the front had positive therapeutic effects that led to frequent, automatic "rapid cures" of those neuroses that were born of fear and the drive to self-preservation. Nonne, in fact, reported that some units commonly forced neurotics into areas of heavy fire, a therapeutic measure that he found ethically dubious.[181]

These strategies reflected the enduring view that the front was a hygienically and psychologically superior setting to the domestic world. Despite the obvious dangers of combat and the extraordinary numbers of casualties and illnesses that the war produced, psychiatrists continued to glorify the front environment and held the *Heimat* rather than the war responsible for the prodigious numbers of neurotics. Many agreed that neurotics "get better under the favorable conditions of the front, where the patient stands in close contact with his fighting comrades and under the influence of the front spirit."[182]

Thus, in contrast to the pathogenic world of the *Heimat*, doctors still celebrated the "authentic" and salutary experience of life on the front. The "contagion" (*Ansteckungsstoff*) believed to cause epidemics of war neurosis was ubiquitous, Liebermeister warned, but it could be found in "high concentration" only far from the front. While the front experience consisted of frequent and often severe psychic and physical shocks, "there only a little neurotic contagion is present, because it has gradually come about that there the people are almost exclusively . . . immune to it. The greater spread of neurosis on the front is decisively inhibited by the healthy and sturdy mental constitution of the comrades there."[183] In the Etappe, on the other hand, psychic traumas occurred far less frequently, but, "the concentration of neurotic contagion grows the further one gets behind the front."[184] There, he cautioned, danger arose from the proximity to the war-disabled, women, and patients' relatives, who acted like "disease carriers," spreading the infectious forces of pity, charity, and sympathy. Liebermeister's views were common, and many of his colleagues shared the belief that neuroses could be treated relatively easily near the front, but once men were transported far from the lines they were, in all likelihood, never to be fit to return.[185]

Yet these prophylactic efforts faced two serious obstacles: The army lacked both experienced neurologists and psychiatrists in the field and appropriate facilities for dealing with nervous casualties there. As a solution to the latter, Liebermeister advocated the construction of psychiatric wings at war-hospitals (*Kriegslazarette*) close to the front lines—a strategy, he noted, that had already been carried out by the enemy in France.[186] The British, in fact, had opened their first front station as early as December 1916. One of these stations, created in August 1917 in the Ypres area, was placed some twelve miles behind the front lines, and eight thousand patients passed through it before the end of the war. The center was staffed by one medical specialist, who had an assistant during particularly busy times. Patients rested and participated in outdoor games and gymnastics, and those who showed no signs of improvement after ten days were evacuated to a special psychiatric facility at the base.[187]

Gaupp endorsed Liebermeister's suggestion and declared his full support for the construction of neurosis stations near the front, writing, "The more neurosis sections built into war hospitals behind the front, the better, as I have been repeatedly and emphatically stating."[188] By early 1918 every German army on the western front had placed a neurosis station in the Etappe.[189] And military-medical officials fully endorsed this solution, writing that whenever possible, "freshly" stricken neurotics be sent to facilities within the field of operations. Indeed, according to General Schultzen, "The longer the neurosis has existed and the more strongly the *Heimat* with its softening and disturbing influences has affected the neurotic, all the more firmly will the feeling of illness be anchored in his psyche, which causes the familiar symptoms, such as insufficiency of the will, pension addiction, the tendency to relapse, etc."[190] The front stations were seen as so beneficial that several doctors proposed transporting difficult cases there from home hospitals.[191]

But the lack of appropriately trained medical personnel created great problems. Psychiatrists working within Germany often complained that doctors in the field frequently failed to recognize hysteria and other functional disorders and sent such patients to reserve hospitals at great financial and medical cost.[192] This was probably aggravated by the fact that doctors with training in neurology and psychiatry had generally been removed from the field around 1917 and transferred to neurosis stations in home territory. Consequently, medics had to be trained to recognize and treat neuroses.[193]

Stier wrote that all medics should receive a week or two of training in a neurosis station to prepare them for the serious responsibility of tending to the nervous strength of their units. For the highly agitated soldiers who had to be sent back to the Etappe, unit doctors were instructed to avoid writing terms like nervous shock and nervous illness on their charts, for fear that they could cause nascent neuroses to become fixed by planting the illusion of a somatic—that is, "real"—disorder.[194] Kurt Schneider reported that letting these would-be neurotic soldiers rest and relax and assuring them a few days rest before resumption of duties often sufficed to restore their combat fitness.[195] Gaupp described the following procedure for unit doctors to deal with nascent neuroses in the field:

> He [the unit medical officer] must approach the man—who has been shaken up by terror, fear and agitation and exhibits psychogenic symptoms—with a calm and friendly tone; patiently listen to his complaints; examine him thoroughly if he so desires; absolutely avoid any insulting words (coward, malingerer, chicken, etc.); remove him from the zone of fire for several days; suggestively nip the nascent neurotic symptoms in the bud with a confident, authoritative manner; and not allow the thought to develop that a temporary excitement such as that would suffice to be sent home from the front.[196]

Only those who exhibited severe psychopathologies or "feeble-mindedness," Gaupp wrote, were to be removed from their units because they would not likely be able to return to action anyway and risked damaging the morale of the others. Gaupp conceded that during periods of especially heavy fighting, unit doctors would not be able to spare the time to deal with neurotics and should send them to the general wounded clearing stations for evacuation to war hospitals in the field or special base facilities. Nevertheless, he called for a program of enlightenment, in which neurologists and psychiatrists would lecture sanitary officers at the front and in the Etappe about neuroses and their treatment to counteract the popular view that neurotic symptoms guaranteed a discharge.[197]

By 1917 treatment and organizational successes encouraged Germany's nerve doctors to take on yet another vexing problem and hence further tighten their control over the thousands of men considered war neurotics. In addition to treating the new patients sent to them from the field and garrison hospitals, doctors turned their attention to those men who had been discharged and pensioned before hysterical disorders were considered treatable. The success of active treatment in transforming war neurotics into productive workers and eliminating pension payments inspired deputy commands to begin reenlisting pensioned neurotics so that they could be subjected to the new therapeutic procedures in the new neurosis stations. As a Bavarian official wrote: "In view of the outstanding success of the treatment methods developed in the war, it is the duty of the military administration to bring belatedly the benefits of treatment to all previously discharged neurotic pension collectors."[198]

When they were originally discharged, these men had generally been assured of a five-year waiting period before their pension awards would have to be reevaluated. However, the disparity between many of the neurotics discharged early in the war—who were often collecting pensions of 60 percent or higher—and those men who had undergone active treatment—who generally received no pensions—caused military officials to overturn prior policy and call for the yearly reexamination of highly pensioned neurotics.[199] The men who were targeted by these new measures included relapsed neurotics, neurotics who had never been subjected to a full therapeutic regimen, and those who had been successfully treated but who were not participating in the war economy.[200] Even nervously ill officers were eligible to be reenlisted for further treatment.[201] The stated goals of this program were not only to claim more workers for the war economy and simultaneously trim the state's pension budget but also to remove war-disabled beggars and peddlers—many of whom were supposedly war neurotics—from the streets.[202]

The "invalid re-examination" was conducted by the Deputy General Commands, and its characteristics varied from region to region. In the three Bavarian Army Corps, the 1917 procedure included all neurotics who had been pensioned at 65 percent or higher; neurotics with pensions lower than 65 percent were not scheduled for reexamination until 1922.[203] Doctors from the deputy commands of each of the three corps reviewed the hospital records of all of these neurotics and summoned appropriate cases for reexamination. Before being sent on to treatment facilities, these neurotics had to be examined by a specialist in an observation station or by a board of special medical advisors to verify that their conditions were indeed psychogenic and that they could be cured with active treatment in a neurosis station.[204] Under no circumstances were these men to be sent to general military hospitals; military medical protocols established that, after examination, they were to go directly to a specialized psychiatric station, where they were clothed in proper military attire and subjected to active treatment.[205]

Rationalization and the Modern Soldier

To measure the success of active treatment and the newly coordinated system of psychiatric services in late May 1918 the Bavarian Ministry of War circulated a questionnaire to the directors of all of the neurosis stations in the region's three corps districts. The survey posed three questions: "How many sufferers of the so-called war neuroses have been treated since the creation of this neurosis section? In how many cases was a renewed ability to work or a higher ability to serve reached? How many officers were included in the above?"[206]

The responses indicate that the organization of psychiatric services in Bavaria came very close to meeting its stated goals. In the neurosis station Marienheim in the town of Speyer, for example, 248 soldiers were subjected to active treatment between the creation of the facility in May 1917 and the report's date, June 1918.[207] Only 17 of these were released as unfit. Of the remaining 231, 1 was sent back into the field, 2 were serving at garrisons in the field, 25 at garrisons in home territory, and 203 were discharged as capable of long-term full-time work.

At the 100-bed nerve section of the reserve hospital Münzschule in Würzburg, which was opened on January 1, 1917 and expanded to 150 beds a year later, more than 1,200 patients had been treated by June 1918, and 98.5 percent of them had been restored to the full capacity to work.[208] In Ludwigshafen, where Fritz Kaufmann directed the neurosis station, some 95 percent of the approximately 1,500 patients treated in the two years before June 1918 were released as symptom-free, and at least 90 percent received a designation of at least "capable of work."[209] In sum, in the three neurosis stations in the territory of the Second Bavarian Army Corps, a total of 2,950 war neurotics were treated before June 1918, 2,764 (94 percent) of whom were released with a designation of "capable of work" or higher. (Only 24 officers were treated in that period.)[210]

Although these impressive, but not at all atypical figures should certainly be taken with some skepticism, it cannot be denied that active treatment, when conducted in an appropriate setting, was extremely successful in removing debilitating symptoms from the overwhelming majority of patients and in restoring the ability to work in tens of thousands of disabled men. Freeing these men from their symptoms essentially meant restoring their ability to work. Indeed, the act of treating neurotics was increasingly linked with the process of channeling them into war-related work to the extent that the boundaries between psychiatric treatment and posttreatment work were increasingly blurred. Evocative of the thousands of *Prothetiker,* war amputees fitted with artificial limbs, who were often quite literally plugged into industrial machinery, men with psychological afflictions were channeled into work situations considered appropriate for their mental strengths and abilities.[211]

Wartime economic programs accelerated the transformation of the German worker into what one historian called "an exchangeable item in the industrial processes of the nation."[212] Psychiatric treatment and organization furthered an analogous process. To serve the needs of the war effort, that is, the war economy, more efficiently, psychiatrists and neurologists oversaw the standardization and centralization of medical facilities, with the result that a whole category of patients, deemed nervously or mentally unfit to serve the war in the field, could be swiftly channeled out of overcrowded hospitals and into industry. Simultaneously, work itself—and industrial work in particular—was integrated into the core of the therapeutic process, and the industrial workplace rather than the hospital was conceived of as the site of psychic and nervous healing. As medicine accommodated itself to the logic of rationalization, the individual subject was swept up into a sealed system, which was itself designed for the efficient production of efficient workers.

In the modern, increasingly interventionist state where medicine competed for its share of power and prestige, a deep compatibility developed between psychiatrists and social and economic planners. These changes saw the systematic assertion of psychiatric control over all phases of the diagnosis, treatment, and rehabilitation of war neurotics, in constructing a system that stretched from battlefield to observation center to neurosis station to factory. For wartime doctors, then, treating men with hysterical disorders did not mean releasing them from the traumatogenic forces of modern war and industry but rather submerging them more fully in the economistic discourse of rationalization and the exigencies of the German economy. Significantly, the conditions once considered the cause of hysteria were increasingly adopted as its cure: whether they faced the shocks of the Kaufmann method or the jolts of a Baden factory, soldiers diagnosed with hysteria were no longer removed from shocking situations but forced to accommodate themselves to them, while being "safely" sequestered from soothing toxins like sympathy and charity. Such treatment, moreover, can be seen as an attempt to remasculinize the hysterical soldier by forcing him to become a self-sufficient, contributing member of society, thus reflecting a kind of cultural anxiety around the proliferation of hysteria among German men.

These developments intersected with a broader transformation in the role and representation of the German soldier. The image of the idealistic, enthusiastic volunteer of 1914 charging into battle with the national hymn on his lips was, amid the stagnation and prolongation of the war, replaced with another, more "modern" image: the soldier as worker, a dutiful cog in a mechanized system designed for the "efficient production of violence."[213] Ernst Jünger's influential depiction of the soldier-worker is perhaps the most vivid evocation of this thoroughly modern, technologized man.[214] But Jünger was only one of a number of writers to note the similarities between industrial workers and modern warriors. Indeed, the vision of the worker-soldier as a "depersonalized function in a technologized environment"—celebrated by Jünger and bitingly satirized by the period's cultural critics—bears a striking resemblance to the type of German man that rationalized psychiatry strove to produce.[215] Psychiatrists indeed sought to damn the "flow" of hysterical men that "flooded" their clinics and to make the hysterical body steely and hard.[216] They shared a vision of the healthy German man as thriving amid the shocks and horrors of combat and selflessly submerging himself in the national cause.

Nevertheless, despite its apparent successes and the medical, economic, and cultural impulses it served, rationalized psychiatric treatment and organization were not without their critics. Opposition came from the patients' side, as trauma and its treatment became, once again, a volatile political issue. As soldier morale deteriorated in the war's final months, the psychiatrist-patient relationship was anything but immune to the broader social and political fissures that became increasingly visible and bitter. As a consequence, ever increasing numbers of patients resisted active treatment or protested against the actions of their doctors, culminating most notably in the hospital mutinies during the revolutionary events of November 1918.[217] There were also medical objections to active treatment, and several doctors found fault with their colleagues' emphasis on speed and efficiency over patients' subjective states. These doctors, many of whom belonged to the psychoanalytic movement, conceived of war neuroses as complex conflicts that required gentler treatments and deeper psychic investigations.

CHAPTER 6

The Discovery of the Mind
Psychoanalytic Responses to War Hysteria

Our analysis has actually also had trouble. No sooner does it begin to interest the world on account of the war neuroses than the war ends. . . .
But hard luck is one of the constants of life. Our kingdom is indeed not of
this world.

SIGMUND FREUD, Letter to Sándor
Ferenczi, 17 November 1918

When the war broke out, the study of hysteria was in a peculiar situation.
Freud was hated, but he was believed in.

ERNST KRETSCHMER,
"Zur Kritik des Unbewußten"

With psychoanalysis we cannot achieve in two years what faradization
can do in two hours or isolation in a few weeks.

OTTO PÖTZL

CONSPICUOUS AMONG THE few doctors who criticized active
treatment and the rationalized system that was constructed
around it were those influenced by the theories and practice of
psychoanalysis. During World War I, several of Freud's followers critiqued suggestion-based treatments and challenged the conflation of work and mental
health that was so central to psychiatric assumptions. Others found fault with
the reductionist diagnoses and etiologies put forward by their psychiatric colleagues and looked beyond the simple wish for pensions and fear of the front,
arguing that deeper, psychodynamic processes were at work. And unique
among psychiatrists and neurologists, several Freudians focused on the sexual
roots of war neuroses, bringing homosexuality and libidinal theory into the etiological picture.

It is not surprising that members of Freud's circle had something to say about
male hysteria and posttraumatic neuroses. Freud, after all, had been concerned
with hysteria in men since his visit to Charcot's Salpêtrière in 1885, and he presented a paper on the topic to the Vienna Medical Society the following year.[1]
Trauma, furthermore, lay at the core of Freud's early therapeutic breakthroughs

and his original theories of neurosis. In the "Preliminary Communication" of 1893, for example, Freud and Joseph Breuer attributed hysterical symptoms to traumatic memories, and the five cases in their subsequent *Studies on Hysteria* illustrated this connection abundantly.[2]

Equally unsurprising, in view of the history of psychoanalysis, is the fact that Freud's followers broke ranks with the medical majority and, at least in part, rejected the therapeutic strategies and the diagnostic language of most neurologists and psychiatrists.[3] But the distance between the views of psychoanalysts and orthodox psychiatrists was not always wide. Indeed, what might defy common expectations are the ways in which Freudian approaches occasionally complemented those used by the medical mainstream and how they found strong support in the least likely of places, among state and military authorities in Germany, Austria, and Hungary.

The war and the massive onset of war hysteria presented both problems and opportunities for psychoanalysts. War conditions threatened the movement's existence by halting international scientific collaboration and diverting the attention of patients and potential benefactors—Freud described himself in December 1914 as living "in [a] private trench"—and yet it simultaneously offered psychoanalysis unprecedented exposure and approval in several of the belligerent lands.[4] While Ernest Jones was active in England, a number of Freud's close Central European followers worked in military psychiatry for the Central Powers, including Karl Abraham and Max Eitingon in Germany, Viktor Tausk and Edward Hitschmann in Austria, and Sándor Ferenczi and Sándor Radó in Hungary. Moreover, a handful of other doctors wearing German, Austrian, and Hungarian uniforms, who were not (or not yet) members of the International Psychoanalytic Association, experimented with psychoanalysis, looked to unconscious processes or sexual conflicts to understand the war neuroses, and developed therapeutic alternatives to the often brusque methods of active treatment. These doctors, most notably the Berlin physician Ernst Simmel, transformed psychoanalysis into a viable treatment for war hysteria and began to report significant therapeutic success with methods that derived from Freudian ideas. Such methods, however, parted from psychoanalytic tenets in important ways, and psychoanalysts alternately downplayed and emphasized these differences.

The story of psychoanalysis in World War I is suffused with questions and contradictions. While some doctors interpreted the war hysteria phenomenon as an irrefutable vindication of Freud's ideas, others saw it as their ultimate refutation. State officials, curiously, began to show great interest in psychoanalysis toward the end of the war, and high-ranking medical officers from the Hungarian, Austrian, and German armies looked on as Abraham, Ferenczi, and Simmel discussed their approaches to war hysteria at a psychoanalytic congress in Budapest in September 1918. Impressed by what they heard, they then endorsed the creation of special wartime psychoanalytic facilities, a plan that was derailed only by the unforeseen, rapid military collapse of the Central Powers.

What explains this peculiar, albeit short-lived partnership between psychoanalysts and the state? And why weren't state officials satisfied with the extraordinary therapeutic results claimed by mainstream neurologists and psychiatrists? Why, furthermore, were members of the socially conservative military command suddenly receptive to and interested in psychoanalysis, with its psychosexual theories of neurosis and its often arcane theoretical vocabulary? And finally, in what ways did psychoanalytic responses represent a dissenting voice from active treatment and rationalized psychiatry?

Psychoanalysis at War

The early reception of Freud's theories in mainstream psychiatry and neurology was far more ambiguous than the tale of betrayals and rejections that Freud himself set down.[5] Scholars now know, for example, that Freud's 1886 paper on male hysteria did not incite a riot as he later claimed and that, due to the writings of Charcot and others, "hysteria virilis" was no longer particularly controversial by the late 1880s.[6] Historians have also shown that many German physicians occupied a middle ground somewhere between Freud's close followers and his adamant detractors; many psychiatrists and neurologists were influenced by certain parts of psychoanalytic theory, while other doctors experimented with forms of psychoanalysis in the clinical environment without subscribing to the entirety of Freudian thought. This helps explain why the greatest strides in adapting psychoanalysis to the treatment of war neurotics were actually made not by members of the Psychoanalytic Association but by several physicians who fall into this middle category.

Two formidable obstacles militated against practicing psychoanalysis in the wartime environment. First, proper analysis required an enormous amount of time and patience, and conditions in the hospital stations, as well as the need to quickly treat and rehabilitate great numbers of men, made this impossible.[7] Second, Freud had written that psychoanalysis could only be effective on well-educated patients, who were free of superstitions, trusted medical science, and fully comprehended the analytic procedure.[8] Proper psychoanalysis, unlike the methods of active treatment, depended on the voluntary participation of the patient. The patient was not an object to be manipulated and controlled through therapy, but rather an active agent who had to understand psychoanalytic theory and embrace its methods. This naturally excluded the majority of war neurotics, most of whom came from the working class and the peasantry. By contemporary medical accounts, these patients were usually uneducated and were often mistrustful, if not downright afraid, of their doctors. The doctor, of course, was typically his patient's superior in both military rank and social standing, and by the middle of the war mounting social tensions visibly strained the doctor-patient relationship, further reducing the likelihood that recalcitrant patients would voluntarily participate in their own treatment and rehabilitation. Freud's close followers, such as Abraham and Ferenczi, were therefore reluctant to psychoanalyze war hysterics for both practical and tactical reasons, and they cautioned that the method was only occasionally suitable for isolated cases.[9]

Nevertheless, despite these formidable obstacles, several doctors did use psychoanalysis in the neurosis stations and worked to shape it into a practicable wartime treatment. Not formally affiliated with the psychoanalytic movement, such doctors may have felt free from its dogmas and were thus able to modify its methods and compromise with the demands of war in ways that the movement's leaders would have neither conceived nor condoned. The story of psychoanalysis in World War I is largely the story of these relatively unknown figures.

The first article describing the psychoanalytic treatment of war neurosis to appear in the German medical press was written by a general practitioner named Fritz Stern, who served in a voluntary war hospital in Berlin-Charlottenburg.[10] Stern oversaw the hospital's 300-bed section for nervous illness, where some two-thirds of the patients suffered from functional neuroses. Wartime military life, Stern theorized, created an atmosphere conducive to the development of hysteria. Basing his analysis on Freud and Breuer's 1895 book, *Studies on Hysteria*—and Freud's early, mechanistic model of trauma—Stern wrote that military conditions inhibited the healthy processing of the tremendous affect created by war service. "Military discipline, the forced community of men of the most diverse classes, the exclusion of the usual intellectual pursuits, the unusual activities prescribed by duty, the demand to endure life-threatening situations without displaying fear. Defenselessness in enemy fire, the need to conform to military standards and many other factors make the processing of affect impossible, with the result that it can have pathogenic consequences."[11] It was thus the combination of the manifold traumas of war with the strictures of military life that forced soldiers to repress their strong emotional reactions and, as a consequence, convert them into the somatic symptoms of war neurosis.[12]

Like Freud and Breuer, Stern wrote of a kind of cathartic "talking cure" that uncovered repressed memories and discharged unresolved affect. For this cure to be effective under such extraordinary conditions, he noted, it had to achieve results within several sessions. The only acceptable way of accomplishing this was to guide the patient through a process of questioning and answering and to prod him to recover his buried traumatic memories. Tricks designed to increase suggestibility (such as pressing on the patient's head or instructing him to lie down with his eyes closed), which were the basis of so many variations of active therapy and early Freudian experimentation, were to be avoided because they could arouse fear and confusion in the minds of the uneducated and could have a hypnotic effect on educated patients.

Stern's brief 1916 article provided few details about the procedure he somewhat dubiously termed psychoanalytic treatment. Yet, he did describe one case that well illustrates the distance between his wartime method and what was conventionally practiced by psychoanalysts. In this case a twenty-seven-year-old waiter suffered from a range of neurotic symptoms, including functional deafness, stuttering, a gait disorder, severe tremors of the body and head, and a dramatic regression into childhood. "He said that he was eight years old, spoke in the infinitive, for example 'no hit,' had pronounced childlike movements, called everyone temporarily 'mama and papa,' could no longer read block printing, paged through a picture book with great interest, demanded his mother vehemently, and had to be dressed and undressed."[13] (Stern did not explore the psychological ramifications of this infantile regression, a phenomenon that constituted the key to the etiology of war neurosis for Ferenczi and Abraham.)

After the usual methods of treatment had utterly failed, Stern decided to "psychoanalyze" the patient. He began by contacting the man's mother, from whom he learned that the patient had been an unusually tender child and had never felt comfortable in the army. Upon further questioning, the patient's mother reconstructed the events that precipitated the outbreak of her son's symptoms. On his long-awaited first leave, the young man had rushed homeward, eager to be reunited with his mother. A message stating that she was ill and could not meet him at the train station failed to reach him in time, and at his arrival the shock and disappointment of her absence purportedly triggered his descent into illness. During the therapeutic session, Stern confronted the patient with this information and requested that he recount the events surrounding his arrival at the station. The key to the symptoms, for Stern, lay in the fact that the man had been literally shaking with excitement to see his mother and had then, upon not finding her, stood frozen on the platform as though paralyzed. But so that he would not be conspicuous to the station authorities, he suppressed his shaking and concealed his agitation.

> He wanted to turn to an official, but could not speak for agitation, and since that point, speaking has been difficult for him. Suddenly the station guard demanded to know what he was doing there, and he was so terrified that he lost his hearing. At further prodding on what else occurred to him, he explained that as a child he had once lost his mother on the street, which had agitated him very much . . . since then he depended on her so.[14]

Even as the patient described these events, his verbal fluency and hearing began to return. The session lasted a total of two hours, after which he regained many of his functions. Although his anxiety persisted, by the next day the man's condition had improved markedly. This therapeutic approach was based, of course, on Freud's early theory of abreaction, by which hysterical symptoms derived from the emotions that accompanied past events, and the therapist's task was to make the events known to the conscious mind, which would cause the symptoms to disappear. As Freud and Breuer wrote in the "Preliminary Communication": "[E]ach individual hysterical symptom immediately and permanently disappeared when we had succeeded in bringing clearly to light the memory of the event by which it was provoked and in arousing its accompanying affect, and when the patient had described that event in the greatest possible detail and had put the affect into words."[15] Significantly, in this case, the precipitating event had nothing to do with combat trauma but resulted from the patient's return to the *Heimat* and the expected contact with his mother, a finding that was consistent with the assumptions of wartime psychiatry, which construed home territory and female kin as pathogenic and the all-male military world as healthy.

Stern cautioned that these remarkable results could not be expected in every case. In fact, he devoted the greater part of his short essay to discussing his method's limitations. Chief among them was that only a narrow group of patients was suitable for this sort of treatment. To Freud's caution that psychoanalysis was only appropriate for educated patients, Stern countered that the type of war neurotic most suited for his treatment was indeed intelligent but was, unlike Freud's refined, haute bourgeois clientele, actually rather uneducated. In patients with too much education, who were perhaps well suited to civilian private practice, military conditions were likely to create inhibitions that were too great for the method to overcome, and the military subordination to the treating doctor might lead to transference. Stern preferred intelligent, but uneducated patients, the simple "civilian proletariat," who sincerely desired to recover; they were most likely to place their faith in doctors, and their symptoms represented the uncomplicated expressions of simple conflicts. Unlike complex and overwrought bourgeois neurotics, then, working-class men proved to be ideal patients for this sort of psychoanalysis because of their simple minds and sincere faith.

Willibald Sauer, a Munich physician serving in a general field hospital, also reported that he had successfully applied Freud's ideas to the treatment of war hysterics. In a 1917 article Sauer aimed to demonstrate "how worthwhile it can be to assume the Freudian point of view even with the war neuroses."[16] Not fully satisfied with the usual suggestive methods, which, he asserted, only treated neurotic *symptoms,* Sauer was concerned with finding the psychic roots of these conditions so that he could treat them according to their causes. He based his method on the work of Ludwig Frank, a Zurich psychiatrist who had been influenced by Freud and Breuer's theories of hysteria.[17] Not affiliated with the psychoanalytic movement, Sauer, like Frank, felt free to discard "everything in the Freudian theories which can be assumed to be pure speculation and artifice"[18]—this amounted to roughly two decades of psychoanalytic investigation and most of the insights Freud considered crucial to the development of psychoanalysis.

Sauer's "psycho-cathartic" method relied on the same principle as Stern's; namely, the Breuer-Freud insight that recovery of a repressed memory would cause the disappearance of its attendant hysterical symptoms. But in contrast to Stern, Sauer turned to hypnosis, which Freud had rejected almost two decades earlier on the grounds that it concealed resistances and transference, which had become the essential elements in his analytic work. Once they were hypnotized, Sauer induced his patients to re-create verbally—or to reenact physically—the repressed traumatic experiences that were, he believed, the source of their suffering.

Sauer described a case in which a patient suffered from nausea, diarrhea, and a range of neurotic digestive disorders. His attempts to remove the symptoms through suggestive hypnosis were unsuccessful. In fact, each time Sauer tried to suggest away the gagging and vomiting, the symptoms forcefully returned at the mere mention of the words. Thus, Sauer concluded that there must be an association in the patient's mind between the symptoms and events that were unknown to him. He questioned the patient while awake and learned that the symptoms had first appeared two years earlier while the patient's unit had been pinned down under heavy artillery fire. He then placed the patient in a light hypnotic state and directed him to cast his glance forward, as if watching a film, until he saw images and scenes that he had experienced during the attack. In other words, when reliving his traumatic experiences in the hospital, the patient should endeavor to distance himself from them, to watch passively as the images rolled by. Sauer's equation of recalling traumatic memories with watching a film is an analogy that runs through the cultural history of trauma.[19]

Sauer dramatically recounted an example of the curious procedure in the following passage:

> I asked him to imagine the impact of the shells on June 6, 1915, in a lively manner. After a short pause noticeable uneasiness, acceleration of breath and pulse. (Do you see the image? [I asked.]) Yes, I see it coming through the woods. (Do you see it?) I hear the whistling. One explodes on the street, (gasping) one to the left of the town, two fly past it. ([He] throws his head to the side, his knees quiver, he presses himself tightly against the wall. His voice is choked. Keep going.) I hid among the others, and then I am sick and I have to vomit (violent belching that gradually becomes gagging). Then it was so that nothing could be done, company retreat. The company marched away. He remains alone with his comrade F. (The gagging increases steadily, and while he is reliving the scene it turns into vomiting.)[20]

Already upon waking from this session the patient felt better, and after several more hypnotic sessions, his symptoms completely disappeared. Soon he returned to his unit deemed fully capable of duty. Consistent with the arguments of Frank and Breuer-Freud, then, the symptoms disappeared when the repressed memory was successfully brought into consciousness and the affect thus discharged.

By no means did Sauer restrict himself to the psycho-cathartic method; in fact, he considered it viable only in certain cases and situations. The methods made famous by Nonne, Kaufmann, and Muck were all plausible, he conceded, only their results were less secure than those of psycho-catharsis. Sauer explained the common observation that active treatment worked best on "hardened," older cases by positing that neuroses cured themselves over time, as the trauma-induced affect discharged itself. Accordingly, Kaufmann's "miraculous" success with long-standing cases was no miracle at all—the longer the symptoms persisted, the closer they would be to disappearing on their own.

While soldiers treated with suggestive methods were considered capable of returning to the field only very rarely, Sauer waxed optimistically about his psycho-cathartic cures. In contrast to Nonne, Kaufmann, and the great majority of his colleagues at work in German territory, Sauer discharged his patients as capable of renewed field duty, and as he reported in the 1917 article, they served effectively without relapse. Indeed he boasted that "the cathartic treatment renders patients even healthier and more resistant than they were before their illness."[21] This seemed to be confirmed in the words of one grateful patient whom Sauer had treated and discharged back to his unit: "'I am doing well and am healthy. . . . I feel like the healthiest man alive since I was in treatment with you.'"[22]

Fritz Mohr, who had practiced various forms of psychotherapy and hypnosis long before the war, was the author of a third article that discussed the psychoanalytic treatment of war neurotics.[23] Mohr contrasted psychoanalysis favorably with the suggestive methods of active treatment, arguing, like Sauer, that the latter merely removed neurotic symptoms, while only psychoanalysis, which investigated the causal link between symptoms and experiences, could achieve a true and lasting cure. But no description of the method or case history appears in Mohr's account.

Mohr did, however, propose an innovative solution to psychoanalysis' wartime obstacles—restricting the method to those patients who really deserved it. How did Mohr determine who "deserved" this attention and individualized care? A patient's worth, he argued, was a function of his utility to the national community:

> Naturally, one undertakes such time-consuming and exhausting work only for those men who are so valuable, that their rehabilitation is desired for the community. . . . In choosing a method of psychological treatment we must especially now be a bit economical with our energies and not attempt to cure everyone with the same method, but rather depending on the type and value of each single case, we will either simply remove the symptoms or treat the whole man. This warning seems advisable in view of the fact that frequently one comes upon individuals about whom one can say in advance, that nothing permanent and complete will be achieved with them even with a great expense of time and energy. For simpler cases . . . the simpler methods of suggestion or shock are appropriate; for more complicated cases, which are often the more socially valuable ones, another kind of procedure [is called for].[24]

Historians tend to assume that psychoanalysis was more progressive (in both a political and a medical sense) than orthodox psychiatry. José Brunner, for example, has argued that psychoanalytic interventions had a humanizing effect on wartime psychiatry, while Elaine Showalter portrays quasi-analytic approaches as more enlightened and curative.[25] While it is true that psychoanalytic theories were more sophisticated and analytic treatments less physically or psychologically brutal than those practiced by mainstream psychiatrists, Mohr's views show that the ideas themselves were not inherently humane, democratic, or egalitarian and that they could also serve the instrumental approaches of wartime psychiatry. Psychoanalysts, like their mainstream orthodox counterparts, also subscribed to hierarchies of patient value, and many submerged individual health to a concern with the needs of the national community.

Ernst Simmel, however, applied psychoanalytic insights in a strikingly different manner. A Berlin physician, whose 1918 monograph on *War Neurosis and Psychic Trauma* captivated Freud, Simmel made the most important and enduring contributions to the psychoanalytic study and treatment of war neurosis.[26] Working in a neurosis station in Posen (*Festungslazarett* 19), Simmel had experienced a number of therapeutic failures with suggestive hypnosis before he gained the support of the station's director, Dr. Adolf Schnee, to try out treatment with the "psychoanalytic method."[27] Pure psychoanalysis, Simmel noted in a nod to Freud, would not be effective on his Posen patients because they lacked the education to understand and take an active part in their treatment. To compensate, Simmel turned to hypnosis as an analytic tool; hypnosis sped up and simplified psychoanalysis and made it suitable to the treatment of large numbers of patients.[28]

Simmel emphatically rejected the form of hypnosis promoted by Max Nonne. Rather than actually curing a malady, he charged, Nonne's hypnotherapy—and the other methods of active treatment—only eliminated symptoms by forcing or suggesting them away, and this strategy could have disastrous long-term consequences. Treating war neurotics through their (heightened) suggestibility without addressing the essence of their illness, the greater cause of the symptoms, he wrote, "is tantamount to deepening the sickness and not curing it."[29] Indeed, in his critique of Nonne, Simmel condemned hypnotic suggestion as the "rape of the mind" (*Vergewaltigung der Psyche*) and warned that symptoms, having simply been suggested away, would easily return in the presence of a new pathological association.[30]

In contrast to Nonne's "psychological rape," Simmel characterized his form of hypnosis as a "psychoanalytic X-ray," a formulation that evokes Charcot's use of the practice to reveal latent pathological states. He conceived of hypnosis as a tool for placing his patients into a dreamlike state, in which they would reveal the events and associations that lay beneath their neuroses.[31] Furthermore, Simmel's treatment required the active and voluntary participation of the patient; rather than viewing patients as passive material, Simmel displayed a unique level of concern for their comfort and subjective states.[32] In contrast to the practitioners of active treatment, who were content to rid patients of their symptoms so that they could work without interruption, Simmel's therapeutic goal—like that of Willibald Sauer—was to resolve long-standing conflicts and make his patients healthier than they were even before the onset of neurotic symptoms. The physical symptoms of a neurosis, Simmel claimed (echoing Freud), functioned as a sort of "security vent" to prevent the mind from overloading with affect and to protect it from long-term damage in the form of a psychosis. The appearance of neurotic symptoms thus marked the beginning of the body's self-healing. Forcefully suggesting these symptoms away worked against this natural healing; it could be dangerous for the patient and often resulted in subsequent outbursts of rage or hysterical attacks as the repressed affect forced its way out.[33]

Due to its theoretical subtlety and deep psychological orientation, Simmel's work with war neurosis bears a far closer resemblance to true psychoanalysis than the methods outlined by Sauer and Stern. Dream interpretation, absent from the other accounts, played a central role in Simmel's procedure; "I do not treat any patient whose dreams I do not know," he wrote.[34] Like Freud, who called dreams the "royal road to the unconscious," Simmel saw dreams as his path into patients' unconscious mentation. He thus had patients narrate their dreams to him in the analytic sessions or, as he preferred, bring him written versions that they had recorded immediately on waking in the morning. Simmel then performed what he termed his "mining work" into the unconscious by isolating recurring dream images or figures and having his patients free-associate with them, a procedure that derived from the methods of Carl Jung: "We take a word or sentence structure which seems peculiar from the dream narration and have him [the patient] make associations, that is, say what randomly occurs to him. In this we again seize on what is most conspicuous and have him once again express the results of his associations."[35]

One patient, for example, dreamt of hiking in the mountains with his brother until a "great white mass" pinned them both to the ground. In the subsequent analytic session, the patient quickly associated the great white mass with snow, which "knocked him to the ground instead of helping him."[36] *Schnee*, the German word for snow, happened to be the name of Simmel's chief at the Posen hospital, and it was Dr. Schnee who first tried to treat this patient through what Simmel described as an aggressive and prolonged hypnotic rape. Thus, the white avalanche represented Dr. Schnee and the patient's experience of his abusive therapeutic procedure. The mountain, Simmel theorized further, symbolized the man's psyche, with its chasms of pent-up affect.[37]

In addition to dream interpretation, Simmel's method borrowed from Freud in other ways. He was also attentive to slips and the other "psychopathologies of everyday life," approaching all involuntary movements, tics, or utterances—

in short anything that got past the unconscious' "gatekeeper"—as a potential clue to the psychic basis of a patient's malady. Here Simmel proceeded with the same associative method that he used with dream interpretation, seizing on recurrent, conspicuous, or odd facial expressions or turns of phrase and investigating their deep psychic associations.

Many of the conditions that Simmel confronted occurred in men who were buried after an unexpected shell explosion.[38] Simmel argued that this so-called burial neurosis (*Verschüttungsneurose*), a common theme in the psychiatric literature, was brought about by the sudden and violent destruction of the soldier's personality complex, that is, the weakening of his Ego, with the result that he lost the ability to discharge the concurrent affect. Hence, the unprocessed affect would cling to a single organ or the entire man, which explained the persistent symptoms. The simple act of having the patient recall the repressed events—or "rolling the film again," as Simmel (and Sauer) called it—sufficed to rid the patient of his symptom complex and to bring about a cure. That Simmel devoted a great deal of attention to burial neurosis is consistent with the general verticality of his analysis: the image of a solider buried in rubble evokes the repression or burial of traumatic memories; the mind in his cases is depicted as either a mountain or a mine; suggestive treatment pushes symptoms further underground, while psychoanalysis unearths them and exposes them to the light.

Simmel typically began treatment by asking his patients to recall and write out the events surrounding the onset of their conditions. He then discussed these accounts with them until more memories came back, which he subsequently asked the patient to record as well. Simmel continued this procedure until he had found associations to use as an entry point in hypnosis. In a comment most likely aimed at Nonne and other practitioners of so-called magical cures, Simmel noted that he avoided giving his patients the impression that his procedure was "supernatural" or mystical. While certain doctors intentionally created mystical impressions to enhance the power of their suggestive treatments, Simmel pointedly rejected such gimmickry: "Thus I do not play the part of the magician, whose hands have 'magnetic healing' powers. Such behavior would make the patient suspicious, if he is critically disposed, and would make the necessary 'friendly' relationship between doctor and patient impossible. I dispassionately instruct him about the character of the hypnotic state, in which everything that is 'tensed up'—in a physical as well as a psychological sense—can work free."[39]

Yet, Simmel confessed that he was not completely honest and forthright with his patients. He conceded that the psychogenic nature of these conditions would have been incomprehensible and rather puzzling to most of them. Precisely to avoid creating the impression of mysterious, supernatural forces, which, Simmel feared, could shock patients and hence hinder their participation in the treatment, he intentionally misled them that their ailments—and his hypnotic treatment—operated through organic mechanisms. He also introduced several "minor deceptions" to help suggest patients into the hypnotic state: "I have them gaze upon a staff, whose tip I gradually lower. The eyes, naturally, follow slowly after it, and I explain, 'Your eyelids are shutting because you are tired.' With my free hand I press lightly from above on the eyebrows, so that the sunken eyelids have to now close, and I explain, 'Your eyelids are closing because you are tired.' Misapprehending the actual cause, he feels himself surrendering to my suggestive soporific influence and has already been subdued by it."[40] Simmel lulled his patients into a deeper hypnotic sleep by letting his voice rise and fall soothingly.

Simmel grouped his patients together according to their symptoms. While many of his contemporaries would have condemned this practice as risking the prolonging of "psychic contagion," Simmel believed that patients with similar symptoms could benefit each other. Because neurotic symptoms carried symbolic meaning, placing patients side by side could stimulate the associative process and significantly aid his own psychoanalytic "mining work."[41]

Clearly Simmel's psycho-cathartic treatment was gentler and less dangerous than the various methods of active treatment. Like Sauer and Stern, Simmel aimed to treat the "whole person" and thus tried to resolve patients' unconscious conflicts. Active treatment successfully removed the physical symptoms of thousands of neurotic soldiers and transformed them into fit workers. Its practitioners concentrated on making their patients' bodies useful to the war and most often showed but a passing concern with the conflicts and anxieties that plagued their minds. As a result, hysterical symptoms most often reappeared once soldiers were returned to their units or exposed to frightening conditions. Psycho-catharsis, however, strove to cure soldier-patients in a deeper sense. Rather than simply eliminating their symptoms, Simmel aimed to enlighten his patients and render them healthier than they were before the appearance of their neurotic conditions. Consequently, many of the patients treated with psycho-catharsis were not considered merely "capable of work," but were discharged from the hospital as able to return to the field.[42] This poses a serious ethical question. Was Simmel really doing his patients a favor by rendering them fit to return to action? It is one of the great ironies in the history of wartime psychiatry that Simmel's ostensibly more humane and ethically sound procedure was potentially of greater service to the war effort and ultimately more life-threatening to patients than the often opprobrious methods of active treatment. This dilemma dramatizes what Freud later called the "insoluble conflict" between the universalistic-humanitarian aims of medical practice and the particularistic-national demands of the state.[43]

Simmel's success explains why medical officials from the Central Powers took a sudden interest in psychoanalysis. Their presence at the Budapest Congress appears to have had little, if anything, to do with the intricate sophistication of psychoanalytic theories of neurosis and the nuances and subtleties of

Freudian thought. It is far more likely that the success of what was (albeit some-what misleadingly) presented as psychoanalytic treatment piqued their inter-est.[44] The fact that active treatment failed in restoring combat fitness to war neurotics may have prompted health officials to look elsewhere, at which time they most likely got word of Ernst Simmel and his success with "psycho-cathar-sis."[45] Furthermore, the Kaufmann method and other aggressive and danger-ous techniques were increasingly under attack; patient complaints about psychiatric brutality were by this time the subject of newspaper reportage and parliamentary debate. The outcry against electrotherapy motivated health offi-cials to seek out safer, less offensive alternatives to active treatment, and psy-choanalysis presented itself as an appealing option.[46] In a memorandum by a health official from the Austrian Ministry of War in early September 1918, just weeks before the Budapest Congress, psychoanalysis was sanctioned as a new tactic against "stubborn" war neurotics, and the creation of special psychoan-alytic neurosis stations was taken under advisement.[47]

Naturally, believing that state backing and a vital, visible role in the war could only help their "cause," psychoanalysts cultivated the state's nascent in-terest. Psychoanalysts, then, like the psychiatric profession as a whole, sought to inflate their national importance and professional standing through the war neurosis experience. Two years later Freud critiqued military medicine for per-verting doctors' humanitarian obligations, but in 1918 he did not hesitate to cast his lot with the national cause.[48] Indeed, at the outbreak of war, various marginal groups in German society enthusiastically responded to the call of mo-bilization and, in so doing, hoped to show their patriotic commitments and fur-ther their acceptance by the mainstream. The same could be said of the psychoanalysts. Freud was preoccupied by his movement's fragility and his own outsider status, and he jumped at the chance to use psychoanalytic success with the war neuroses to move from the periphery to the center of German-speak-ing medicine and society. Indeed, in August 1914, Freud basked in his feelings of "Austrianness"; four years later—although he had grown deeply cynical about the war—he hoped to compensate for his alienation from the psychiatric establishment by serving the state and army.[49]

The Budapest Congress: Sex and Psyche

Thirty-two members of the International Psychoanalytic Association and fifty-five guests—including local doctors, members' spouses, and Ernst Sim-mel—convened in the auditorium of the Hungarian Academy of Sciences on September 28, 1918. "Everybody was in uniform, except Freud," recalled Sándor Radó, the Budapest analyst who served as the congress secretary.[50] The uniforms were not the meeting's only peculiarity. For one, the Fifth Interna-tional Psychoanalytic Congress was hardly international. With the exception of two visitors from the neutral Netherlands, Doctors van Emden and van Ophuijsen of The Hague, it consisted entirely of members from Central Powers coun-tries. (Nevertheless, the meeting's international status was upheld after the war by the newly reunited International Association.) The absence of Ernest Jones and other English analysts, furthermore, must have conspicuously marked the congress' atmosphere, as did the unprecedented attendance of state and mu-nicipal officials.[51] Indeed, the Lord Mayor of Budapest was in the audience, as were high-ranking medical officials from the Hungarian, Austrian, and German armies.[52] Furthermore, the attendees, according to subsequent accounts, were warmly and graciously received in the Hungarian capital amid much pageantry. Budapest officials housed the visiting analysts in the city's new "Thermal Ho-tel" and even placed a special Danube steamer at their disposal. Such a recep-tion was a novelty for the participants who were accustomed to indifferent, begrudging acceptance by their host cities. In fact, due to the favorable re-ception of his ideas in Hungarian circles and the influence of several wealthy benefactors, Freud often speculated that Budapest would one day become the movement's new home.[53]

Sándor Ferenczi, who was then serving as the chief neurologist at the Maria Valeria base hospital in Budapest, delivered the keynote address. During the war, for both personal and political reasons, Ferenczi had become Freud's closest confidant and collaborator, and the two remained in regular contact throughout the war years. When conditions permitted, Freud continued his pro-tracted analysis of Ferenczi. At other times, the two corresponded about a range of professional and personal matters, including Ferenczi's "inner theater of war," his love triangle with the unhappily married Gizella Pálos and her daugh-ter Elma.[54]

Ferenczi began his Budapest address with an allegorical anecdote intended to illuminate the position of psychoanalysis within psychiatry. According to the story—related by a Hungarian colleague who had witnessed the recent revolu-tionary events in Russia—the leaders of the new Russian state had consolidated their power and constructed a polity based on the laws of historical material-ism. But they encountered unforeseen resistance in trying to implement the new social order. Steeped in their materialist ways, Russian Marxists were at first blind to the source of this resistance. However, they ultimately saw that the ma-terialistic conception of history was too narrow, and that by taking only eco-nomic and political relations into account, they had overlooked one significant factor: the emotional and intellectual life of people; in short, the complexities of human subjectivity (*das Seelische*). The cost of the Bolshevik experiment, ac-cording to Ferenczi, was astronomical, and many thousands of lives were lost, but out of the failure came a crucial discovery, "the discovery of the mind" (*die Entdeckung der Seele*).

Just as the "failure" of the revolution led the Bolsheviks to discover the psy-chological, the tragic devastation of war, claimed Ferenczi, brought about an analogous discovery in German mental medicine.

The war produced nervous diseases on a massive scale, and they demanded explaining and curing, but the up-to-then accepted organic-mechanical explanation—which roughly corresponds to the materialistic view of history among sociologists—failed completely. The great experiment of the war has shown manifold severe neuroses where there could be no possibility of a mechanical effect, and the nerve doctors likewise came around to the understanding that something was missing from their conception, and this something was, once again, the mind [*die Seele*].[55]

Significantly, for Ferenczi, the new awareness of the psyche represented the victory of psychoanalysis over mainstream psychiatry and neurology.

Ferenczi then sketched the origins of psychogenic thinking in contemporary neuroscience and attributed its foundation to Freud's and Breuer's work on hysteria. Nonne, he allowed, had correctly labeled the war neuroses as hysteria and had used his therapeutic success with hypnosis to support his contention. But neither Nonne nor any of his supporters could demonstrate how psychogenesis operated—they were ignorant about the psychophysical mechanisms that actually produced a neurotic condition. Then, showing how a number of leading neurologists and psychiatrists, such as Bonhoeffer, Gaupp, and Alfred Hauptmann, had accepted the principles of psychogenesis and the ideogenic basis of neurosis, Ferenczi concluded that they subscribed to the theories of psychoanalysis without acknowledging it. "So you see, ladies and gentlemen: the experiences with the war neurotics gradually led further than the discovery of the mind—they nearly led neurologists to the discovery of psychoanalysis."[56]

Clearly, Ferenczi's analysis turns on a misrepresentation of the landscape of contemporary mental medicine. He depicted prewar psychiatry as completely materialistic and mechanistic, failing to take into account the different currents that had begun already in the 1880s and 1890s. Indeed, doctors such as Gaupp, Bonhoeffer, Hellpach, and Sommer, the emerging leaders of university mental medicine, stood firmly in the psychogenic camp by the turn of the century and were influenced not by Freud and Breuer but by figures such as Emil Kraepelin, not by bourgeois neurotics but by accident hysterics and the debates around traumatic neurosis. Thus, when Ferenczi divided psychiatrists into the somaticists and the Freudians, he was drawing a false dichotomy that overlooked the psychological turn in late-nineteenth-century German psychiatry. Perhaps Ferenczi's description applied to the world of private neurological clinics, but he was ignoring the most influential members of his profession—one wonders whether the misrepresentation was willful and if it was intended to inflate the contribution and acceptance of psychoanalysis for the nonspecialist officials in attendance. Ferenczi's assertion that the war hastened the acceptance of psychogenicism is indeed plausible, but his equation of psychogenic theories with psychoanalysis views the history of medicine through a Freudian prism and does not stand up to scholarly scrutiny.[57]

At this point in his presentation, Ferenczi turned to the question of psychic constitution. Neurologists and psychiatrists had failed to reach a consensus on the issue of whether neuroses could develop in any individual or if a certain psychopathological disposition was a necessary precondition. Psychoanalysis, he argued, took a middle position in the disposition debate. Freud had conceived a scale that offset the precipitating traumatic event and the individual psychic disposition as "reciprocal values." Accordingly, a mild predisposition coupled with an extraordinary shock would produce a neurosis, just as a strong predisposition would require only a minimal trauma. To round out the equation, individuals with but a slight predisposition could survive minor traumas unscathed. Still, as Ferenczi's later remarks made clear, the psychoanalytic concept of predisposition differed significantly from the more mechanistic notions touted by nonanalysts.

Ferenczi then turned to an area where the teachings of mainstream mental medicine seemed most irreconcilable with the tenets of psychoanalysis: sexuality, and specifically the psychoanalytic belief in the sexual basis of hysteria. Freud had famously written that all neuroses had their origin in sexuality, and this insight remained a cornerstone of psychoanalysis and simultaneously the source of much ongoing controversy. Nonne was one of many critics who seized on this point. Nonne argued that evidence from the war confirmed much of Freud's thinking, and, in a 1922 article, he even included Freud, along with such doctors as Bonhoeffer, Gaupp, and himself, in a list of the men who had contributed most to understanding war neurosis, adding that "psychoanalysis is thoroughly justified—theoretically and in practice—in the treatment of military neurotics."[58] But ultimately, for Nonne, the war exposed the bankruptcy of psychoanalysis because war experiences definitively refuted the sexual etiology of hysterical neurosis.[59] Indeed, on this point Nonne was in accordance with the great majority of German neurologists and psychiatrists, for whom the sources of war neurosis simply had nothing to do with sexuality. Ferenczi naturally discounted this point, and like Abraham in the presentation that followed, he took great pains to introduce sexuality into the etiology and symptomatology of the war neuroses.

Ferenczi argued that views like Nonne's derived from a misinterpretation of the psychoanalytic conception of sexuality. Psychoanalysis did not understand sexuality as purely a matter of the genitals, Ferenczi argued; rather, the mechanism at work in the war neuroses and indeed all posttraumatic neuroses involved a broader conception of sexuality, one that was grounded in the Platonic conception of "Eros."[60] He explained: "Psychoanalysis returns to this ancient point of view when it treats all sensual and affectionate relationships of the individual to the opposite and to the same gender, emotions toward friends, relatives, any fellow person, even the affect relationship to one's own Ego and to one's own body in the rubric of 'eroticism' that is, 'sexuality.'"[61] In the war neuroses, Ferenczi argued, the key to the sexual question lay in narcissism, or self-love.

Ferenczi conceded that the libidinal dimensions of war neurosis were not easily discernible. But he advised skeptics to return to Freud's theories of hysteria and let themselves be convinced of the sexual basis of (nontraumatic) neurosis: "Then you will be much more easily persuaded of the correctness of the sexual theory of the neuroses; an appreciation of the sexual basis of the war neuroses will then become self-evident. In any case, gloating over the fall of the sexual theory is somewhat premature."[62] (Freud later added that lack of evidence for the sexual theory is not the same thing as proof of the theory's incorrectness; in other writings he often quoted Charcot's line: "Ça n'empêche d'exister"—"[not seeing it] does not preclude its existence.")[63] In addition to this somewhat circular logic, Ferenczi offered another strand of evidence for the sexual basis of war neurosis; he cited the common observation that post-traumatic neuroses usually brought prolonged disturbances of the sexual drive, if not complete impotence.[64] This observation alone, according to Ferenczi, should suffice to establish that there was a link between the war neuroses and sexuality and to prove that Nonne's judgment was too hastily made.

In the final section of his address, Ferenczi returned to the theme of narcissism. Among the most frequent war neurotic symptoms were outbursts of rage, fear, and depression, all of which Ferenczi traced to a kind of self-absorption or "oversensitivity of the Ego," which reflected that the neurotic's object relations were stunted. "Not infrequently, this increased self-love degenerates into a kind of infantile narcissism: the patients want to be coddled as children, cared for and pitied. Thus one can speak of a regression into the childish stage of self-love."[65] (This certainly applied to Stern's case of the waiter who was overcome with excitement at the reunion with his mother.)

Narcissism was also the key to the predisposition question. An individual highly disposed toward narcissism would be more likely to develop a post-traumatic neurosis, although, Ferenczi allowed, no one was immune because the stage of narcissism represented an important point in the libidinal development of all healthy people. Furthermore, Ferenczi found confirmation of his views in the observation that "infantile narcissism" figured prominently among the characteristics commonly exhibited by war neurotics. "The complete personality of most traumatics [*Traumatiker*] conforms to that of a naughty, unscrupulous child, scared and cowering as a result of a shock. The excessive weight which nearly all traumatics place on a good meal fits with this image. . . . Most do not want to work, they want to be supported and nourished like children."[66] Here Ferenczi alluded to one of the salient differences between the psychoanalysts and their rivals. The factors most doctors emphasized to explain war neurotics' symptoms—pensions, fear of the front—were only what Freud would call the secondary gain of a neurosis. The primary motivation must lay much deeper in their development, in their early childhood experiences. In these cases, it was usually the desire to return to an infantile situation that they had only very reluctantly left in the first place. That the resulting conditions could simultaneously guarantee their safety or financially support them might have contributed to the symptoms' development or prolongation but should not be mistaken for their cause.

Elsewhere Ferenczi had argued that multisymptomatic neurotics, in particular those with strongly debilitating disorders of gait, resembled the developmental stage of children in their first year (he cited as evidence a nurse's offhand comment that one neurotic patient looked like a small child just learning to walk).[67] But regression was not simply a matter of returning to an early childhood state. According to psychoanalytic theory, neurotic symptoms were expressed in symbolically meaningful ways, and Ferenczi interpreted some neurotic conditions as representations of atavistic states. A very strong burst of affect, he argued, could cause an individual to regress back to a state that was not a part of his own development but figured significantly in the development of our species. Hence, neurotic symptoms could symbolize atavistic characteristics made obsolete by human evolution; the inability to stand, to take one common symptom, connoted our ancestors before they learned to walk upright.[68]

Ferenczi concluded by asserting that the psychoanalytic view of war neurosis opened up many avenues of observation that had been ignored by neurologists. It was to be expected, he noted, that in the future psychoanalysis would bring further explanations and even "radical cures" to this malady.

Karl Abraham, at the time Freud's closest German follower, delivered the second presentation on war neurosis. Abraham, whose cousin Hermann Oppenheim had financially supported his psychoanalytic pursuits despite holding them in low regard, was a Berlin-based psychiatrist who headed the psychiatric department at an army hospital in East Prussian Allenstein.[69] Abraham began his presentation where Ferenczi had left off.[70] Like his Hungarian colleague, Abraham claimed that the war had brought mainstream neurology ever closer to the psychoanalytic perspective, but he defined two areas where significant differences still obtained, the unconscious and the sexual. He turned his attentions to the latter subject, and set out to show that the experience with war neurosis confirmed the sexual basis of neurosis and proved the correctness of the psychoanalytic view of sexuality. Wartime neuroses and even psychoses, Abraham argued, could not be understood without recourse to sexual mechanisms.

The posttraumatic neuroses had long been held up to refute the sexual basis of neurosis because their source seemed so obviously external and their content nonsexual. From his clinical experience, however, Abraham had become skeptical of this assumption. One clue to their sexual nature was that among peacetime posttraumatic neurotics, "the impotent male" and "the frigid woman" had stood out as two archetypes; these symptom complexes closely resembled the conditions shown by the majority of the war neurotics Abraham had encountered. Both types of patient suffered from shaking, restlessness, sensitivity, sleeplessness, headaches, fear, depression, and general feelings of inadequacy.

Like Ferenczi in the prior lecture, Abraham brought sexuality into the picture by positing that traumatic experiences induced a regression to a state of infantile narcissism. "Trauma affects the sexuality of many people in the sense that it occasions a regressive change, which tends toward narcissism. Let me note that both of us [i.e., Ferenczi too] came to this view, which we expressed today, without having discussed it in the slightest beforehand."[71] To illustrate the role of sexuality, in particular as it pertained to the predisposition question, Abraham presented the case histories of two men: the first had survived multiple woundings and eagerly returned to the front each time without developing neurotic symptoms, while the second man, startled during combat one night, fell into a trench, and although he suffered no physical damage, immediately developed a condition of severe neurotic shaking. Why did one man become a neurotic after only a minor trauma and the other survive severe traumas without a neurosis? The answer, Abraham explained, lay in their differing psychic constitutions. Based on his clinical findings, he concluded that the majority of war neurotics were already before the war "labile men, particularly with respect to their sexuality."[72]

Like most other German psychiatrists and neurologists, Abraham thus stigmatized his neurotic patients and located their pathologies not in the traumatic experiences of war, but in internal, constitutional deficiencies. Such men, he charged, were perpetual underachievers who lacked the initiative and energy to meet the demands of life squarely. Abraham's approach, then, reinforced mainstream psychiatric judgments with the added dimension of sexuality; that is, neurotics' difficulty working and supporting themselves was mirrored by their sexual inadequacy. "Without exception their sexual activities became infrequent, their libidos inhibited through fixation; many of them were of weak potency already before the war or were potent only under certain conditions. Their attitude toward the female gender was more or less disturbed through partial fixation of the Libido in the developmental stage of narcissism."[73]

Using the categories and terms of psychoanalysis, Abraham valorized national unity and subordination to the national community in a manner akin to the doctors who designed and carried out active treatment and rationalized psychiatry. For Abraham, meeting the demands of war required sacrificing one's Ego to the community, or suppressing one's self-love or narcissism for the greater, national cause. And this feat could be achieved only by a constitutionally healthy man, one capable of transferring his love to external objects. The predisposed neurotic, on the other hand, was developmentally stunted. He was incapable of that crucial step and (pathologically) placed his own survival ahead of the collective good. When external conditions forced him to repress his self-love, a neurotic breakdown would most likely result.

Abraham also linked the predisposition to war neurosis with latent homosexuality. Both denoted a lack of male potency. Men with strong homosexual tendencies often used their wives as a kind of psychological crutch, or they changed sexual partners frequently in search of constant confirmation of their virility and sexual potency. The sudden absence of heterosexual sexual activity in army life placed such men in a vulnerable psychic state, in which a traumatic experience could easily throw them off kilter. To be sure, the all-male military milieu and the wide "cultural" gap between mobilized men and the women they left at home made the question of homosexuality particularly relevant during the war. Even Ferenczi complained of often powerful homosexual urges when he served at a garrison in the remote Hungarian town of Pápa.[74] (Freud had written in his 1905 *Essays on the Theory of Sexuality* of "contingent inverts," essentially heterosexual men who practiced homosexual sex when deprived of female company, as in prison or the army.) Yet, Abraham's assumption that homosexuals were more prone to war neurosis was at odds with most of the contemporary sexological literature on the topic. In an article on sexual questions in war, for example, one doctor conceded that homosexuals, not being bound to the family structure, were less loyal and dutiful toward the national community. However, he claimed that their "sense of adventure" and their natural passion for war (*Kriegslust*) made them excellent soldiers, ironically enough, often far superior to "whole men."[75]

Like Ferenczi, Abraham observed a regression into infantile narcissism in many war neurotics and spoke of a patient who regressed to the level of a two year old in the aftermath of a mine explosion. He also claimed to have observed cheerfulness, even celebratory atmospheres, in hospital wards for amputees, which also served to confirm the libidinal theory of neurosis. These men rejoice, he theorized, out of self-love and the erotic fetishization of their wounded bodies. Abraham described the behavior of four hospitalized men, each of whom had lost an eye in the same explosion:

> They jumped, danced, laughed in an exuberant state, somewhat like children who work themselves up into a joyous frenzy. Here too it is a matter of a regression to narcissism. These patients repress the fact that through mutilation they have experienced some degree of debasement [Entwertung], especially in the eyes of the female gender. What they lose in external love, they replace henceforth with self-love. The injured body part receives new importance as an erogenous zone.[76]

Then Abraham turned to the question of pensions and the common view that the wish for a pension explained the development and prolongation of neurotic symptoms in (physically or psychologically) wounded veterans. He asserted that a sexual mechanism, and not greed or indolence, was at work here too. Psychoanalysis gave new meanings to the notion of compensation. That these men were fighting for a pension to compensate for a missing finger or neurotic shaking was only an illusion. In reality, their need for compensation was to redress the psychological consequences of their wounding; that is, they sought pensions to compensate not for their measurable decline in earning power but for their subjective loss of object love. Reduced to a state of childlike narcissism, the wounded soldier lost his capacity to devote himself to anything but himself and became a slave of his avarice and self-serving impulses.

Abraham concluded that psychoanalysis could serve the Central Powers as a powerful therapeutic tool. Methods of active treatment had proven less effective than once thought. Their "cures" were of short duration, and they had other, undesired side effects. Despite the fact that he had only used a rudimentary form of psychoanalysis on a limited number of patients, Abraham conjectured that only psychoanalysis could attain a deeper, enduring cure because of all methods, it alone addressed the causes and structural basis of a neurosis.[77]

Ernst Simmel was the third and final speaker at the Budapest Congress. Simmel had only recently come to the attention of the psychoanalytic world. That February, never having met or corresponded with any of the leading psychoanalysts, he sent Freud his war neurosis monograph. Freud read it quickly and responded enthusiastically.[78] That Simmel based his work on Freud's early theories and relied on hypnosis, a technique Freud had discarded long before, was, Freud wrote, understandable given the wartime circumstances and the nature of his patient pool.[79] Freud emphatically recommended the book to Abraham and Ferenczi. As he wrote to Abraham, "This is the first time that a German physician, basing himself firmly and without patronizing condescension on psycho-analysis, speaks of its outstanding usefulness in the treatment of war neuroses, backs this with examples, and is also completely honest on the question of sexual etiology. . . . I think a year's training would make a good analyst of him. His attitude is correct."[80] Several months later, Freud decided to award Simmel the first of a new annual prize for the best book in psychoanalysis. And in September 1918 Simmel stood in Budapest before the assembled analysts and presented the day's third lecture.[81]

Simmel began his presentation by stating that the study of war neurosis had proven Freud's theories correct in that these conditions represented the physical conversion of psychological processes. But then his lecture diverged significantly from the two that preceded it. While Abraham and Ferenczi had stressed the relevance of sexual factors to every kind of traumatic neurosis, Simmel took a more equivocal position on the sexual question. As he bluntly stated, "the unconscious meaning of war neurotic symptoms is . . . mostly not of a sexual nature, rather therein are revealed all the war related effects of shock, fear, anger, bound up with ideas which correspond to the immediate experience of war."[82]

Simmel did not completely discount the etiological relevance of sexual factors; they contributed significantly to an individual's disposition or susceptibility to neurosis. Childhood sexual trauma, he pointed out, was revealed to lie at the basis of the neuroses of several soldiers whom he had treated. In other cases, an Oedipal father resentment or an unhealthy mother attachment had rendered men unable to hold up under rigorous military discipline. Furthermore, for Simmel, war neurosis generally arose out of a conflict between the drive to self-preservation and a soldier's sense of duty.[83] The drive to (both physical and mental) self-preservation was the most primitive human instinct, and, Simmel asserted, it was naturally deeply bound up with sexuality.

Not surprisingly, Simmel's equivocation on the sexual question generated some unease among the psychoanalysts, and Freud and Abraham came to regard his contributions with a degree of skepticism. A month after the Congress Abraham cautioned that Simmel's views did not conform to current psychoanalytic thinking. In particular, Simmel's treatment of the sexual question tempered Abraham's enthusiasm toward him as a potential colleague. As Abraham wrote to Freud: "On the return journey from Budapest, and also more recently in Berlin, I have become more closely acquainted with Simmel. He has not yet in any way moved beyond the Breuer-Freud point of view, has strong resistances against sexuality which he is not yet clearly aware of, and, unfortunately, actually stressed at the Berlin meeting that according to his own experience, sexuality does not play an essential part, either in war neurosis or in analytic treatment. Perhaps he will develop further, but we must not overrate him."[84]

That Simmel seemed to show more sympathy for war neurotics than Abraham and Ferenczi may reflect the way he spent the war. His heavy involvement in day-to-day treatment dictated, perhaps, his greater attention to the distressing conditions his patients endured and was less conducive to the more abstract speculations of the two analysts. Indeed, the personality type that Abraham and Ferenczi pathologized as narcissistic, Simmel described in terms of the normal instinct for self-preservation. Rather than addressing neurotics' lack of virility or constitutional weaknesses, Simmel emphasized the manifold traumas of the war experience. He thus stressed the exogenous over the endogenous, recent traumatic events over early developmental miscues. "One must have experienced the events of the war oneself or their recapitulation in analytic-cathartic hypnosis, in order to understand the assaults on the mind thrust on a man, who, after multiple woundings, must return to the field, who is apart from his family for important occasions for the unforeseeable future, who sees himself thrust beyond help into the ghastly terror of a tank or the approach of an enemy gas attack. . . ."[85]

In his address Simmel described war neurosis as the mind's method of protecting itself from the effects of these traumatic states. A neurosis acted as an internal defense, shielding the mind from greater psychic dangers like psychosis; the relative rarity of war psychoses, in turn, could only be explained by the frequency of neuroses. In a neurosis, Simmel theorized, the personality splits under the cumulative impact of the psychological effects of military discipline and prolonged mental and physical exhaustion, coupled with abnormally high demands.[86] The feeling of being no more than an expendable component of a larger body, the eclipsing of subjectivity and individuality and the necessity of submitting oneself to authority—the very conditions so many psychiatrists celebrated in 1914—were psychologically dangerous for Simmel in that they undermined the soldier's Ego and diminished his ability to deal with trauma.[87]

Traumatic events or a posttraumatic loss of consciousness worked to blot out (*auslöschen*) the Ego and open up the gate to the unconscious. The conversion of the psychic into the physical represented the mind's method of self-defense against its overtaxing; experiences too terrible to be worked through consciously were processed by the unconscious and converted into physical symptoms. This also accounted for the common observation that officers showed different, "less crude" symptoms than regular soldiers. Raised above "the mass" and presumably better educated, officers had a greater capacity to sublimate traumatic experiences. Since the onset of symptoms represented the mind's attempt to discharge affect, for Simmel, "the [outbreak of the] illness is . . . simultaneously the beginning of the healing process."[88] The same could be said of a patient's dream life, and Simmel viewed his patients' dreams also as attempts at self-healing.[89]

These unconscious processes, Simmel found, revealed themselves in hypnosis: "In hypnosis the soldier recounts or experiences again everything which he took in only unconsciously while in this condition. We learn of agonizing pains, which in the state of blockage never came into conscious apperception. In such hypnoses we see his fear, [we see] his terror work free, his anger rise up, [all of] which in the moment of excitation were instantly sent into the unconscious."[90] To illustrate this point, Simmel provided the example of a soldier with a functional paralysis of the arm. In a conscious state, despite all attempts to enlighten him, the soldier believed that he could not move his arm. But under hypnosis, he recovered the repressed, traumatic events. The soldier had, it seems, lost his senses during artillery fire. The impact of shrapnel had thrust his arm behind him, causing a sudden fear that it had been torn off. That fear entered the man's unconscious and through autosuggestion, a common mechanism in posttraumatic neuroses of this sort, the idea was planted that the arm was indeed gone.

Despite any disagreements between Simmel and the other speakers, the Budapest Congress, which Freud called a "beautiful success," had its desired effect.[91] Freud wrote that he was "swimming in satisfaction" with the results, which would protect his life's work, and Ferenczi noted that the psychoanalysts had "greatly impressed the Budapest physicians."[92] Not long after the Congress, Hungarian officials endorsed the idea of creating special psychoanalytic war hospitals and planned to open the first one in Budapest, a thirty-bed experimental clinic under Ferenczi's direction.[93] The German and Austrian administrations seemed likely to follow suit.

Psychoanalysis beyond Trauma: Freud and the Death Drive

Just weeks after the Budapest Congress, the Central Powers collapsed both militarily and politically. The war's end, of course, obviated the planned psychoanalytic stations and abruptly ended the cooperation between psychoanalysts and the Central European states.[94] Three weeks after the Congress, aware that the psychoanalytic stations would not come about, Abraham sought to downplay this missed opportunity. As he wrote in a letter to Freud, "I do not like the idea that psycho-analysis should suddenly become fashionable because of purely practical considerations. We would rapidly have acquired a number of colleagues who would merely have paid lip service and would afterwards have called themselves psychoanalysts. Our condition as outsiders will continue for the time being."[95] And, as Freud opined to Ferenczi six days after the cease-fire, this was a case of bad luck; the war's cessation would put an abrupt end to official interest in psychoanalysis and push Freud's science back to its marginal status. Indeed, in the aftermath of the cease-fire and motivated also by the anti-Semitism unleashed in the Hungarian counterrevolution, Freud and his followers withdrew from political affairs and retreated even deeper into psychoanalysis.[96] Freud, furthermore, passed up a chance to condemn mainstream psychiatry when his rival, psychiatry professor Julius von Wagner-Jauregg, was investigated for therapeutic brutality and incompetence by an Austrian commission shortly after the war.

Yet, the war's end seemed to herald a greater acceptance of psychoanalysis and the wider proliferation of its teachings among both doctors and lay intellectuals. Immediately after the war in Hungary, Béla Kun's Hungarian Soviet appointed Ferenczi to the world's first professorship in psychoanalysis.[97] (However, the position was swept away with the counterrevolutionary tides that soon overtook the rump Hungarian state.) Shortly thereafter, the psychoanalytic movement attained a more secure foothold on German soil with the founding of the International Psychoanalytic Press in 1919 and the opening of the Berlin Psychoanalytic Polyclinic and Institute in 1920.[98] Writing just months after the Treaty of Versailles was signed, Freud credited the war, and specifically the war neuroses, with bringing mainstream medicine closer to the tenets of psychoanalysis:

> Medical men who had hitherto held back from any approach to psychoanalytic theories were brought into closer contact with them when, in the course of their duties as army doctors, they were obliged to deal with war neuroses. . . . Some of the factors which psychoanalysis had recognized and described long before as being at work in peace-time neuroses—the psychogenic origin of the symptoms, the importance of *unconscious* instinctual impulses, the part played in dealing with mental conflicts by the primary gain from being ill ("the flight into illness")—were observed to be present equally in the war neuroses and were accepted almost universally.[99]

But Freud also recognized the ways in which the war experience called attention to and even deepened the differences between psychoanalysis and contemporary psychiatry. "There is," he added, "no need to consider that these approaches to psychoanalysis imply any reconciliation or any appeasement of opposition."[100] He and his colleagues, furthermore, retained their marginal position. They opted out of the debates that engaged most German psychiatrists and neurologists; they did not attend the Munich Congress or many other significant wartime meetings; and they did not participate in the traumatic neurosis controversy, with the exception of the occasional, scathing attack on Oppenheim. Although many of the analysts themselves, like their subsequent historians, focused on the ways in which the war narrowed the gap between Freud and German psychiatry, this narrowing has certainly been exaggerated, as has, conversely, the original rejection of Freudian ideas by mainstream medicine.

Both Freud and Ferenczi, for example, strongly implied that in the prewar years they alone had acknowledged the role of the psychological in nervous and mental illness. A more balanced view, however, would locate Freud within a broader shift, a more general psychological turn among the leaders of late-nineteenth-century mental medicine. As such, Freud's early ideas did not represent as dramatic a departure from mainstream medicine as he claimed. Other than a handful of vocal critics, including Alfred Hoche and Emil Kraepelin, many psychiatrists and neurologists viewed Freud's early writing on hysteria as a viable model for the interaction of the mind and body—it was his later emphasis on sexuality that most considered to be excessive if not perverse.[101] Even Robert Gaupp, an emerging leader of orthodox German psychiatry, wrote in a 1911 article that he accepted much of Freudian theory. Claiming that he agreed for the most part with Freud's and Breuer's 1895 *Studies on Hysteria,* in which hysterical symptoms were explained in terms of the conversion of unprocessed affect, Gaupp noted that, in addition to other feats, the two Viennese doctors had "convincingly clarified the manner by which mental activity expresses itself in strange physical symptoms."[102]

Gaupp's 1911 position reflected commonly held views that lay somewhere between Freud's supporters and his adamant critics. Even Hoche—Germany's most venomous opponent of psychoanalysis, who at a 1912 meeting of the German Association for Psychiatry, blasted the movement as "valueless except as a cultural historical episode"—did not stand as far from Freud as he may have liked to believe, sharing at least the belief in the ideogenic basis of nervous disease.[103] And Robert Sommer, a far more moderate critic of psychoanalysis, thought that the technique could be valuable on patients who inhabited the sexually degenerate milieu of the big cities.[104]

Thus, Freud's early model of hysteria can be viewed as one element of a broader transformation in German mental medicine. During the war, many mainstream doctors described neurotic conditions in terms similar to those used by Breuer and Freud in 1895, invoking such concepts as the "flight into illness" and the "conversion of affect." Perhaps this owed to the unacknowledged, "passive penetration" of Freud's ideas into the general medical profession; on the other hand, it may have resulted from broader trends that encompassed both positions.[105] In either case, significant differences still obtained; for example, doctors such as Bonhoeffer, Nonne, and Stier generally ascribed primary etiological significance to the wish for a pension or the desire to escape service, factors that Freud considered to be only the secondary gain.

But Freud's post-1900 writings, in which he focused more intensely on patient resistances and the stages of sexual development, found little acceptance—

or even acknowledgment—among university psychiatrists and neurologists in Germany. And the war did little to alter this; while it may have increased the exposure of psychoanalytic ideas, it scarcely improved their reception among mental health leaders. In fact, few mainstream doctors subscribed at all to theories of the unconscious. Convinced that war hysteria was essentially a problem of will and wishes, doctors like Nonne trumpeted the downfall of Freud and psychosexual theories because of the war neurosis experience.[106] And psychoanalysts themselves remained somewhat hesitant to grapple with the posttraumatic neuroses and never found satisfying results. Indeed, in his first major postwar text, *Beyond the Pleasure Principle,* Freud referred to traumatic neurosis as a "dark and dismal subject" and noted that "no complete explanation has yet been reached either of war neuroses or of the traumatic neuroses of peace."[107]

Many of the doctors discussed above, including Sauer, Stern, and Frank, called their methods "psychoanalytic" even though they were based on the 1893 to 1895 theories, ideas that Freud had essentially dismissed years before the war. And Freud and his followers paid little, if any, attention to these other doctors, viewing Simmel as the first German doctor to publish on the psychoanalytic treatment of war neurotics. But even Simmel equivocated on the sexual question and devoted little attention to it, which caused Freud and Abraham to approach him with a degree of skepticism and caution. However, through Simmel's therapeutic success, the psychoanalysts saw an opportunity to better their position and thus overlooked their differences with the Berlin physician and used him to court the state's interest.

Although psychoanalytic ideas seem to have had only a minor impact on German psychiatry and neurology, evidence suggests that the war greatly furthered their diffusion elsewhere.[108] In Britain, where the orthodox psychiatric profession had paid significantly less attention to hysteria before the war—and, in contrast to French and German medicine, had scarcely recognized the possibility of male hysteria—the one medical branch that concerned itself with the disease was gynecology, which as late as the early twentieth century still located the disease source in female anatomy.[109] Thus, one historian has argued, the onset of the war neurosis problem created a vacuum, which at once discredited prior theories of hysteria and overturned the Victorian attitudes they reflected, making room for psychoanalytic and psychosexual views within mainstream neurology and psychiatry.[110] And in the United States, where Simmel and numerous other psychoanalysts fled between the wars, Freudian ideas—carrying the prestige of Central European science—deeply influenced the psychiatric profession and greatly informed military psychiatry in World War II.[111]

In World War I Germany, in contrast, only a handful of psychiatrists and neurologists showed interest in either psychoanalysis or the various sexological studies that were conducted. German psychiatrists continually emphasized issues of will, work, and psychic constitution and essentially ignored questions of sex and gender identity.[112] Those physicians and eugenicists who were concerned with sex approached it primarily as a public health matter, seeking ways to prevent the spread of sexually transmitted diseases, alternately through preaching abstinence (or marital fidelity) or by confining prostitution to supervised brothels.[113] In Britain, on the other hand, as exemplified by the celebrated clinical encounter between the noted neurologist and anthropologist W. H. R. Rivers and the poet Siegfried Sassoon, questions of masculinity and sexual identity were often accepted as integral to the hysteric's condition and mental state.[114]

Whether or not the war changed the mainstream medical reception of psychoanalysis, war events certainly changed psychoanalytic thought itself. As Louise Hoffman has argued, the war experience revolutionized psychoanalysis; it forced Freud and his followers to confront harsh social realities and helped reorient Freudian thought along new axes, leading to a fuller development of ego psychology and a new attention to social circumstances.[115]

The complex, often contradictory story of psychoanalysis in World War I also reflects Freud's ongoing difficulties with the concept of trauma and his shifting strategies for dealing with posttraumatic pathologies within a psychoanalytic framework.[116] Theorizing trauma—and indeed coming to terms with the war's enormous impact on the world and on his own life—led Freud to introduce new categories in his first major postwar work. And through a discussion of war trauma—and specifically the nightmares in which subjects repetitiously return to the scene of a traumatic event—Freud arrived at the repetition compulsion and the death drive, key categories in subsequent elaborations of psychoanalytic theory.

Significantly, by focusing not on the traumatic moment itself but rather on the memory of that moment as the source of posttraumatic pathology, Freud effectively relativized trauma. For Freud, a neurosis was caused not directly by a traumatic event—a rupture of the mind's protective shield—but by a subject's subsequent recollections of the event and the emotions it unleashed. This served to "interiorize" trauma, making it a function of the patient's mind rather than the properties of the accident experience, which then rendered the accident itself essentially irrelevant and called attention only to the subject's way of experiencing, processing, and remembering (or fantasizing of) it. While these thoughts might sound more nuanced and subtle than anything Nonne wrote during the war, they actually reinforced mainstream psychiatric ideas by undermining the (pathological and economic) value of traumatic events and stressing the hysterical predisposition, even if that predisposition was the result of developmental rather than congenital factors. In the end, neither Freud's theories nor Simmel's treatments effectively challenged the assumptions and approaches that prevailed in mainstream psychiatric circles.

PART III

Aftermath
*Hysteria, Trauma,
Memory*

CHAPTER 7

Dictatorship of the Psychopaths
Psychiatrists and Patients through Defeat and Revolution

> One day the authorities will wake up and realize what a great social danger the war hysterics represent.
>
> ERNST RITTERSHAUS, "Zur Frage der Kriegshysterie"

> The psychopaths are always around. In calm times we study them, but in times of upheaval, they rule over us.
>
> ERNST KRETSCHMER, *Gestalten und Gedanken*

EVEN AS FREUD and his followers were touting the merits of psychoanalysis before military authorities in Budapest, the German war effort was beginning to unravel. After the *Reichswehr's* desperate spring offensive was halted in the west, its troops' retreat was dissolving into chaos. Morale among German men was declining markedly as it became increasingly clear that further military action was pointless. Old social fissures, temporarily suppressed at the war's beginning, resurfaced with a new intensity; just weeks after the Budapest Congress naval mutiny catalyzed the outbreak of revolution, leading to the Kaiser's abdication and the rapid dissolution of the imperial state.

In the context of military collapse and open social and political conflict, the male hysteria problem entered a new phase. The diagnosis began to take on new connotations, and political and social change had a tremendous impact on psychiatric practice. Because active treatment depended on suggestion and subordination, its success was linked to the morale of—and relationships between—soldier-patients and doctors. Furthermore, growing patient discontent with brusque psychiatrists and painful treatments was finding an eager audience in a more politicized press and public. As a result, complaints against doctors received greater publicity, and psychiatrists—even active treatment as a whole—came under scrutiny by the lay public and political leaders, culminating in a remarkable parliamentary debate in June 1918.

Always inherently political, war psychiatry—and indeed the whole trauma question—became explicitly and sharply politicized amid military defeat and revolution. Increasingly the object of patient resistance and recalcitrance toward the end of the war, psychiatrists became targets of revolutionary furor in November 1918, in some cases, literally having to run for their lives from bands of angry soldiers. This experience and their old political allegiances drew most psychiatrists into stalwart opposition to the revolutionary events that toppled the old order and threatened their power and status. Karl Bonhoeffer, for example, denounced the Revolution as a dictatorship not of the proletariat but of "the psychopaths."[1] Diagnosing a national nervous collapse, doctors used the language of psychiatry to describe political events and to pathologize revolutionary actors, equating war hysteria with political radicalism, unpatriotic behavior, and biological inferiority. Their writings, ultimately, helped shape an alternative memory of war and trauma, a narrative in which psychiatrists displaced patient suffering and construed themselves as the war's true victims.

Life against Medicine: Active Treatment on Trial

"Even in times of peace, medicine was, sadly, powerless against death. But today to a much greater extent, life is powerless against medicine."[2] The critic Alfred Polgar penned this radical critique of military medicine at the height of the war. "How have doctors," he asked, "whom war has empowered, exercised their power? . . . How have they fulfilled their role of determining the fates of their fellow-men? How have they avoided the danger of becoming brutal, cruel, derisive, conniving? . . . this will be decided on the day when the judges will be judged and the doctors will be 'examined.'"[3]

Polgar's critique of military medicine was part of a broader attack on military, political, and medical authority that began to emerge in the middle of the war. The fleeting, if not merely illusory national unity achieved around mobilization in the summer of 1914 was by then a distant memory as Germans continued to suffer under the effects of the grueling war. Furthermore, by 1917 old social and political divisions reentered the spotlight—strike actions, starting in the spring of 1916, soon turned into outright opposition to the war effort. As the Social Democrats split over their support for the war, and the far right wing pressed for annexations in the east, economic pressure from the British blockade was increasingly taking its toll on domestic life.[4] In addition, new sources of tension emerged during the war, born of the experiential gaps based on gender, generation, and rank, which came to haunt Germany's political culture in the war's later phases and beyond.[5]

The clinical encounters between doctors and patients were far from immune from these external changes because the psychiatrist-patient relationship was embedded in surrounding social and political circumstances. Medical power and control were considered necessary for active treatment and derived, in part, from doctors' superiority in rank and status. Thus, political and social conflict almost inevitably crept into the treatment room. As representatives of the war-making state and purveyors of frightening cures, psychiatrists became a target of both concerted left-wing opposition and spontaneous patient outbursts. Psychiatric leaders, in turn, fought hard to preserve their profession's tenuous status and reputation amid these attacks and the broader political and social changes at hand.

Soon after the Munich Congress of September 1916, health officials had called for a "more vigorous" approach to the war neurosis problem to reverse the rising tide of nervous patients.[6] The new, aggressive methods were, by military and medical standards, very successful and resulted in stunning therapeutic breakthroughs. Soon, however, the new vigor gave rise to vociferous criticism, which was amplified in the spring and summer of 1918, a time marked by plummeting morale among soldiers amid news of Entente advances and the mass surrender of German troops. The strict discipline and harsh treatment, which many doctors deemed essential to active treatment, encountered increasing resistance and opposition both within and outside the neurosis stations. Rumors had spread about long-term damage and even deaths resulting from the Kaufmann cure, and new patients began steadfastly to resist its application.[7]

Other practitioners attributed growing patient intransigence to a "smear campaign against psychiatrists," a kind of psychiatric "witch-hunt," fed by rumors, rabble-rousing speeches, and newspaper articles that precipitously attacked active treatment. In a spring 1918 lecture, Arthur Schüller, a Vienna neurologist, warned that this popular outcry would only worsen matters by forcing doctors to refrain from painful but therapeutically necessary measures, which was certainly not in the best interest of the neurotics.[8]

Schüller was convinced that popular criticism of the medical profession reflected nothing more than lay ignorance of the neuroses and their treatment. While all other areas of medicine had been well served by the public's interest and philanthropy, he noted, only "the difficult job of the nerve doctor encounters a lack of public understanding, which inspires mistrust and antipathy toward its achievements."[9] As a response Schüller called for a campaign of popular enlightenment to salvage the reputation of his profession and prevent the treatment of the nervously ill from "falling into the hands of the quacks."[10] Indeed, their role as guardians of national strength and collective mental health required that psychiatrists and neurologists have the nation's respect and faith.

The treatment of war neurotics, which at first seemed to solve psychiatry's crisis, had begun to provoke widespread challenges to psychiatric authority and competence, which were starting to undo the profession's fragile wartime gains. When Gaupp lectured in Stuttgart in April 1917, he remarked that he felt like "a defendant, filled with concern for the honor and appearance of the medical profession and obligated to justify to the public what I and numerous other nerve doctors accomplish in our professional work."[11] Gaupp deftly deflected responsibility for these complaints from doctors onto their patients. As Hoche had done decades before, Gaupp blamed Germany's accident pension legislation for creating undesirable, ungrateful patients, men who were simply seeking pensions and pity and had no interest in rehabilitation. As a consequence of these laws, Gaupp bemoaned, "many a soldier believes that he has the right to a military pension, because he was out there and 'held his head up.' Merely for fulfilling their duty to the Fatherland, they demand a reward, which they seek to force through numerous unverifiable complaints."[12]

Not only had patients begun to resist particular treatments and procedures, but they (or their relatives) also began to take complaints to their political representatives. Around the time of Gaupp's lecture, this discontent became the subject of parliamentary debate throughout Germany. When the Bavarian Diet took up the issue of war hysteria and its treatment in 1917, an SPD delegate from Munich reported complaints that "particular doctors regard [war neurotics] as swindlers and simulators which they express with words that it is astonishing to hear used at all by a learned man, a doctor."[13] Other deputies charged that doctors approached neurotic patients with too little sympathy or understanding. Similar critiques were voiced in the Baden and Württemberg Houses over the course of 1917 and 1918.[14]

In the summer of 1918 these concerns made it to the *Reichstag,* where several deputies took issue with active treatment and psychiatric pension practices. The first to speak out on the issue was the Center Party deputy and future chancellor Joseph Karl Wirth, who was concerned that the atmosphere in the neurosis stations fostered not mercy but rather harsh discipline. On June 11, 1918, Wirth stood before the assembly and read one patient's complaints. The man had been injured in the spine and discharged with a pension and then reenlisted and subjected to electrotherapy in the Billingen hospital station in the Black Forest. He had pretended that he felt better and willingly sacrificed his pension to escape the painful treatment procedure. To shouts of approval from the center and left, Wirth denounced such practices, proclaiming: "We want there to be a mild and merciful spirit in these hospital stations, and the doctors who work in them must refrain from any statements which could have a repellent effect on the misfortunate men who come in. . . . We must forbid greeting an arriving war invalid with the words: 'The state cannot pay your pension'—the German people can and will, and the doctors must refrain from any such utterances."[15]

Wirth revealed that several *Reichstag* deputies had already clashed with the government over these issues in private committee sessions, but he refrained from publicizing the contents of those meetings.[16] Furthermore, he was careful to dissociate himself from the more radical critiques that were to come from the left side of the chamber and claimed to speak from a humanitarian rather than a revolutionary perspective. Indeed, Wirth proposed no radical changes in either military-medical organization or pensioning policies; he limited his critique to the deficiencies of the hospital atmosphere and seemed more interested in the appearance of Germany's medical practitioners than in actual conditions in the treatment rooms.

Patient discontent was rapidly growing, Wirth observed, especially in Baden and Württemberg—the sites of the most developed psychiatric systems, where many complaints against individual doctors had been brought to the regions' political representatives. He beseeched medical officials from the War Ministry to provide a satisfactory corrective to this rising discontent, "so that our *Volk* can look upon the work of the doctors in these hospitals once again with amity and trust."[17] After a brief explication of the principles of suggestive therapy, Wirth noted that brusque behavior by neurosis station personnel threatened their otherwise miraculous results. As evidence of the shocking conditions in these hospitals, he claimed that none other than the Baden Minister of State had expressed outrage upon witnessing the application of these "tortures." Significantly, Wirth shrank from condemning active treatment on principle, ceding that question to medical authorities. His point was that the misapplication of these treatments would harm the reputation of German psychiatrists, which would thereby diminish their therapeutic effectiveness. When Social Democratic deputies enthusiastically cheered his words, Wirth silenced them caustically.[18] He also participated in the medical discourse of the miraculous, continually referring to active treatment as a "miracle cure" and demanded only that "when the men are brought in for electric treatment, the staff avoid all utterances, which may offend their religious sensibilities. Otherwise the brilliant successes are diminished. . . . We want the hospitals wiped clean of this nasty mood; then they can be good and effective."[19]

Wirth concluded his long oration by imploring Germany's military-medical authorities to act to protect the reputation of its doctors and neurosis stations: "Prevent what the leftists did in the committee and what has been publicized throughout Germany, that these stations deserve the name 'pension squeezers' or 'pension removal wards' [*Rentenentbindungsantalten*]: they should not be that, they should be a divine garden of mercy for philanthropy to the misfortunate, and even the religious should not have to fear entering these stations, even if the spirit which obtains there is not yet the spirit of science and the authentic German soul."

Later that same day, Georg Schöpflin, a Majority Social Democrat from Saxony, declared his agreement with much of Wirth's presentation, adding that electric current, starvation, and isolation in a dark room were not treatments that befit soldiers who had fought and risked their lives for the Fatherland. On the following day, General Georg Friedrich Wilhelm Schultzen, the commander of the army's sanitary services, appeared in the chamber to address a series of medical issues, chief among which was the treatment of war neurosis. Schultzen devoted much of his talk to refuting "the severe attacks of Herr Wirth." By publicizing patient complaints, Schultzen charged, Wirth further weakened doctors' standing. Schultzen's defense invoked the same principles that doctors such as Gaupp and Kaufmann used to justify electrotherapy to medical critics. He argued that the collective benefit of these treatments, their tremendous service to the national community, justified any individual suffering and made isolated cases of discontent inconsequential. Occasional complaints, he reasoned, even if justified, were statistically negligible and did not tarnish active treatment's wondrous utility:

> The general benefits which are achieved with this kind of treatment have been too seldom noted, while the individual complaints have come to the fore too often. Allow me to emphasize that we have treated at least 60 to 70,000 of these neurotics so far in our neurosis stations throughout Germany. What does it suggest if several hundred out of every thousand cases really have made such complaints, as it has been claimed here. Out of these 60 to 70,000 far more than ninety percent have been cured. . . . Gentlemen, in my opinion that is quite an achievement.[20]

Having ordered the full, nationwide implementation of active treatment in the preceding year, Schultzen continued to advocate aggressive, active methods over milder, ineffective treatments for the good of both the state and the patients themselves.[21] "I am of the conviction that it is far better when one returns the ability to work to such men, rather than discharging them with a pension so that they will end up running around the streets as shakers and beggars, inciting large-scale agitation and unrest."[22] Although many doctors had implicitly associated pension collection with a lack of patriotism, Schulzten in his *Reichstag* address made explicit the equation between uncured, pensioned neurotics and political agitators. His words add another dimension to medical views of work; namely, that steady work prevented radicalization and deterred political agitation. Active treatment, thus, became more than a psychiatric matter; it represented a way of saving Germany from the perils of revolution.

Schultzen conceded that cases of maltreatment and abuse occurred. He admitted to his *Reichstag* audience that active treatment looked dreadful, but he appealed to them to appreciate its successes and overlook its appearance for the good of the national community. He urged that critiques not be publicized further: Criticism of psychiatrists would only serve to weaken their standing, which in turn would diminish their ability to treat patients.

The *Reichstag* debate continued two days later when several more deputies from various parties spoke to the matter of medical abuses. The War Ministry responded by blaming relatives for riling patients up, which made necessary the application of aggressive, even punitive medical measures. By 1918, then, relatives were seen not only as detrimental to patient prognosis but as an explicit political threat.

Georg Davidsohn, a Majority SPD deputy from Silesian Liegnitz, was the final speaker to address the *Reichstag* on the war neurosis issue. Davidsohn, who had served as a front soldier from May 1915 until he was wounded in August

1916, was instrumental in organizing Germany's Association for War Wounded (*Reichsbund der Kriegsbeschädigten*). In his *Reichstag* speech he expressed a seldom-voiced concern with the psychological effects of active treatment: "Herr *Generalarzt* Dr. Schultzen can say all he wants that in the institutions which use electric current—and earlier even used confinement in the dark and starvation cures—things are done in a manner that conforms to exact science, but he cannot do away with the fact that the majority of all the soldiers who are subjected to this treatment leave the institution terribly bitter . . . that they ultimately take an enormous amount of bitterness, rage and hate with them, from this treatment into their families."[23]

But like the other speakers, Davidsohn did not mount a direct challenge to medical authority. As a layperson, he yielded to medical expertise and accepted that active treatment was for the good of the patients. His objection was thus neither to active treatment itself nor to its goal of restoring fitness for working; rather he protested that its practitioners lacked a sufficient awareness of their patients' psyches. Despite the fact that many methods of suggestive treatment were based on deception and used patient ignorance to therapeutic advantage, Davidsohn demanded that patients be informed about the procedure so that they would know what to expect and could be assured that it involved "a scientifically tested method" for their own good. "Those who do not know this, since in effect the greater part of this treatment ends with the result that the man receives no more pension, say to themselves, 'I was treated this way so that my pension could be taken away'—and they cannot be blamed for having the simplistic view of a lay person. They see only the 'post' and don't know the 'propter' and say, 'I was forced into this, that is outrageous, terrible, and anyway I will fall prey to the nervous attacks and shaking once again.'"[24]

Davidsohn described a case in which a soldier was forced to sit blindfolded on a chair and endure an unspecified procedure, which was so unpleasant that it led him to contemplate suicide. He pleaded that Schultzen return to the *Reichstag* and explain how such a thing could happen. But like Wirth, Davidsohn, and the other deputies who criticized active treatment in the *Reichstag,* only objected to its appearance and the manner in which it was often carried out. The appropriateness of using the collection of painful and curious methods of active treatment on psychologically debilitated patients went unquestioned. Indeed, psychiatric matters were immune from criticism as long as they were considered "scientifically approved." Occasionally delegates paid lip service to the fact that war neurotics, having risked their lives for the nation, deserved better medical treatment, but psychiatrists and neurologists were spared outright condemnation. Lay politicians could not conceive of challenging the nation's doctors, who were armed with the legitimacy of science and whose dedication to the national good went unquestioned. Most political critics—at least before November 1918—shared the limited goal expressed by Davidsohn in his concluding statement, in which he demanded that "this system be further improved so that individuals come in and out of it at least with other ideas about the intentions of this frightful treatment."[25]

The Patients Protest

Complaints against active treatment were also dealt with by juridical authorities from the Deputy General Commands, which handled accusations against individual doctors. No less than Emil Kraepelin, Germany's preeminent psychiatrist and a consulting doctor for the First Bavarian Army Corps in Munich, was accused of mistreating at least one neurosis patient. A Captain Müller, whom Kraepelin examined in the Munich psychiatric observation station in May 1918, complained that his rights and dignity had been violated by the psychiatrist, who allegedly denied that he was ill and refused to show him his chart.[26] The charge was not taken seriously, and Kraepelin's actions were deemed appropriate.

Likewise, an NCO named Gustav Meyer, who was treated at a Munich reserve station for hysterical disorders of gait and psychosomatic pains, complained to the Deputy General Command in May 1918 that he had been placed in a tiny room where the sole window was covered by an iron grate and that he was denied emergency dental care and the company of other patients.[27] To the former complaint, officials responded that the measure was taken to prevent him from escaping; the other charges were denied and the dental care was considered unnecessary. In light of Meyer's "nervous condition" officials "generously" demurred from pressing charges against him for insubordination.

This situation was more serious in Württemberg, where two doctors, Martin Freund and Gustav Liebermeister, became the objects of vociferous patient complaint and ultimately military investigation. On March 13, 1918, Albert Pflüger, a deputy in the Württemberg Diet, appealed to the Deputy Command of the Thirteenth Army Corps in Stuttgart on behalf of a patient in the Bad Rötenbach neurosis station. The patient, one Philipp Kussmaul, who had served with Field Artillery Regiment 13, had been buried in the rubble of an explosion a year and a half before. When he emerged, he suffered from a hysterical inability to walk. Months later, Kussmaul found himself in the Rötenbach station, where, according to his wife, he was severely mistreated. As Frau Kussmaul reported to Pflüger, her husband was subjected to a five-hour treatment session that he had to endure unclothed. In addition, she claimed that he was underfed, bound around the feet and confined to his bed, placed in solitary confinement, and prevented from writing to her. Frau Kussmaul feared that "if this treatment goes on much longer, there won't be anything left of [my] husband."[28]

Frau Kussmaul's complaint was forwarded to the Sanitary Department of the Thirteenth Corps which, in turn, solicited a reply from Martin Freund, the physician in charge of the Rötenbach station. Freund countered that many of the complaints were inaccurate and that Pflüger's account was inherently one-sided because it was based exclusively on the patient's perspective. And Freund was quick to point out several scientific inaccuracies in Pflüger's letter.[29] According to Freund's account, on March 7, 1918, Kussmaul was treated with electric current and exercises meant to strengthen and train his muscles. After some six hours of treatment, he had learned how to stand when held in place, but as soon as he tried to walk on his own, Kussmaul fell back into his abnormal gait. Freund then isolated him so that he would not negatively influence the station environment. Since the electric current did not seem to be working, Freund had the patient's legs bound for two hours every day, a practice that, he claimed, usually worked with psychogenic paralysis of this type by creating the illusion of a somatic effect.[30] He denied holding back Kussmaul's mail and noted that rather than submitting a postcard to the hospital administration to be stamped and forwarded, Kussmaul mailed it himself secretly, an act of insubordination for which he could have been punished. Moreover, Freund averred, this patient had received his meals just as all the others, so the rumors about his starvation were unfounded.

Freund concluded his testimony by defending his use of electric current, claiming that his own technique was "incomparably milder" than what was done at Hornberg, Baden's model station.[31] The problem, Freund maintained, was that doctors did not have enough authority and influence over their patients, which impaired their ability to cure.[32] The result of Kussmaul's complaints are not clear, but it is highly unlikely that Freund's actions were found to be a violation of acceptable conduct, and he continued to direct the Rötenbach station until the end of the war.

Gustav Liebermeister, director of the Ulm neurosis station, likewise came under attack for "acting against regulations," and several representatives from the Württemberg Diet appealed to military juridical authorities to investigate. Letters from at least four deputies complained about Liebermeister's conduct and the painful method of electrotherapy he used. One letter implied that Liebermeister "experimented" on his patients; others charged that he cursed at them, calling them pigs, parasites, and malingerers; another maintained that German soldiers were treated better in French prison camps than in their own neurosis stations. A fourth letter appealed on behalf of an NCO named Leist. Leist had written in February 1917 that Liebermeister seemed to want to kill him, although he later retracted the charge.[33]

The military court turned to Gaupp for testimony about Liebermeister's character and conduct, and Gaupp used the opportunity to defend not only the reputation of a close colleague but the practice of active treatment as a whole. Like his 1917 Stuttgart speech, Gaupp's reply in the Liebermeister affair shifted the blame for alleged instances of medical brutality onto the patients. He flatly denied the charges against Liebermeister by attacking the credibility of the ac-

cusers. Gaupp emphasized that Liebermeister was a competent and humane
doctor, but then he went a step further. Even as he denied that Liebermeister
dealt with patients in an inappropriate manner, he tried to show how the patients probably deserved harsh treatment anyway:

> If it were true that he [Liebermeister] called the patients in his ward "bastards"
> and "swine," then I would condemn it, but not if it could be shown that among
> those were simulators and agitators. The mere evidence that he ever said such a
> thing *to his patients* has never been provided, rather the opposite has been
> shown to be the case. In view of my knowledge of the personality of the ac-
> cused, I completely deny that he used such profanities . . . with his patients.
> Now it is, of course, completely different if he once privately said to his assis-
> tants—under the influence of the anger from the bad wills of several hysterics or
> simulators he confronted—that they [the patients] were a band of swine.[34]

Gaupp acknowledged that moral judgment usually had no place in medical
practice, but hysteria required different standards because it was often combined with—and was hard to disentangle from—deceitfulness and "moral inferiority."

> To understand how a doctor could come to such conclusions about "patients"
> . . . you must know how often with the hysterics, the illness goes hand in hand
> with moral inferiority, with lying, with agitation and slander, how shamelessly
> we psychiatrists are lied to, not infrequently, unfortunately; how strongly pitiful
> selfishness, which exploits the war to make a profit, can arise, and how difficult
> a struggle it is for the doctor who, aware of his social responsibility, has to deal
> with such dishonest men.[35]

By placing the word *patients* in quotation marks, Gaupp effectively undermined
the status of hysteria as a legitimate disease and further blurred the distinction
between hysterical disorders and moral shortcomings.

Gaupp contrasted war hysterics, safely harbored in hospitals, with men who
remained in the field and continually risked their lives for the national cause.
He asked: "Should a man who—completely healthy physically—has fled into
hysterical symptoms and complaints out of weakness of will, cowardice or even
avarice, receive a reward? Shall it come to the point when the morally healthy
and self-sacrificing are out there bleeding to death, while the weak-nerved and
egoistic hide behind headaches, dizziness, shaking and complaints and direct
their perverse energies to securing and keeping the highest military pension possible?"[36] On another occasion Gaupp bemoaned that "the best sons of our *Volk*
have fallen, while the weak and sickly survive. Never before in the history of
the world has a war brought such negative selection. . . . The mentally deficient
are promptly removed from the exhaustion and horror of the war . . . The more
this occurs, and naturally it must occur, all the more frightfully is the burden of
fighting and the inevitability of death forced on the healthy and fully vigorous
part of masculine Germany."[37]

When soldiers broke down, then, they not only drained the economy but they left the fighting to healthier and stronger men, men who were more valuable to the national community. In view of these circumstances, Gaupp implied that any truth to the charges against Liebermeister would actually reflect positively on the doctor; that is, the frustration that his overzealousness betrayed demonstrated Liebermeister's enthusiasm for treating these patients and restoring them to the service of the Fatherland. Hence, Liebermeister's truculence demonstrated his extraordinary dedication to the national cause: "The stronger the patriotism and social conscience of a doctor today," wrote Gaupp, "all the more *self-sacrificing* and *energetic* he will be in curing hysterics and in the battle against the obsession with pensions, which makes social parasites and miserable hypochondriacs out of physically healthy young men. Hence the zeal of the accused in the practice of his treatment is . . . a sign of the moral gravity with which he approaches his responsibility, and he has earned the gratitude of the Fatherland as well as those patients whom he has cured."[38]

Gaupp also noted that many routine medical procedures, such as pulling teeth, performing surgery, and administering injections, were similarly painful and yet only psychiatric interventions were subjected to complaints and legal review. He asked why a "dignified doctor" who only wanted to cure his patients by means of a treatment that happened to be painful should arouse so many complaints. The answer lay in the quality of the patient pool: "These patients *do not want to be cured*," he charged, "or due to their moral inferiority, they lack the moral strength to achieve health by withstanding a little pain."[39] Many stubbornly clung to their symptoms in a desperate attempt to hold onto their pension claims or to avoid combat. To refrain from active treatment because of patient protest, then, would mean caving in to the "whining" complaints of hysterics and thereby "decimating the military and breeding an army of pension collectors, who will become worthless members of the body populace."[40]

In Gaupp's view, hysterical patients, ultimately, were duplicitous, untrustworthy witnesses. Their desire not to be cured made them see doctors as their enemies; their preference for the safety and financial gain guaranteed by hysterical symptoms made them view active treatment as a threat that could remove their symptoms and hence their potential pensions. In this vein, Gaupp wrote of a patient who suffered from hysterical shaking for many months. When the symptoms were quickly removed in a single hypnotic session, the man flew into a rage over his undesired curing. As Nonne wrote several years later, "The neurotic, due to his psychological constitution, will always declare that he was treated too harshly, just as he will try to get away with achieving less than is demanded of him."[41]

Gaupp's position reasserted the importance of the will as a moral and medical category. Just as at the war's beginning strength and unity of will were celebrated as the source of Germany's national health and military success, after four years of war, military decline and instances of disobedience were often attributed to weakness and disunity of wills. In the collectivist, organistic frameworks that many doctors embraced, hysterical soldiers represented the weakness and disobedience that seemed to be increasingly plaguing the body politic and fragmenting the nation. For Gaupp, then, treating neurotics was part of a larger political and social struggle against "softness, the addiction to pensions and all other forms of the anti-social mentality."[42] Consequently, nervous symptoms were, in the minds of many psychiatrists and neurologists, even further removed from traumatic antecedents and more closely associated with pathological predispositions, which were now cast in explicitly political terms. As one health official observed: "Rare are the 'good' hysterias and the severe neuroses of the years '14, '15 and '16. Now it is chiefly a matter of getting out of military service."[43] In other words, the good old days early in the war produced many authentic cases of traumatization, cases caused by the direct effects of a shock experience. Later in the war, however, as morale steadily declined, the will to combat diminished, and the men who started filling the psychiatric clinics were of a lesser moral quality. Indeed, many had never even seen combat.

This shift further blurred the already hazy distinction between simulators and authentic neurotics—for Gaupp, both suffered from weakness of will, moral inferiority, and a lack of patriotism—and helped justify increased medical force. "The fight against the hysterical disorder of will [*Willensverirrung*] is often a difficult struggle; it takes a lot of strength and sweat before the doctor's will becomes master over the will of the patient. But because the doctor's will is good, and that of the patient bad, the doctor has the moral right to force his will."[44] Gaupp observed, furthermore, that Germany's heightened manpower needs and the consequential lowering of recruiting standards brought a dramatic increase in the number of "dishonest" and "unpatriotic" men in the army.[45] Remarking that such men tended to land in the army's psychiatric facilities, Gaupp characterized them as follows in his Stuttgart lecture of 1917:

> Among these people, many of whom are mentally limited or even feeble-minded, can be found some whose whole lives unambiguously indicate their social inferiority. Among the hysterical inmates in our clinic, are now—in contrast to the war's first year—quite a few criminals, degenerates, and mentally and morally defective men, what's more [there are] men without any love of the fatherland, totally averse to the demands of military service, born and raised in Switzerland, without any German sensibility, unstable, emotional men, who react to every disciplinary demand with either anger or depression, fanatics who refuse to be obedient for religious reasons, crafty fellows who want to create life-long pensions out of a short military stint, irascible trouble makers and agitators who will shrink from no lie or slander to fulfill their dishonest goals.[46]

In a further attack on the credibility of these patients, Gaupp provided the example of a patient named Holzinger who had made incriminating accusations against Liebermeister. Gaupp knew this patient personally, having observed him in his Tübingen station. That the man was missing his left index finger led Gaupp to suspect that he had mutilated himself intentionally to escape his military duty. Such a man, he warned, could not be believed, so whatever charges he had made against Liebermeister were to be viewed skeptically.

Gaupp emphatically concluded that Liebermeister was innocent of the accusations made against him. He reaffirmed his faith in his colleague, who, he assured, had not strayed from medically acceptable conduct and who "through his exceptional amount of work and self-sacrifice has earned the gratitude not only of his patients, but also of the Fatherland, to which he has returned many patients—who before had remained uncured in spite of long treatment and stood in danger of remaining incurable—cured and socially fit."[47]

The military court considered the case against Liebermeister for several months before finally clearing him of all charges.[48] Yet Liebermeister was so embittered by the experience that he tendered his resignation, claiming that he was no longer able to muster the necessary confidence for the successful performance of active treatment. Representing the concerns of Württemberg's psychiatrists, Gaupp appealed to the medical department of the War Ministry in Berlin at the beginning of August 1918. He asked for assurance that "doctors enjoy full protection and energetic defense by War Ministry officials against the unjustified attacks on the part of neurotics and their relatives."[49] Unless they knew that the War Ministry stood firmly behind them, doctors would not have the "freshness and flexibility" to carry out their work.

Gaupp conceded that there were abuses in the neurosis stations, and he asked the War Ministry to ensure that only "humane" doctors, who could control themselves and who would never allow themselves to get angry or denounce their patients as malingerers, be permitted to treat neurotics.[50] In general, he called for doctors to proceed with more self-control. He did not want them to shrink from the energy and discipline of active treatment, but suggested that they approach their patients with greater psychological sensitivity. In such a way, Gaupp concluded, doctors could, without changing their therapeutic strategies or diminishing treatment success, avoid most of the complaints against them and thus protect the profession's reputation and status.

In seeking explanations for the rising tide of discontent, military-medical authorities also conceded that particular doctors became overzealous when carrying out active treatment and that many emphasized eliminating (undeserved) pensions far too vigorously and vocally.[51] "Indeed," wrote General Friedrich K. E. von Ammon of the Medical Department of the Bavarian War Ministry in an August 1918 memorandum, "the disadvantageous effects on numerous neurotics of collecting pensions, or collecting *high* pensions, cannot be disputed, but too sharp and careless an emphasis of this point of view leads to misinterpretation and to the assumption that the neurosis stations were created solely for the removal or lessening of pension payments."[52] Young doctors seemed to be the source of most complaints. Conceding that patient discontent was not without justification, Ammon feared that younger practitioners often showed greater interest in achieving "dazzling curing statistics" than in more appropriate medical goals. He added that these doctors frequently became "irritable" when they failed to effect sudden cures and charged that they were too quick to blame these failures on their patients, implicitly regarding them as simulators and even verbally abusing them. What distressed him most was the sense that the nation had lost faith in its neurologists and psychiatrists, a common theme in medical writings at the end of the war.

Ammon proposed that hospital staff members be better screened, trained, and supervised so that unprofessional behavior could be prevented. Furthermore, he advised that doctors "absolutely avoid everything which could give them the reputation of working for financial interests and not for the good of the patient and the national community."[53] He also suggested that medical men take a more active role in "enlightening" the public by lecturing on active treatment, that neurosis stations be open to visits by members of the press, and that station administrators work more closely with the voluntary war-disability associations. Ultimately, Ammon's proposals betray the fact that the War Ministry was less concerned about breeches of medical ethics or the fates of maltreated patients than with the standing—and therefore, the effectiveness—of the nation's physicians. He assured doctors that the Ministry had no intention of either limiting their freedom in choosing treatments or regulating their activities. His primary concern was to prevent popular discontent or patient resistance from diminishing the success of active psychiatric treatment.[54]

To develop a coordinated response to growing popular discontent, military-medical authorities convened 150 psychiatrists, neurologists, and military officials, including the army's chief medical official, *Sanitätsinspekteure* Otto von Schjerning, at a special meeting in Berlin on October 9, 1918.[55] General Schultzen chaired the discussion, which covered current treatment methods as well as broader, theoretical issues about neurosis.[56] Schultzen indignantly reported on his encounters in the *Reichstag*. That laypeople were meddling into military-medical affairs, he added, poisoned the therapeutic air, making treatment increasingly difficult. Other participants observed that the morale in the neurosis stations was deteriorating and feared that doctors had acquired an undeserved reputation as "pension squeezers."

The doctors in attendance presented a united front, perhaps for the benefit of the military onlookers. During the general discussion, none—not even Karl Abraham or Ernst Simmel, who had made each other's acquaintance in Budapest several weeks earlier—rose to condemn active treatment. Nor did neurologist Kurt Singer encounter opposition when he affirmed that energetic treatment, and not pity, should continue to define the neurosis station atmosphere. Nevertheless, the Berlin discussants did support several policy changes. First, they agreed to favor hypnosis over electrotherapy. Electrotherapy with strong, sinusoidal current, had been banned by the War Ministry on December 22, 1917, but many doctors continued to use milder currents, while others employed the electrotherapeutic apparatus without the current to exploit its powerful suggestive effects.[57] This practice was criticized for furthering the popular perception that strong currents were still in use, which, in the minds of the participants, greatly contributed to popular discontent.

Second, the participants resolved that the character of the neurosis stations should change. The stations had originally been conceived of as small spaces, where doctors could provide individualized care and easily control the prevailing atmosphere. At the Berlin meeting, however, it was decided that a limited number of large, well-equipped, and highly visible stations should replace the network of small facilities, to make the results of active treatment more evident and hence generate greater public sympathy for the role of war psychiatry. Despite the therapeutic advantages of the small stations, many feared that they "obscure the impression which the neurosis station should make on the general public."[58] Public relations, then, dictated that the miracle of active treatment should no longer be hidden in obscurity.

Third, the attendees agreed that patients should be better screened before their transfer to neurosis stations. Foremost among the patients to be excluded were the so-called psychopaths, those who did not want to be cured and showed no desire to work, those men, in short, who were less authentically neurotic and who most likely had not seen heavy action.[59] Indeed, the "proliferation of psychopaths"—and not the frightful methods of treatment—was blamed for causing several suicides and general disciplinary problems in the neurosis stations. According to one doctor's account of the discussion, it was agreed that "men who do not *want* to become healthy will not be treated, rather discharged immediately; they spoil the whole atmosphere. However, they may not be released from the military, but should be brought closer to the front—either to a neurosis station at the front or to worker battalions."[60]

The participants ultimately showed more concern with their own working conditions than with the comfort and fate of their patients; they shared the sentiment that treating neurotics was itself a nervously draining and exhausting occupation. Bemoaning the widespread ignorance about neuroses and their treatment in the military as well as among the general populace, Schultzen encouraged doctors to hold lectures before groups of lawyers, businessmen, and labor unions and to open up all neurosis stations to visits by members of the press and others in public service.[61]

At the time of the conference, Schultzen released a new version of the War Ministry's official "neurosis memorandum" on the "principles for the treatment and evaluation of the so-called war neurotics."[62] In older versions, the following passage had appeared in the section on treatment: "Energetic methods are advisable whenever a lack of will to recover obstructs treatment."[63] But in the revised memorandum the section contained an addendum, intended to moderate medical behavior and, no doubt, mollify its critics: "Here it is absolutely im-plored, that in striving for therapeutic success, the treating doctor proceeds in a state of emotional calmness, avoiding any damaging utterance and refraining from using the expressions 'simulator,' 'malingerer' etc., and if he notices that he has lost his calm, he must break off the treatment at once."[64]

Following the spirit of the October meeting and also reflecting General Am-mon's August proposals, officials of the Bavarian Second Army Corps invited a delegation of reporters to visit the Münzschule neurosis station in Würzburg on October 30, 1918.[65] This station, where men from most of the corps dis-tricts east of the Rhine were treated, consisted of three sections: the main clinic, which contained 120 beds for neurotic patients; the section for agricultural la-bor, whose 30 beds were attached to the Werneck *Vereinslazarett*; and a 20-bed sanitarium for neurasthenics. The treatment techniques practiced included iso-lation (the "psychic abstinence cure"), the Kaufmann method, suggestive hyp-nosis, and long baths. In all other ways, the station was typical. It featured gymnastics facilities for posttreatment exercise and boasted workshops for woodworking, basket making, and cobbling.[66]

In an article that appeared the following day in a Würzburg newspaper, one reporter noted that 97 to 98 percent of the station's patients were "cured," that is, able to work again. This very success, he hoped, would strengthen patients' faith in their doctors. "The manner and certainty of curing is astounding," he wrote, "Men who had lost the ability to speak were cured in one minute with-out force, simply with electricity (and not at all strong current) and sugges-tion. . . . The war neurotic gives up his cane upon admission to the station. An impressive collection of these canes is now standing unused in a corner."[67] En-thusiastic about the speed and effectiveness of active treatment, this author had little patience for the station's critics who had likened it to a prison or torture chamber.[68]

That reporter's opinions were shared by other members of the press delega-tion, all of whom appeared to be deeply impressed by what they witnessed. An-other observer, a doctor from Speyer, was moved to dismiss lay criticisms, declaring: "Before you publicly condemn a method of treatment which works so beneficially in the interest of the patients and for the economic welfare of the people—even in the *Reichstag* and *Landtag* and based merely on the testi-monies of individuals and in part on wholly untrustworthy patients—you should become better informed about it by consulting with the doctors in ques-tion, rather than only taking into account the testimony of one side."[69] A sec-ond Würzburg reporter similarly paid little heed to the popular condemnations of the neurosis stations, or the rumored "imprisonment" and "ruthless appli-cation of strong current"; he observed: "Whoever can just once get a look at this kind of treatment will agree right off that modern, active treatment, which skilled specialists have arrived at in the course of the war, deserves to be called the best imaginable and most ideal [treatment]."[70]

The Kaufmannization of the Mind: The November Revolution and Medical Memory

Weeks later the war ended, and the armistice went into effect on November 11, 1918. On the morning of the ninth, exactly a month after the Berlin meeting, as psychiatry professor Karl Bonhoeffer walked from Berlin's Lehrter Rail Station to his office at the Charité clinic, he encountered "troop units marching in disarray, mixed with civilians carrying placards which read 'Do not shoot!' pale, emaciated figures, covered with sweat, who gesticulated wildly and shouted at the soldiers."[71] Bonhoeffer had walked right into the swelling ranks of the November Revolution. When he tried to enter the psychiatric clinic, he later recalled: "The porter confronted me on the stairs with a red cockade, apparently with the intention of barring my entry into my office, or at least of coming to blows with me about it."[72] That same day, Social Democrat Phillip Scheidemann leaned out a *Reichstag* window and declared a republic; two hours later, Karl Liebknecht proclaimed a socialist republic; and the coming months saw eruptions of violence between right-wing militants, left socialists, and the army, which the Ebert-led SPD brought in to restore order.

Bonhoeffer, like most psychiatrists in Germany, responded to the revolutionary upheaval with fear, confusion, and steadfast conservatism. Just as the declaration of war in August 1914 had inspired many psychiatrists to reflect on war in philosophical and psychological terms, the German Empire's military and political collapse also generated a groundswell of meditations among mental health professionals. While the 1914 writings uniformly welcomed war and celebrated its putatively beneficial effects on mental and nervous health, many of the works of late 1918 and 1919 blamed Germany's devastating defeat and the toppling of the old order on the exhaustion of the nation's nerves. Filled with dire predictions about the fate of the German people, these gloomy tracts looked to isolate the causes of Germany's "nervous collapse" and sounded a "medical alarm" to halt the nation's descent into moral and political chaos.[73]

The November Revolution, like so many modern revolutions, had a pronounced psychiatric dimension. Indeed, the history of psychiatry and the fate of the mentally ill have long been entangled with revolution.[74] French psychiatric hagiography venerated Philippe Pinel for unshackling the insane during the French Revolution; 1848 in Germany was associated with more liberal attitudes toward the mentally ill; and Russian psychiatrists strongly sympathized with the Revolution of 1905 and condemned the czarist regime as detrimental to the peoples' mental health.[75]

But the relationship between psychiatry and revolution has another side. Opponents and victims of revolutionary change have also invoked psychiatric terms, often viewing revolutions as outbursts of mass insanity and using the categories of mental illness to police boundaries in times of social and political turmoil. The category of the "psychopath"—a product of late-nineteenth-century classification schemes—reveals the constructedness of psychiatric diagnoses with particular clarity, and recent historians of psychiatry have assumed that the notion of psychopathology served to enforce social and political norms, acting as a thinly veiled, scientific-sounding way of denouncing and pathologizing threats to the bourgeois order.[76]

Thinking about the Revolution, however, was not so abstract for most practitioners of active treatment—political events, in many cases, changed their working conditions and threatened their careers and even lives. Revolutionary times palpably altered the relations between psychiatrists and their staffs, as clinic employees expressed their workplace grievances and made new demands such as the eight-hour day.[77] But the Revolution, and the mutinies that catalyzed it, had an even greater impact on psychiatrists' relations with their patients. In the neurosis stations, patient intransigence, having begun as early as spring 1917, now attached itself to a larger political cause. As a result, several psychiatrists and neurologists, accustomed to absolute disciplinary authority in their clinics, experienced terrifying reversals of power at the hands of hospital soldier councils and vengeful patients. Nonne, for example, recalled that a mood of "passive resistance" obtained in his Hamburg hospital, where discipline suddenly evaporated. "Naturally, military drills and exercises disappeared. . . . I declared that I would only cure those who personally asked me to and absolutely submitted themselves to my discipline."[78]

Nonne observed that the Revolution worsened prognoses by doing away with the discipline and subordination necessary for active treatment. "Curing percentages," he wrote, "were far lower than before, doubtlessly because the mood of the ward no longer embodied the prerequisites for success."[79] Kurt Singer also noted that the reversal of power relations in the neurosis stations made active treatment futile. Neurosis patients could no longer be convinced to submit themselves to electrotherapy, and the sense of medical authority and military discipline, so central to successful psychiatric treatment, had disappeared.[80] Hence, formerly stellar treatment statistics showed an abrupt decline, and the celebrated rapid cures could no longer be reproduced. The neurosis station at the Görden asylum near Brandenburg, for example, had reported nearly perfect curing percentages during the war's final phase. However, in 1919 this number plummeted from nearly 100 to 8 percent, and a startling 42 percent of its patients did not even show the slightest improvement.[81] In that year the Freiburg neurologist Heinrich Stern observed a sudden reversal: The doctor's military authority, which had been therapeutically necessary, had become a great liability due to neurotics' "sensitive attitude" toward anything military. Without the force of military rank, it was scarcely even possible to get patients to submit to painful treatments; in effect, political events forced psychiatry to abandon its great achievement, the rapid cure.[82]

Yet, these same events had even more dramatic consequences that eclipsed the sense of therapeutic crisis. Active treatment was seldom necessary anymore; the armistice and the Revolution seemed suddenly to cure thousands of debilitated neurotics. "My station," recalled Robert Wollenberg, "which until that point had been fully occupied, immediately emptied out, and many paralytics and shakers, who just before were still hobbling around on crutches, at once found their strength again and could suddenly walk around remarkably well."[83] Such testimonies of the instantaneous disappearance of manifold neurotic symptoms heralded a sudden end to the neurosis problem.

For some doctors this phenomenon provided final, seemingly incontrovertible proof of the psychogenic nature of the neuroses and the fallacy of traumatic neurosis.[84] "Is it true," asked Freud in a letter to Sándor Ferenczi, "that all the war neurotics suddenly became healthy, except for one? What will Oppenheim say to that?"[85] Significantly, few interpreted this phenomenon to mean that most neuroses had been simulated. Rather, it was widely believed that the ceasefire abrogated the need for neuroses; once there was no longer any danger of being called to the front, there was no more use for hysterical reactions. More sympathetic approaches claimed that the Revolution cured real neuroses by removing the fear of the front and hence resolving the conflict between duty and self-preservation. The Revolution, then, acted as an effective, collective cure.[86]

Erwin Loewy-Hattendorf, a clinical nerve doctor from Steglitz in southern Berlin, sought an explanation for this peculiar phenomenon in a 1920 essay on war, revolution, and accident neuroses.[87] On the one hand, Loewy noted, the Revolution worsened prognoses by freeing neurotics from the bonds of military and medical obedience, a prerequisite of active treatment. But at the same time, the war's end removed the fears at the core of so many neuroses. Hence, numbers of new cases declined sharply, and in older cases symptoms often disappeared spontaneously. In short, "the reasons which could cause a soldier to flee into illness were essentially eliminated by the Revolution."[88]

But there was another, more explicitly political dimension to this phenomenon. It was not only the end of the war and the threat of the front, according to many observers, but also the political and psychological achievements of the Revolution that were at work. For Singer, the Revolution fundamentally altered all aspects of the "neurotic problem."[89] In an April 1919 lecture he argued that the sudden end of the war brought positive therapeutic effects by "empowering" working-class soldiers: "The strongest emotional pressure, which burdened the neurotic and neurotically susceptible soldiers, that is, the fear of the trenches, the resistance to war as a collective concept for everything dangerous, depriving, grueling—this severe stress seemed to have been immediately lifted from the soldiers."[90] Without irony, Singer compared this therapeutic benefit to the electric shocks of the infamous Kaufmann method: "Even more favorable was that the resolution of these tensions occurred suddenly and worked exactly like a therapeutic affect shock. It was the greatest Kaufmannization of the mind without current."[91]

Yet Singer displayed a deeper sensitivity to soldier suffering than the majority of his colleagues. He argued that the perception of new social conditions and power relationships healthfully lifted the self-esteem of the common soldier:

> Above all, the Revolution brought the class which comprised the main contingent of neurotics, that is, the working proletariat, with one stroke into a position in which neurotic complexes, as the expression of protest of inferiors, the oppressed, and the subordinate were ruled out. Compensation for feelings of inferiority . . . the flight into illness, tricks, and exaggeration were in this moment no longer necessary, since the prior power relationships were so completely turned around. . . . The feelings of insecurity and inferiority at the basis of neuroses were removed through the fiction of a higher self esteem among soldiers. The psyche no longer needed to escape its plight through illness, once it was proclaimed that even the least significant soldier and worker carried the baton in his knapsack, so to speak.[92]

Many other doctors equated the work of the revolutionaries with the goals of neurotics, but more typically this association was made to condemn the unpatriotic, parasitic behavior of the two groups. Doctors cited the sudden transformation of many patients from disabled neurotics into energetic revolutionary leaders to show that the Revolution was directed by psychically unhealthy men and that the hysterics had been barely ill at all. Nonne, for example, recalled that a "refractory shaker" in his ward, a man who had often complained of being treated too harshly, suddenly shed his symptoms and served most effectively on the soldiers-patients' council.[93] And Kretschmer wrote of a hysteric who was about to be examined just as rumors of revolution swept into his Mergentheim neurosis station. Kretschmer recounted that the patient immediately fled, running to the fountain in the town's market square to deliver a fiery political oration to an excited crowd.[94] Singer, also linking neurosis station inmates with revolutionary leaders, wrote that "a pseudo-neurotic took charge of the soldiers' council in the hospital; eight days earlier he had begged on hand and foot not to be discharged, claiming that he couldn't even climb up and down the stairs because of his headaches. This NCO directed the organization of the new hospital regime—running back and forth between the *Reichstag* and the hospital—with astonishing competence and stamina."[95]

Soldier councils did form in many neurosis stations, and in other kinds of war hospitals as well, and often intervened directly in the treatment of the remaining patients.[96] These councils did what the politicians had not done; they responded to patient complaints by blocking unpleasant treatments like the Kaufmann cure and isolation therapy.[97]

The Munich psychiatrist Karl Weiler recounted that life in the Bavarian Kempton neurosis station was irreversibly disrupted when local residents stormed it to "liberate" the neurotic inmates. However, he also observed that as a consequence of the revolutionary upheaval, "very many [neurotics] who were still in treatment recovered almost instantly, in that their shaking disappeared, their ability to speak returned, etc."[98] Many of the neurosis facilities in the First Bavarian Corps District were closed as a result, but two in Munich and one in Augsburg remained open. Weiler noted the positive therapeutic consequences of the fact that only "authentic" hysterics were left in these stations once all the others cleared out with the arrival of revolution; "since at that point only people with authentic hysterical symptoms were admitted, treatment no longer encountered great difficulties, although the widespread lack of discipline was not exactly conducive to it."[99]

Just as Alfred Polgar had prophesied in 1917, the war's end gave patients a chance to sit in judgment on their doctors. And the Revolution undermined medical authority within the clinics to the point where many psychiatrists—particularly those known for excessive therapeutic zeal or brutality—had to flee from throngs of vengeful men.[100] As Gaupp recalled years later, many of his least desirable patients had become revolutionary "heroes," and it took tremendous effort to "save one of my station's most successful doctors from a terrible fate."[101] Similarly, Robert Wollenberg portrayed the Revolution as the disruption of order in his Strasbourg neurosis station: "In the shortest time all discipline and order were gone," he wrote, ". . . Dangerous psychopaths, who had gone into the city out of curiosity, returned to the station with loaded weapons and had to be disarmed, so that they did not cause serious damage."[102] Nonne, it seems, had to slip out his hospital's back door to avoid the advancing "mob."[103]

These accounts of the Revolution show how many psychiatrists portrayed themselves as the targets of revolutionary events and rapid political change. Patients, in these descriptions, blocked clinic entrances, interfered with therapeutic practices, and disrupted hospital order, literally threatening the lives of their doctors. These depictions, thus, represented the final step in a gradual process by which Germany's psychiatrists sought to displace their patients by casting themselves in the role of the war's true victims. The process had begun in the middle of the war when psychiatrists complained of the strain of carrying out difficult treatments on intransigent hysterics; it intensified amid the complaints of a smear campaign by "ungrateful" relatives and "meddling" politicians; and it reached its fruition in the political and economic turmoil of the Weimar Republic, a time in which competing claims of victimization carried ever greater cultural currency.[104]

Simultaneously, psychiatric theories increasingly denied the traumatizing impact of war, explaining hysteria among soldier-patients as a reflection of constitutional pathologies and morbid wishes and fears. Indeed, the politically charged condemnation of the neurotic as a weak-willed parasite who placed his own welfare before that of the national community intensified in the postwar period. War neuroses, a growing number of doctors came to believe, had essentially nothing to do with the war, meaning that the tens of thousands of nervously ill casualties could not be considered, in any real sense, the war's victims. War, then, was not to blame for psychological suffering; the problem was caused by an overly sympathetic society and the misguided actions of ignorant doctors.

Equating revolutionary actors with hysterical patients completed the picture. Patients thus not only had to cede their victim status to their doctors, but actually assumed the role of perpetrators. Psychiatrists ultimately scapegoated their (hysterical) patients for both calamitous military defeat and contributing to the economic vicissitudes of the 1920s through their "pension-greed" and their role in the Revolution. Psychiatrists' interwar writings, which helped shape the enduring medical memory of the war, simultaneously stripped war of its negative psychological consequences and furthered divisions between good, healthy, self-sacrificing Germans and hysterics and psychopaths, whose moral inferiority and weakness of will infected the republic they helped to create.[105]

The Nervous Collapse: Psychiatrists Diagnose the Nation

Although many psychiatrists later came to accept the republic—by "reason" if not by conviction—in general the profession longed for the restoration of an imagined old order and its attendant values. Associating the recent political events with the actions of hysterics and psychopaths was one way in which doctors used their medical expertise and status to discredit the Revolution and critique the nascent Weimar system.

A series of articles written just after the war sought to demonstrate that revolutionary leaders were motivated not by acute political awareness or a sensitivity to the suffering brought on by war and capitalism but by personal gain, the thrill of "running amok," and even delusion and severe mental illness. Kurt Hildebrandt, a psychiatrist at the Dalldorf asylum in northern Berlin, divided "psychopathic" revolutionaries into two groups in a 1919 lecture: egoistic antisocial types who joined the movement for their own personal gain and power-hungry swindlers and braggarts.[106] Hildebrandt focused on the case of M., a painter, who had exited the war through hysterical symptoms but only after he had "made millions" through forgeries and swindling. Providing a long, detailed account of the case history of the painter turned Spartacist, Hildebrandt concluded that M.'s participation in the Revolution owed not to political conviction—which he had never before demonstrated—but to the pursuit of material gain and "his pathological obsession with playing a momentous role."[107]

The bitterest antirevolutionary writing came out of Munich, site of the short-lived Bavarian Soviet and then a wave of counterrevolutionary and anti-Semitic violence.[108] In response to the revolutionary events, several Munich doctors published case histories of revolutionary actors and typologies of the pathologies of radicalism. Eugen Kahn, a doctor at the psychiatric clinic of the University of Munich and a member of Kraepelin's German Research Institute for Psychiatry, lectured in August 1919 on the psychiatric profile of revolutionary leaders and followers. Kahn based his study on the assumption that "the psychiatrist must always be ready to judge in an impartial, politically neutral manner according to his best knowledge and conscience."[109] His analysis of a sample of sixty-six—seventeen revolutionary leaders and forty-nine followers—led Kahn to conclude that "scarcely one of the sixty six can in any way be viewed as completely psychically intact."[110] Although he was reluctant to condemn the Revolution itself as a psychopathic occurrence or judge every revolutionary actor as mentally inferior, Kahn selected fifteen cases that he believed described typical revolutionary characteristics. Those cases could be divided further into four basic types: hysterical personalities, ethically defective psychopaths, fanatic psychopaths, and manic depressives.

Of the four cases with hysterical personalities, three had been treated in military psychiatric facilities for war hysteria. All, according to Kahn, were selfish, melodramatic men who thrived on attention, which they gained at times through pity. The locksmith and toolmaker in the group, both of whom had histories of criminal activity, overlapped with Kahn's "ethically deficient" category; the one Jewish hysteric, a law student, represented the prototype of the "degenerate hysterical intellectual."[111] Among Kahn's sample of revolutionary psychopaths, several historians have shown, can be found thinly disguised descriptions of the Munich revolutionary leaders Kurt Eisner, Erich Muhsam, and Ernst Toller, who had been examined in the clinic after the downfall of the short-lived Bavarian Soviet.[112]

Kraepelin himself regarded the Revolution as a political and medical catastrophe. In the eye of the revolutionary storm, he joined up with the Munich leaders of Germany's racial hygiene movement to try to prevent the nation from "degenerating into a criminal, malingering and feeble-minded mass" and harbored such reactionary medical zealots as Alfred Ploetz and Fritz Lenz, hiding them from Munich Soviet authorities in his psychiatric clinic at the university.[113] And in a solemn and now notorious 1919 treatise, Kraepelin offered a psychiatric perspective on current events and national health.[114]

Kraepelin attributed the political upheaval to the wearing down of the national psyche and the weakening of the national will after four years of grueling warfare and asserted that, as a psychiatrist, he was obligated to address and help solve these problems. Citing the precedents of the Paris Commune and the Russian Revolution of 1905, Kraepelin noted that it was common for nations to experience revolutionary currents in the aftermath of military defeat. To explain he drew an analogy between revolution and hysteria: "[Hysterical symptoms] occur," he wrote, "when a severe emotional shock disrupts calm, objective reason, and the instinctual discharging of internal tensions replaces rational action."[115] Kraepelin compared hysterical reactions in individuals with collective acts of political radicalism: "In every mass movement we encounter traits which clearly indicate a deep affinity with hysterical symptoms. Above all, we may assume that the actual leaders of such movements, the greater part of the mentally deficient comrades, are unsuited for the intuitive, instinctual resolution of the struggle for existence."[116]

Revolutionary leaders and hysterics, Kraepelin observed, shared a lack of foresight and perspective; both groups suffered from weakness of will and were enslaved by their momentary passions and instincts. In addition to the delusional youth, utopian poets, and manic depressive schemers, Kraepelin singled out Jews as disproportionately numerous among the revolutionary leaders and followers. The "Jewish race," he argued, showed an abnormally high disposition toward psychopathology, as revealed by their "talent in languages and in acting," their ambition, and their skill as "piercing critics."[117]

Kraepelin approached Germany's political problems with a crude embrace of social Darwinism. He had nothing but scorn for the Revolution's democratic pretensions, which, as he saw it, threatened to reverse nature's meritocracy and tragically subordinate Germany's "most noble and capable sons" to the whims of the masses. Having witnessed so many of these "most able and self-sacrificing men" fall in the war, while the "unfit and self-serving" were spared through war neurosis, Kraepelin advocated "the breeding of outstanding personalities, who can manage our fate in the difficult days to come."[118]

The war's degenerative impact, that is, its reversal of the workings of Darwinian selection, was a theme that echoed throughout postwar psychiatric writing. Bonhoeffer, whose earlier research had addressed the observed increases in vagabondage, alcoholism, and suicide in German society, returned to the topic of degeneration soon after the war. Bonhoeffer bemoaned that more than two million healthy young men had given their lives to the national cause, while a stream of hysterics and psychopaths survived unscathed. The war, he wrote, had the unfortunate dysgenic effect of increasing the relative numbers of "inferiors" within German society.[119] Postwar conditions tragically reflected the domination of biological inferiors, and for Bonhoeffer this necessitated increased medical intervention in public affairs.

Gaupp also condemned the revolutionary events, which he characterized as a national "nervous collapse." Postwar political change, for both Bonhoeffer and Gaupp, resulted from a state of "mass hystericization," which made the war-weary populace vulnerable to political and social depravity.[120] It was not the shock or exhaustion from fighting but rather "moral debasement" and "political proselytizing" that transformed naïve men into revolutionary socialists. "Today they are the fellow-travelers of the Spartacists, whose motivations are less clear political conviction than the joy in destroying and rabble-rousing and the living out of primitive and crude instincts."[121]

Even Oppenheim, who cautioned that the category of mental illness was invoked too lightly and carelessly by laypeople in their attempts to understand the revolutionary upheaval, discussed the role of the feebleminded, manic depressives, and psychopaths in the Revolution. Published in a Berlin daily a month before his death, Oppenheim's reflections aimed to enlighten the public about the relationship of revolution and mental illness. Like Gaupp and Krae-pelin, the neurologist attributed the Revolution to a state of national nervous exhaustion, a condition that rendered good people uncharacteristically vulner-able to political agitation and propaganda. His account differed, however, in his greater sympathy for wartime suffering and the more direct connection he drew between the state of the nation's nerves and the actual experience of war. "The great majority of our people," wrote Oppenheim, "have suffered an enor-mous loss of nervous strength and resistance through the frightful excitements and deprivations of the long war, with the result that they are far more suscep-tible to incitements and provocations than in times of good health, and lend an open ear to wild rumors and agitation which, if nervously strong, they would reject. Thus the sickly mental state of the individual as well as the masses has contributed much to the upheavals in which Germany now finds itself."[122]

As several historians have argued, medical and state officials, threatened by the dissolution of the old order, looked with fear at the breakdown of social and political authority structures. Their outrage at the perceived moral chaos and licentiousness of the revolutionary days, Richard Bessel writes, betrayed a deep concern with their own status and security.[123] Doctors' quickness to di-agnose "mass psychoses" and to cast themselves in the role of protectors of the general public must be understood in this light and seen as a response both to growing antipsychiatric sentiment and to the outbreak of revolution around Eu-rope.[124]

A number of tracts written by psychiatrists in the immediate aftermath of the war and Revolution support Bessel's contention. Many grimly reflected on the nation's moral and mental crisis, condemned the excesses associated with the Revolution, and displayed a profound fear of a communist insurgency.[125] Strik-ingly, psychiatric critiques of the political and cultural avant-garde as immoral, unpatriotic, and degenerate shared key assumptions with the cultural policies and propaganda of the Nazis.[126] Certainly, Kraepelin's writings helped fan the flames of anti-Semitism, which increased sharply in the immediate postwar pe-riod. On the whole, however, psychiatric texts were more conservative than fascistic; they advocated a kind of medical authoritarianism to steer Germany out of its national nervous collapse and restore social and political calm. Sig-nificantly, the solutions these doctors reached reflect the persistence of wartime priorities in the postwar era. They show how psychiatrists devoted greater at-tention to issues of collective mental health and sought a heightened interven-tion in the concerns of daily life. These agendas set the stage for Weimar-era psychiatry, with its emphasis on treatment outside of the asylums and its pur-suit of eugenic solutions to public health crises.

"And so our era," mused Erwin Stransky months after the end of the war, "instead of bringing higher status to psychiatrists, has temporarily had the op-posite effect and actually caused the smear campaign against psychiatrists to break out in a new phase."[127] Lecturing before the German Psychiatric Association on "the mental reconstruction of the German people and the task of psychiatry," the Vienna psychiatrist called on his colleagues to become "the apostles of a better future for our people."[128] He urged psychiatrists to quit their ivory towers and abandon old, ineffective forms of activity and learn from the propaganda methods of mobilized political parties and even the Catholic Church. Most distressing of all to Stransky was the very "un-German" decline in the will to work that, as he observed, accompanied this mass hystericization. The populace, he complained, had succumbed to pathological short-sightedness, as demonstrated most vividly by the terrifying fanaticism of the Munich Soviet. Hence, the task that fell to psychiatrists, namely instilling the will to work and therefore preventing revolution, acquired particular urgency and heightened political significance in this context.[129]

Robert Sommer also vigorously opposed the Revolution and invoked medical categories to explain and assess it. A nationalist opponent of the Versailles treaty, Sommer feared that Germany's severe economic deprivation had significant psychological consequences, which doctors were obligated to address. Equating Bolshevism with insanity, he warned, in his 1919 "medical alarm":

> Under these circumstances, as a doctor it is my duty to proclaim that through this ordeal the starving German people are being propelled more and more into a mass sickness, which I am convinced will erupt in two forms, namely: 1. as nervous depression; 2. as political insanity with anarchic character. If the Entente is really serious about the struggle against Bolshevism, then it must not continue to provoke a mass illness by paralyzing the German people economically—if [mass illness] has really broken out as seriously in Germany, the heart of Europe, as in Russia, then it will certainly spread over all of Europe just as the mental epidemics of the Middle Ages.[130]

Reports of a series of suicides among "respectable" German men led Sommer to recognize the severity of the nation's suffering. Indeed, he suspected that without external aid, Germany would succumb to the "disease" of Bolshevism within a month or two. Sommer called on his medical and psychological colleagues abroad to lobby in order to halt the economic devastation of vanquished Germany so that "the suffering body and spirit of the German people can be granted the peace and quiet to rebuild a Central European, German economic and cultural life."[131] Without economic relief, Sommer feared that the conditions that gave rise to the Revolution would sabotage the approaching National Assembly: "If [our economy] remains destroyed, as it now is, then the coming National Assembly has, from a medical and psychological perspective, a poor prognosis, since the state of nervous exhaustion and over-stimulation—which lies at the basis of the radical and violent explosions currently coming to the surface, especially in Berlin—will continue to worsen and will lead to general destruction. In place of the new *Reich* we will have the struggle of all against all."[132]

A number of doctors diagnosed Germany with a case of collective neurasthenia, in the words of Willy Hellpach, a "mass neurosis," brought on by the arduous and exhausting four years of war."[133] An assumption that consistently ran through these writings was that restoring Germany's mental health and nervous vigor—and thus its political well-being—depended on the nation's psychiatrists and neurologists. For Hellpach, "the liquidation of war neurasthenia is the great social problem which will stand before us mind doctors after the war."[134] And the solution, many concluded, was for Germany's doctors and psychologists to play a greater role in the nation's social and legal affairs.[135]

Relations between mental health practitioners and patients, already strained by wartime social tensions and conflicts over active treatment, only deteriorated in the contentious atmosphere of the postwar years. Many patients who were examined for war-related nervous or mental disorders complained that doctors harassed them, suspected them of political subversion, and cast aspersions on their patriotism—after the war, this hostility played itself out very visibly in psychiatric pension deliberations. And the depiction of psychiatrists as untrustworthy and villainous could be found across Weimar culture, from Alfred Döblin's *Berlin Alexanderplatz* to *The Cabinet of Dr. Caligari*, a 1919 film that featured a demented, brain-washing asylum director who bears a striking resemblance to Charcot and a somnambulist whose movements, one scholar has pointed out, resemble typical war neurosis symptoms.[136] One of the film's writers, in fact, had been treated by a psychiatrist for a war neurosis.

Doctors, in turn, feared for their lives against an increasingly angry patient population. According to Hoche, whose official Freiburg University portrait was torn down and trampled by leftist students in 1919, some psychiatrists kept loaded weapons in their offices during consultations out of fear that patients would attack doctors who did not support their pension claims. Hoche himself held on to a heavy, steel table leg "with which one could, if necessary, accomplish quite a lot."[137]

In Austria, where relations between psychiatrists and patients were every bit as contentious as in Germany, active treatment burst onto the national stage and received a highly publicized official hearing. In 1917 Polgar had longed for the day when the doctors would be examined; three years later, he noted in the *Weltbühne,* the left-wing journal of cultural criticism where he published his satire, "That day is now here."[138] Indeed, the day came when Julius von Wagner-Jauregg, noted professor of psychiatry at the University of Vienna, was tried by the Commission for the Investigation of Derelictions of Military Duty—a body created by Austria's provisional National Assembly in December 1918—for allegations of wartime misconduct and incompetence. The psychiatrist's treatment of war hysterics was the main area of inquiry. According to the diary of one Lieutenant Walter Kauders, who had been a patient at the Vienna University Clinic, Wagner-Jauregg and his associates had handled the war's nervous casualties with great disdain and brutality, hardly showing them the concern and humanity that befit the country's combatants.

On December 11, 1918, *Der Freie Soldat* (The Free Soldier), a Social Democratic weekly, ran an article denouncing the activities of Austrian psychiatrists
in the war. The article stated:

> One of the most revolting chapters in the story of the Austrian army medical
> services is the treatment of war neurotics. These pitiable victims of the refined
> methods of modern warfare were taken in hand in a most peculiar way. Since a
> complete cure demands time, trouble and good nursing, which the revered army
> command was not prepared to lavish on the "common" soldier, the accommo-
> dating doctors found a way of clearing the neurological wards of their patients
> in a surprisingly short time. Electrical power currents were passed through the
> bodies of . . . war neurotics, causing them such excruciating pain that many
> died during treatment, but most of them escaped the torture by taking flight
> from the hospital—without, of course, having been cured. . . . More than one
> patient in these infamous hospitals has committed suicide. The score must be
> settled to the full with these worthy doctors.[139]

Several months later, the newspaper published a second article that singled
out Wagner-Jauregg as guilty of medical brutality and grave violations of patient dignity and rights. "One of the methods used was treatment with electric
power currents, of which all who were favored with it said that the pain it
caused was beyond description. There is more than a suspicion that these electrical currents were not used as a cure at all, but simply as a means of torture.
This method of electrical treatment was used particularly at the Wagner-Jauregg
clinic."[140] The author based his attack on the Kauders diary; he continued:
"Exactly after the manner of medieval torturers, Professor Wagner's assistant,
Dr. Kozlowski, first threatened [Kauders] with faradization, then made him
watch wretched victims of electrical treatment twisting and howling with pain,
and finally subjected him to this agony himself."[141]

Because of Wagner-Jauregg's notoriety—he was among Austria's leading medical figures—the trial aroused a great deal of media attention. Wagner-Jauregg's
subsequent fame (for his Nobel Prize–winning research on malaria and general
paralysis of the insane) and Freud's participation as an expert witness helped
make the trial a momentous event in the history of psychiatry and psychoanalysis.[142] Although the commission exonerated Wagner-Jauregg of all charges,
the fact that an esteemed professor of psychiatry in Vienna had to defend himself in this way indicates the extent of popular rage and suspicion against psychiatrists after the war and the consequential loss of status and security that
psychiatrists feared in Central Europe's new republics.[143]

Responding to the altered doctor-patient relationship during and after the
Revolution and to the unfavorable reputation the nation's psychiatric community had acquired, some psychiatrists and neurologists strove to create a new
role for themselves as the protectors of imperiled national nervous and mental
health. To define this new role, many doctors turned even further away from
individual patients and toward the state; having lost the respect and affection

of great numbers of their patients, many psychiatrists based their new status claims on designing technocratic and bureaucratic solutions to collective national health problems. These tendencies existed before the war and were amplified by wartime diagnostic debates and therapeutic breakthroughs, but they became even more widespread in the years after the war, whose consequences so diminished the value of individual life.

Conspicuous among these doctors were Gaupp and Bonhoeffer, whose interest in eugenic solutions increased through the 1920s. In a 1919 essay, Gaupp complained about the decreasing influence of doctors over the German people.[144] What made this situation particularly egregious, he argued, was that medical influence had waned precisely when it was most needed, when war and revolution had plunged Germany into a deep, "national sickness." "A sick people needs doctors to make it better," wrote Gaupp, "it requires the training and leadership of those whose mental and moral education have prepared it for this task."[145] But this task was complicated by the fact that popular faith in doctors and all other social elites had been greatly diminished.

Hoche, one of the shrillest psychiatric voices of the period, responded to the depreciation of human life brought on by war and the postwar economic desperation by embracing radical medical measures. The medical organicism he articulated early in the war developed into support for a kind of eugenic euthanasia, in which the needs of the national community determined the value of individual lives. In a notorious 1920 treatise, which he cowrote with the lawyer Karl Binding, Hoche advocated the termination of lives deemed "unworthy of life" in view of the welfare costs they generated. Hoche conceived of euthanasia as a "national duty" and estimated that some 500,000 "idiots" and another 10,000 "congenitally crippled" could be found in Germany.[146]

To be sure, Hoche's views were extreme for his time and were only (partially) realized two decades later, after Hitler had had six years to consolidate his power and a world war to divert attention. And the Hoche and Binding book generated much controversy within medical and legal spheres in Germany. Yet, these views did reflect broad assumptions that were shared by a wide range of medical thinkers—both on the right and left—that mental health professionals had a crucial role to play in national reconstruction and that collective, national solutions should be sought for the urgent medical and economic problems at hand. A number of other psychiatrists joined the Racial Hygiene Association after the war and devoted increasing attention to researching the biological bases of mental illness. And the close connection Hoche made between issues of mental health and a concern for the national economy was central to medical views of neurosis during the war and new modes of psychiatric treatment introduced in the 1920s.

As Gaupp addressed a group of doctors not long before the war's end, he still hoped that psychiatrists could shape German men into obedient subjects and devoted workers. He urged his colleagues to have the courage to turn away undeserved pension claims even in bleak economic times and to "strengthen the joy in working and the will to work . . . so that in the new times ahead we will find before us a generation of men fit and able to carry out the great tasks that lie before them."[147] Facing unfathomable loss of life, dizzying political change, and deep economic anxiety, psychiatrists retrenched as the new state brought new struggles.

CHAPTER 8

Pension War

Nervous Veterans and German
Memory in the Weimar Republic

Why does such a man lie whimpering in bed year after year for a couple
pennies of accident pension, when he could earn good money every day
and sing, drink, and dance by night?

ERNST KRETSCHMER, "Hysterie"

A whole new race, smart, strong and filled with will. What reveals itself
here as a vision will tomorrow be the axis around which life revolves still
faster and faster. The path will not always, as here, have to be forged
through shell craters, fire and steel; but the double-quick step with which
events are prosecuted here, the tempo accustomed to iron, that will
remain the same. . . . This war is not the end, but the prelude to violence.

ERNST JÜNGER, "Feuer"

"I WAS A HEALTHY man when I became a soldier, and was discharged
a cripple . . . ," declared Franz Müller, an erstwhile iron worker, as
he reinitiated military pension proceedings in July 1925.[1] Nine years
earlier Müller had experienced what doctors described as a "nervous shock"
and landed in a Bavarian war hospital where he remained for two months. He
then returned to action on the eastern front, but soon complained of gastric and
rheumatic pains. In 1918, according to Müller's fragmented medical records,
after falling and bruising his chest, he was found to be in a state of severe agitation and disorientation and was placed under observation in several clinics
around Berlin. He was finally discharged in January 1919, and five months later
he applied for a pension, claiming that his poor health prevented him from
working. Müller's was, in many ways, a typical trajectory for the men who
drifted in and out of the murky world of war psychiatry and thus remained on
the margins of legitimate illness and financial compensation. Indeed, between
the original 1916 incident and his final pension review in 1925, Müller was examined by numerous doctors, treated with many treatments, and rediagnosed
multiple times, and each time his compensation award was adjusted accordingly.

"Had I never been a soldier," Müller claimed in a pension hearing, "and never been in the war, I would not have these nervous pains."[2] This formulation, and the assumptions it reflects, represented the subjective experience of thousands of World War I veterans. "[I was] with the Prussians in the trenches . . . and am no longer a man," declared Franz Biberkopf, the protagonist of Alfred Döblin's *Berlin Alexanderplatz*.[3] The idea that war destroyed men in body and mind, that it shattered their health and extinguished their virility, was a common way of recalling the war experience that had profound cultural resonance in all the major belligerent countries.[4] It also raises the broader historical question of the war's collective impact on German society, politics, and culture. That the physical and psychological effects of prolonged exposure to mass death and violence undermined the Weimar Republic's democratic possibilities by creating a cadre of brutalized subjects has been a historiographic mainstay, yielding the common conclusion that the republic was doomed from its contentious beginnings.[5] The cultural historical corollary, that Weimar literature, art, and film can be understood as a "culture of trauma," a collective, unconscious attempt to work through repressed war trauma, has a similarly powerful grip on our historical imagination.[6]

Was Germany "traumatized" by the war? Can a nation—in this case fifty million people bitterly divided by social, political, religious, and regional distinctions—be seen as a sort of collective historical subject that undergoes the same psychological processes as an individual? This was certainly the assumption of contemporary psychiatrists such as Gaupp and Sommer when they diagnosed Germany's collective nervous exhaustion. But cases like Franz Müller's—and psychiatric responses to them—challenge these assertions. They help problematize the relationship between the war and the postwar, between military violence and political violence, and between wartime trauma and interwar culture.

More specifically, Müller's claims retrospectively shaped his various war experiences into a coherent narrative, a narrative that conformed to medical models of traumatic pathogenesis. Accordingly, he asserted a particular chronological and causal relationship between his war service and his long-term nervous and psychological condition and blamed a specific event—in this case, the 1916 shock—for turning him from a healthy man into a cripple. Müller's suffering was quite real and enormously debilitating, but the form in which he presented it, his traumatic narrative, was also a reflection of one strand of trauma theory and indeed German pension policies.

However, the medical experts who decided Müller's case challenged his traumatic narrative and posited an alternative story. Their version of events undermined the etiological significance of any discrete shock episode and pointed instead to the presence of a preexisting pathological constitution. For one doctor the evidence could be found in Müller's "insufficiently formed testicles" and the "unsatisfactory development of his secondary sex traits."[7] Others reported that he overreacted to relatively minor physical pain, yet another sign of a psychopathic character. "[T]he minor accident," wrote Dr. Kraft of the psychiatric clinic at Berlin's Charité hospital, "consciously or unconsciously offered the occasion for producing psychogenic symptoms, which gave him the possibility of escaping the most unpleasant realities of war service."[8] Müller's symptoms, then, represented a "flight into illness." Kraft did diagnose a war neurosis, but concluded that like "countless neurotics," Müller entered the war already a sickly man. The allegedly traumatic event, therefore, could not be seen as a *cause*, but rather an excuse "with which the neurotic once again hopes to fulfill his wish of escaping the difficulties of daily life."[9] Müller's narrative was rejected, and a pension was out of the question.

The gap between Müller's position and that of his psychiatric antagonists typified the pension application experience for veterans who claimed to be mentally or nervously impaired by war service. Their struggles over compensation show how the war's effects lingered long into the postwar period and continued to structure social reality, particularly in the years before the economic and political stabilization of 1923–1924. Postwar pension matters also reveal the persistent psychiatric valorization of work; while economic concerns were central to notions of mental and nervous health before and during the war, they played perhaps an even greater role in the war's aftermath, when state agencies and veterans' groups alike celebrated labor's therapeutic and patriotic value. And while wartime psychiatric practitioners devoted much energy to the pension issue, in the postwar period, pension questions increased in significance, particularly amid the hyperinflation and general economic insecurity of the early Weimar years.

The peculiarities of psychiatric pensioning meant that wartime debates over hysteria and trauma continued long after Hermann Oppenheim's defeat and death. And these debates played themselves out not only in the compensation struggles between psychiatrists and patients but also in the deepening divide between psychiatric specialists and the general practitioners who staffed Germany's new welfare offices. Pensioning represents the key to understanding the status of "nervous veterans" in Weimar society—it was one area where individual and collective memories of the war were constructed and contested. Indeed, in psychiatric pension proceedings, Germans not only struggled over vital financial questions, they also began to work out the memory and meaning of the war for the lives and health of individuals and for the nation as a whole. Psychiatric thinking about trauma had serious consequences for individual patients, the medical profession, and the political and cultural battles that loomed beneath the Weimar Republic's fragile consensus.

Interwar pension cases, then, add a material dimension to discussions of historical memory, which are often abstract and pay scant attention to the realities and struggles of daily life.[10] That is, most of the burgeoning scholarship on collective memory has focused on either high culture—literary and artistic renderings of war experience and grief—or on war memorials and monuments, which implies that memories can be imposed from above and (literally) set in stone. Looking at pension proceedings, on the other hand, facilitates seeing memory as a fluid part of lived experience.[11] Memory thus emerges as a contested realm, an area of negotiation between official master narratives and divergent personal experiences.[12] In this case, memories of World War I were the source of struggle between largely working-class claimants and bourgeois psychiatrists, a subject with great material and ontological implications.

Looking at this struggle also opens up new perspectives on trauma; rather than using it as a category of historical analysis—that is, as a way of describing German (and indeed all European) reactions to the tremendous devastation brought by the war—it can be seen as a historical actor, a concept that was constructed, contested, and ultimately overturned in the encounters between veterans and psychiatrists and psychiatrists and general practitioners. To assume that Germany was collectively traumatized by the events of World War I is to ignore the constructedness and historicity of the trauma concept itself.

The Neurotics of 1920

The experience of World War I unquestionably left a deep and lasting imprint on Weimar culture, and a sense of utter despair and devastation pervades early Weimar writings. In social terms, many of the conflicts that the war unleashed continued to haunt Germany for many years to come.[13] Among the war's lasting legacies was the problem of war hysteria, which did not disappear with the November Revolution. Although the Revolution's immediate effect was to clear out the neurosis stations and make most hysterical symptoms vanish with stunning speed, when the first waves of revolutionary excitement dissipated, many men started making their way back to the clinics, their shakes and stutters having mysteriously returned. "The streets have filled up with hysterical shakers and paralytics," noted neurologist Kurt Singer in 1920. "Among these can be found many who simply simulate, who appear first thing in the morning at the square, where the pitying public flings money, and in the evening, upon terminating their collection activity, disappear, once again free from shaking and paralysis."[14]

Around this time, public officials began reporting alarming increases in begging and peddling. Amputees, cripples, even "shakers," situated themselves on street corners throughout Germany and collected donations from pitying passersby. Medals dangling on their chests, these unfortunate figures appealed to the public's sense of charity and gratitude for their tremendous sacrifices. Through the paintings of Otto Dix, among others, the war-disabled beggar endures as a powerful symbol of the period and denotes the Weimar state's apparent indifference toward the war's most abject victims.[15] But this conception has not stood up to historical scrutiny. In fact, it did not even stand up to contemporary investigations. After a series of studies, welfare officials and veterans groups concluded that most of these men were not war casualties but peacetime beggars who found that their intake increased substantially if they slipped on a uniform.[16] Those beggars who were actually war disabled often held down jobs during the week and supplemented their income with occasional weekend panhandling. In one, albeit probably fraudulent, confession, a Hannover man "admitted" to deceiving the "stupid folks" and netting over one thousand marks in three days of feigned shaking.[17]

Yet most psychiatrists agreed that many of the shakers who sat in the streets and crowded the welfare offices were not simply simulating. "What is it with the neurotic of 1920?" asked Singer in an article that year. Singer and other doctors wondered why the shakes and stutters of the war years had begun to return after their abrupt disappearance in the Revolution. The answer, for many observers, lay in the altered social conditions of the postwar world. In particular it was the arduous transition back to civilian life, an adjustment made all the more difficult by Germany's economic woes, that caused these men to break down again. Fearing the "specter of unemployment," many former war neurotics returned to the "comfortable bed of neurotic symptoms."[18] Psychiatrists, in effect, compared the vicissitudes of Weimar life, the political violence and economic upheavals that marked the Republic's early years, with the conditions of war. In both contexts, hysteria could be seen as a survival strategy, an escape from the struggle for existence (*Existenzkampf*) for men who shrank from life's difficulties.[19]

In the early 1920s, given the demands of earning a living in an era of hyperinflation, the war retrospectively emerged as actually relatively comfortable and pleasant in some accounts.[20] Soldiers always knew where their next meal was coming from and adapted to a routine that, despite being arduous and monotonous and posing the continual threat of the front, did offer a degree of security and indeed solidarity. Postwar life, psychiatrist Karl Pönitz argued, showed many veterans how good they had had it in the army and presented a set of unforeseen difficulties to men who had previously longed for their freedom. Relapsed neurotics, then, were said to be taking flight back into their symptoms as crutches to avoid the harsh realities of postwar life, much as their original symptoms had represented attempts to flee the threat of front duty and possible death—the same line of reasoning Dr. Kraft used in his ruling against Franz Müller. Weimar society, Kraft and Pönitz both implied, provided its own traumas for men not quite up to the challenges of daily life, a theme that took on increasing resonance later in the 1920s.

"By the end of this period of upheaval," Singer had cautioned in a 1919 article, "doctors must be well prepared, so that we do not head from the Scylla of the war neuroses to the Charybdis of the peace-time, accident and pension neuroses."[21] Singer was one among many doctors who feared that the psychiatric odyssey was far from over. Warnings about the postwar pension problem had become a conspicuous part of psychiatric discourse by the middle of the war and had figured prominently in the traumatic neurosis debate of 1915–1916. Loss of military manpower (or war-munitions workers) was obviously no longer a concern after the war. At this point the male hysteria problem was becoming primarily a social and economic issue, and compensation claims looked to be a formidable threat to the national economy as Germans faced the daunting task of rehabilitating and reintegrating the hundreds of thousands of disabled men returning from the field.[22]

A 1922 study concluded that veterans with nervous disorders—broadly defined to include such disparate disabilities as rheumatism, progressive paralysis, and so-called heart neuroses—were costing the state as much as one billion marks annually and that they accounted for nearly half of all military pension claimants.[23] Hysteria and other functional conditions represented a sizable share of this sum. This led Berlin psychiatrist Ewald Stier to assert that "compensation for nervous disorders is not simply the most difficult part of pensioning, but is, in short, the central problem of the whole war pension issue. It is impossible to overestimate its significance for the national economy . . ."[24]

What made matters all the more vexatious was the sense that most psychiatric pensions were undeserved. Indeed, to explain these prodigious numbers, Stier did not look to the conditions and consequences of war service but rather to the false diagnoses and misplaced sympathy of his medical colleagues. He blamed Oppenheim. And most of all he bemoaned the persistence of Oppenheim's ideas in the medical world. "Even doctors," Stier complained, "frequently succumb to the exaggerated general opinion that sees war as having a 'damaging' effect on the nerves."[25] To be sure, leading psychiatrists and neurologists had long dismissed the theory of traumatic neurosis, but nonspecialists, among them the general practitioners who were in the trenches of what would soon be called the pension war, still clung to the notion that war trauma directly caused lingering disabilities. In such a way, Stier feared, out of pure ignorance, countless undeserved pensions were continually being awarded to the detriment not only of the state but of the individual patients as well. The situation was intolerable, he later recalled, because the "Social-Democratically led state" lacked the will to turn away undeserving pension seekers.[26]

Functional conditions, for Stier, seldom deserved financial compensation. But the lay public, and even trained doctors, were repeatedly fooled, falling prey to "the sad and heart-wrenching image of the stuttering, shaking and writhing neurotics, supported by canes and crutches, which we encounter everywhere."[27] Erroneously attributing their suffering to burial or nervous shock, ignorant observers treated war neurotics with pity and assistance—which, according to psychiatric dogma, only prolonged and deepened their illnesses—rather than the sterner measures that were medically indicated. As Pönitz reported: "[L]ay people see the 'pitiful shakers,' approach half out of curiosity, half out of horror, and shower the 'unfortunate' with donations."[28]

This skepticism was typical of psychiatric professionals during and after the war. Many sought to combat these misperceptions in the general populace and even the War Ministry. Gaupp observed that "the opinion has arisen among the lay public that war is a source of severe nervous or mental illnesses," and declared: "This is, for God's sake, incorrect."[29] Not only laypeople, warned Nonne, but educated doctors who should know better also believed in the allegedly pathological impact of war. Nonne, who evaluated nervous and mental disability claims in Hamburg after the war, was frustrated that "in spite of the long experiences of peace-time and war, doctors at the welfare offices still frequently lack the ability to see 'behind the curtain' and to judge the entire personality and all that goes with it."[30] Extending his attack to military officials, Nonne added, "The whole problem with the War Ministry is that the pension chasers [*Rentennörgler*] are—at least up to now—always appeased."[31]

Psychiatry and the Problem with Pensions

Germany's military pensioning system was established with a series of laws in 1906 and 1907. It was separate from, but parallel to, the labyrinthine social insurance bureaucracy that had been instituted two decades earlier under Bismarck. The 1906–7 legislation, which remained in effect through the war, defined military disabilities largely in terms of loss of earning power, making the German system unique among the belligerent powers.[32] Thus, much more than the (medical) severity of an injury, its economic significance was what determined the size of a pension award. Disabled men were examined by medical experts who ascertained the percentage that their earning power had been diminished: while an amputated leg amounted to a 90 percent disability, the loss of a foot ranked as 30 percent.

Military rank also helped determine the size of pension awards. For example, in 1916 a private declared 100 percent disabled would be pensioned at 540 marks per year; a corporal would earn 600 marks; a sergeant 720 marks; and a sergeant-major, 900 marks.[33] In view of cost-of-living estimates—for blue-collar workers food, clothing, utilities, rent, taxes, and other expenditures amounted to between 744 and 888 marks per household head—these pensions alone could only guarantee a meager existence.[34] Even a full pension for a high-ranking officer would scarcely cover escalating living costs, and as the war progressed, even these scant provisions came under increasing fire for their allegedly excessive generosity.

But military pensions were not designed to be a substitute for work. They were seen, rather, as a supplement to wages and a safety net for periods of unemployment. The central goal of Germany's welfare system remained rehabilitation.[35] The state believed it owed wounded veterans the restoration of their ability to earn, not compensation for their sacrifices. Only by working could men step into their socially sanctioned role as breadwinners and household heads; work restored their dignity, enabled their societal reintegration, and hastened their recovery.

The pension system remained the province of military authorities throughout the war, and the regional war ministries as well as the colonial and naval offices administered their own pension sections.[36] Just months before the war's end, due to the enormous burden of war-related pension claims, veterans offices were created in each of Germany's twenty-five deputy corps districts, and these offices oversaw an extensive network of local and regional bureaus.[37] Under pressure to conform to the limitations that the Treaty of Versailles placed on the size of the army, in October 1919 German authorities transferred the military pension system from the Ministry of War to the Ministry of Labor and essentially merged it with the preexisting civilian welfare organization.[38] In practical terms this meant that veterans were provided health care through the medical arm of the national insurance system and that the military pension courts were grafted onto the existing insurance courts. The broader consequence of this consolidation was that in the 1920s the war neurosis issue was fully swept into the larger issue of postaccident neuroses, which all but completed the conflation of war trauma with peacetime accident trauma.[39]

Pension proceedings, at best complex and vexed, were especially troublesome in psychiatric cases and presented a unique set of problems for psychiatrists, the state, and the patients themselves. While physically disabled veterans formed seven national associations and divided into subgroups for specific types of wounds (blindness, amputations, etc.) war neurotics lacked their own organization. Often suspected of shirking, they were spurned by other veterans and unwelcome in the ranks of the "really war disabled."[40] If, like Franz Müller, a veteran believed that he suffered from a war-induced nervous condition that diminished his earning power, it certainly fell within his rights to initiate pension proceedings. These proceedings, however, required that he submit himself to further examination and treatment, and many men must have hesitated before subjecting themselves to a regimen of electric current, suggestive hypnosis, or one of the other therapeutic possibilities.

The pensioning of war neuroses even became the subject of parliamentary debate soon after the war. On June 4, 1919, Ernst Beyer, a doctor and Social Democratic deputy from Königsberg, who had served under the psychiatry professor Ernst Meyer at a West Prussian neurosis station, stood before the Prussian diet and decried the pension policy toward neurotics.[41] Beyer was outraged that the state was shirking its financial responsibility for psychologically damaged soldiers. He charged that doctors were sacrificing scientific truth and social justice for economic concerns.

Beyer disputed the principles shared by the majority of Germany's psychiatrists and neurologists, including Meyer, and took a position somewhat akin to Oppenheim's. That is, unlike most neurologists and psychiatrists, he believed that the traumatic neuroses of war constituted a distinct type of illness that directly resulted from the travails of war service. He was convinced that somatic damage lay at the root of these conditions, but, he allowed, microscopic technology had not yet advanced far enough to enable the detection of these anomalies. Nevertheless, Beyer emphatically concluded that the state must take responsibility for these casualties.

Beyer also complained that active treatment was seldom practiced in the aftermath of the war, which meant that many untreated war neurotics were left to fend for themselves.[42] And even when they did report to hospitals, Beyer claimed, neurotics were often placed in asylums for the mentally ill where they were locked up and ignored. In a striking reversal, then, active treatment, which had been the source of patient opprobrium and protest, emerges as the only humane solution for Beyer. Hence, on the floor of the *Landtag*, he demanded that all neurotics receive active treatment at once:

> It is high time that these neurotics, whom we see everywhere, disappear from the streets. It is degrading that these sick individuals are peddlers, what with their symptoms, with the shaking and the other conspicuous signs of illness. We must demand of the state and the *Volk* that it take in these war disabled and do everything it can to bring them a cure. We must demand that active treatment be made available to these nervously ill men and that they be given a capital settlement or that they are guaranteed the possibility of working on the land and earning for themselves.[43]

Dr. Otto Martineck, chief medical officer of the Prussian War Ministry, who had intervened at the end of the Oppenheim debate, rose to address Beyer's charges. Martineck disputed the assumption that neurotics were automatically excluded from the war disabled and referred to the War Ministry's rules for pensioning neurological and psychological illnesses. He asserted that pension claims for neuroses were evaluated on a case-by-case basis and that when a causal connection between neurotic symptoms and war service could be established, neurotics were indeed entitled to compensation.

Martineck's assurances scarcely mollified the voices on the left. First, an Independent Social Democrat, a Dr. Wehl, spoke out against Martineck and condemned medical pension policies as state oppression of the working class. Then Beyer returned to the podium. He opposed the notion that pension claims for neurotics should be evaluated individually and proposed that doctors acknowledge the experience of the war and its general pathogenic effects on the psyche. He pleaded: "Neurotics are human beings and must be dealt with as such; indeed they are exceptionally sensitive people whose psyches cannot simply be disregarded, but rather must be taken into account in all cases. I want to reach the point where we do not try to ascertain whether a shell exploded near a patient or whether a man was buried or was grazed or hit squarely by a shot, but instead where we ask how the man has suffered subjectively."[44] Beyer's belief in the general psychopathological effect of war was out of step with contemporary psychiatric thinking. This gap only widened over the 1920s, as psychiatrists increasingly denied the traumatizing impact of war events and—returning to pre-1914 notions—even, in the face of overwhelming evidence to the contrary, extolled war's psychological, physical, and cultural benefits.

Beyer was named psychiatric advisor to the Prussian Ministry of Welfare in 1920, but his appointment aroused the opposition of several conservative activists. At a psychiatric conference that May, several doctors sought to discredit him and block his appointment. According to a Dr. Baumann, an asylum director in East Prussian Landsberg, Beyer had entered the war as a political conservative and, after a short tour of duty, emerged as a "November Socialist." In addition to this radical political change, itself construed as a sign of opportunism and even psychopathology, Beyer had another skeleton in his closet: He had been treated in the psychiatric ward of a Danzig hospital—for a war neurosis.[45]

The Weimar System and the Unified Approach to Pensions

As part of its ambitious and wide-ranging system of social welfare, the Weimar state introduced sweeping pension reforms in May 1920. The new law (*Reichsversorgungsgesetz* [RVG]) sought to simplify and rationalize the unwieldy pension system inherited from the imperial era. It established that veterans or their widows had to apply for compensation through local welfare offices (*Fürsorgestellen*). Consulting doctors, who were most often general practitioners, then determined whether there was a causal connection between a man's war service and the disabilities in question and then, when appropriate, calculated the extent to which the disabilities decreased his earning power. Loss of earning power was measured on a scale of 10 to 100 percent, and numbers were rounded to the nearest even ten. The medical determination was then passed on to pension bureaucrats who calculated the pension sum, which was based on the percentage disability plus a range of other factors such as medical expenses, cost of living allowances, and inflationary adjustments.[46]

Like the wartime system, the new approach continued to emphasize rehabilitation to work. It also established quotas to force firms into hiring war-disabled workers. Soon career counseling centers and occupational retraining programs for disabled men appeared in most German cities and towns.[47] In an effort to reduce the welfare rolls, in 1920 the state paid capital settlements to all veterans with a disability under 10 percent. In 1923, men with disabilities under 25 percent were paid off, cutting some half a million more men off the pension rolls. Capital settlements had long been favored by psychiatrists who believed that they prevented discharged men from becoming "pension addicts" and encouraged their swift return to work; indeed, Hoche's capital settlements resolution received unanimous support at the Munich Congress in September 1916.[48] Nevertheless, in 1924 there were still more than 720,000 veterans entitled to military pensions.[49]

All military pensions that were allotted before the 1920 pension law had gone into effect had to be approved by the new pension offices. When veterans or war widows disputed the rulings made in the pension offices, they could appeal to local pension courts, which were directed by judges and civil servants and which acted in consultation with medical experts. Although the pension offices were not strictly bound by the decisions of their medical consultants, medical authority over these matters was seldom challenged.[50] Disputed decisions could be further appealed to the National Pension Court in Berlin, a supreme court of pension appeals. However, between 1920 and 1923, as the mark's value steadily plummeted, the National Court was woefully overburdened and appallingly inefficient. Despite its continuous expansion, the Court worked with an enormous backlog, and even five years after the war, literally millions of pension claims remained unresolved.[51] The frustrating delays and the slow, often humiliating process of applying for a pension raised veteran discontent, and the pension bureaucracy remained a primary target of veterans' rancor despite the Weimar system's relative generosity.

In general, the new system defined a service-related disability (*Dienstbeschädigung* [DB]) as a "health disorder [*Gesundheitsstörung*] which occurred in consequence of the execution of duty or through an accident that took place during the execution of duty or was caused or worsened by the conditions of military service."[52] Within that category, a war disability (*Kriegsdienstbeschädigung* [KDB]), then, was a service-related disability that "can be traced to the particular conditions of the war and was suffered in the time between the beginning of the war and the end of the demobilization."[53] Judging cases of war disability was not an exact science, and doctors were instructed to evaluate the *probability* that an illness resulted from the conditions of war.[54] Thus, the connection between a disability and military service "needs not be proven; it suffices when it is shown to be sufficiently probable. On the other hand, the mere possibility of a causal connection is generally not sufficient for the medical judge to assume a war disability."[55]

These guidelines made sense for somatic wounds and illnesses, but they brought little clarity to psychiatric cases. The relationship between wartime traumas and posttraumatic states continued to arouse controversy in medical circles despite the wholesale rejection of Oppenheim's traumatic neurosis theory. Doctors were still divided on the notion of predisposition or hysterical constitution, a question that became pivotal in pension deliberations.

At the heart of the problem was the peculiar nature of shock and psychological trauma. While early theorists of trauma drew analogies between the way a physical blow affects the body and the way a shock acts on the mind, such rigidly mechanical models had been abandoned long before the war.[56] Trauma cases, furthermore, confounded attempts to establish direct causal and even chronological connections. Only Oppenheim posited an absolute, direct relationship between shock events and postevent symptoms, and he struggled to explain why many war neurotics had never seen combat action and why the conditions appeared so infrequently in prison camps. Neurologists such as Freud and Charcot, on the other hand, theorized that an event becomes traumatic only in a subject's imaginative reconstruction of it; accordingly, trauma inheres not in an event but in an individual's subjective experience or memories of it.[57] Physical or emotional shocks, thus, cannot be objectified or quantified. They become psychic traumas only through—simultaneous or subsequent—mental processes, processes that can occur long after the initial stimulus. Trauma emerges, thus, through a series of repetitious acts and images.[58] And in Freudian theory the "reality" and objective characteristics of the traumatic event were immaterial. Only the mind's memory work or the degree of its preparedness for a shock were pathologically relevant.[59] Seen in this light, cases of psychic trauma did not conform to the chronological parameters of pension criteria, since it is not the actual accident *event* (Ereignis) but rather the subjective *experiencing* (Erlebnis) of the event that leads to posttraumatic conditions.[60]

To be sure, neither the Ministry of Labor nor psychiatrists such as Stier showed much interest in the nuances of psychoanalytical trauma theory. Yet, more conventional thinkers, who were far more integral to Germany's medical landscape and more influential on its pension practices, nonetheless shared Freud's belief in the inherent subjectivity and problematic chronological status of the traumatic event. Already in the trauma debates of 1915–1916, many psychiatrists noted that when two men experienced the same combat ordeal, often one broke down and the other remained healthy. Furthermore, breakdowns often happened long after the traumatic event or even in the absence of an identifiable trauma. Could conditions that only appeared years after the war be seen as the legitimate result of a wartime event? Was there a statute of limitations for the state's responsibility? Furthermore, what was the relationship between the psychic predisposition and the shock episode? Did a psychic predisposition mean that the state bore no responsibility?

While a soldier with demonstrably somatic injuries would have had no trouble proving that, say, he had two legs before a mine explosion, war neurotics were faced with a more challenging task. To establish the necessary causal and chronological chain, they had to prove that they were mentally and nervously healthy before the war, and this meant swimming against prevailing psychiatric currents. As the pension protocols stated: "A more exact examination of the earlier personality reveals that even the neurotic and psychopathic disorders which seem to have been caused by the war, according to unanimous attestations, develop on the basis of a predisposed psychopathic constitution."[61] And the psychopathic constitution remained such a slippery and inexact concept that evidence for one could normally be supplied by perusing any patient's case history; a childhood sickness, poor performance in school, and even such factors as a "nervous," sickly, or alcoholic relative or persistent marital strife sufficed as evidence.[62] If such a predisposition was deemed the source of a neurosis, a pension was ruled out.[63]

Furthermore, if a man's neurotic symptoms were removed through active treatment, he lost his right to a pension because his ability to work was, in theory, fully restored. But what happened when the symptoms returned after the war? Were the "neurotics of 1920" pension eligible?

This determination was up to the discretion of the examining doctor. If further treatment failed, there was a window of pension eligibility between the poles of predisposition and pure pension greed or simulation. The protocols clearly did not rule this out: "The fact that [hysteria] is by nature simply a matter of temporary forms of reaction in an unaltered constitution does not mean that DB or KDB is to be rejected, if the symptoms of this reaction persist at the time of discharge"[64]—even as they upheld the opposition between receiving a pension and getting healthy: "The consideration that recognizing a DB in a psychopath can promote symptoms that suggest an illness and prevent a cure, must not be the deciding factor in judging DB or KDB."[65]

The new laws and the vagueness of constitutional theory thus left a gray area within pension policy, opening up space for doctors' individual interpretations and judgments. Consequently, the prevailing approach to pensioning was, in the words of psychiatrist Ernst Kretschmer, "a contradictory, subjective, instinctive decision of the individual arbiter."[66] Kretschmer took it upon himself to rectify this and—with the support of the Württemberg War Ministry and the backing of Gaupp—proposed a unified approach for pensioning war and accident hysterics shortly after the war.[67] Kretschmer's central goal was to find a systematic way of establishing to what degree a subject's symptoms were directly dictated by his will. But hysterical neuroses lay on a spectrum, extending from pure simulation to severe sickness and encompassing all points in between—this further complicated his attempts to find objective, scientific criteria for determining questions of compensation and accountability.

Kretschmer's solution introduced new analytical categories to pensioning questions. He broke the issue down into two scales: a neurological and a psychiatric. On the neurological scale, hysterical reactions ranged between *reflexive* and *willed* behaviors, terms he found preferable to the Freudian categories of conscious and unconscious.[68] This determination could be made by observing patient behavior. Patients whose symptoms persisted over a long period and in the apparent absence of onlookers were more likely to be reflexive hysterics. Willed hysteria, on the other hand, was more blatantly opportunistic and instrumental. Patients who had been hard workers before the war, or those who worked despite the persistence of painful symptoms, were not likely candidates. Likewise, men who stopped enjoying life by, for example, giving up meat for aggravated stomachs, probably had no sickness of will; engaging in pleasure-seeking activities, on the other hand, was a sign of willed hysteria, as was the sudden disappearance of symptoms immediately after a medical examination.

The hysteric's willed muscle activity, Kretschmer observed, often hardened into a kind of habitual behavior or "hysterical habituation," an intermediate category that lay between reflexive and willed conditions. Such symptoms as a shaking right hand, facial tics, and paresis of the ankle (*Spitzenfuss*) were signs of a likely habituation. While nearly all hysterical conditions resulted from a combination of these elements, the neurological analysis sought to identify the dominant source. In those patients where the will to be sick predominated, the psychiatric question also had to be addressed—here doctors had to ask whether the patient's will lay within the scope of the normal or the pathological.

The neurological scale was designed to determine the ability to work and therefore pension eligibility, while the psychiatric scale concerned criminal accountability (for simulating or exaggerating symptoms). Patients judged to be legitimately sick by both neurological and psychiatric criteria, and who had not responded to treatment, would be entitled to a pension. And men who showed their will to recover and behaved decently could be rewarded with small, transitional pensions. But, Kretschmer warned, pensions should never be granted to threatening or paranoid patients. When awarded, psychiatric pensions should be kept low (not to exceed 25 to 30 percent) and should remain lower than the pensions awarded for superficially similar maladies with organic basis.

In August 1919 Kretschmer and Gaupp circulated these proposals to neurologists and psychiatrists with experience treating war neurosis—including Nonne, Kaufmann, Ferdinand Kehrer (a key architect of the Baden system), and Liebermeister—to psychiatric clinics throughout Germany and Austria and to General Schultzen at the War Ministry. They sought feedback and practical tips that could be passed on to doctors acting as psychiatric experts.[69] Gaupp asked for guidelines for making the neurological judgment on speech, sight, and hearing disorders; for differentiating accident neurosis after a blow to the head from physical brain trauma; and for detecting simulation and exaggeration.

While the respondents generally praised Kretschmer for his industriousness and his thoughtful contributions, they raised a number of reservations. Several doctors warned that the plan was too complex and unwieldy and introduced too much new terminology into clinical practice. Furthermore, feared Kurt Schneider, the use of a "neurological scale" would mislead many doctors into falsely attributing the cause of these psychogenic symptoms to somatic nerve damage.[70] A Dr. Schröder from the Greifswald psychiatric clinic pointed out that Kretschmer's scheme was no more scientific than other approaches and that there could be no purely objective grounds for distinguishing hysteria from simulation.[71] Psychiatrist Friedrich Mörchen chided Kretschmer for failing to emphasize that war hysteria is not really an illness but rather a manner of reacting in those with a weak, primitive constitution.[72] Ultimately, then, neither Kretschmer's thoughtful if somewhat abstruse proposals nor legislative efforts were able to unify psychiatric pension procedures; they continued to be con-

tested in psychiatric circles and remained a source of great conflict between patients and psychiatrists. The psychiatric crusade continued on a case-by-case
basis.

Memory Matters: Case Histories as Traumatic Narratives

"If this doctor had returned from the field sick or had spilled his blood for
the Fatherland, he would certainly not see a war disability as only a means to
an end. . . . The war-disabled man is also a human being and not a dog as so
many think today sadly. I demand justice for myself, and for every dignified
German man."[73] These words, written by a pension petitioner after he was examined at a Hannover neurosis ward and accused of exaggerating his symptoms, attest to the continued hostility between patients and their psychiatric
examiners. At a 1922 demonstration of a war-disabled association in Munich,
for example, psychiatrist Karl Weiler was singled out for his unfavorable pension rulings and publicly denounced as a "pension squeezer" (*Rentendrücker*).[74]
The economic hardships of the immediate postwar years further strained already acrimonious psychiatrist-patient relationships. Patients often feared being examined, suspecting doctors of maliciously wanting to take away their
pensions.[75] While the rapid devaluation of their savings made veterans and
their families more desperate to receive disability compensation from the state,
these same forces rendered the state less able or willing to pay them. Indeed, the
window of pension eligibility for war neurotics narrowed appreciably over the
course of the Weimar years as psychiatric campaigns bore fruit first in 1926 and
again in 1929.

The Neurological and Psychiatric Clinic of Berlin's Charité hospital was a
major setting for evaluating psychiatric pension claims—military as well as
civilian. The clinic, under Bonhoeffer's direction, served in this capacity for the
local Berlin Pension Office, the National Pension Office, and for many munic-
ipal and regional offices throughout Germany; it was the nation's highest authority for psychiatric pension claims.[76] When pension appeals were evaluated
at the Charité, the medical arbiter received a dossier containing the patient's
complete medical history and, where appropriate, his military record. The resulting rulings (*Obergutachten*), often richly detailed discourses on the state of
psychiatric science, offered doctors a forum for debating the significance of war
service on individual life and health. They reveal the rivalries between psychiatrists and nonspecialists over pension eligibility and show that the conflict between hysteria and traumatic neurosis—still a clash between two medical
subcultures—continued long after the war. These rulings make it possible to
track changes in psychiatric policy over the Weimar years and reveal the shifting status of the war and war-related trauma in the postwar period. They present an ideal source for analyzing the formation of the war's medical memory.

Ernst Mann was a tailor who had served one year at a garrison when he was hit by a train door. Complaining of headaches, dizziness, and heart palpitations, Mann entered the Spandau garrison hospital in 1916, where a doctor reported that his hands shook and he stuttered. Over the following months, Mann was transferred back and forth between hospitals and his unit, and was hypnotized with minor success in a neurosis station. When he was examined at the Görden asylum near Brandenburg—the same institution where such illustrious figures as Oskar Maria Graf and George Grosz had been pronounced insane[77]—he was characterized as "a pension neurotic of the most unpleasant variety" and as "whining, weak-willed and listless."[78] Despite his lingering complaints, Mann was discharged without a pension. He applied for reconsideration after the war, tracing his ongoing suffering to his year of garrison duty and in particular the train door incident.

Ewald Stier examined Mann in Berlin in 1919 and concluded that there was no illness. Stier wrote that the symptoms were essentially fabricated for the sake of a pension and thus had no causal relationship with war trauma. However, in another examination later in the same year, a general practitioner sympathetic to the patient's claims rejected Stier's ruling and estimated that Mann's earning power was diminished by 75 percent and that his symptoms were the direct result of the wartime occurrence. Mann's case ultimately wound up at the Charité for adjudication, and Bonhoeffer ruled on it in the spring of 1922. The question for Bonhoeffer was whether a causal connection could be established between the 1916 incident and Mann's subsequent troubles.

Bonhoeffer flatly rejected the veteran's claims. The diagnosis he reached was "war hospital hysteria" (*Lazaretthysterie*), which indicated that the symptoms arose not from traumatic war conditions but from the influence of other patients in a hospital station:

> Experience leaves no doubt that the primary mechanism in the hospital hysteric is grounded in the desire to have the symptoms observed in others, which occasions him—whether consciously or not—to recapitulate them. During the war this wish was based on the fear of military, that is, front duty. As a consequence, with the cessation of these fears, that is, with the declaration of unfitness or after the end of the war, these symptoms observably disappear; in those isolated cases where they persist, their durability can be seen without exception as the wish for a compensatory pension.[79]

This peculiar diagnosis reflected the wartime assumption that hospitals, as hotbeds of suggestion and bad influences, were detrimental to men susceptible to war neuroses and that true recovery had to occur at the workplace. As evidence, Bonhoeffer argued that the hypnotic treatment at Görden had succeeded in curing Mann of his hysterical symptoms. It was only when he saw another patient suffering a tremulous attack that Mann became agitated and his hysterical symptoms reappeared. For Bonhoeffer, then, it was the infectious proximity of other psychopaths, together with the wish for compensation, rather than any catalyzing trauma, that accounted for Mann's lingering symptoms.

In his ruling Bonhoeffer may have anticipated an objection. The fact that Mann's hysterical condition arose from his experience in the hospital station would seem to dictate the state's assumption of responsibility. However, Bonhoeffer firmly stated that the ultimate cause of Mann's suffering could be traced back to his psychopathic constitution. "The precondition for such a reaction," he wrote, "is a particular constitution, usually an in-born psychopathology. . . . A causal relationship between the neurotic condition and the accident is to be denied."[80]

Psychiatric experts applied similar logic to the case of Otto Schmied, a construction worker who was originally discharged from service with a 30 percent pension for hysterical symptoms. In 1925 Schmied was thrown in a building site explosion. After the accident he showed the classic clinical picture of a traumatic neurosis: he lost his powers of speech and saw the return of his wartime symptoms, tremulous shaking and difficulty walking. Finding that his ability to earn was further reduced and claiming that his new health problems represented a worsening of his war-related nervous condition, Schmied applied for additional compensation, which necessitated that his military pension be reevaluated. In March 1926, however, the Imperial Insurance Office ruled that Schmied's ability to earn had not diminished and that the accident was not the cause of his suffering.

After an appeal, Dr. Kraft of the Charité upheld that ruling in his 1926 report. Current psychiatric knowledge, Kraft wrote, disputed the notion that hysteria was an actual illness.

> Even the acknowledgment of DB for "hysteria," on which grounds S. is still receiving a thirty percent pension, does not conform to the current state of hysteria research. It is, in fact, not possible to speak of hysteria as of a unified illness. . . . It is rather a matter of reactions which can be found in individuals with in-born psychopathic constitutions. Such psychopaths are more troubled by the difficulties of daily life than the so-called normal, average person and need an enormous amount of psychic labor to carry out its requirements. As a consequence, they break down, even under normal circumstances, but especially in heightened difficulties, and flee—a characteristic of hysterical reactions—into illness.[81]

The so-called trauma, Kraft continued, could only be seen as an excuse, a trigger for behaviors that were deeply rooted in the psychopathic constitution and its attendant survival strategies. Because these hysterical reactions represented unconscious behavior patterns, they often seemed to be authentic expressions of illness, which made them all the more difficult to detect. Only trained specialists, the psychiatrist maintained, were in a position to identify such conditions. No wonder, then, that laypeople often failed to grasp the reality behind war neurosis and bestowed misplaced sympathy and charity on these men. Kraft upheld the 1926 decision and concluded that Schmied (unconsciously) exploited the accident of the preceding year to produce a set of psychogenic symptoms for the sake of a pension and thus should not be entitled to compensation.

Fritz Hinze, a third example, had been a barber who served with the *Landsturm* (home guard) from November 1914 through the spring of 1915 when he was hospitalized for a lung infection. Afterwards he returned to the field, but was removed in 1918 due to advanced age (forty-four), at which time he was transferred to a horse depot. There in November 1918, Hinze was kicked in the head by a horse and was treated for head trauma in a Freiburg hospital. Months later, after he was discharged, he worked first for a police department and then in a barber shop. At some point in 1919 Hinze was observed to shake. Eventually his shaking interfered with his work and apparently cost him his job. Stating that he was unable to work, Hinze filed for military compensation and traced his nervousness and tremors back to the horse depot accident.

A Düsseldorf pension court declared his capacity for work reduced by 70 percent due to the "nervous consequences" of the head injury. But that ruling was overturned by a Koblenz examiner who attributed the shaking to the hysterical wish for compensation. The case was ultimately sent to the Charité where, in October 1923, a Dr. Hoenig made his recommendation. Hoenig doubted that there was a causal relationship between the accident and the hysterical symptoms, in view of the time that had elapsed before the symptoms appeared. But, declaring himself unable to reach a verdict with the material before him, Hoenig suggested that Hinze be referred to a nerve clinic in Cologne or Düsseldorf for further evaluation. The results of the case are unclear, but in view of the prevailing patterns, it is unlikely that the compensation claim was honored.

Consider also the case of Georg Bamberg, a Schwerin-born NCO who was hospitalized twice during the war for nervous symptoms.[82] Bamberg spent a month in a Posen hospital for neurasthenia in the summer of 1916 and was placed in a reserve hospital for three weeks in 1918, again with neurasthenic symptoms. He was released that November, and nine months later he applied for a pension, complaining of headaches, lethargy, and pains in his limbs. After a January 1920 examination, Bamberg was sent on to the observation station at the Görden asylum. There he complained of occasional hysterical attacks that prevented him from working for weeks at a time. Although the examining doctor suspected Bamberg was exaggerating his symptoms to inflate his pension allotment, he nevertheless diagnosed "psychogenic nervous weakness" caused or at least worsened by his war service, and he awarded a pension of 25 percent.

Bamberg applied for a pension increase in 1923 and again in 1925. The first time he was paid off in the form of a capital settlement as part of the wave of capital settlements of that year. The second time his case was eventually sent to Berlin for evaluation, and his pension was revoked in a December 1926 decision. The author of the ruling was Dr. Christel Roggenbau, a psychiatry assistant at the Charité. Roggenbau reversed the earlier diagnoses and instead attributed Bamberg's condition to hysterical wishes and desires (*Begehrungsvorstellungen*) in the presence of a psychopathic constitution.[83] Roggenbau included an excursus on the current state of knowledge about hysteria, clearly intended to inform nonspecialists about hysteria's nature and to stop the practice of pensioning its symptoms:

> A hysterical condition is not an illness, but the reaction of a psychopathic personality. A hysterical reaction is a particular form of mental disposition which is taken on to attain a certain goal. This disposition can be given up at any time when it seems useful. . . . It can be assumed that the goal of the hysterical symptoms in B. was satisfied by a good working income, and that upon the disappearance of these favorable circumstances the old hysterical symptoms reappeared in 1925. . . . The war service was only the occasion which aroused in B. a certain kind of wish complex."[84]

In Roggenbau's summation, as in case after case, psychogenic symptoms were attributed not directly to traumatic experiences but to various wishes or imaginative desires, and the return of such symptoms in the postwar context was equated with pension neurosis. Another example of this equation can be found in the case of Erich Jost, a furnace maker from lower Silesian Schweidnitz who had no history of illness before entering the army.[85] Jost served on the western front in the Second Grenadier Regiment of Schweidnitz and on August 24, 1915, was thrown and partially buried in an explosion near the Vimy Ridge, probably in the British offensive of Messines. Knocked unconscious, Jost was taken to a nearby field hospital and several days later found himself in a reserve hospital facility in Halle. The records from Halle reveal that he had frightening dreams (filled with fires and Cossacks), underwent drastic mood changes, claimed to hear artillery fire, and suffered from fainting spells. But with a week's rest, Jost showed signs of recovery and was sent back to his battalion. However, after only several weeks on the eastern front he reported to another hospital station with new nervous symptoms. This time Jost was sent home to the reserve hospital Volksgarten in Schweidnitz, where he complained of pain in the back of his head, constant exhaustion, and persistent insomnia.

Doctors could find no organic basis underlying Jost's condition. They observed a severe shaking of the fingers and tongue and noted extreme sensitivity in the scalp. His examiners also reported loss of memory; it seems Jost had no recollection of the several days between the initial explosion and his arrival in Halle. On a more subjective note, the doctors recorded Jost's state of confusion. He seemed to have no understanding of what was going on around him, and he came across as unintelligent. In October 1916, more than a year after the initial explosion, he was released from military service. An examining doctor ruled that his ability to earn had been reduced by 75 percent, and he was pensioned accordingly. His diagnosis was simply, "stupefaction and chronic headaches due to burial."

After his release Jost found work in a munitions factory. There he crushed a finger in a machine accident, an occurrence that reinitiated the compensation process and occasioned review of his military pension. In the meantime, Jost joined the *Freikorps* (the militant bands of anti-Semitic, anti-Slavic, and anti-communist freebooters that formed after the war), and his unit sent him to a Görlitz nerve station for reexamination, and there he was treated for hysteria. The rest of his life was marked by frequent reexaminations, rediagnoses, and pension adjustments until his death from a stroke in 1922. But the case did not end there. Jost's widow then filed for military compensation, claiming that the death was a direct result of nerve damage suffered during his military service. The final opinion in this case was written by Dr. Crutzfeldt, another psychiatric assistant at the Charité, in May 1926. Crutzfeldt established that the death was causally related to neither the shell explosion of 1915 nor the subject's history of hysterical symptoms. The hysteria, he concluded, could be traced to wish complexes—the sign of a pure pension neurosis—and could not be linked to his war service.

With remarkable consistency these cases show how veterans used narratives of trauma to pursue their pension claims; that is, they put forward accounts that retrospectively identified one or several central traumatic moments as the source of their long-term suffering. (Interestingly, many of these accounts revolved around noncombat events, as the train door incident and the horse kick, for example.) Veterans' traumatic narratives were often supported (or possibly even proposed) by general practitioners and other nonpsychiatrists in whom these men frequently found a sympathetic ear, and they were crafted—consciously or not—to conform to trauma theory and pension parameters. Psychiatric specialists, on the other hand, steadfastly opposed these narratives of trauma with another version of events, a version that rewrote the traumatic story with an alternative narrative by positing an inborn psychopathic constitution and by emphasizing the power of wishes and pension greed to provoke symptoms. Seldom calling these men simulators, psychiatrists nonetheless cast doubt on the authenticity of their symptoms and consistently defined hysteria as a pathological type of reaction. In such accounts the precipitating trauma lost any meaning except, possibly, as an excuse for developing symptoms.

This narrative disparity had important economic consequences, particularly as the grim economic picture pitted veterans and their representatives against the state in a bitter struggle for shrinking resources, at least until the economic stabilization of the mid-1920s (and then with even greater ferocity after the crash of 1929). The significance of these encounters, however, was more than just economic—it was also political and cultural. Indeed, for veterans the dehumanizing effects of the pension system became a subject of literary parody and political ire.[86] Franz Müller, for example, the veteran with whose case this chapter began, exclaimed to his examiners: "You all think that you can just dictate, and I'll dance. Dictatorship has been fought from the beginning in the Prussian Republic, and I will fight you all now too, and am not to be placated. . . ."[87]

Over the course of the 1920s, it became steadily more difficult for men to receive financial compensation for war-related psychological suffering, and psychiatric opposition grew increasingly steadfast. According to Stier, the doctor "stands between two patients, which are here represented on one side by the allegedly or actually injured man and on the other side by the community of the working and tax paying population . . ."[88] Denying pensions, thus, was seen to serve both the collective good of the nation and the welfare of the individual patient.

By the middle of the decade growing numbers of doctors absolutely opposed compensation for all postaccident nervous symptoms, whether incurred in peacetime or war, allegedly for the good of both the patients and the whole nation. The Freiburg psychiatrist Alfred Hauptmann, for example, declared a "war against pension hysteria" in 1925, writing that, "to give a hysteric an accident pension does not mean compensating him, but rather debilitating him."[89] And in 1926 Friedrich Panse, a Berlin asylum psychiatrist, compared the responses of accident victims in different national and historical contexts and concluded that neurotic illnesses only arose where pension systems existed. He thus explained the symptoms through the awareness of the possibility of compensation; hence, for Panse, "the absolute refusal of all compensation for purely neurotic conditions after accidents can be generally implemented without any negative consequences."[90] Doctors such as Hoche had made that point, the ideogenic critique of social insurance, already in the 1890s, but when Panse put forth similar conclusions in the postwar era, the object of his attack was the war neurotics. In view of the war's prodigious and peripatetic casualties, Panse's article reinforced the separation of war neurotics from the war's legitimate victims and agitated against the former's compensation.

That year Stier presented a list of ten principles (*Leitsätze*) in which he declared that cutting off pensions was the only humane approach to dealing with accident hysterics.[91] Stier's principles and a landmark 1926 ruling were recognized as the guidelines for pension decisions by the National Pension Court and the Imperial Insurance Office, which effectively reversed the path-breaking decision it had made in 1889 to accept traumatic neuroses as actionable.[92] The revised ruling was based on the assumption that the pension application process itself was damaging to mental and nervous health, and thus as many people as possible should be spared from it; hence, psychiatrists argued, pension eligibility had to be sharply circumscribed.[93] The decision, then, reaffirmed that for both war hysterics and accident neurotics a swift return to work was the only therapeutically viable option. "If accident neurosis is an illness," Stier wrote, "then curing it with money is impossible."[94] In the same year, in an effort to "bury the so-called traumatic neurosis once and for all," Bonhoeffer wrote that accident hysteria cases should be sent for psychiatric-neurological evaluation as quickly as possible and that doctors should hold to the principle that hysterical reactions are not to be pensioned.[95] Thus, ten years after the Munich War Congress and thirty-seven years after the initial ruling, traumatic neurosis was, at least in theory, laid to rest. The 1926 decision, in fact, was recognized as valid by the Nazi state in 1939 and the Federal Republic of Germany in 1957, although it was modified five years later.[96]

Yet, the 1926 decision was not the last word on the subject for Weimar-era psychiatrists. In 1929 a conference in Berlin addressed the pension problem once again. Otto Martineck, who had become medical director in the Imperial Labor Ministry, presided over the three-day event, which included lectures by such psychiatrists as Stier, Hoche, Weiler, and Bonhoeffer, who was represented by his assistant Dr. Jossmann. The lecturers were asked to address four interrelated questions. Are nervous symptoms worthy of compensation when they (1) make themselves felt only years after the initial event; (2) reappear years after being cured or done away with; (3) become worse after having stabilized for a number of years; and (4) remain long after compensation?[97] With the exception of the Berlin psychotherapist Arthur Kronfeld, who criticized prevailing pension policies and the notion of the psychopathic constitution, most lecturers attacked the 1926 ruling for not going far enough. There was essentially no disagreement that the answer to all four questions should be an emphatic *No.*

Masculinity, Memory, and the Will to Trauma

Historian Michael Geyer has theorized that war trauma was "inverted" between the two world wars.[98] Identifying the confrontation with mass death as the central thread in Germany's twentieth-century trajectory, Geyer observes a process in the interwar years whereby trauma was, in a sense, mastered, as both the individual body and the imaginative, social body were hardened to the consequences of physical and emotional distress and shock.[99] While the shocks of World War I overwhelmed combatants and civilians in both body and mind, Germans began to steel themselves to the industrialized slaughter—military and ultimately genocidal—of World War II, facing its trials, according to Geyer, with a studied apathy. Applied to psychiatry, these insights suggest that German psychiatrists played a role in the inversion of trauma through their wartime and postwar practices. Psychiatric theory helped give trauma positive connotations and thereby contributed to a collective forgetting of war's potential psychopathological impact.

Geyer characterizes the confrontation with mass death as a "cultural field of contention."[100] But while he historicizes the experience of man-made death, he accepts trauma as a transhistorical, essentialized category. However, the pension struggles between veterans and psychiatrists—indeed the vexed history of traumatic neurosis—show the category's very constructedness, that it was constituted by patients and some doctors, contested by psychiatrists, and ultimately devalued in the discursive field between psychiatrists and veterans.

Indeed, war trauma was yet another casualty of the war. Wartime psychiatry gradually stripped the shocks, jolts, and stresses of the battlefield of their harmful (psychological) consequences. After an initial period of uncertainty in the face of unpredictably high numbers of neuroses, Germany's psychiatrists began to return to prewar views of trauma, which located pathologies in the patient's constitution rather than in external events. A crucial step in this transformation came in the traumatic neurosis debate of the middle of the war, when Oppenheim's opponents began to rally around evidence that decoupled traumatic antecedents and allegedly posttraumatic symptoms. Breakdowns, therefore, could not be explained by the horror of a blinding explosion, the terror of being buried alive, the sudden sight of a dead or maimed friend; far more dangerous was the allure of the pension for men of weak mental constitution.

By the middle of the war, the front and military spirit entered psychiatric discourse as healthier alternatives to civil society. Furthermore, soldiers often rejected and disdained the pity and sympathy of their loved ones at home. Analogously, medical writers consistently asserted the toxicity of sympathetic displays by female relatives and strove to protect war neurotics from their "damaging" influence, sequestering patients, when possible, in an all-male environment. The *Heimat,* a world where women held down men's jobs, was condemned as a site of deviance and decay; its "softening and disturbing influence," psychiatrists believed, bred weakness of will, laziness, and addiction to pensions.[101] And Weimar-era welfare measures only intensified these threats, meaning that for the highly suggestible male hysterics, peacetime was actually far more dangerous than war.[102]

In contrast to the pathologies of the *Heimat,* the experience of mobilization had been characterized as authentic and salutary, and writers favorably juxtaposed the front community to the sentimentality and mawkishness of the women at home.[103] Indeed, the closer to the front one went, psychiatrists came to believe, the less neurotic "contagion" could be found. The home front, on the other hand, was continually condemned as rife with bad influences and psychological "disease carriers" such as the war disabled, beggars, and doting female relatives, not to mention shirkers and war profiteers.[104] If war neurosis was contagious, then it was most likely to be caught in German territory in a hospital or a welfare office, or in any place where men sat around dwelling on their symptoms rather than working. And by this logic, the sites of psychological safety and well-being were those closest to the physical dangers and ever-present risks of war.

These premises represented the resumption of prewar ideas—ideas formed before anyone could have predicted the dreadful realities of modern, total war. Psychiatrists, among others, had extolled war as a solution to the ills of the Wilhelmine era, indeed as a means of uniting a fragmented people and as a medical prescription for soft, emasculated German men, which presaged fascist notions of the hardened male body.[105] The "natural" wartime environment was construed as a healthful antidote to the deteriorating conditions of Germany's expanding cities and the perceived decadence and degeneration of imperial society, which could rescue the nation's mental and moral health from the corrosive effects of technology and industrial growth.[106]

Psychiatric treatment also reflected this attempt to normalize the extraordinary conditions of war, by which the "traumatic" was construed as healthy and the "normal" as pathogenic. The infamous Kaufmann method, for example, sought to cure war neurosis by recreating the shocks of the battlefield within the treatment room, demonstrating to these unfortunate patients that a stay in the hospital was hardly an escape from the terrors of military life. And even verbal treatments, which generally operated through hypnosis or suggestion, aimed to convince men that they were not sick and strove to replace the self-serving, hysterical impulses of the patient with the hard, disciplined will of the doctor. Treatments, thus, also contributed to this reversal, turning the hospital into a site of "trauma" and construing work and war service as the domain of the healthy German man.

A final step in the transformation of trauma began in the later 1920s, a time when, Geyer writes, the inverted approach became ascendant.[107] This new view was best embodied by Ernst Jünger, whose writings embraced the confrontation with industrial slaughter as a baptism of fire. Jünger celebrated the transformative power of the front experience; his war narrative, like those of psychiatric pension petitioners, claimed that he was no longer the same man after his war experience. Jünger, however, turned the formulation on its head. Unlike the veterans who claimed to be destroyed by the war, to have returned from Flanders' Fields as broken men, for Jünger the war experience forged a new man, a thoroughly modern, mobilized identity, born of the rigors of the front ordeal.[108] The confrontation with death brought rebirth and transcendence. Though not a specifically Nazi vision, this conception had much in common with the militant struggles of Weimar's far right, with its discourse of permanent war and constant mobilization. And it merged with powerful associations that the Nazis drew on in their mythology of World War I and their attempts to sacralize the memory of the war dead and to cast their militant struggle as the continuation of Germany's national cause.[109]

The Nazi movement repeatedly vilified the Weimar state for not honoring the war's victims. In the Nazi vision, the republic's founders, a cabal of Jews and Marxists, were responsible for sabotaging the war effort and had stabbed the nation in the back. War hysterics were similarly implicated.[110] Psychiatric responses to pension claims intersected with and reinforced these revisionist memories. Accordingly, Weimar welfare provisions, rather than the war, were cast as the true threat to mental health and national efficiency. While the militant right derided the Weimar state for failing to sufficiently honor the war's victims, it charged, conversely, that the state was coddling the hysterics. Psychiatric experts, by denying the pathological impact of wartime shock on the individual, served these new narratives that rewrote war's brutal consequences and found the key to Germany's redemption and resuscitation in military (and indeed total) mobilization. With the war's unprecedented carnage just a dozen years in their past, many Germans came to believe that a war-making state could cure their malaise.

Of course, the connections between World War I psychiatry and "Nazi medicine" are not so simple, and only several of the doctors discussed in this book became Nazi Party members or worked closely with the National Socialist regime. There was certainly much psychiatric support for and cooperation with the Nazis' medical measures, as evidenced by the sterilization laws of July 1933 and psychiatric participation in the mass murder of the mentally ill starting in September 1939. Yet among psychiatrists such outright collaboration with Nazi atrocities was most common among the younger generation.[111] Most of the leaders of World War I psychiatry were politically conservative, not radically right wing, and many of the authorities on war hysteria, already in their midsixties by 1933, saw the Nazi takeover as an opportune time for retirement. Many others, Jews and leftists in particular, were forced to flee; several, such as Ernst Simmel and Kurt Goldstein, were fortunate enough to reestablish their careers abroad.

Nevertheless, the Nazi project did fulfill many common psychiatric goals, inasmuch as the Nazis sought to base politics on biomedical principles, gave certain doctors heightened influence over state policy, and promised to rejuvenate and rebuild the nation.[112] As champions of a eugenically informed and highly instrumentalized psychiatry—that is, an approach to mental health that prioritized the needs of the nation over the welfare of the individual patient—leading World War I psychiatrists may have contributed to the mentalities that made possible the path from "mass well-being" to "mass annihilation."[113]

More broadly, psychiatric approaches to the hysteria problem furthered a kind of bureaucratic rationalization, which did not necessarily prefigure the brutalities of Nazi-era psychiatry but characterizes a much more general medicalized modernity. However, psychiatric views of trauma did overlap powerfully with the fascist celebration of war and violence and its allegedly salutary effects on men and nations.

The inverted approach to trauma, the valorization of war's dangers was, of course, only one of many competing discourses on war and trauma in Weimar Germany. It would be naïve to deny that many individuals and groups continued to mourn the immense destruction brought by the Great War, and the wrenching sadness of wartime devastation scarred Weimar's cultural landscape, from the sculptures of Käthe Kollwitz to the lugubrious strains of *Nosferatu*. A traditional, sentimental culture of grieving infused many of the Weimar period's commemorative efforts and persisted through the 1920s and 1930s. Indeed, there was hardly an outpouring of war enthusiasm in 1939.[114] But war memories were not homogeneous. They were carried by different groups and were shaped and reshaped by postwar circumstances and social conflicts. They often took the form of contested narratives with high material stakes that focused the nation's political, social, and economic struggles. As such the medical science of memory actively participated in a collective act of forgetting, as psychological suffering was increasingly marginalized and trauma was subsumed into a celebration of war's rigors. In the process psychiatrists helped the Weimar state manage its crippling war expenses. Psychiatric theory and the state's financial needs converged to dictate the denial of traumatic memory.

While psychiatrists had reported phenomenal success at bringing neurotics into industrial and agricultural work during the war, in the Weimar period they believed they faced more formidable obstacles. "The hardships of our time," warned psychiatrist Friedrich Mörchen, "are particularly favorable circumstances for the development of neurotic reactions."[115] Peacetime, it turned out, posed a far greater health danger than the shocks and strains of modern warfare, and psychiatrists feared the consequences of the Weimar Republic's toxic combination of rampant unemployment and public assistance. It seemed only fitting, then, that it would take another war to reestablish a healthy national community. By the time Nazi Germany dragged the world back into war, German psychiatry had long been mobilized for its own war. Hermann Oppenheim's legacy still had to be defeated.

Conclusion

HISTORICAL ACCOUNTS OF posttraumatic stress disorder conventionally assert a lineage that begins with John Eric Erichsen in the 1860s and passes through a number of other major medical figures—Charcot, Janet, Freud—before ending up with the PTSD diagnosis and more contemporary trauma theorists. The wars and catastrophes that scarred the twentieth century gave trauma progressively greater attention and brought, in turn, newer, more sophisticated theories of traumatic suffering. In a trajectory that runs from railway spine to survivor guilt, from shell shock through the Shoah to Gulf War syndrome, doctors, psychologists, and policy makers have endlessly debated the long-term impact of the horrifying ordeals of war, violence, and genocide on the mind and nerves.

This book has drawn on and engaged with the intellectual history of trauma in several ways. Above all, it has sought to insert Hermann Oppenheim into that history and has claimed that his traumatic neurosis diagnosis deserves an eminent place in trauma's historical lineage. However, the preceding chapters have also identified a kind of counterhistory of the trauma idea, a significant strand of German thought that rejects the trauma model of psychological suffering. Beginning with the opposition to Oppenheim, the refusal of trauma comprises a striking source of psychiatric continuity from the 1880s through the 1920s. While different arguments and evidence were used in different situations, a continuous thread runs from Oppenheim's earliest opponents—Strümpell, Schultze, and Seeligmüller in the late 1880s—through Gaupp, Nonne, and Hoche during World War I. It culminates in the efforts of such figures as Stier and Bonhoeffer in the 1920s, as they sought to put an ultimate end to traumatic neurosis and its allegedly disastrous impact on Germany's collective health and national strength.

Modern male hysteria is a product of the shadow side of trauma's history. As this book has argued, the diagnosis arose in imperial Germany as an alternative to traumatic neurosis, its popularity overdetermined by a confluence of scientific change, economic anxiety, and social division. Indeed, hysteria had the great advantage of releasing the state from responsibility for the suffering of workers and soldiers because it located the pathological source within the subject rather than in an external accident or combat event. Whether they were the volatile bourgeois daughters of the fin de siècle or the constitutionally unfit German war neurotics, hysterics—psychiatrists believed—lacked willpower and self-control. Their symptoms served the flight into illness; hysterical soldiers succumbed to their fear of death and pension greed and shirked their duty to the national cause. The specter of the male hysteric, then, haunted the German imagination as the nation progressed along the path to modernity: He sapped Germany's economic power, undermined its military strength, and ran amok in the revolutionary chaos of 1918–1919. To the conservative, stridently nationalistic psychiatric profession, male hysterics symbolized Germany's social, political, and economic catastrophes.

A second intellectual tradition often intersected with and cross-fertilized the medical rejection of trauma. This discursive strain valorized qualities such as willpower and physical and emotional hardness as the fundament of a revived German masculinity. This thinking is palpable from the Wilhelmine culture of male honor through the celebrations of war's salubrious spiritual powers in 1914. It informed psychiatric critiques of Germany's pathological modernity and helped inflame the backlash against social insurance legislation. This sanctification of work and masculine hardness resonated in wartime active treatment and in the atmosphere of the specialized neurosis stations—to be made back into a proper man, the male hysteric required a strong dose of masculine virtue, the company of his front comrades, or the rewards of labor. Indeed, the countertrauma discourse prefigured interwar notions of mobilized male identity and, in its most extreme guise, evokes the figure of the Weimar freebooter, who refused to demobilize and sought out the shocks and dangers of battle long after the war's end.

This book began by critiquing some commonly assumed German continuities. It concludes by asserting other continuities. It has argued against the idea that war psychiatry in Germany was uniquely brutal and nationalistic in a way that directly foreshadowed the medical crimes of the Nazi regime. It emphasized, instead, psychiatry's role in a broader modernization process, a general tendency of increased medical control over individual life and the eclipsing of subjectivity in a faceless administrative modernity. On the other hand, this book has pointed to a continuous countertrauma trajectory. Although the Weimar right's traumatophilia, its celebration of the redemptive power of violence, was certainly swept up into the Nazi cause, the countertrauma discourse has had a far broader resonance in Western society, culture, and medicine. Indeed, we still lack a satisfying framework for making sense of serious emotional distress and remain skeptical—often for good reasons—about trauma's rather uncertain pathological reality. Because of our persistent medical materialism we continue to stigmatize suffering that is invisible and less "real"—we often wish survivors and veterans would stop talking and get back to work. Ultimately, the dialectic of trauma and countertrauma inheres in and complicates our continued ambivalence toward traumatic suffering. We are, I suspect, far more sympathetic to the countertrauma discourse, and even the worker-patient ideal, than we care to admit.

Abbreviations

AfP	*Archiv für Psychiatrie und Nervenkrankheiten*
AZP	*Allgemeine Zeitschrift für Psychiatrie und psychisch-gerichtliche Medizin*
BA RAM	Bundesarchiv, Berlin, Reichsarbeitsministerium
BA RMdI	Bundesarchiv, Berlin, Reichsministerium des Innern
BayHSta	Bayerisches Hauptstaatsarchiv, Munich
BKW	*Berliner klinische Wochenschrift*
DMW	*Deutsche medizinische Wochenschrift*
DZN	*Deutsche Zeitschrift für Nervenheilkunde*
GehStA	Geheimes Staatsarchiv Preußischer Kulturbesitz, Berlin
HUB	Archiv der Humboldt Universität zu Berlin
MA	Militärarchiv Württemberg, Stuttgart
MK	*Medizinische Klinik*
MMW	*Münchener medizinische Wochenschrift*
MPN	*Monatsschrift für Psychiatrie und Neurologie*
NZ	*Neurologisches Centralblatt* (renamed *Neurologisches Zentralblatt*)
SHSA	Sächsisches Hauptstaatsarchiv, Dresden
UAG	Archiv der Justus-Liebig-Universität, Giessen
UAT	Universitätsarchiv Tübingen
WKW	*Wiener klinische Wochenschrift*
WMW	*Wiener medizinische Wochenschrift*
ZfS	*Zeitschrift für Sexualwissenschaft*
ZgNP	*Zeitschrift für die gesamte Neurologie und Psychiatrie*

Notes

Introduction

1. A number of accounts of the German medical profession and National Socialism appeared in the late 1980s and 1990s, and the literature continues to grow. These works have emphatically overturned older assumptions that saw medicine as a victim of Nazi tyranny and revealed doctors' deep complicity in designing and carrying out the sterilization and "euthanasia" programs of the Third Reich. See Weindling, *Health, Race, and German Politics;* Kater, *Doctors under Hitler;* Proctor, *Racial Hygiene;* Friedlander, *The Origins of Nazi Genocide.* On psychiatry, see Burleigh, *Death and Deliverance;* Bock, *Zwangsterilisation im Nationalsozialismus;* Walter, *Psychiatrie und Gesellschaft in der Moderne.*

2. On eugenics and the continuities/discontinuities with National Socialism, see the works cited in note 1 and the following: Weiss, *Race Hygiene and National Efficiency;* Weingart, Kroll, and Bayertz, *Rasse, Blut, und Gene;* Berg and Cocks, eds., *Medicine and Modernity;* Wetzel, *Inventing the Criminal.*

3. For a recent discussion of the *Sonderweg* debate, see Eley, "Introduction: Is There a History of the *Kaiserreich*?" See also Moeller, "The Kaiserreich Recast?"

4. See, e.g., Blasius, *"Einfache Seelenstörung."*

5. Siemen, *Das Grauen ist Vorprogrammiert,* esp. 7–51; K.-H. Roth, "Die Modernisierung der Folter in den beiden Weltkriegen," 8–75; Fischer-Homburger, "Der Erste Weltkrieg und die Krise der ärztlichen Ethik," 122–34; Riedesser and Verderber, *Aufrüstung der Seelen;* idem, *Maschinengewehre hinter der Front;* Komo, *"Für Volk und Vaterland."* Exceptions (i.e., works that place war neurosis within different contexts and approach it from different perspectives) include D. Kaufmann, "Science As Cultural Practice: Psychiatry in the First World War and Weimar Germany," 125–44; Ulrich, "Nerven und Krieg: Skizzierung einer Beziehung," 163–91; Fischer-Homburger, *Die traumatische Neurose;* Leed, *No Man's Land.* On Austrian psychiatry in the war, see Hofer, "Nerven-Korrekturen," 249–68.

6. Above all, see Siemen, *Menschen Blieben auf der Strecke.*

7. For comparative perspectives, see the special issue on shell shock in the *Journal of Contemporary History* 35 (Jan. 2000) and Lerner and Micale, "Trauma, Psychiatry, and History," 1–30. Among the many works that discuss the British case, see Shephard, *A War of Nerves;* Leese, *Shell Shock;* Stone, "Shellshock and the Psychologists," 242–71; Bogacz, "War Neurosis and Cultural Change in England, 1914–22," 227–56; Feudtner, "'Minds the Dead Have Ravished,'" 377–420. On other national contexts, see T. Brown, "Shell Shock in the Canadian Expeditionary Force, 1914–1918," 308–32; Cox, "Invisible Wounds," 280–305; and works cited in note 8.

8. On the French case, see Roudebush, "A Battle of Nerves" (Ph.D. diss.). On Italy, Bianchi, "Psychiatrists, Soldiers, and Officers in Italy during the Great War," 222–52; idem, "La Psychiatrie Italienne et la Guerre," 118–31.

9. On Yealland, see Shephard, *War of Nerves;* Showalter, *The Female Malady,* esp. 167–94.

10. See Rabinbach, *The Human Motor;* Campbell, *Joy in Work, German Work.*

11. Esther Fischer-Homburger was the first historian to set the war neurosis problem within the context of German debates on trauma and "traumatic neurosis." See Fischer-Homburger, *Die traumatische Neurose.* See also Eghigian, *Making Security Social;* Mülder-Bach, ed., *Modernität und Trauma.*

12. Max Weber, "Science As a Vocation" and "On Bureaucracy," 129–56, 196–244.

13. Peukert, *The Weimar Republic.*

14. Peukert, "The Genesis of the 'Final Solution,'" 234–52.

15. See Mary Nolan, *Visions of Modernity;* Campbell, *Joy in Work.* On the cultural and gender-historical consequences of rationalization, see Reese et al., eds., *Rationale Beziehungen?;* Tröger, "The Creation of a Female Assembly-Line Proletariat," 237–69; Grossmann, *Reforming Sex;* idem, "The New Woman and the Rationalization of Sexuality in Weimar Germany," 159–71; idem, "*Girlkultur* or the Thoroughly Rationalized Female," 62–80.

16. Whalen, *Bitter Wounds,* esp. 89.

17. On the psychiatric reform movement after the war, see Walter, *Psychiatrie und Gesellschaft,* 225–322.

18. See Labisch, *Homo Hygienicus;* Cocks, "The Old As New," 193–213; Berg and Cocks, eds., *Medicine and Modernity.* On rationalization and war, see Daniel Pick's important study: *War Machine: The Rationalisation of Slaughter in the Modern Age.* See also Cooter and Sturdy, "Of War, Medicine, and Modernity," 1–21.

19. The classic study of hysteria's history is Veith, *Hysteria: The History of a Disease.* The most useful work on hysteria's historiographical, methodological, and bibliographical dimensions is Micale, *Approaching Hysteria: Disease and Its Interpretations.* See also Sander L. Gilman et al., *Hysteria Beyond Freud;* Shorter, *From Paralysis to Fatigue;* Slavney, *Perspectives on "Hysteria";* and works cited in notes 20 and 21.

20. For an interesting methodological model, see Shorter, "Mania, Hysteria, and Gender in Lower Austria, 1891–1905," 3–31.

21. Porter, "The Body and the Mind, the Doctor and the Patient," 225–85.

22. See, e.g., Weindling, *Health, Race, and German Politics;* Grossmann, *Reforming Sex.*

23. On Foucault's impact on the historiography of psychiatry, see Micale and Porter, eds., *Discovering the History of Psychiatry;* Scull, "Psychiatry and Its Historians," 239–50. See also Jan Goldstein, *Console and Classify;* Blasius, *Der verwaltete Wahnsinn.*

24. Foucault, *Madness and Civilization;* idem, *Power/Knowledge.*

25. For a historiographic survey of hysteria, see Micale, *Approaching Hysteria.* Here I am referring respectively to Showalter, *The Female Malady;* Smith-Rosenberg, *Disorderly Conduct;* Goldstein, *Console and Classify;* and Porter, "The Body and the Mind."

26. Showalter, *Female Malady,* esp. chap. 7; idem, "Hysteria, Feminism, and Gender," 286–344; idem, "Rivers and Sassoon: The Inscription of Male Gender Anxieties," 61–69.

27. Leed, *No Man's Land,* esp. chap. 5. See also idem, "Fateful Memories," 85–100.

28. For a recent exception, see Goldberg, *Sex, Religion, and the Making of Modern Madness.* Sander Gilman's work constitutes another important exception. See, e.g., "The Image of the Hysteric," 345–452; *The Case of Sigmund Freud.* Surprisingly, only one treatment of war neurosis in Germany incorporates a gender-historical approach. See Link-Heer, "Männliche Hysterie: Eine Diskursanalyse," 364–96.

29. The study of masculinity in German history has only begun in recent years. Important studies include Kühne, *Männergeschichte, Geschlechtergeschichte;* Frevert, *Ehrenmänner: Das Duell in der bürgerlichen Gesellschaft;* G. L. Mosse, *The Image of Man;* and Theweleit's masterful study, *Male Fantasies.*

30. See, e.g., Deborah Cohen, *The War Come Home.* On the war's cultural consequences, see Eksteins, *Rites of Spring;* Eberle, *World War I and the Weimar Artists.* The war's memory has inspired a flurry of historical writing in recent years. Key works include Winter, *Sites of Memory, Sites of Mourning;* Fussell, *The Great War and Modern Memory;* and Sherman, *The Construction of Memory in Interwar France.*

31. See Winter, "Shell-shock and the Cultural History of the Great War," 7–11.

32. For a historiographical and bibliographic guide to this rapidly growing body of scholarship, see Lerner and Micale, "Trauma, Psychiatry, and History: A Conceptual and Historiographical Introduction." See also Young, *The Harmony of Illusions;* Leys, *Trauma: A Genealogy;* Mülder-Bach, ed., *Modernität und Trauma;* Fischer-Homberger, *Traumatische Neurose.*

33. See, e.g., Israëls and Schatzman, "The Seduction Theory," 23–59.

34. See Eissler, *Freud As an Expert Witness*. On psychoanalysis in the war, see Brunner, *Freud and the Politics of Psychoanalysis*, 106–22; Büttner, "Freud und der Erste Weltkrieg"; Hoffmann, "War, Revolution, and Psychoanalysis," 251–69; Reichmayr, "Psychoanalyse im Krieg," 36–58.

35. On Janet, see Ellenberger, *The Discovery of the Unconscious*, chap. 6; van der Hart, Brown, and van der Kolk, "Pierre Janet's Treatment of Post-Traumatic Stress," 379–95; van der Hart and Friedman, "A Reader's Guide to Pierre Janet on Dissociation," 3–16.

36. On insurance and welfare legislation in Germany, see Eghigian, *Making Security Social;* Hong, *Welfare, Modernity, and the Weimar State, 1919–1933;* Crew, *Germans on Welfare.*

37. On Charcot and trauma, see, e.g., Micale, "Jean-Martin Charcot and 'les névroses traumatiques,'" 172–90.

38. For a different approach to this question, see E. T. Dean Jr., *Shook over Hell.*

39. Young, *Harmony of Illusions;* Hacking, *Rewriting the Soul;* Antze and Lambek, eds., *Tense Past;* Merridale, "The Collective Mind," 39–56.

40. See Antze and Lambek, "Introduction"; Young, "Bodily Memory and Traumatic Memory."

41. The study of memory has become a vibrant area of historical scholarship. For an introduction to the topic in German studies, see Fritzsche and Confino, eds., *The Work of Memory.* A thorough review of new works on memory can be found in Fritzsche, "The Case of Modern Memory," 87–117. On German memory and World War I, see G. L. Mosse, *Fallen Soldiers;* Bessel, "The Great War in German Memory," 20–34; Ulrich and Ziemann, eds., *Krieg im Frieden.*

Chapter 1. Pathological Modernity

1. On the history of psychiatry in Germany, see Blasius, *"Einfache Seelenstörung"*; Engstrom, "The Birth of Clinical Psychiatry"; Schindler, "Psychiatrie im Wilhelminischen Deutschland."

2. See Shorter, *A History of Psychiatry,* esp. chap. 3.

3. See, e.g., Eulner, *Die Entwicklung der medizinischen Spezialfächer.*

4. Weindling, *Health, Race, and German Politics,* 167–68; Peukert, "The Genesis of the 'Final Solution.'"

5. See McClelland, "Modern German Doctors: A Failure of Professionalization?" 81–98.

6. On professionalization in Germany, see especially McClelland, *The German Experience of Professionalization.* See also Cocks and Jarausch, eds., *German Professions, 1800–1950;* Kater, "Professionalization and Socialization of Physicians in Wilhelmine and Weimar Germany," 677–701; and on psychiatric professionalization in France, Goldstein, *Console and Classify,* esp. chap. 1.

7. Schindler, "Psychiatrie im Wilhelminischen Deutschland."

8. Psychiatry became a requirement in 1906. Eulner, *Die Entwicklung,* 261. For a detailed discussion of university psychiatric clinics, see Engstrom, "The Birth of Clinical Psychiatry."

9. On the differentiation between neurology and psychiatry, see Hirschmüller, *Freud's Begegnung mit der Psychiatrie,* 29.

10. On Griesinger, see Engstrom, "Birth of Clinical Psychiatry," chap. 3; Shorter, *History of Psychiatry,* chap. 3.

11. See, e.g., Matthias M. Weber, *Ernst Rüdin.*

12. Quoted in Schindler, "Psychiatrie im Wilhelminischen Deutschland," 90.

13. Ibid., 19.

14. Ackerknecht, *A Brief History of Psychiatry,* 82. See also Eulner, *Die Entwicklung,* 257.

15. Shorter, *History of Psychiatry.* On German asylums in the early nineteenth century, see Goldberg, *Sex, Religion, and the Making of Modern Madness.* On nineteenth-century British asylums, see Scull, *Museums of Madness;* idem, ed., *Madhouses, Mad-doctors, and Madmen.*

16. Walter, *Psychiatrie und Gesellschaft in der Moderne,* 129; Kraepelin, *Lebenserinnerungen,* 12–13.

17. Goldberg, "A Reinvented Public"; Engstrom, "The Birth of Clinical Psychiatry," 425–52.

18. Examples of this interpretation can be found in Blasius, *Umgang mit Unheilbarem;* Scull, "Psychiatry and Social Control in the Nineteenth and Twentieth Centuries," 149–69.

19. See Goldberg, *Sex, Religion, and the Making of Modern Madness.*
20. Blackbourn, *The Long Nineteenth Century,* 352. On the historiography of the German Empire, see Chickering, ed., *Imperial Germany: A Historiographic Companion;* Eley, ed., *Society, Culture, and the State in Germany, 1870–1930.*
21. See Schubert-Weller, *"Kein schönrer Tod . . ." Die Militarisierung der männlichen Jugend.*
22. Weindling, *Health, Race, and German Politics,* esp. 81.
23. Schindler, "Psychiatrie im Wilhelminischen Deutschland," 92.
24. Blasius, *Umgang mit Unheilbarem,* 59–60.
25. See the files in the collection: "Schriften zur Frage des Irrenwesens," GehStA, Berlin-Dahlem, Rep. 76, VIIIB, Akte 1827; Schindler, "Psychiatrie im Wilhelminischen Deutschland," 91–93.
26. Shorter, *History of Psychiatry,* chap. 2.
27. Nordau, *Entartung.*
28. On degeneration, see Pick, *Faces of Degeneration;* Nye, *Crime, Madness, and Politics in Modern France;* Chamberlin and Gilman, eds., *Degeneration: The Dark Side of Progress.*
29. Wetzell, *Inventing the Criminal,* 46–47.
30. Ibid., 49.
31. For a discussion of the idea of the psychopathic constitution, see Fränkel, "Über die psychopathische Konstitution bei Kriegsneurosen," 287–309.
32. Bonhoeffer, "Ein Beitrag zur Kenntnis des großstädtischen Bettel- und Vagabondentums," 1–65.
33. Quoted in Schindler, "Psychiatrie im Wilhelminischen Deutschland," 32.
34. Hellpach, *Nervenleben und Weltanschauung.*
35. See Weiss, *Race Hygiene,* esp. 10–11.
36. Weindling, *Health, Race, and German Politics,* 80–81.
37. On the rise of eugenics in German science and medicine see Proctor, *Racial Hygiene;* Weindling, *Health, Race, and German Politics;* Weiss, *Race Hygiene;* Weingart, Kroll, and Bayertz, *Rasse, Blut, und Gene;* Berg and Cocks, eds., *Medicine and Modernity.*
38. On the history of the research institute, see Matthias M. Weber, " 'Ein Forschungsinstitut für Psychiatrie . . . ,' " 74–89.
39. Sommer, *Familienforschung und Vererbungslehre.*
40. Schindler, "Psychiatrie im Wilhelminischen Deutschland," 35.
41. Ibid., 24–25.
42. Wetzell, *Inventing the Criminal,* 100–101.
43. See Proctor, *Racial Hygiene,* in addition to works cited in n. 37. On eugenic psychiatry in North America, see Dowbiggin, *Keeping America Sane.*
44. Weindling, *Health, Race, and German Politics,* esp. chap. 5.
45. See Weiss, *Race Hygiene.*
46. See Walter, *Psychiatrie und Gesellschaft,* esp. 204–11.
47. Caplan, "Trains and Trauma in the American Guilded Age," 57–77; idem, "Trains, Brains, and Sprains," 387–419. See also Schivelbusch, *The Railway Journey.*
48. Trimble, *Post-Traumatic Neurosis;* Fischer-Homburger, *Traumatische Neurose;* Lerner and Micale, "Trauma, Psychiatry, and History."
49. See Fischer-Homburger, *Traumatische Neurose.*
50. Caplan, "Trains, Brains, and Sprains," 392.
51. Quoted ibid.
52. See Veith, *Hysteria;* Gilman, "The Jewish Psyche," 60–104.
53. Quoted in Micale, *Approaching Hysteria,* 161.
54. For a contemporary German treatment of this issue, see Placzek, *Das Geschlechtsleben des Hysterischen,* 14. Historical discussions include Micale, "Hysteria Male/Hysteria Female," 200–42; Showalter, *Female Malady.*
55. See Micale, "Hysteria Male/Hysteria Female," 227.
56. Quoted in Caplan, "Trains, Brains, and Sprains," 393.
57. Paraphrased in Fischer-Homberger, *Traumatische Neurose,* 59.

58. See Caplan, "Trains and Trauma."

59. See Goldstein, *Console and Classify,* 351–77; Harris, *Murders and Madness,* esp. 155–207.

60. Micale, "Charcot and the Idea of Hysteria in the Male," 370; idem, "Hysteria Male/Hysteria Female," 203.

61. On Charcot's theories of traumatic hysteria, see Micale, "Jean-Martin Charcot and 'les névroses traumatiques,'" 172–190; idem, "Hysteria Male/Hysteria Female."

62. Micale, "Jean-Martin Charcot and 'les névroses traumatiques,'" 116.

63. Ibid., 124.

64. Gaupp, "Über den Begriff der Hysterie," 457.

65. For discussions of hysteria, women, and gender, see Showalter, *Female Malady;* idem, "Hysteria, Feminism, and Gender"; Shorter, "Mania, Hysteria, and Gender"; Gilman, "The Image of the Hysteric."

66. Micale, *Approaching Hysteria,* 116–20.

67. Goldstein, *Console and Classify,* esp. 322–77. See also Roudebush, "A Battle of Nerves," chap. 2; Porter, "The Body and the Mind."

68. For Charcot's lectures, see Charcot, *Clinical Lectures on Diseases of the Nervous System.*

69. For descriptions, see, e.g., Showalter, *Female Malady,* 147–55; Goldstein, *Console and Classify.*

70. Micale, "Hysteria Male/Hysteria Female," 207; idem, "Charcot and the Idea of Hysteria in the Male."

71. See Decker, *Freud in Germany,* 73–87.

72. Fischer-Homburger, *Traumatische Neurose,* 112.

73. Nonne, *Anfang und Ziel meines Lebens,* 76.

74. Ibid., 177–78. See also Löwenfeld, *Über den Nationalcharakter der Franzosen;* Sommer, *Krieg und Seelenleben.*

75. Ellenberger, *The Discovery of the Unconscious;* Levin, "Freud's Paper 'On Male Hysteria,'" 377–97.

76. See Lerner, "From Traumatic Neurosis to Male Hysteria," 140–71, for more biographical details on Oppenheim. This account of his life and career is based primarily on the following sources: Emil Herz, "Hermann Oppenheim: Auszug aus den Erinnerungen," unpublished manuscript, n.d., Emil Herz Collection, AR 2538, archive of the Leo Baeck Institute, New York; idem, *Denke ich an Deutschland in der Nacht;* Selbach, "Über Hermann Oppenheim," Vortrag auf der Eröffnungsfeier der Jahresversammlung der Deutschen Gesellschaft für Neurologie am 4.10.1978, Emil Herz Collection, AR 2538, archive of the Leo Baeck Institute; Cassirer, "Hermann Oppenheim," 669–71; A. Stern, *In bewegter Zeit.*

77. H. Oppenheim, *Die traumatischen Neurosen,* 2d ed., 2.

78. H. Oppenheim, "Über einen sich an Kopfverletzungen und allgemeine Körpererschütterungen anschließenden cerebralen Symptomenkomplex," 725. For a description of the reactions to his lecture, see idem, *Die traumatischen Neurosen,* 2d ed., 8.

79. H. Oppenheim, *Die traumatischen Neurosen.*

80. Ibid., 119–22.

81. H. Oppenheim, *Die traumatischen Neurosen,* 2d ed., 121–22. On the misrepresentation of Oppenheim's ideas, see Cassirer, "Hermann Oppenheim," 669–71.

82. H. Oppenheim, *Die traumatischen Neurosen,* 178. See also the 1894 edition of his neurology textbook, *Lehrbuch der Nervenkrankheiten für Ärzte und Studierende.*

83. H. Oppenheim, *Die traumatischen Neurosen,* 2d ed., 6.

84. Ibid., 6–7.

85. "Ausstellung und Besoldung von Professoren sowie Einrichtung neuer Lehrstuhle, 1886–1893," HUB, Medizinische Fakultät, Akte 1381, Bd. 5.

86. On Althoff, the condition of the German universities at this time, and the politics of the academic profession, see Jarausch, *Students, Society, and Politics in Imperial Germany;* McClelland, *State, Society, and University in Germany, 1700–1914,* esp. 239–322.

87. See Kater, "Professionalization and Socialization," 677–701, esp. 689, for a discussion of

medical anti-Semitism in the 1880s and 1890s and the obstacles that made it difficult for Jewish physicians to attain university chairs in medicine.

88. On the radicalization of medical professionals in late-nineteenth-century Germany, see Jarausch, *Students, Society, and Politics;* on the rise of anti-Semitism in the 1880s and 1890s in the medical profession, see Weindling, *Health, Race, and German Politics;* Kater, "Professionalization and Socialization," esp. 689–94. Likewise, several current authors write that anti-Semitism prevented Oppenheim from becoming a professor. See Decker, *Freud in Germany,* 86; Weber, *Ernst Rüdin,* 35.

89. S. Braun, "Aus der Geschichte einer Westphälisch-jüdischen Familie," *Allgemeine Düsseldorf,* 24 July 1964, 11, Emil Herz Collection, AR 2538, archive of the Leo Baeck Institute; the suggestion that Oppenheim marry a non-Jewish woman was recounted by Oppenheim's student Arthur Stern. Stern, *In bewegter Zeit,* 55. However, another account dismisses these allegations of anti-Semitism as unlikely in view of the fact that Althoff's own daughter had married the Jewish doctor Alfred Goldscheider. Selbach, "Über Hermann Oppenheim," 4.

90. Oppenheim, *Lehrbuch der Nervenkrankheiten.* On the influence of Oppenheim's textbook, see A. Stern, *In bewegter Zeit,* 56; Selbach, "Über Hermann Oppenheim," 4; Decker, *Freud in Germany,* 86.

91. See Gilman, *The Case of Sigmund Freud.*

92. Kater, "Professionalization and Socialization," 679.

93. See Shorter, *From Paralysis to Fatigue,* 218–20; Efron, *Medicine and the German Jews,* 237. According to Efron, some 50 percent of Berlin's doctors were Jews, and 75 percent of them were in private practice.

94. A. Stern, *In bewegter Zeit,* 65–66.

95. For a discussion of the culture of university medical professors, see Kater, "Professionalization and Socialization," 680–82.

96. Historian Roy Porter has written extensively on the idea of a medical marketplace and the economic pressures on physicians. On psychiatry and hysteria, see Porter, "The Body and the Mind," 256.

97. For an example of his work with Eastern European Jews, see Oppenheim's "Zur Psychopathologie und Nosologie der russisch-jüdischen Bevölkerung," 1–9.

98. H. Oppenheim, *Psychotherapeutische Briefe.*

99. Radkau, *Das Zeitalter der Nervosität.*

100. See Drinka, *The Birth of Neurosis,* esp. chap. 8; Radkau, *Zeitalter der Nervosität,* esp. 185–202; idem, "Die Wilhelminische Ära als nervöses Zeitalter," 211–41; and Rabinbach, *Human Motor,* esp. chap. 6.

101. See, e.g., Binswanger, *Die Pathologie und Therapie der Neurasthenie.*

102. Radkau, "Wilhelminische Ära," 218. See also Baader, "Stadtentwicklung und psychiatrische Anstalten," 239–53.

103. Radkau, "Wilhelminische Ära," 216. On the archetypes of nervousness, see Stekel, *Nervöse Leute: Kleine Federzeichnungen.*

104. See Shorter, *History of Psychiatry.*

105. H. Oppenheim, *Psychotherapeutische Briefe.*

106. Shorter, *From Paralysis to Fatigue,* 220.

107. For a history of insurance in the modern German state, see Eghigian, *Making Security Social.*

108. On the political and legal status of traumatic neurosis, see Fischer-Homburger, *Traumatische Neurose;* Eghigian, "Die Bürokratie und das Entstehen von Krankheit," 203–23; Moser, "Der Arzt im Kampf gegen 'Begehrlichkeit und Rentensucht,'" 161–83; Schmiedebach, "Die 'traumatische Neurose,'" 151–63.

109. H. Oppenheim, "Der Krieg und die traumatischen Neurosen," 258.

110. Quoted in Fischer-Homberger, *Traumatische Neurose,* 61.

111. See Frevert, "Bourgeois Honor." See also Nye, *Masculinity and Male Codes of Honor in Modern France.*

112. Greg Eghigian, "Hysteria, Insurance, and the Rise of the Pathological Welfare State in Germany, 1884–1926" (unpublished paper, 1993).

113. See Weindling, "Bourgeois Values, Doctors, and the State," 198–223.

114. Schmiedebach, "Sozialdarwinismus, Biologismus, Pazifismus: Ärztestimmen zum Ersten Weltkrieg," 97.

115. Jeschal, *Politik und Wissenschaft deutscher Ärzte im Ersten Weltkrieg.* See also Kater, "Professionalization and Socialization," esp. 681.

116. See Efron, *Medicine and the German Jews,* esp. 256.

117. Wollenberg, *Erinnerungen eines alten Psychiaters,* 3.

118. Eghigian, "The German Welfare State As a Discourse of Trauma," esp. 110.

119. Hoche, "Geisteskrankheit und Kultur," 16. Elsewhere Hoche wrote, "The existence of the accident insurance legislation soils [*trübt*] not only nervous and psychological symptom complexes, but in so doing affects everything that goes with it, the personal relationship of the doctors to these patients," "Über Hysterie," 331.

120. Fischer-Homburger, *Traumatische Neurose,* 131–32.

121. Ibid., 61–63.

122. Ibid., 69–70.

123. H. Oppenheim, "Der Krieg und die traumatischen Neurosen," 257.

124. Ibid., 258.

125. Ibid., 259.

126. Quoted in Eghigian, "German Welfare State," 107.

127. Micale, "On the Disappearance of Hysteria," 496–526. On the nineteenth-century expansion of the hysteria diagnosis, see Goldstein, *Console and Classify,* esp. 322–77.

128. Kraepelin, *Psychiatrie: Ein Lehrbuch für Studirende und Ärzte.*

129. Micale attributes the idea of hysterical constitution to Wilhelm Grieseinger; see *Approaching Hysteria,* 24.

130. Gaupp, "Über den Begriff der Hysterie," 458.

131. Bonhoeffer, "Wie weit kommen psychogene Krankheitszustände und Krankheitsprozesse vor," 371–86.

132. Gaupp, "Über den Begriff der Hysterie," 464.

133. See G. L. Mosse, "Masculinity and the Decadence," esp. 252–55; idem, *The Image of Man.*

134. Gaupp, "Über den Begriff der Hysterie," 458.

135. Ibid., 463.

136. Karl Bonhoeffer (1868–1948); Robert Gaupp (1870–1953); Alfred Hoche (1865–1943); Robert Sommer (1864–1937).

137. Weindling, *Health, Race, and German Politics,* 14–20; Weiss, *Race Hygiene,* 16–19.

Chapter 2. Mobilizing Minds

1. Quoted in Ulrich, "Nerven und Krieg: Skizzierung einer Beziehung," 164. See also Singer, "Wesen und Bedeutung der Kriegspsychosen," 177–80.

2. Hindenburg made these remarks to a Spanish journalist. Paraphrasing that quote, Gaupp asked in the same year, "What undermines the strength of nerves . . . more than hysterical despondency?" Gaupp, *Die Nervenkranken des Krieges,* 18. See also Sänger, "Über die durch den Krieg bedingten Folgezustände am Nervensystem," 567.

3. Joachim Radkau deals extensively with these themes in his book *Das Zeitalter der Nervosität.*

4. Singer, "Wesen und Bedeutung der Kriegspsychosen," 177.

5. Ibid.

6. Gaupp, "Krieg und Seelenleben!" 162.

7. Hellpach, "Lazarettdisziplin als Heilfaktor," 1208.

8. For an illuminating discussion of the notion of war enthusiasm and its political consequences, see Verhey, *The Spirit of 1914;* Ulrich and Ziemann, eds., *Frontalltag im Ersten Weltkrieg.* More generally on mobilization and "war enthusiasm," see Kruse, "Die Kriegsbegeisterung im Deutschen Reich," 57–89; Rürup, "Der Geist von 1914 in Deutschland,"

1–30; Horne, ed., *State, Society, and Mobilization in Europe;* Fritzsche, *Germans into Nazis,* 13–82.

9. See Chickering, "Total War: Use and Abuse of a Concept," 13–28.

10. Weindling, "The Medical Profession, Social Hygiene, and the Birth Rate in Germany, 1914–1918," 417–38.

11. Of the former group approximately 1,325 died and 2,149 were wounded. Some 6,000 dentists, 1,800 pharmacists, and many medical students also served in uniform. See Schjerning, *Die Tätigkeit und die Erfolge der deutschen Ärzte im Weltkriege;* Bleker, "Medizin im Dienst des Krieges," 13–28.

12. Bleker and Schmiedebach, eds., *Medizin und Krieg,* 261–62.

13. Jeschal, *Politik und Wissenschaft,* 32–33. See also Schwalbe, *Wissenschaft und Kriegsmoral,* esp. 21–34.

14. Binswanger, *Die seelischen Wirkungen des Krieges,* 12–18.

15. Sombart, *Händler und Helden, Patriotische Besinnungen.* On Sombart, see also Ringer, *The Decline of the German Mandarins,* 183–85.

16. Quoted in Schwalbe, *Wissenschaft und Kriegsmoral,* 21.

17. Schmiedebach, "Sozialdarwinismus, Biologismus, Pazifismus: Ärztestimmen zum Ersten Weltkrieg," esp. 118–22.

18. Tamm, "'Ein Stand im Dienst der nationalen Sache,'" 11–21.

19. For psychiatric texts that purvey stereotypes of the enemy, particularly the French, see Sommer, *Krieg und Seelenleben,* and Löwenfeld, *Über den Nationalcharakter der Franzosen.*

20. For a parallel argument on German criminology in World War I, see Wetzell, *Inventing the Criminal,* 109–15.

21. See Weiss, *Race Hygiene,* 17–19, and the essays in Eckart and Gradmann, eds., *Die Medizin und der Erste Weltkrieg.*

22. The military historian Michael Howard notes that in wars before 1870 deaths from sickness exceeded deaths directly due to combat by a factor of five to one; by the end of World War I, this ratio had been reversed. Howard, *War in European History,* 116. On advances in medical treatment that owed to the war, see Mayer-Gross, "Practical Psychiatry in War-Time," 1327–30; for advances in prosthetics, see Thomann, "'Es gibt kein Krüppeltum,'" 114–21; on advances in blood transfusion techniques, see Schlich, "'Welche Macht über Tod und Leben!'" 109–30. On fighting diseases during the war, see the essays by Weindling, Fantini, Prüll, and Müller in *Die Medizin und der Erste Weltkrieg.*

23. See Goldscheider, "Über die Ursachen des günstigen Gesundheitszustandes unserer Truppen im Winterfeldzuge," 161–75; Hoche, *Krieg und Seelenleben,* 5.

24. Riedesser and Verderber, *Aufrüstung der Seelen,* 10.

25. Quoted in Birnbaum, "Sammelbericht III," 383. See also Schjerning, *Tätigkeit und Erfolge,* 1.

26. Sommer, *Krieg und Seelenleben,* 13–14.

27. Ibid., 60. See also Karl Pönitz, *Die klinische Neuorientierung,* 1.

28. Robert Sommer, "Krieg und Heilkunst," unpublished manuscript, n.d., Robert Sommer Papers, UAG, Bd. 6.

29. For details on Sommer's life and ideas, see Meyer zum Wischen, "*Der Seele Tiefen zu ergründen . . .*" *Robert Sommer und das Konzept einer ganzheitlichen, erweiterten Psychiatrie.*

30. Robert Sommer, "Zur Psychologie des Krieges und der Erfindungen," unpublished manuscript, n.d., Robert Sommer Papers, UAG, Bd. 14, 43.

31. Binswanger, *Seelische Wirkungen,* 10.

32. Roth, "Kriegsgefahr und Psyche," 3.

33. Hofer, "Nerven-Korrekturen." See also Radkau, *Zeitalter der Nervosität.*

34. Quoted in Easton, *Red Count,* 222.

35. Quoted in Ulrich, "Krieg als Nervensache."

36. See Leed, *No Man's Land,* for a discussion of the idea that war represented an escape from society.

37. Binswanger, *Seelische Wirkungen,* 10.

38. Radkau, *Zeitalter der Nervosität,* 422–42. See also Herf, *Reactionary Modernism,* esp. 70–108.

39. G. L. Mosse, "Masculinity and the Decadence," esp. 252–55; idem, *The Image of Man.*

40. G. L. Mosse, "Masculinity and the Decadence." For the British case, see J. Oppenheim, *"Shattered Nerves,"* esp. 148.

41. Sombart, "The Kaiser in His Epoch," 287–312. For France, see Nye, *Masculinity and Male Codes,* 226.

42. See, e.g., Schubert-Weller, *"Kein schönrer Tod . . ."*

43. Quoted in Mommsen, "The Topos of Inevitable War," 26.

44. On this view of the war, see Leed, *No Man's Land,* esp. chap. 2.

45. Cited in Birnbaum, "Sammelbericht III," 317.

46. Sänger, "Über die durch den Krieg bedingten Folgezustände"; Laudenheimer, "Feldärztliche Beiträge über Kriegsneurosen," 1302.

47. Birnbaum, "Sammelbericht III"; Roth, "Kriegsgefahr und Psyche," 1–3.

48. Goldscheider, "Über die Ursachen," 161–75.

49. W. Schweisheimer, "Sinnesschärfung und Sinnesspannung an der Front," *Frankfurter Zeitung* (28 October 1915): 4–7, Robert Sommer Papers, UAG, Bd. 7.

50. Letter from Dr. Fritz Wolf, 9 September 1915, Robert Robert Sommer Papers, UAG, Bd. 7, 1.

51. "Die deutsche Kriegspille," *Frankfurter Zeitung,* n.d., Robert Sommer Papers, UAG, Bd. 7, 12.

52. See Birnbaum, "Sammelbericht III," 320. I am grateful to Heinz-Peter Schmiedebach for this point.

53. Burchard, "Sexuelle Fragen zur Kriegszeit," 375–76.

54. Donath, "Beiträge zu den Kriegsverletzungen und -erkrankungen des Nervensystems."

55. Ibid., 725.

56. See, e.g., Hoche, *Krieg und Seelenleben,* 26–27.

57. Quoted in Chickering, *Imperial Germany and the Great War, 1914–1918,* 9.

58. Hoche, "Über Hysterie," 332.

59. Goldscheider, "Über die Ursachen," 173

60. Wollenberg, *Erinnerungen,* 135.

61. Bonhoeffer, "Psychiatrisches zum Kriege," 435.

62. Gaupp, "Hysterie und Kriegsdienst," 361. Two years later Gaupp wrote: "While before the war you heard people talking about their nervousness everywhere, so that it was almost a disgrace to not be a 'little bit neurasthenic,' now no one has time to be hypochondrically concerned with his nerves." *Nervenkranken des Krieges,* 21–22.

63. Mendel, "Psychiatrisches und Neurologisches aus dem Felde," 3.

64. Binswanger, *Die seelischen Wirkungen,* 11.

65. Ibid., 21–22.

66. Hoche, *Krieg und Seelenleben,* 4–5. See also Redlich, "Einige Bemerkungen über den Krieg und unser Nervensystem," 467.

67. Sänger, "Über die durch den Krieg bedingten Folgezustände am Nervensystem."

68. Hoche, "Über Hysterie," 332.

69. Gottstein, "Die Sterblichkeit in Berlin während des ersten Kriegshalbjahres," 740. This was temporary, and suicide among soldiers in World War I ultimately far exceeded peacetime rates. Hahn, "'Widerstandslose, minderwertige Individuen,'" 273–97.

70. Birnbaum, "Sammelbericht II," 80. See also C. Dean, "The Great War, Pornography, and the Transformation of Modern Male Subjectivity," 65.

71. Wittkower and Spillane, "A Survey of the Literature of Neuroses in War," 2. For a detailed discussion of contemporary studies of the impact of the war on crime rates, see Wetzell, *Inventing the Criminal,* 109–15.

72. Goldscheider, "Über die Ursachen," 170.

73. Ibid. See also Everth, "Von der Seele des Soldaten im Felde," 8.

74. Binswanger, *Seelische Wirkungen,* 18.

75. Hoche, *Krieg und Seelenleben,* 27–29.
76. E. Meyer, "Psychosen und Neurosen in der Armee während des Krieges," 2085.
77. Robert Sommer, "Zur Psychologie des Krieges und deren Erfindungen," unpublished manuscript, n.d., Robert Sommer Papers, UAG, Bd. 14, 26–27.
78. Sommer, *Krieg und Seelenleben,* 8–9.
79. Quoted in Verhey, *Spirit of 1914,* 5. See Peter Fritzsche, *Nation of Fliers,* esp. 29, for similar expressions of organistic unity during air shows.
80. For a comparison of ideas of obedience and military discipline among the belligerent nations, see Smith, *Between Mutiny and Obedience.*
81. See, e.g., Freimark, *Die Revolution als Massenerscheinung,* 27–28.
82. Freud, "Thoughts for the Times on War and Death," 275–300.
83. Wollenberg, "Nervöse Erkrankungen bei Kriegsteilnehmern," 2181–83.
84. Suckau, "Psychosen bei Frauen in Zusammenhang mit dem Kriege," 328–56.
85. See LeBon, *The Crowd.*
86. Stelzner, "Aktuelle Massensuggestion," 371. See also Wollenberg, *Erinnerungen,* 134–36. There are many references to these fears in Karl Kraus's play, *Die letzten Tage der Menschheit.* See Kraus, *The Last Days of Humanity.*
87. Stelzner, "Aktuelle Massensuggestion," 387.
88. See Hoche, *Krieg und Seelenleben,* 35.
89. Bonhoeffer, "Psychiatrie und Krieg," 1777–79.
90. Wollenberg, "Nervöse Erkrankungen," 2181.
91. Fuchs, "Mobilmachungspsychosen," 25.
92. Hoche, *Krieg und Seelenleben,* 10.
93. Cited in Birnbaum, "Sammelbericht I," 329.
94. Alt, "Im deutschen Heere während der Kriegszeit aufgetretene psychische Störungen," 334.
95. As late as May 1915, Hoche praised the beneficial effects of the war on nervous and mental health. See "Über Hysterie," 331–35; see also the comments by Dr. Meyersohn in "Verhandlungen psychiatrischer Vereine," 221.
96. H. Oppenheim, *Die Neurosen infolge von Kriegsverletzungen,* 227.
97. Gaupp, "Hysterie und Kriegsdienst," 361. See also idem, "Krieg und Seelenleben!" 166.
98. This number is a very rough estimate that I have derived by extrapolating from the official *Reichswehr* statistics for one unit. See "Die Krankenbewegung bei dem Deutschen Feld- und Besatzungsheer," vol. 3 of *Sanitätsbericht über das Deutsche Heer im Weltkriege 1914/1918* (Berlin: E. S. Mittler, 1934), 145–49.
99. See Wollenberg, "Nervöse Erkrankungen," 2181–83.
100. See, e.g., Alt, "Im deutschen Heere"; Hoche, *Krieg und Seelenleben,* 21–22.
101. Bonhoeffer, "Psychiatrie und Krieg," 1777.
102. Geuter, "Polemos Panton Pater—Militär und Psychologie im Deutschen Reich 1914–1945," esp. 149. See also Lemmens, "Funktion und Anspruchswandel der militärmedizinischen Tauglichkeitsbeurteilung," 164–73. Mentally ill asylum patients were in principle excluded from the army, but individuals who had spent time in asylums were not, and it is conceivable that mentally ill (or formerly mentally ill) men lied about their medical histories.
103. On the U.S. army's efforts, see Wittkower and Spillane, "A Survey of the Literature," 23. On intelligence testing in the U.S. army, particularly in view of the professionalization of American psychology, see Samelson, "World War I Intelligence Testing and the Development of Psychology," 274–82; Kevles, "Testing the Army's Intelligence," 565–81. For a comparison of U.S. and British approaches, see Thomson, "Status, Manpower, and Mental Fitness," 149–66.
104. See Gaupp, *Nervenkranken des Krieges,* 12. Analogously, the physical standards for recruitment were progressively lowered as the war dragged on. For the British case, see Fussell, *The Great War and Modern Memory,* 9.
105. Letter from Broizem to Kommando des XII. Res. Korps, Dresden, 29 June 1915. "Sanitätsdienst, Allgemeines" in Akte 13539, Generalkom. des XII. Res. Korps, Institut für deutsche Militärgeschichte Collection, SHSA.
106. Robert Gaupp, 18 May 1918, UAT, Akte 308/89.

107. Mendel, "Psychiatrisches und Neurologisches," 3. See also Weygandt, "Versorgung der Neurosen und Psychosen im Felde," 1503–5, for a description of the various drugs used as well as the methods of subduing seriously disturbed soldiers.

108. Bonhoeffer, "Psychiatrie und Krieg," 1778.

109. Mann, "Neue Methoden und Gesichtspunkte zur Behandlung der Kriegsneurosen," 1333.

110. See Mitchell, *Fat and Blood*. For discussions of Mitchell's rest cure, see Drinka, *The Birth of Neurosis*, 197–210; Showalter, *Female Malady*, 140–42.

111. Karl Wilmanns in "Bericht über die Sitzung des bad. Landesausschusses der Kriegsbeschädigtenfürsorge, 26 October, 1917," 43–44, BA RAM, Film 36069.

112. Ibid., 41.

113. Ibid., 42.

114. Quoted in Kaufmann, "Zur Behandlung der motorischen Kriegsneurosen," 1523.

115. Letter from Robert Gaupp to Kriegsgerichte im Bereiche des XIII. (K-Württ.) Armeekorps, Tübingen, 28 January 1916. MA, Stellv. Generalkom. XIII. A.K., Bestand M77/1, Akte 1038.

116. See Hellpach, "Lazarettdisziplin als Heilfaktor," 1208.

117. Pönitz, *Die klinische Neuorientierung*, 26. See also Hoffmann, "Über die Behandlung der Kriegshysterie," 114–17.

118. Hellpach, "Lazarettdisziplin als Heilfaktor." See Bonhoeffer's contributions in "Berliner Gesellschaft für Psychiatrie und Nervenkrankheiten. Sitzung vom 14. Dezember 1914," NZ 34 (1915): 73–78.

119. See, e.g., Hellpach, "Lazarettdisziplin als Heilfaktor."

Chapter 3. Long Live Hysteria!

1. On Robert Gaupp's usage of "*Granatkontusion*," see Schmidt, "Die psychischen und nervösen Folgezustände," 538.

2. See Bonhoeffer, "Granatfernwirkung und Kriegshysterie," 51–58; Sarbo, "Granatfernwirkungsfolgen."

3. Fussell, *Great War and Modern Memory*.

4. Leys, "Traumatic Cures: Shell Shock, Janet, and the Question of Memory," 629 n. On the NYDN diagnosis, see Shephard, *War of Nerves*, esp. 54.

5. Herz, *Denke ich an Deutschland*, 72.

6. H. Oppenheim, "Der Krieg und die traumatischen Neurosen," 258.

7. Ibid., 259.

8. "Berliner Gesellschaft für Psychiatrie und Nervenkrankheiten," NZ 34 (1915): 74. See also H. Oppenheim, "*Die Neurosen infolge von Kriegsverletzungen*," 1.

9. For accounts of the British debate, see Shephard, *War of Nerves*; Leese, *Shell Shock*; Stone, "Shellshock and the Psychologists"; Bogacz, "War Neurosis"; and Feudtner, "'Minds the Dead Have Ravished.'"

10. See Link-Heer, "Männliche Hysterie."

11. On sex and gender in British wartime psychiatry, see Showalter, "Rivers and Sassoon." On the French case, see Roudebush, "A Battle of Nerves" (Ph.D. diss.).

12. Nonne, "Über erfolgreiche Suggestivbehandlung," 192.

13. See Chapter 6 for a discussion of the exceptions.

14. Gaupp, "Hysterie und Kriegsdienst," 362.

15. Hoche, *Krieg und Seelenleben*, 24–25.

16. Hoche, "Über Hysterie," 331.

17. Cimbal, "Die seelischen und nervösen Erkrankungen," 414.

18. Oppenheim certainly understood the passage as an attack on his ideas. He quoted this passage and defended himself in a later edition of the same journal. See H. Oppenheim, "Zur traumatischen Neurose im Kriege," 514–18.

19. On Oppenheim's influence in Berlin, see Bonhoeffer, "Lebenserinnerungen von Karl Bonhoeffer—Geschrieben für die Familie," 86. On Berlin's Jewish doctors, see Kater, "Professionalization," and Shorter, *From Paralysis to Fatigue*.

20. H. Oppenheim, "Der Krieg und die traumatischen Neurosen," 268.

21. Ibid.

22. Liepmann, "Über Hermann Oppenheim," 5.

23. See Chapter 8 for a detailed discussion of pension policy and the difficulties of assessing pension eligibility in trauma cases.

24. Quoted by Schmidt, "Die psychischen und nervösen Folgezustände," 538. For Oppenheim's response, see H. Oppenheim, "Zur traumatischen Neurose im Kriege," 514.

25. H. Oppenheim, "Neurosen nach Kriegsverletzungen," 213.

26. See "Berliner Gesellschaft für Psychiatrie und Nervenkrankheiten," NZ 34 (1915): 73–78. For other accounts of the meeting, see Zeller, "Die Hysterielehre," 126–27; Schmidt, "Die psychischen und nervösen Folgezustände."

27. "Berliner Gesellschaft für Psychiatrie und Nervenkrankheiten," 73.

28. Ibid., 78.

29. Ibid., 74.

30. H. Oppenheim, "Der Krieg und die traumatischen Neurosen," 260.

31. Bonhoeffer, "Lebenserinnerungen," 88.

32. See Mohr, "Die Behandlung der Kriegsneurosen," 131–41. The Wilmanns study is cited in Pönitz, *Klinische Neuorientierung,* 8–10; and Badischer Landesauschuß der Kriegsbeschädigtenfürsorge, "Merkblatt für die Fürsorge für nervöse Kriegsteilnehmer," n.d., UAT, 308/89 "Kriegsneurose," 2; also see Lust, "Kriegsneurosen und Kriegsgefangene," 1829–32.

33. Mörchen, "Traumatische Neurose und Kriegsgefangene," 1188–91; idem, "Der Hysteriebegriff bei den Kriegsneurosen," 1214–15.

34. For psychiatric studies of POWs that took into account issues of morale and national characteristics, see Birnbaum, "Sammelbericht VII," 57; Pappenheim, "Über Psychosen bei Kriegsgefangenen," 518–25. See also Liebermeister and Siegerist, "Über eine Neurosenepidemie im Kriegsgefangenenlager," 350–55; Placzek, *Das Geschlechtsleben des Hysterischen,* 9.

35. Quoted in Pönitz, *Klinische Neuorientierung,* 9.

36. Gaupp, *Die Nervenkranken des Krieges,* 14.

37. "Gaupp spricht über die Neurosen und Psychosen des Krieges," n.d., UAT, 308/42, 4.

38. See Pönitz, *Klinische Neuorientierung,* 9.

39. Ibid., 14.

40. Lewandowsky, "Erfahrungen über die Behandlung nervenverletzter und nervenkranker Soldaten," 1567; "Gaupp spricht über die Neurosen und Psychosen des Krieges," n.d., UAT, 308/42, 2; Jendrássik, "Einige Bemerkungen zur Kriegsneurose," 498.

41. Hauptmann, "Kriegs-neurosen und traumatische Neurosen," 20–32.

42. Gaupp, "Die Behandlung der nervösen Schüttellähmung durch starke elektrische Ströme," UAT, 308/89, 1 (emphasis in text). See also Wexberg, "Neurologische Erfahrungen im Felde," 1410–11.

43. See, e.g., R. Gerz, "Bericht über die vom preus. Kriegsministerium (Sanitätsdepartment) nach Berlin berufene Versammlung der Neurotikerärzte," Würzburg, 14 October 1918, BayHStA, San. Amt II. A.K., Bd. 14, 1.

44. See Nonne, "Soll man wieder traumatische Neurosen diagnostizieren?" 337–39.

45. H. Oppenheim, *Die Neurosen infolge von Kriegsverletzungen,* 266. On hypnosis and other forms of therapy at the museum hospital station in Berlin, see also idem, "Für und wieder die traumatische Neurose," esp. 227.

46. For an elaboration of this position, see Artwinski, "Über traumatische Neurosen nach Kriegsverletzungen," 248.

47. H. Oppenheim, "Zur traumatischen Neurose im Kreige," 515.

48. Hoche, "Beobachtungen bei Fliegerangriffen," 570–73; Jendrássik, "Einige Bemerkungen zur Kriegsneurose," 498. See also Pönitz, *Klinische Neuorientierung,* 40.

49. H. Oppenheim, *Die Neurosen infolge von Kriegsverletzungen,* 230.

50. Ibid., 228.

51. Ibid.

52. Ibid., 216.

53. The psychoanalyst Sándor Ferenczi ridiculed this term and several of Oppenheim's other categories as "unpronounceable" and noted that one of Oppenheim's critics proposed using these terms—"so that they lead to something useful"—as test words for diagnosing functional speech disorders. Ferenczi, "Die Psychoanalyse der Kriegsneurosen," 12n.

54. "Verhandlungen psychiatrischer Vereine," 164.

55. "Verhandlungen psychiatrischer Vereine," 195. See also Hoche, "Über Wesen und Tragweite," 347–67.

56. "Verhandlungen psychiatrischer Vereine," 199.

57. See Schaltenbrand, "Max Nonne," in *Grosse Nervenärzte,* 3:164–73; F. Stern, "Bericht über die Kriegstagung des deutschen Vereins für Psychiatrie in München am 21., 22, und 23. September 1916," 236–39; 249–52.

58. "Verhandlungen psychiatrischer Vereine," 203.

59. F. Stern, "Bericht über die Kriegstagung."

60. "Verhandlungen psychiatrischer Vereine," 209.

61. In a subsequent account, which is probably not terribly reliable, Nonne noted that three out of the thirty-four doctors who participated in the debate supported Oppenheim. See Nonne, "In Memoriam Hermann Oppenheim und Ludwig Bruns," 30.

62. F. Stern, "Bericht über die Kriegstagung," 252.

63. "Verhandlungen psychiatrischer Vereine," 219.

64. Ibid., 226.

65. Ibid., 227.

66. Ibid. Ludwig Bruns, a respected Hannover physician who died in 1917, has been referred to as Oppenheim's "only friend among doctors." See Selbach, "Über Hermann Oppenheim," 5.

67. "Verhandlungen psychiatrischer Vereine," 227.

68. Ibid., 230.

69. Ibid.

70. Ibid., 232.

71. Nonne, *Anfang und Ziel meines Lebens,* 179–80. Actually, Oppenheim lived until May 1919, almost three years after the Munich Congress.

72. H. Oppenheim, "Zur Frage der traumatischen Neurose," 1567.

73. H. Oppenheim, "Stand der Lehre," 1169. See Naegli, *Unfalls- und Begehrungsneurosen.* Oppenheim called Naegli's book, which attacked him harshly, "a work of damnation" (*Verdammungsschrift*). H. Oppenheim, "Stand der Lehre," 1169.

74. H. Oppenheim, "Stand der Lehre," 1169.

75. This characterization is from Birnbaum, "Sammelbericht V," 231.

76. Goldscheider, "Zur Frage der traumatischen Neurose," 1406–11.

77. Gaupp, "Kriegsneurosen."

78. H. Oppenheim "Zur Frage der traumatischen Neurose," 1567.

79. Ibid., 1568.

80. Ibid.

81. Ibid.

82. Ibid., 1569.

83. Ibid.

84. Selbach, "Über Hermann Oppenheim," 6.

85. Oppenheim, "Zur Frage der traumatischen Neurose," 1569.

86. Martineck, "Zur Frage der traumatischen Neurose," 44–45.

87. Cassirer, "Hermann Oppenheim," 669.

88. A. Stern, *In bewegter Zeit,* 59.

89. Nonne, "Zum Andenken an Hermann Oppenheim," 388–89. Years later, recalling how he took over the directorship of the German Neurological Association from Oppenheim, Nonne wrote that Oppenheim "never pulled out of the depression" caused by the Munich Congress. See Nonne, "In Memoriam Hermann Oppenheim und Ludwig Bruns," 30.

90. Jolly, "Über den weiteren Verlauf hysterischer Reaktionen," 590–91. See also Wagner, "Die Dienstbeschädigung bei nerven- und geisteskranken Soldaten," 227.

91. Stier, "Psychiatrie und Heer," 19 (emphasis in text). Stier's assertion that Oppenheim left the meeting early is not indicated in the protocols cited above, nor is it likely because Oppenheim made the third-to-last comment.

92. Hauptmann, "Kriegs-neurosen und traumatische Neurosen," 20.

93. H. Oppenheim, "Der Krieg und die traumatischen Neurosen," 258.

94. See, e.g., Daum, "Science, Politics, and Religion."

95. See Engstrom, "The Birth of Clinical Psychiatry," 120–34.

96. In the words of Oppenheim's Berlin colleague Hugo Liepmann, "If in addition to the scientific need to counter Oppenheim's errors on this subject, there was also an eminently practical, not only financial, but also national-medical [*volkshygienisch*] need, still we cannot overlook the fact that they were rooted in a humane, highly sympathetic character, the trustworthy, sincere and good attitude of the doctor toward the patient, a trait which earned him the love of his countless patients." Liepmann, "Über Hermann Oppenheim," 5.

97. On the "Jew count," see, e.g., Angress, "The German Army's 'Judenzählung' of 1916," 117–37; W. E. Mosse, ed., *Deutsches Judentum in Krieg und Revolution, 1916–1923.*

98. Stier, "Psychiatrie und Heer," 19.

Chapter 4. The Powers of Suggestion

1. Nonne, "Therapeutische Erfahrungen an den Kriegsneurosen in den Jahren 1914–1918," 102.

2. Nonne, *Funktionell-motorische Reiz- und Lähmungs- Zustände bei Kriegsteilnehmern und deren Heilung durch Suggestion und Hypnose* (Hamburg, 1916).

3. The method is only named in the first case. In making this film, Nonne actually used patients whom he had already treated. He hypnotized them so that they would show their prior symptoms for the camera, and then he hypnotized the symptoms away again, a technique he often used in his demonstrations. My thanks to Ulf Schmidt for this information. See Nonne, "Über Psychotherapie mit Filmvorführungen und Lichtbildern," 477–78.

4. For a discussion of these issues in the French context, see Roudebush, "A Battle of Nerves" (Ph.D. diss.).

5. Taking off from Walter Benjamin's discussion of shock and modernity, several works have discussed the role of photography and film in modern war as a means of numbing the traumas of mechanized combat through the "cold gaze" of the camera. See, e.g., Kaes, "The Cold Gaze," 105–17; idem, "War—Film—Trauma," 121–30; Hüppauf, "Experiences of Modern Warfare and the Crisis of Representation," 41–76; Herf, *Reactionary Modernism,* 99–100.

6. Nonne, "Über erfolgreiche Suggestivbehandlung," 216. See also Nonne and Wachsner, "Therapeutische Erfahrungen in der Behandlung sogenannter Neurosen," 271–73.

7. Nonne, "Therapeutische Erfahrungen," 105.

8. Quoted in Nonne, "Über erfolgreiche Suggestivbehandlung," 192.

9. Nonne, "Therapeutische Erfahrungen," 105.

10. Nonne, *Anfang und Ziel,* 178.

11. Ibid.

12. Ibid.

13. For the earlier figures, see Nonne, "Zur therapeutischen Verwendung der Hypnose," 136–38. At the Munich War Congress of September 1916, Nonne reported a success rate of just above 50 percent. This number, he wrote in 1917, "rose in December 1916 to 72% and has now risen to 80%. In the last two months I have cured 83% of my cases, and in the last three weeks, 90%." Nonne, "Über erfolgreiche Suggestivbehandlung," 200. For the later results, see Nonne, "Therapeutische Erfahrungen"; Pönitz, *Klinische Neuorientierung,* 28.

14. Nonne, "Zur therapeutischen Verwendung der Hypnose," 136–38.

15. Nonne, *Anfang und Ziel,* 179.

16. Quoted in Brunner, *Freud and the Politics of Psychoanalysis,* 110. See Nonne, "Therapeutische Erfahrungen," 109–10.

17. Nonne, "Therapeutische Erfahrungen," 105.

18. Nonne, *Anfang und Ziel,* 183.

19. Ibid., 179.

20. Ibid.

21. Smith, *Between Mutiny and Obedience,* 252.

22. See Birnbaum, "Sammelbericht II," 45; Nonne, "Therapeutische Erfahrungen," 109–10.

23. Nonne, "Über erfolgreiche Suggestivbehandlung," 202.

24. Nonne, "Therapeutische Erfahrungen," 109.

25. Ibid. See also Liebers, "Zur Behandlung der Zitterneurosen nach Granatshock," 873.

26. Nonne, "Therapeutische Erfahrungen," 109.

27. Ibid. For a vivid description of this process, see Engelen, *Suggestion und Hypnose,* esp. 22–23.

28. Freud and Breuer, *Studies on Hysteria.* See especially the "Preliminary Communication" of 1893, 3–17.

29. See Leys, *Trauma: A Genealogy,* esp. 87.

30. Nonne himself made the comparison between a neurologist using active treatment and a surgeon. See Nonne, "Therapeutische Erfahrungen," 113.

31. Ibid., 110.

32. Nonne, "Über erfolgreiche Suggestivbehandlung," 207.

33. Nonne, "Therapeutische Erfahrungen, 110.

34. Ibid., 111.

35. Nonne, "Über erfolgreiche Suggestivbehandlung," 207.

36. Schaltenbrand, "Max Nonne"; F. Stern, "Bericht über die Kriegstagung."

37. Nonne, *Anfang und Ziel,* 179; for another account of Nonne's performance, see Mann, "Neue Methoden," 1334.

38. Nonne, *Anfang und Ziel,* 179; idem, "Soll man wieder traumatische Neurosen diagnostizieren?" 337–39.

39. Nonne, "Über erfolgreiche Suggestivbehandlung," 197.

40. Ibid., 198.

41. Nonne, *Anfang und Ziel,* 180–81.

42. Ibid., 181.

43. Ibid.

44. Schaltenbrand, "Max Nonne," 165.

45. Nonne, *Anfang und Ziel,* 184.

46. Ibid., 214–20.

47. Harrington, "Hysteria, Hypnosis, and the Lure of the Invisible," 3:226–46.

48. On Charcot's use of hypnosis, in addition to works cited in chap. 1, see Harris, *Murders and Madness,* esp. chap. 5.

49. Shorter, *From Paralysis to Fatigue,* 181–86.

50. See Gilman, "The Image of the Hysteric."

51. As Sander Gilman points out, the hospital was filled with pictures that documented the hysterical states, making it easy for patients to imitate them. "The Image of the Hysteric," 346–49.

52. See Harris, *Murders and Madness,* 179; Gauld, *A History of Hypnotism,* esp. chap. 16.

53. On the Bernheim–Charcot debate see Ellenberger, *The Discovery of the Unconscious,* esp. 85–101; Harris, *Murders and Madness,* 160–93.

54. Schaltenbrand, "Max Nonne," 164. Nonne later recounted that in 1888, while serving in the army, he had tried hypnotizing soldiers. Nonne, "Über erfolgreiche Suggestivbehandlung," 198.

55. See *Index-Catalogue of the Library of the Surgeon-General's Office.*

56. Quoted in Nonne, "Über erfolgreiche Suggestivbehandlung," 214.

57. See Lerner, "Hysterical Cures," 79–101.

58. The film, *The Cabinet of Dr. Caligari,* which was released shortly after the war, is one example of the public interest in and anxiety over hypnosis. See Kaes, *Wounded Nation.*

59. On the occult in German science, medicine, and culture, see Treitel, "Avatars of the Soul." On Britain, see Owen, *The Darkened Room;* and J. Oppenheim, *The Other World.* On spiritualist practices during and after the war, see Winter, *Sites of Memory,* esp. 54–77.

60. See "Entwurf eines Gesetzes gegen Mißstände im Heilgewerbe," *Verhandlungen des Reichstages* XII Legislative Period, 2. Session, 1909–1911, Bd. 277 (1909/1910), 2759.

61. "Anwendung des Hypnotismus und des Magnetismus zu Heilzwecken," GehStA, Rep. 76 VIII B, Akte 1324. On hypnosis in film, see the correspondence between Herr Bulcke, Leiter der Filmoberprüfstelle, Reichsministerium des Innern, and Karl Bonhoeffer, in HUB Charité Nervenklinik 37 (Gesetzte u. Gesetzentwürfe Reichsgesundheitsamt [Erbgesetz], 1922–1934). On hypnosis and crime in France, see Harris, *Murders and Madness.*

62. Shorter, *History of Psychiatry,* chap. 4.

63. Freud, "An Autobiographical Study," 17.

64. See Ernst Trömner's remarks in "Diskussion zum Vortrag Nonne," 21–22. See also Decker, *Freud in Germany,* 294; Leys, "Traumatic Cures."

65. Nonne, "Therapeutische Erfahrungen," 106.

66. Nonne, "Über erfolgreiche Suggestivbehandlung," 194.

67. Nonne, *Anfang und Ziel,* 177–78.

68. Mohr, "Grundsätzliches zur Kriegsneurosenfrage," 93.

69. Nonne, "Therapeutische Erfahrungen," 113.

70. Ibid., 109.

71. Ibid., 112.

72. Ibid.

73. Nonne, "Über erfolgreiche Suggestivbehandlung," 202.

74. Ibid., 213.

75. Goldstein, "Über die Behandlung der Kriegshysteriker," 751. See also Mann, "Neue Methoden und Gesichtspünkte," 1334.

76. "Verhandlungen psychiatrischer Vereine," 227.

77. Quoted in Birnbaum, "Sammelbericht II," 45. See also H. Oppenheim, "Zur Psychopathologie und Nosologie der russisch-jüdischen Bevölkerung."

78. H. Oppenheim, "Für und wider die traumatische Neurose," 227. Alfred Hauptmann wrote that Oppenheim's lack of experience with hypnosis explained his less favorable success. See Hauptmann, "Kriegs-neurosen und traumatische Neurosen."

79. Kaufmann, "Die planmässige Heilung," 802–4. For Nonne's response, see Nonne, "Über erfolgreiche Suggestivbehandlung," 201. Kaufmann also remarked that his patients resisted hypnosis so intensely that they preferred to be treated with electrotherapy. See Kaufmann, "Zur Behandlung der motorischen Kriegsneurosen," 1520–23.

80. Preuß. Kriegsministerium, Medizinal Abteilung, "Grundsätze für die Behandlung und Beurteilung der sogennanten Kriegsneurotiker," 3, UAT, 308/89.

81. See Eissler, *Freud as an Expert Witness,* 52.

82. Stekel, *The Autobiography of Wilhelm Stekel,* 161.

83. Ibid.

84. Ibid., 160–61.

85. Kretschmer, *Gestalten und Gedanken,* 91.

86. Böttiger, "Diskussion zum Vortrag Nonne," 261–62.

87. Nonne, "Über erfolgreiche Suggestivbehandlung," 214.

88. Simmel, *Kriegs-Neurosen und "pyschisches Trauma,"* 23. For a detailed discussion of Simmel and his hypnotic treatment, see Chapter 6. The same expression was used by Dr. Max Liebers at the Munich Congress. "It is also to be recommended," wrote Liebers, "if possible to avoid using the word hypnosis around patients, since in many it can unleash disturbing thoughts, and since many resist the 'rape [*Vergewaltigung*] of their psyche.'" "Verhandlung psychiatrischer Vereine," 220.

89. Niessl von Maiendorf, "Über pathologische Tremorformen zur Kriegszeit," 236.

90. Ibid. (emphasis in text).

91. Nonne, "Über erfolgreiche Suggestivbehandlung," 204.

92. See Goldstein, *Console and Classify,* chap. 3, for an interesting discussion of Pinel, moral treatment, and the medicoscientific adoption of "charlatan" methods. For an English translation

of Pinel's own published account, see Pinel, *A Treatise on Insanity*. For a view of Pinel's very different from Goldstein's, see Weiner, *Comprendre et Soigner: Philippe Pinel, 1745–1826*.

93. I am grateful to Georg Hofer for biographical details about Kaufmann.

94. Kaufmann protested this reputation, claiming that he was less "Kaufmannish" (i.e., brutal) than other doctors. See "Diskussionsbemerkungen (aktive Behandlung)," Ludwigshafen, 1918, BayHStA, Stellv. Gen. Kom. II. A.K. San. Amt, Bd. 14, Heft 2.

95. Kaufmann, "Die planmässige Heilung," 802–4.

96. Ibid., 802–3.

97. Ibid., 804. Kaufmann wrote that hypnosis was not suitable for the environment in which he worked.

98. Ibid., 803.

99. The following account is drawn from Kaufmann, "Die planmässige Heilung," 802–4.

100. Ibid., 803.

101. Mendel, "Die Kaufmannsche Methode," 190.

102. See Weiler, "Ein Jahr Kriegsneurotikerbehandlung," 402.

103. Stainbrook, "The Use of Electricity in Psychiatric Treatment," 156. See also Hubenstorf, "Elektrizität und Medizin," 241–57; Rowbottom and Susskind, *Electricity and Medicine*.

104. See Mann, *Elektrodiagnostik und Elektrotherapie*.

105. Stainbrook, "Use of Electricity," 175. See also H. Oppenheim, *Psychotherapeutische Briefe*.

106. Quoted in Loewy-Hattendorf, *Krieg, Revolution, und Unfallneurose*, 3.

107. Freud, "Autobiographical Study," 9.

108. See Kaufmann, "Zur Behandlung der motorischen Kriegsneurosen," 1522; Goldstein, "Über die Behandlung der Kriegshysteriker," 753.

109. R. Weiß, "Behandlung der Kriegsneurotiker," clipping from unidentified newspaper, n.d., in BayHSta, San. Amt II. A.K., Bd. 14, 1.

110. Mann, "Neue Methoden und Gesichtspunkte," 1336.

111. For discussions of the differences between faradic and galvanic current in electrotherapy, see Drinka, *Birth of Neurosis*, 222–24; Eissler, *Freud as an Expert Witness*, 378–82.

112. Mendel, "Kaufmannsche," 182. The review that Mendel refers to appeared in *NZ* 35 (1916): 566.

113. Mendel, "Kaufmannsche," 182.

114. "Verhandlungen psychiatrischer Vereine," 187; Liebers, "Zur Behandlung der Zitterneurosen," 874.

115. Cited in Kehrer, "Zur Frage der Behandlung der Kriegsneurosen," 11.

116. "Verhandlung psychiatrischer Vereine," 220.

117. Lewandowsky, "Über den Tod durch Sinusströme," 1169; Mann, "Neue Methoden"; Boruttau, "Todesfälle durch Sinusströme," 808–9.

118. Nonne, "Therapeutische Erfahrungen," 108; Loewy-Hattendorf, *Krieg, Revolution, und Unfallneurose*, 10. On Austria see A. Schüller, "Die Kriegsneurosen und das Publikum," 1091.

119. Rothmann, "Zur Beseitigung psychogener Bewegungsstörungen bei Soldaten in einer Sitzung," 1278.

120. Kaufmann, "Die planmässige Heilung," 804.

121. Gaupp, "Die Behandlung der nervösen Schüttellähmung," UAT 308/89 (emphasis in text).

122. Jellinek, "Kriegsneurose und Sinusstrom," 1085–88.

123. Gaupp, "Die Behandlung der nervösen Schüttellähmung," 3.

124. Gaupp, *Nervenkranken des Krieges*, 18.

125. Ibid., 16.

126. Weichbrodt, "Zur Behandlung hysterischer Störungen," 521.

127. Gaupp, "Die Behandlung der nervösen Schüttellähmung," 3.

128. Kehrer, "Zur Frage der Behandlung, 2.

129. In "Verhandlungen psychiatischer Vereine," 205.

130. Ibid., 191.

131. Ibid.

132. Kaufmann, "Zur Behandlung der motorischen Kriegsneurosen," 1522. Ludwig Mann agreed: "The Kaufmann treatment is not as awful as it seems in print." In "Verhandlungen psychiatrischer Vereine," 212.

133. Kaufmann, "Zur Behandlung der motorischen Kriegsneurosen," 1523.

134. See, e.g., Wagner, "Die Dienstbeschädigung," 234–35.

135. Letter from Schultzen, preuß. Kriegsministerium to württ. Kriegsministerium Stuttgart, 29 January 1917, UAT, 308/89. This meeting took place on December 18, 1916, and is described in the cited letter.

136. Wilmanns "Bericht über die Sitzung des bad. Landesausschusses," BA RAM, Film 36069, 43–44.

137. Gaupp, "Die Behandlung der nervösen Schüttellähmung." Gaupp continued: "The treatment was quickly adopted throughout Germany (incidentally in France, Austria, and Hungary as well) and from all sides came the most glowing reports of success." Ibid., 2.

138. Birnbaum, "Sammelbericht V," 241.

139. Kaufmann did not specify the methods he used, but one can assume that he used suggestive electrotherapy in many of the cases. See Kaufmann, Ludwigshafen, 6 June 1918, in BayHStA, Stellv. Gen. Kom. II. A.K., San. Amt, Bd. 14, Akte 2.

140. Raether, "Neurosen-Heilungen nach der 'Kaufmann-Methode,'" 491.

141. Goldstein, "Über die Behandlung der Kriegshysteriker," 751.

142. See Nonne, "Über erfolgreiche Suggestivbehandlung," 195.

143. On the use of ether and electric current, see Hirschfeld, "Aus der Praxis der sogenannten aktiven Psychotherapie," 687.

144. Bickel, "Über die Kriegsneurosen, ihre Entstehung und die Erfolge ihrer Behandlung," 209.

145. Raether, "Neurosen-Heilungen nach der 'Kaufmann-Methode,'" 492–93.

146. Ibid., 518.

147. Ibid.

148. G. Oppenheim, "Zur Behandlung des Zitterns," 622.

149. Ibid., 622–23.

150. Ibid., 623.

151. Mohr, "Aus der Praxis der Psychotherapie," 1119.

152. Goldstein, "Über die Behandlung der Kriegshysteriker," 751.

153. Quoted in Nonne, "Über erfolgreiche Suggestivbehandlung," 194.

154. Letter from Seydel, Bayerisches Kriegsministerium, Medizinal-Abteilung, to the health offices of the three Bavarian Army Korps, Munich, 3 December 1917. BayHStA, Stv. I. A.K. San. Amt, Bd. 156.

155. Schulzten, Kriegsministerium, Medizinal Abteilung Berlin, 29 January 1917, UAT, 308/89.

156. Nonne, "Therapeutische Erfahrungen," 106.

157. "Gaupp spricht über die Neurosen und Psychosen des Krieges." See also Birnbaum, "Sammelbericht II," 46; G. Oppenheim, "Zur Behandlung des Zitterns," 620.

158. See Nonne, "Über erfolgreiche Suggestivbehandlung," 195; Wachsner, "Zur Behandlung funktioneller Störungen," 1104; Oehmen, "Die Heilung der hysterischen Erscheinungen in Wachsuggestion," 463–66.

159. Kehrer, "Zur Frage der Behandlung der Kriegsneurosen," 13.

160. Rothmann, "Zur Beseitigung psychogener Bewegungsstörungen"; Goldstein, "Über die Behandlung monosymptomatischer Hysterie bei Soldaten," 842–52. See also Singer, "Prinzipien und Erfolge der aktiven Therapie bei Neurosen," 227.

161. Goldstein, "Über die Behandlung." See also Joseph and Mann, "Erfolge der Rothmann'schen Narkosenmethode bei Kriegshysterie, insbesondere bei hysterischem Schütteltremor," 674–76.

162. Goldstein, "Über die Behandlung," 754.

163. Ibid., 754. For a different perspective, see Weichbrodt, "Zur Behandlung hysterischer Störungen," 521.

164. See Kehrer, "Zur Frage der Behandlung," 18.

165. Dub, "Heilung funktioneller und motorischer Leiden," 293–94.

166. Sommer, "Beseitigung funktioneller Taubheit, besonders bei Soldaten, durch eine experimental-psychologische Methode," 574–75.

167. I am grateful to Brigid Doherty for calling my attention to the Moede device. See her "Montage and the Body at Work," chap. 3 of the dissertation, "Berlin Dada: Montage and the Embodiment of Modernity, 1916–1921." On psychotechnical devices during and after the war, see Rabinbach, *Human Motor,* 263–66.

168. See Nolan, *Visions of Modernity,* 89.

169. Sommer, "Beseitigung funktioneller Taubheit," 68.

170. Robert Sommer, letter to Dr. O. Schultze, Giessen, 3 August 1917, Robert Sommer Papers, UAG, Bd. 65, no. 135, Blatt 733.

171. Sommer, "Beseitigung funktioneller Taubheit," 68–69.

172. Ibid., 71. Apparently, a similar method was practiced in a war hospital in Leipzig. See Letter from E. Zimmerman to Sommer, 23 January 1917. Robert Sommer Papers, UAG, Bd. 65, no. 131, 727–28.

173. Muck, "Heiligungen von schwerer funktioneller Aphonie," 441.

174. Ibid.

175. Ibid.

176. Muck, "Über Schnellheilungen von funktioneller Stummheit," 165–66. For the latter number, see Muck, *Beobachtungen und praktische Erfahrungen aus dem Gebiet der Kriegsneurosen,* 10.

177. O. Schultz as quoted in Muck, *Beobachtungen und praktische Erfahrungen,* 12.

178. Muck, "Über Schnellheilungen," 166.

179. Weichbrodt, "Zur Behandlung hysterischer Störungen," 519–25.

180. Ibid., 523.

181. M. Meyer, "Behandlungsmethoden hysterischer Bewegungstörungen bei Kriegsneurosen," 256–57.

182. Graf, *Prisoners All,* 160.

183. Other kinds of water and bath treatments were certainly practiced on war neurotics, but references to them in the literature of the time are scarce. See Forster, "Hysterische Reaktion und Simulation," 298–324; letter from Gaupp to K. Württ. Gericht der stellv. 53. Infantriebrigade in Ulm, Tübingen, 24 May 1917, UAT, 308/42. These should not be confused with the gentle and soothing baths that were often prescribed for neurasthenic officers and soldiers with organic wounds.

184. "Verhandlungen psychiatrischer Vereine," 185.

185. Kaufmann, "Zur Behandlung der motorischen Kriegsneurosen," 1520–23.

186. See "Verhandlungen psychiatrischer Vereine," 185. Nonne described this treatment as "truly cruel." See Nonne, "Therapeutische Erfahrungen," 113.

187. Kretschmer, "Hysteriebehandlung im Dunkelzimmer," 825.

188. Pönitz, *Klinische Neuorientierung,* 30.

189. Lewandowsky, "Was kann in der Behandlung und Beurteilung?" 991; Weichbrodt, "Einige Bemerkungen zur Behandlung von Kriegsneurotikern," 266.

190. Lewandowsky, "Was kann in der Behandlung und Beurteilung?" 991. See also Jendrássik, "Einige Bemerkungen zur Kriegsneurose," 499.

191. Hirschfeld, "Zur Behandlung im Kriege erworbener hysterischer Zustände," 195–205; idem, "Zur Behandlung der Kriegszitterer," 824–25.

192. Hirschfeld, "Zur Behandlung der Kriegszitterer," 825.

193. Ibid.

194. Hirschfeld, "Aus der Praxis," 687–88.

195. Forster, "Hysterische Reaktion und Simulation."
196. See Kraepelin, "Hundert Jahre Psychiatrie," 161–275. This point was made by a contemporary doctor. See Specht, "Einige historische und äesthetische Nebengedanken," 1406–7.

Chapter 5. The Worker-Patient

1. Hoffman, "Über die Behandlung der Kriegshysterie," 115–21.
2. Ibid., 119.
3. Pönitz, *Klinische Neuorientierung*, 32. See also Hoffmann, "Über die Behandlung der Kriegshysterie," 119; Birnbaum, "Sammelbericht V," 241.
4. Lewandowsky, "Was kann in der Behandlung und Beurteilung der Kriegsneurosen erreicht werden?" 1028.
5. See R. Gerz, "Leitsätze," Würzburg, n.d., BayHStA, San. Amt II. A.K., Bd. 14, 1; Mayer-Gross, "Practical Psychiatry," 1327; Wilmanns, "Die Wiedertüchtigung der an funktionellen Neurosen leidenden Kriegsbeschädigten," 138.
6. Singer, "Prinzipien und Erfolge," 275.
7. Nolan, *Visions of Modernity*; Campbell, *Joy in Work*; Reese et al., eds., *Rationale Beziehungen?*; Grossmann, "The New Woman and the Rationalization of Sexuality."
8. Stone, "Shellshock and the Psychologists"; Daniel Pick, *War Machine: The Rationalisation of Slaughter in the Modern Age*, esp. chap. 12. For a wartime treatment of the rationalization of military (but not medical or economic) organization, see Stern, *Gedanken über Heeresorganisation*; on rationalization, discipline, and soldiers' bodies, see Foucault, *Discipline and Punish: The Birth of the Prison*, esp. 135–69; Theweleit, *Male Fantasies*, vol 2., *Male Bodies: Psychoanalyzing the White Terror*. See also Hüppauf, "Langemarck, Verdun, and the Myth of a *New Man* in Germany after the First World War."
9. On the rationalization of wartime industry, specifically in terms of resource allocation by the War Raw Materials Office (KRA), see Feldman, *Army, Industry, and Labor*, esp. 46–52; and Mendelssohn-Bartholdy, *The War and German Society*, chap. 13.
10. See Weindling, "The Medical Profession"; Whalen, *Bitter Wounds*, esp. chap. 7. See also Cooter and Sturdy, "Of War, Medicine, and Modernity."
11. Ulrich, "Die Desillusionierung der Kriegsfreiwilligen von 1914." On Ernst Jünger and the notion of the "soldier-worker," see Herf, *Reactionary Modernism*, esp. 70–108.
12. On the nationalization of voluntary welfare associations during and after the war, see Whalen, *Bitter Wounds*, chap. 7; Cohen, *The War Come Home*, 61–100. See also the memorandum from the Württemberg Ministry of War, Kriegsministerium, Stuttgart, 25 June 1915, UAT, 308/89. On work, welfare, and therapy, see Eghigian, *Making Security Social*, 117–58.
13. Hirschfeld, "Aus der Praxis," 688. Hirschfeld was paraphrasing psychiatrist Karl Wilmanns.
14. Kriegsministerium, "Nachprüfung beim Prüfungsgeschäft," Munich, 14 May 1917, BayHStA, Stellv. Gen. Kom I. A.K., Bd. 156.
15. Dienstanweisungen für die neue Behandlungslazarette, Munich, 13 April 1918. UAT, 308/89.
16. Hoffmann, "Über die Behandlung der Kriegshysterie," 146; Edel and Hoppe, "Zur Psychologie und Therapie der Kriegsneurosen," 839.
17. "Beschäftigung der Verwundeten," SHSA, Stellv. Gen.-Kdo des XII. A.K., no. 12708, 12.
18. Edel and Hoppe, "Zur Psychologie," 839. See also Letter from Stellv. Intendantur of the XIIth Army Korps, Dresden, 19 March 1917, SHSA, Stellv. XII A.K., Akte 12708, 77.
19. Foucault, *Madness and Civilization*, esp. 38–64.
20. Schultzen, Kriegsministerium, Berlin, 9 January 1917, UAT, 308/89.
21. Muck, "Heilungen von schwerer funktioneller Aphonie," 441.
22. Raether, "Neurosen-Heilungen nach der 'Kaufmann-Methode,'" 518. See also "Die Kriegsneurotiker," [author unknown] *Bayerische Landeszeitung* 33 (n.d.), BayHStA, San. Amt II. A.K., Bd. 14, 1.
23. See, e.g., A. Schüller, "Die Kriegsneurosen und das Publikum," 1091.

24. Singer, "Prinzipien und Erfolge," 282.
25. See Gaupp, "Hysterie und Kriegsdienst," 363; Nonne and Wachsner, "Therapeutische Erfahrungen," 271–73.
26. Singer, "Prinzipien und Erfolg," 282.
27. Schultzen, Kriegsministerium, Berlin, 9 January 1917, UAT, 308/89. See also Goldstein, "Über die Behandlung monosymptomatischer Hysterie"; Wagner, "Die Dienstbeschädigung," 242.
28. Feldman, *Army, Industry, and Labor,* 64.
29. Bessel, *Germany after the First World War,* 13–14.
30. Ibid., 13.
31. On the centrality of the capacity to work (*Erwerbsfähigkeit*) to notions of individual health and social organization after the war and as a component of the social welfare tradition in Germany, see Michael Geyer, "Ein Vorbote des Wohlfahrtstaates," esp. 245–49.
32. Schjerning, *Die Tätigkeit und die Erfolge,* 9.
33. Siemen, *Menschen blieben auf der Strecke,* 29.
34. Pönitz, *Klinische Neuorientierung,* 30.
35. Letter from Gaupp to Kriegsgerichte im Bereiche des XIII A.K., Tübingen, 28 January 1916, MA, M77/1 Stellv. Gen. Kom. des XIII. A.K., Akte 1038.
36. Gaupp, *Nervenkranken des Krieges,* 12.
37. Letter from Lasser, Stell. GK XIII. A.K., Stuttgart, 24 January 1916, UAT, 308/89.
38. Schultzen, Kriegsministerium, Medizinal-Abteilung, Berlin, 29 January 1917, UAT, 308/89.
39. Letter from Gaupp to Lasser, Tübingen, 21 November 1916, MA, M1/8 Kriegsministerium, Med. Abt. IV.1.1.5.
40. Schultzen, "Gründsätze für die Behandlung und Beurteilung der sogen. Kriegsneurotiker," Berlin, 29 January 1917, UAT, 308/89.
41. See Mayer-Gross, "Practical Psychiatry," 1327; Hellpach, "Lazarettdisziplin als Heilfaktor," 1207–11.
42. Wollenberg, "Nervöse Erkrankungen."
43. Wilmanns, "Behandlung der Kranken," 427–28.
44. Wilmanns, "Wiedertüchtigung," 135.
45. Wilmanns, "Behandlung der Kranken," 427.
46. Gaupp, *Nervenkranken des Krieges,* 15.
47. See Wilmanns, "Bericht über die Sitzung des bad. Landesausschusses der Kriegsbeschädigtenfürsorge," 33. For Württemberg, see the memorandum, Kriegsministerium, Stuttgart, 25 June 1915, UAT, 308/89; Schjerning, *Tätigkeit und Erfolge,* 5.
48. Nonne, "Therapeutische Erfahrungen," 118. See also the memorandum from General Schultzen, Berlin, 29 January 1917, UAT, 308/89, and letter from Liebermeister to Gaupp, Ulm, 28 January 1918, UAT, 308/89.
49. Mayer-Gross, "Practical Psychiatry," 1329. See also Schultzen, "Grundsätze für die Behandlung und Beurteilung der sogenannten Kriegsneurotiker (Neurotiker-Merkblatt)" (this document has no date, but it can be inferred from surrounding documents that it probably was written in 1918), 2. BayHStA, San. Amt II. A.K., Bd. 14, 1.
50. Schultzen, "Behandlung und Beurteilung von Kriegsneurotikern," Berlin, 7 September 1917, UAT, 308/42.
51. Hofbauer, Sanitätsamt des I.A.K., "Dienstanweisung für die Neurotiker-Behandlungslazarette," Munich, 13 April 1918, UAT, 308/89.
52. Letter from von Stroebel, Stuttgart, 3 March 1917, UAT, 308/89.
53. The Elisabethenberg station was intended only for functional hearing disorders. Lasser, Stuttgart, 10 December 1917, UAT, 308/42.
54. Hofbauer, Sanitätsamt des I.A.K., "Dienstanweisung für die Neurotiker-Behandlungslazarette," Munich, 13 April 1918, UAT, 308/89.
55. Ibid.
56. Hoffmann, "Über die Behandlung der Kriegshysterie," 118.
57. It was also suggested that stays in the observation stations be limited to fourteen days. Dr.

Kimmel to Sanitätsamt des II. bayerischen A.K., "Besprechung dringenden dienstlichen Fragen in der Kaiser-Wilhelm Akademie Berlin," Würzburg, 20 December 1916, BayHSta, Stellv. Kom. II A.K. San. Amt, Bd. 15, Akte 3.

58. Gaupp to Med. Abt. des K. W. Kriegsministeriums, Tübingen, 3 November 1917, UAT, 308/89; Kimmel, "Besprechung dringenden dienstlichen Fragen."

59. "Kriegsbeschädigte als Hausierer und Bettler," Berlin, 19 December 1917, BA RAM, Film 8861.

60. Dr. Kimmel, "Besprechung dringenden dienstlichen Fragen in der Kaiser-Wilhelm Akademie Berlin," Würzburg, 20 December 1916, BayHStA, Stellv. Kom. II A.K. San. Amt, Bd. 15, Akte 3.

61. Wilmanns, "Behandlung der Kranken," 427–28.

62. Schultzen, "Grundsätze für die Behandlung und Beurteilung der sogenannten Kriegsneurotiker (Neurotiker-Merkblatt)," 2. BayHStA, San. Amt II. A.K., Bd. 14, 1.

63. Gaupp to württ. Kriegsministerium, San. Amt, Tübingen, 9 January 1918, MA, M77/1, no. 1038.

64. Gaupp to Medizinal Abteilung Stuttgart, Tübingen, 3 November 1917, UAT, 308/89. See also letter from Dr. Kimmel, BayHStA, Stellv. Gen. Kom. des II. A.K. San. Amt, Bd. 15, Akte 3; and Schultzen, "Grundsätze für die Behandlung und Beurteilung der sogenannten Kriegsneurotiker," 1, UAT, 308/89.

65. "Gaupp spricht über die Neurosen und Psychosen des Krieges," UAT, 308/42, 1–2.

66. Buttersack to Gaupp, Heilbronn, 18 September 1918, UAT, 308/89.

67. R. Gerz, "Bericht über die vom preus. Kriegsministerium (Sanitätsdepartment) nach Berlin berufene Versammlung der Neurotikerärzte," Würzburg, 14 October 1918, BayHStA, San. Amt II. A.K., Bd. 14, 1.

68. Wilmanns, "Behandlung der Kranken." On war neuroses among officers, see Curschmann, "Zur Kriegsneurose bei Offizieren," 291–93.

69. "Gaupp spricht über die Neurosen," 6–8.

70. "Zusammenkunft der Kriegsneurotiker-Ärzte," *MMW* 65 (1918): 1226–27. On self-inflicted wounds, which were not a serious concern for military psychiatrists, see Schultzen, "Grundsätze für die Behandlung und Beurteilung der sogenannten Kriegsneurotiker," 8, n.d., UAT, 308/89.

71. Quoted in Eissler, *Freud as an Expert Witness*, 62.

72. For a discussion of this problem in the British context, see Cooter, "Malingering in Modernity."

73. See, e.g., Gaupp, *Nervenkranken des Krieges*, 12.

74. Quoted in Birnbaum, "Sammelbericht I," 343.

75. Kretschmer, "Hysterische Erkrankung und hysterische Gewöhnung," 64–91.

76. Ibid., 88.

77. Pönitz, *Klinische Neurorientierung*, 32. See also A. Schüller, "Die Kriegsneurosen und das Publikum," 1091.

78. Two doctors reported detecting simulation in no more than two of two hundred treated patients. Edel and Hoppe, "Zur Psychologie und Therapie der Kriegsneurosen," 836–40.

79. Goldberg, "Die ambulante Behandlung der Kriegsneurotiker in Ambulantenstationen für Nervenkranke," 119.

80. Nonne, "Therapeutische Erfahrungen," 106.

81. Schultzen, "Grundsätze für die Behandlung und Beurteilung der sogenannten Kriegsneurotiker," 2, n.d., UAT, 308/89.

82. Quoted by Gaupp in a letter to K. Württ. Gericht der Stellv. 53. Infantriebrigade in Ulm, 24 May 1917, Tübingen, UAT, 308/42.

83. See Hoffmann, "Über die Behandlung der Kriegshysterie," 125.

84. Kimmel to Sanitätsamt des II. Bayerischen A.K., Würzburg, 20 December 1916, BayHStA, Stellv. Kom. II A.K. San. Amt, Bd. 15, Akte 3. See also Gerz, "Leitsätze."

85. See, e.g., Nonne, "Über erfolgreiche Suggestivbehandlung," 213.

86. Kretschmer, *Gestalten und Gedanken*, 89. Kretschmer described the sanitarium as "old-fashioned" and "small."

87. See Liebermeister, *Über die Behandlung von Kriegsneurosen,* 3.

88. Hoffmann, "Über die Behandlung der Kriegshysterie," 122. On the concept of "boring to death," see Kehrer, "Zur Frage der Behandlung," 3.

89. Hofbauer, Sanitätsamt des I.A.K., "Dienstanweisung für die Neurotiker-Behandlungslazarett," Munich, 13 April 1918, UAT, 308/89. These rules were issued to station directors in Bavaria, but it is most likely that they applied to Württemberg as well.

90. On the importance of the station staff to the suggestive atmosphere, see Ammon, "Behandlung von Kriegsneurotikern," Munich, 8 August 1918, BayHStA, San. Amt II. A.K., Bd. 14, 1.

91. On Freund, see letter from Württ. Landstände zweite Kammer to K. Stellv. Intendantur, Stuttgart, 13 March 1918, UAT, 308/89; for Liebermeister, see letter from Gaupp to K. Württ. Gericht der Stellv. 53. Infantriebrigade in Ulm, Tübingen, 24 May 1917, UAT, 308/42.

92. Kretschmer, "Hysteriebehandlung im Dunkelzimmer," 825.

93. Seydel, Kriegsministerium, Medizinal-Abteilung, to K. San. Ämter des I. II. und III. A.K., Munich, "Behandlung von Kriegsneurotikern," 3 December 1917, BayHSta, Stellv. GK. I. A.K. San. Amt, Bd. 156; Stellv. XIII. A.K. Versorgungsabteilung, "Militärische Einkleidung der Kriegsneurotiker vor ihrer Einweisung in die Nervenlazarette," Stuttgart, 16 June 1917, UAT, 308/89. See also Singer, "Prinzipien und Erfolge," 281–82.

94. Hofbauer, "Dienstanweisung für Neurotiker-Lazarette," 2. For a discussion of the therapeutic benefits of gymnastics, see Ollendorf, "Turnen in der Behandlung der psychogen bewegungsgestörten Soldaten," 765–66.

95. Nonne, "Über erfolgreiche Suggestivbehandlung," 207. On the use of treated neurotics as attendents in both home territory and the field, see Gerz, "Bericht über die vom preuß. Kriegsministerim (Sanitätsdepartement) nach Berlin einberufene Versammlung der Neurotikerärzte." For Gaupp's objections, see his letter to Lasser, Chef der Med. Abt. Stuttgart, Tübingen, 13 March 1918, 2, UAT, 308/42.

96. Mohr, "Die Behandlung der Kriegsneurosen," 139. On agricultural work and animal husbandry, see Hartmann, "Die k.u.k. Nervenklinik Graz im Dienste des Krieges," 1162–1258.

97. Hofbauer, "Dienstanweisung für Neurotiker-Lazarette," 2.

98. See "Beschäftigung der Verwundeten"; Hartmann, "Die k.u.k. Nervenklinik Graz im Dienste des Krieges."

99. On station atmosphere, see Hirschfeld, "Zur Behandlung der Kriegszitterer," 824–25; Pönitz, *Klinische Neurorientierung,* 27. On "spontaneous healing," see Nonne, *Anfang und Ziel,* 178; Paschen, "Zur Behandlung funktioneller motorischer Störungen nach Kaufmann," 169–70.

100. Hoffmann, "Über die Behandlung der Kriegshysterie"; Kehrer, "Behandlung und ärztliche Fürsorge bei Kriegsneurosen," 159; Mayer-Gross, "Practical Psychiatry," 1329.

101. See Hellpach, "Lazarettdisziplin als Heilfaktor," 1207–11; Wilmanns, "Bericht," 33.

102. Lewandowsky, "Was kann in der Behandlung und Beurteilung der Kriegsneurosen erreicht werden?" 990.

103. Nonne, "Therapeutische Erfahrungen"; Weichbrodt, "Einige Bemerkungen," 266. On the importance of uniforms and military hierarchy, see Lewandowsky, "Was kann in der Behandlung und Beurteilung der Kriegsneurosen erreicht werden?" 990; Forster, "Hysterische Reaktion und Simulation."

104. Pönitz, *Klinische Neurorientierung,* 26.

105. Ibid.

106. Hellpach, "Lazarettdisziplin als Heilfaktor," 1210.

107. Stier, "Wie kann der Entstehung von Kriegsneurosen bei der Feldarmee vorgebeugt werden?" 60–72.

108. Pönitz, *Klinische Neurorientierung,* 26.

109. Hellpach, "Lazarettdiszpilin als Heilfaktor," 1209.

110. See J. Oppenheim, *"Shattered Nerves,"* esp. 214–15.

111. Kehrer, "Zur Frage der Behandlung der Kriegshysterie," 22.

112. On the image of the nurse, see Domansky, "Der Erste Weltkrieg," 315–18. See also Theweleit, *Male Fantasies,* esp. 1:124–36.

113. See Domansky, "Erste Weltkrieg," 317–18.

114. See, e.g., Hoffmann, "Über die Behandlung der Kriegshysterie."

115. Mann, "Über Granatexplosionsstörungen," 345. See also Hellpach, "Lazarettdisziplin," 1211.

116. "Grundsätze für die Behandlung und Beurteilung der sogenannten Kriegsneurotiker," 2, n.d., UAT, 308/89. See also Wilmanns, "Die Behandlung der Kranken mit funktionellen Neurosen im Bereiche des XIV A.K.," 427.

117. "Gaupp spricht über die Neurosen," 5.

118. Otto Pötzl, quoted in Eissler, *Freud as an Expert Witness,* 88.

119. Wilmanns, "Die Wiedertüchtigung der an funktionellen Neurosen leidenden Kriegsbeschädigten," 138.

120. Quoted in Gaupp, "Kriegsneurosen," 388 n.

121. Hoffmann, "Über die Behandlung der Kriegshysterie," 118–19.

122. Dr. Maring, "Vorschläge zur Neurotikerfürsorge. Ergänzung des badischen Systems," Ulm, 15 March 1918, UAT, 308/89.

123. See, e.g., Wilmanns, "Die Behandlung der Kranken mit funktionellen Neurosen," 427; Mohr, "Grundsätzliches zur Kriegsneurosenfrage"; Hirschfeld, "Zur Behandlung der Kriegszitterer," 824–25.

124. For the results of studies conducted early in the war, see Chapter 2. See also Birnbaum, "Sammelbericht III," 326; Jolly, "Kriegshysterie und Beruf," 873–82; Rittershaus, "Die psychiatrisch-neurologische Abteilung im Etappengebiet," 272.

125. "Kriegsbeschädigte als Hausierer und Bettler," Berlin, 19 December 1917, BA RAM, Film 8861.

126. R. Hirschfeld, "Zur Behandlung im Kriege erworbener hysterischer Zustände," 200.

127. Wollenberg, *Erinnerungen,* 137–38.

128. See Wilmanns, "Wiedertüchtigung," 138.

129. Schultzen, "Behandlung und Beurteilung von Kriegsneurotikern," 15, Berlin, 7 September 1917, UAT, 308/89; Gerz, "Bericht über die vom preuß. Kriegsministerium (Sanitätsdepartement) nach Berlin einberufene Versammlung der Neurotikerärzte."

130. Gaupp to Medizinalabteilung des württ. Kriegsministeriums, Tübingen, 3 November 1917, UAT, 308/89.

131. Goldstein, "Über die Behandlung," 756.

132. Gaupp, *Nervenkranken des Krieges,* 15.

133. Seydel, Kriegsministerium, Medizinal-Abteilung, to K. San. Ämter des I. II. und III. A.K., Munich, "Behandlung von Kriegsneurotikern," 2, 3 December 1917, BayHStA, Stv. GK, I. A.K. San. Amt, Bd. 156.

134. Gaupp [probably] to Med. Abt. des K. Kriegsministerium, Stuttgart, 10 May 1918, UAT, 308/42; Liebermeister, "Über die Behandlung von Kriegsneurosen," 31.

135. Stroebel, "Verwendung von Psychopathen, Neurotikern . . . ," Stuttgart, 16 April 1917, UAT, 308/89.

136. See Nonne, "Therapeutische Erfahrungen," 111.

137. Ibid.

138. Schultzen, Kriegsministerium Berlin, "Neurotiker-Merkblatt," 6, n.d., UAT, 308/89.

139. Ibid.

140. Schjerning, *Tätigkeit und Erfolge,* 5.

141. Kehrer, "Behandlung und ärztliche Fürsorge bei Kriegsneurosen," 161–62. See also Wilmanns "Wiedertüchtigung," 129, on the pioneering role of Baden in the organization of neurosis treatment.

142. Wilmanns, "Wiedertüchtigung," 135.

143. Kehrer, "Behandlung und ärztliche Fürsorge bei Kriegsneurosen," 158–64.

144. Ibid., 161.

145. Kehrer, "Behandlung und ärztliche Fürsorge bei Kriegsneurosen," 161; Pilzecker, "Der Lazarettnachweis im Reservelazarett Triberg (Schwarzwald)," 165–70.
146. Wilmanns, "Wiedertüchtigung," 137. See also Wagner, "Arbeitstherapie und Rentenabschätzung bei Kriegsneurotikern," 274.
147. Wilmanns, "Bericht," 43.
148. Pilzecker, "Lazarettnachweis," 168.
149. Ibid.
150. Wilmanns, "Bericht," 44.
151. Hoffmann, "Über die Behandlung der Kriegshysterie," 142.
152. Pilzecker, "Lazarettnachweis," 167.
153. Wilmanns, "Bericht," 44.
154. Ibid.
155. Hoffmann, "Über die Behandlung der Kriegshysterie," 142. This measure was adopted throughout Germany; see "Grundsätze für die Behandlung und Beurteilung der sogenannten Kriegsneurotiker (Neurotiker-Merkblatt)," UAT, 308/89; Pönitz, *Klinische Neuorientierung,* 32.
156. Wilmanns, "Bericht," 44.
157. Hoffmann, "Über die Behandlung der Kriegshysterie," 143. Details about the Baden "neurotic battalions" have been difficult to obtain; however, it is clear that a company of five hundred neurotics was formed in Karlsruhe. R. Gerz, "Bericht über die vom preuß. Kriegsministerium (Sanitätsdepartement) nach Berlin einberufene Versammlung der Neurotikerärzte."
158. Hoffmann, "Über die Behandlung der Kriegshysterie," 143.
159. Pilzecker, "Lazarettnachweis," 169.
160. Wilmanns, "Bericht," 44; idem, "Die Behandlung der Kranken mit funktionellen Neurosen im Bereiche des XIV A.K.," 427.
161. Hoffmann, "Über die Behandlung der Kriegshysterie," 143.
162. Ibid.
163. Fritz Kaufmann, "Äußerung zu dem Anschreiben des K. Sanitätsamt Nr. 18851 vom 17.4.1918," Ludwigshafen, 27 April 1918, BayHStA, San. Amt II. A.K., Bd. 14, 1.
164. Schultzen, in *Verhandlungen des Reichstages, XIII. Legislaturperiode II Session, Stenographische Berichte,* vol. 313 (Berlin, 1918), 5434; Weiler, "Ein Jahr Kriegsneurotikerbehandlung," 401–5; A. Schüller, "Die Kriegsneurosen und das Publikum," 1090–91.
165. Domansky, "Erste Weltkrieg"; Daniel, "Women's Work in Industry and Family, Germany, 1914–1918," 267–96. More generally on women and work during the war, see Daniel, *The War from Within;* Davis, *Home Fires Burning.*
166. Dr. Maring, "Vorschläge zur Neurotikerfürsorge. Ergänzung des badischen Systems," Ulm, 15 March 1918, UAT, 308/89.
167. Maring, "Vorschläge zur Neurotikerfürsorge," 2–3.
168. Wilmanns to Gaupp, Heidelberg, 9 June 1917, UAT, 308/43.
169. Schäfer, "Einrichtung einer besonderen Rentenabteilung für Neurotiker," Stuttgart, 28 May 1918, MA, M77/1–26, 1.
170. Schäfer, "Einrichtung einer besonderen Rentenabteilung für Neurotiker," 1; Kretschmer, *Gestalten und Gedanken,* 89.
171. Gaupp, "Hysterie und Kriegsdienst," 363.
172. The sources do not reveal when the unit actually opened; they provide only this scheduled date.
173. Letter from Liebermeister to Gaupp, Ulm, 28 January 1918, UAT, 308/89.
174. Maring, "Vorschläge zur Neurotikerfürsorge," 2.
175. Letter from Gaupp to K. Sanitätsamt, Tübingen, 23 September 1918, UAT, 308/89.
176. Schäfer, "Einrichtung einer besonderen Rentenabteilung für Neurotiker."
177. Ibid.
178. See Bostroem, "Neurologische und psychologische Fronterfahrungen eines Trupenarztes," 1310–14.
179. Letter from Gaupp to K. Sanitätsamt, Tübingen, 23 September 1918, UAT, 308/89.

180. Gaupp, no title, Tübingen, 18 May 1918, UAT, 308/89.
181. Nonne, "Therapeutische Erfahrungen," 114.
182. Wilmanns, "Bericht," 41.
183. Liebermeister, "Verhütung von Kriegsneurosen," 308.
184. For an American view, see J. H. W. Rhein, "War Neuroses as Observed in Army Neurological Hospitals at the Front," 179.
185. Mayer-Gross, "Practical Psychiatry," 1328; K. Schneider, "Einige psychiatrische Erfahrungen als Truppenarzt," 311–12.
186. Liebermeister, "Verhütung," 309. For the French side, see Roudebush, "Battle of Nerves," 104–5.
187. Dillon, "Treatment of Neuroses in the Field," 119–27; Hargreaves, Wittkower, and Wilson, "Psychiatric Organisation in the Services," 163–79.
188. Letter from Gaupp to K. Sanitätsamt, Tübingen, 23 September 1918, UAT, 308/89.
189. Stier, "Wie kann der Entstehung von Kriegsneurosen bei der Feldarmee vorgebeugt werden?" 66.
190. Schultzen, "Grundsätze für die Behandlung und Beurteilung der sogenannten Kriegsneurotiker (Neurotiker-Merkblatt)," n.d, 9.
191. Nonne, "Therapeutische Erfahrungen," 119; Lewandowsky, "Was kann in der Behandlung und Beurteilung?" 1028.
192. Gaupp, no title, 18 May 1918, UAT, 308/89.
193. Gaupp [probably] to Med. Abt. des K. Kriegsministerium, Stuttgart, 10 May 1918, UAT, 308/42; Gaupp, no title, Tübingen, 18 May 1918, UAT, 308/89, 5.
194. Stier, "Wie kann der Entstehung von Kriegsneurosen bei der Feldarmee vorgebeugt werden?" 66. The British Army acted in a similar fashion when it banned the term "shell shock" and replaced it with "NYDN" (not yet diagnosed nervous). See Shephard, *War of Nerves,* esp. 54.
195. Schneider, "Einige psychiatrische Erfahrungen als Truppenarzt," 311.
196. Gaupp, no title, Tübingen, 18 May 1918, UAT, 308/89, 6.
197. Nonne, "Therapeutische Erfahrungen," 119.
198. R. Gerz, "Leitsätze."
199. Seydel, Kriegsministerium, Medizinal-Abteilung, to K. San. Ämter des I. II. und III. A.K., Munich, "Behandlung von Kriegsneurotikern," 3 December 1917, BayHSta, Stellv. Gen. Kom. I. A.K. San. Amt, Bd. 156.
200. "Neurotiker-Merkblatt," n.d., UAT, 308/89, 9–11.
201. Memorandum from Lasser, Kriegsministerium, Stuttgart, 5 June 1918, UAT, 308/89.
202. Stellv. Korpsarzt II. A.K. to Kreisausschuß für Kriegsbeschädigten-Fürsorge, Würzburg, 13 December 1917, BayHStA, Stellv. Gen. Kom. II. A.K. San. Amt, Bd. 14, Heft 2; Kriegsamt, Berlin, 19 December 1917, "Kriegsbeschädigte als Hausierer und Bettler," BA RAM, Film 8861.
203. Stellv. Gen. Kom. I.A.K. to San. Amt I.A.K., 21 August 1917, Munich; BayHStA, Akte 156.
204. Seydel, Kriegsministerium, Medizinal-Abteilung, to K. San. Ämter des I. II. und III. A.K., Munich, 3 December 1917, BayHSta, Stellv. Gen. Kom. I. A.K. San. Amt, Bd. 156. On curability, see "Neurotiker-Merkblatt," 5, UAT, 308/89.
205. "Militärische Einkleidung der Kriegsneurotiker vor ihrer Einweisung in die Nervenlazarette," Stellv. Gen Kom XIII. A.K. Versorgungsabteilung, Stuttgart, 16 June 1917, UAT, 308/89.
206. Seydel, Kriegsministerium, to San. Amt I.II.III b.A.K. Munich, 31 May 1918, BayHStA, Stellv. Gen Kom II. A.K. San. Amt, Bd. 14, Akte 2.
207. Gerz, Würzburg, 9 June 1918, BayHStA, Stellv. Gen. Kom. II. A.K. San. Amt, Bd. 14, Akte 2.
208. Ibid.
209. Kaufmann, Ludwigshaften, 6 June 1918, Stellv. Gen. Kom. II A.K. San. Amt, Bd. 14, Akte 2.
210. Gerz, Würzburg, 9 June 1918, BayHStA, Stellv. Gen. Kom. II A.K. San. Amt, Bd. 14, Akte 2.

211. See Doherty, "'See: We Are All Neurasthenics,' or the Trauma of Dada Montage," 82–132; Kienitz, "Der Krieg der Invaliden," 367–402. On care for the orthopedically wounded, see Thomann, "'Es gibt kein Krüppeltum.'" For the case of England, see Koven, "Remembering and Dismemberment," 1167–1202; Cohen, *The War Come Home.*

212. Mendelssohn-Bartholdy, *The War and German Society,* 214.

213. Michael Geyer, *Deutsche Rüstungspolitik 1860–1980,* 99; Ulrich, "Desillusionierung"; Hüppauf, "Langemarck, Verdun, and the Myth of a *New Man.*"

214. Ulrich, "Desillusionierung," esp. 121; Herf, *Reactionary Modernism,* esp. 72–75.

215. The phrase is from Hüppauf, "Langemarck, Verdun, and the Myth of the *New Man,*" 92.

216. The frequent use of terms such as "flow" and "flooded" by psychiatrists evokes Klaus Theweleit's discussion of the body and the representation of women and Bolshevism in the writings of men in the *Freikorps,* the violent bands of freebooters in the postwar period. See Theweleit, *Male Fantasies,* esp. vol. 1.

217. See chap. 7.

Chapter 6. The Discovery of the Mind

1. Levin, "Freud's Paper 'On Male Hysteria.'"

2. Freud and Breuer, *Studies on Hysteria.*

3. Sándor Ferenczi, for one, wrote to Freud that he had "no desire" to engage in electrotherapy, hypnosis, or suggestion, all of which "went against [his] grain." Falzeder and Brabant, eds., *Correspondence of Freud and Ferenczi,* 138.

4. Letter to Sándor Ferenczi, 15 December 1914, *Correspondence of Freud and Ferenczi,* 36.

5. Freud, "On the History of the Psychoanalytic Movement," 1–66.

6. Ellenberger, *Discovery of the Unconscious;* Levin, "Freud's Paper 'On Male Hysteria.'" For a discussion of the early reception of Freud's ideas in German medicine, see Decker, *Freud in Germany.*

7. See, e.g., Eissler, *Freud as an Expert Witness,* 93–94.

8. Simmel, *Kriegs-Neurosen und "psychisches Trauma,"* 23.

9. See Ferenczi, "Über Zwei Typen der Kriegsneurosen," 131.

10. F. Stern, "Die psychoanalytische Behandlung der Hysterie im Lazarett," 1–3.

11. Ibid., 1.

12. Recent historical work has employed a similar model to explain war neurosis. Elaine Showalter, for example, points to the conflict between adhering to rigid Edwardian masculine codes and handling the intense emotionality of war. See Showalter, *Female Malady,* esp. 171–72.

13. F. Stern, "Psychoanalytische Behandlung," 2.

14. Ibid., 3.

15. Freud and Breuer, *Studies on Hysteria,* 6.

16. Sauer, "Zur Analyse und Behandlung der Kriegsneurosen," 26.

17. Frank, "Zur Psychanalyse (Behandlung psychoneurotischer Zustände)," 65–75.

18. Sauer, "Zur Analyse," 28; Frank, "Zur Psychanalyse," 70.

19. A brief discussion of these connections can be found in Kaes, "War—Film—Trauma," 125–26.

20. Sauer, "Zur Analyse," 31.

21. Ibid., 44.

22. Ibid., 32.

23. Mohr, "Aus der Praxis der Psychotherapie," 1116–19.

24. Ibid., 1118.

25. Brunner, *Freud and the Politics of Psychoanalysis,* 106–22; Showalter, *Female Malady,* 167–94.

26. Simmel, *Kriegs-Neurosen und "psychisches Trauma."*

27. Schnee, "Gleitwort," in Simmel, *Kriegs-Neurosen und "pyschisches Trauma,"* 3.

28. As he later recounted, Simmel saw some two thousand neurotic patients over the course of the war, half of whom he treated himself. See Simmel, "Kriegsneurosen," 205.

29. Simmel, "Zweites Korreferat," 47.

30. Simmel, *Kriegs-Neurosen und "psychisches Trauma,"* 23.

31. Ibid., 30.

32. Simmel, "Zweites Korreferat," 47.

33. Nevertheless, Simmel acknowledged that he used suggestive hypnosis in many cases, in view of the need for mass treatment (*Massenbehandludng*) in the neurosis stations. Simmel, *Kriegs-Neurosen und "psychisches Trauma,"* 83.

34. Simmel, "Zweites Korreferat," 51.

35. Simmel, *Kriegs-Neurosen und "psychisches Trauma,"* 20.

36. Ibid.

37. Ibid., 39–40.

38. Ibid., 25.

39. Ibid., 28.

40. Ibid.

41. Ibid., 33.

42. See Heinze, "Über die Behandlung und Beurteilung der Kriegsneurosen," 195.

43. Freud, "Memorandum on the Electrical Treatment of War Neurotics," 211–16.

44. Freud wrote in 1920, "In 1918 Dr. Ernst Simmel, head of a hospital for war neuroses at Posen, published a pamphlet in which he reported the extraordinarily favorable results achieved in severe cases of war neurosis by the psychotherapeutic method introduced by me. *As a result of this publication,* the next Psycho-Analytical Congress, held in Budapest in September 1918, was attended by official delegates of the German, Austrian, and Hungarian Army Command, who promised that Centres should be set up for the purely psychological treatment of war neuroses." "Memorandum on Electrical Treatment," 215 [emphasis mine].

45. See Jones, *Life and Work of Sigmund Freud,* 2:197–98.

46. See "Zusammenkunft der Kriegsneurotiker-Ärzte," *MMW* 65 (1918): 1226–27.

47. Cited in Büttner, *"Freud und der Erste Weltkrieg,"* 35.

48. Freud, "Memorandum on Electrical Treatment," 214.

49. Freud wrote at the beginning of the war, "I feel like an Austrian for the first time in some thirty years, and am set to give it another try with this not very hopeful empire." Quoted in Büttner, "Freud und der Erste Weltkrieg," 50. Büttner argues that Freud saw in the war a chance to overcome the setbacks his movement suffered with the parting of Jung, Adler, and Stekel.

50. Sándor Radó, transcribed interview with Bluma Swerdloff, Columbia University Oral History Project, 13.

51. Reichmayr, "Psychoanalyse im Krieg," 38–39.

52. The list of participants, a schedule, and a brief report can be found in "Bericht über den V. Internationalen psychoanalytischen Kongreß in Budapest, 28.–29. September 1918," *Korrespondenzblatt der Internationalen Psychoanalytischen Vereinigung* 1 (1919): 31–37. The guests included Freud's wife Marthe and his son Ernst; this was the only conference in which members of Freud's family, other than his daughter Anna, participated. Jones, *Life and Work,* 2:197. The original intention was to hold the conference in Breslau, but it was moved to Budapest at the last minute for unclear reasons. Büttner suggests that participants from Austria-Hungary were having difficulty arranging their visas. Büttner, *"Freud und der Erste Weltkrieg,"* esp. 72–77.

53. Jones, *Life and Work,* 2:198; Abraham and Freud, eds., *A Psycho-Analytic Dialogue: The Letters of Sigmund Freud and Karl Abraham, 1907–1926,* 278. On the status of psychoanalysis in Hungary, Ferenczi wrote: "It is nonetheless remarkable what has been mobilized by psychoanalysis. The minds in Hungary are more or less under its influence." *Correspondence of Freud and Ferenczi,* 150.

54. *Correspondence of Freud and Ferenczi,* 110.

55. Ferenczi, "Die Psychoanalyse der Kriegsneurosen," 9–10.

56. Ibid., 19.

57. For a discussion of the "Freudian historical teleology," see Micale, *Approaching Hysteria,* 125–29.

58. Nonne, "Therapeutische Erfahrungen," 104, 112.

59. Nonne, "Über Kriegsneurosen und ihre Behandlung," 358. See also Mörchen, "Das Problem der Hysterie," 1220.

60. See Freud, "Einleitung," 4.

61. Ferenczi, "Die Psychoanalyse," 26.

62. Ibid.

63. Freud, "Einleitung," 7.

64. See, e.g., Bloch, "Über traumatische Impotenz," 135–41; Pick, "Über Sexualstörungen im Krieg," 1418–20. For different observations, see Lissmann, "Neurosexologische Beobachtungen in der Front," 295–96.

65. Ferenczi, "Die Psychoanalyse," 26.

66. Ibid., 28.

67. Ferenczi, "Über zwei Typen," 141.

68. Ferenczi, "Die Psychoanalyse," 28–29; idem, "Über zwei Typen," 141.

69. A. Stern, *In bewegter Zeit,* 58. Oppenheim in turn was periodically mocked by Freud and his associates.

70. K. Abraham, "Erstes Korreferat," 31–41.

71. Ibid., 32.

72. Ibid., 33.

73. Ibid.

74. *Correspondence between Freud and Ferenczi,* 39.

75. Burchard, "Sexuelle Fragen zur Kriegszeit," 373–80. See also Juliusberger, "Zur Kenntnis der Kriegsneurosen," 305–18; Wexberg, "Neurologische Erfahrungen."

76. K. Abraham, "Erstes Korreferat," 38–39.

77. Ibid., 41.

78. Letter from Freud to Simmel, Vienna, 20 February 1918. Library of Congress, Sigmund Freud Collection, Correspondence, B19.

79. Ibid.

80. Letter from Freud to Abraham, Vienna, 17 February 1918, in *Psycho-Analytic Dialogue,* ed. Abraham and Freud, 270–71. The rest of the passage reads: "I received a brochure from Germany a few days ago that is bound to be of special interest to you. I cannot send it to you, because I want it to be generally known here, but you will be able to get it easily. It is called *War Neurosis and Psychical Trauma. Their reciprocal relations presented on the basis of psycho-analytical and hypnotic studies* by Dr. Ernst Simmel, now a medical superintendent of a special hospital for war neurotics. . . . It is true that he has not gone the whole way with psycho-analysis, bases himself essentially on the cathartic standpoint, works with hypnosis, which is bound to conceal resistance and sexual drives from him, but he correctly apologises for this because of the necessity of quick results and the large number of cases with which he has to deal." Letter from Freud to Abraham, Vienna, 2 December 1918, in *Psycho-Analytic Dialogue,* 281–82. See also Freud's letter of February 17 to Ferenczi, where he writes: "[Simmel's book] should also interest and delight you very much. It . . . is unreservedly on analytic ground, even though it is essentially a 'cathartic' work, and it shows that German war medicine has taken the bait." *Correspondence of Freud and Ferenczi,* 264–65.

81. Simmel, "Zweites Korreferat," 42–60. This essay has been reprinted in Hermanns and Schultz-Venrath, eds., *Ernst Simmel: Psychoanalyse und ihre Anwendungen,* 21–36.

82. Simmel, "Zweites Korreferat," 44–45.

83. See Simmel, *Kriegs-Neurosen und "psychisches Trauma,"* 29–30.

84. Letter from Abraham to Freud, Allenstein, 27 October 1918, in Abraham and Freud, *Psycho-Analytic Dialogue,* 280. Nevertheless, after the war Simmel went through training analysis under Karl Abraham and went on in 1927 to establish the first psychoanalytic sanitarium, in Belin-Tegel. See Schultz and Hermanns, "Die Entdeckung der Psychosomatik," 50–67.

85. Simmel, "Zweites Korreferat," 45.

86. The personality of the war neurotic, Simmel wrote, lay between the hero and the malingerer, having the altruistic sense of duty of the former and the egoistic self-absorption of the latter. Unable to commit to either side of his personality, he "flees into illness." Simmel, *Kriegs-Neurosen*

und "psychisches Trauma," 31. Freud described this splitting as follows: "The conflict is between the soldier's old peaceful ego and his new warlike one, and it becomes acute as soon as the peace-ego realizes what danger it runs of losing its life owing to the rashness of its newly formed, parasitic double." In "Introduction to Psycho-Analysis and the War Neuroses," 209.

87. Simmel, "Zweites Korreferat," 45.

88. Ibid., 46.

89. Ibid., 54.

90. Ibid., 46.

91. *Correspondence of Freud and Ferenczi,* 296.

92. Ibid., 296, 297.

93. Jones, *Life and Work,* 2:197; *Correspondence between Freud and Ferenczi,* 299.

94. Freud, "Einleitung," 3.

95. Letter from Abraham to Freud, Allenstein, 27 October 1918, in *Psycho-Analytic Dialogue,* 279–80.

96. As Ferenczi wrote to Freud, "It is a good thing that one has a Jewish and a psychoanalytic ego along with the Hungarian, which remain untouched by these events." *Correspondence of Freud and Ferenczi,* 297.

97. *Correspondence of Freud and Ferenczi,* 353.

98. Fallend et al., "Psychoanalyse bis 1945," 122–24. On the founding of the Berlin Psycho-analytic Institute, see H. Abraham, "Die Anfänge der psychoanalytischen Vereinigung in Berlin (1908–1933)."

99. Freud, "Introduction to Psycho-Analysis and the War Neuroses," 207–8 (emphasis in text).

100. Ibid., 208.

101. Decker, *Freud in Germany.*

102. Gaupp, "Über den Begriff der Hysterie," 463.

103. See "Verhandlungen psychiatrischer Vereine: Bericht über die Jahresversammlung des Deutschen Vereins für Psychiatrie zu Breslau am 13. und 14. Mai 1913," *AZP* 70 (1913): 779–96.

104. See Sommer's letter to Hoche, 10 May 1913. Robert Sommer Papers, Bd. 65, no. 20, Blatt 528.

105. For the former view, see Albrecht Hirschmüller and Renate Kimmig, "'Pénétration pacifique'? Zur Rezeption der Psychoanalyse in der deutschen Psychiatrie der Zwanzigerjahre," unpublished paper. See also Hoffman, "War, Revolution, and Psychoanalysis"; Cocks, *Psychotherapy in the Third Reich.*

106. See, e.g., Kretschmer, "Zur Kritik des Unbewußten."

107. Freud, *Beyond the Pleasure Principle,* 12, 6.

108. For the reception of psychoanalytic (and psychogenic) ideas in British psychiatry and society, see Stone, "Shellshock and the Psychologists," 242–71, and E. Dean, "War and Psychiatry," 61–82.

109. Micale, "Hysteria Male/Hysteria Female," esp. 227.

110. Ibid.

111. See Gilman, "The Struggle of Psychiatry with Psychoanalysis: Who Won?" 293–313; Shephard, *War of Nerves.*

112. A rare exception can be found in Erich Schneider, "Zur Klinik und Prognose der Kriegs-neurosen," 1295–1303.

113. For a discussion of these issues, see Sauerteig, "Militär, Medizin, und Moral: Sexualität im Ersten Weltkrieg," 197–226; Daniel, *War from Within,* 138–47.

114. See Showalter, "Rivers and Sassoon."

115. Hoffman, "War, Revolution, and Psychoanalysis."

116. See the insightful discussion by Leys in *Trauma: A Genealogy,* 18–40.

Chapter 7. Dictatorship of the Psychopaths

1. Bonhoeffer, "Lebenserinnerungen," 93.

2. Polgar, "Faradische Ströme," 589.

3. Ibid.

4. For an account of these social tensions, see, e.g., Ryder, *The German Revolution of 1918*, 48–109; Weitz, *Creating German Communism, 1890–1990*, 62–99. On women and gender, see Davis, *Home Fires Burning*.

5. See Bessel, *Germany after the First World War,* 5–10.

6. On the more vigorous treatment (tatkräftigere Behandlung) see, e.g., Seydel, "Behandlung von Kriegsneurotikern" Munich, 19 February 1917, BayHStA, San. Amt II. A.K., Bd. 14, 1.

7. Hirschfeld, "Aus der Praxis."

8. A. Schüller, "Die Kriegsneurosen und das Publikum," 1090.

9. Ibid., 1091.

10. Ibid. On psychiatric attempts to combat quackery, see Lerner, "Hysterical Cures." For a contemporary source that reflects the growing concern with quackery after the war, see E. Schultze, "Zur sozialen und sanitätspolizeilichen Bedeutung der Hypnose," 260.

11. Gaupp, *Nervenkranken des Krieges*, 2.

12. Ibid., 19.

13. "Verhandlungen der Kammer der Abgeordneter des bayerischen Landtags," 36. Landtag, Ausserord. Session, 1917, *Stenographischer Bericht*, Bd. 15, 369. Sitzung, 8 March 1917, 393.

14. See Ammon, "Behandlung von Kriegsneurotikern," Kriegsministerium, Medizinal-Abteilung, Munich, 8 August, 1918, BayHStA, San. Amt II. A.K., Bd. 14, 1.

15. *Verhandlungen des Reichstages, XIII. Legislaturperiode II Session, Stenographische Berichte* vol. 313 (Berlin, 1918), 5390.

16. Ibid.

17. Ibid.

18. To an unidentified deputy from the SPD, Wirth shouted, "The reason for your cheerfulness eludes me, Herr Colleague. I do not know whether it concerns what I have said." Ibid., 5391.

19. Ibid., 5392. Here Wirth may be referring to the tendency to diagnose "religious fanatics" and particularly "conscientious objectors" to war as psychopaths. For examples of this phenomenon see "Gaupp spricht über die Neurosen"; A. Hübner, *Über Wahrsager, Weltverbesser, Nerven- und Geisteskranken im Kriege.*

20. *Verhandlungen des Reichstages, XIII. Legislaturperiode II Session, Stenographische Berichte* vol. 313 (Berlin, 1918), 5434.

21. Schultzen, "Behandlung und Beurteilung von Kriegsneurotikern," Berlin, 7 September 1917, UAT, 308/42. The original order concerning the implementation of active treatment may have been given earlier—in his June 12 speech, Schultzen said that he had ordered this eighteen months earlier.

22. *Verhandlungen*, 5434.

23. Ibid., 5828.

24. Ibid.

25. Ibid.

26. Letter from Hofbauer to Sellv. Gen. Kommando des I.A.K., 7 June 1918, BayHStA, Stellv. Gen. Kom. I. A.K. San. Amt, Akte 142. It was a standard regulation that patients not be allowed to see their charts.

27. Letter from Meyer, 17 May 1918, Munich to Chefarzt des Res. Laz. München K, BayHStA, Stellv. Gen. Kom. I. A.K. San. Amt, Akte 142.

28. Letter from A. Pflüger, Landtagsabg. to K. Stellv. Intendantur, Stuttgart, 13 March 1918, UAT, 308/89.

29. Letter from Freund, Bad Rötenbach, 30 March 1918 to Kgl. Sanitätsamt XII A.K., UAT, 308/89.

30. The letter from Pflüger refers to a "Strickverband," which connotes that the patient was bound with rope or cord. In his response Freund calls attention to Pflüger's error and writes of a "Streckverband" (bandage).

31. Letter from Freund, Bad Rötenbach, 30 March 1918 to Kgl. Sanitätsamt XII A.K.

32. Ibid.

33. Gaupp, letter to K. Württemberg Gericht der stellvertr. 53 Infantriebrigade, Ulm, 24 May 1917, UAT, 308/42.

34. Ibid., 4–5 (emphasis in text).

35. Ibid., 5.

36. Ibid.

37. "Gaupp spricht über die Neurosen und Psychosen des Krieges," 9.

38. Gaupp, letter to K. Württemberg Gericht der stellvertr. 53 Infantriebrigade, 5 (emphasis in text).

39. Ibid., 5–6 (emphasis in text).

40. Ibid., 10.

41. Nonne, "Therapeutische Erfahrungen," 116.

42. Gaupp, *Nervenkranken des Krieges*, 20.

43. R. Gerz, "Bericht über die vom preus. Kriegsministerium (Sanitätsdepartment) nach Berlin berufene Versammlung."

44. Gaupp, letter to K. Württemberg Gericht der stellvertr, Gen. Kom, 11.

45. See also Kraepelin, "Psychiatrische Randbemerkungen zur Zeitgeschichte," 172–73.

46. Gaupp, *Nervenkranken des Krieges*, 16.

47. Gaupp, letter to K. Württemberg Gericht der stellvertr, Gen. Kom, 12.

48. Gaupp, letter to Sanitätsdepartement des K. Kriegsministeriums, Tübingen, 5 August 1918, UAT, 308/89.

49. Ibid., 2.

50. Ibid., 3.

51. Ammon, "Behandlung von Kriegsneurotikern."

52. Ibid. (emphasis in text).

53. Ibid.

54. Ibid.

55. "Verfassungsgebende Preußische Landesversammlung. 30. Sitzung am 4. Juni 1919," 2320. BA RAM, Film 36206, Akte 9338.

56. My account of the proceedings is based on the published account in: "Zusammenkunft der Kriegsneurotiker-Ärzte," *MMW* 65 (1918): 1226–27; and an unpublished report by one attendee: R. Gerz, "Bericht über die vom preus. Kriegsministerium (Sanitätsdepartment) nach Berlin berufene Versammlung."

57. Nonne, "Therapeutische Erfahrungen," 108; Loewy-Hattendorf, *Krieg, Revolution, und Unfallneurose*, 10; for Austria, see Schüller, "Die Kriegsneurosen und das Publikum," 1091.

58. Gerz, "Bericht," 4.

59. See Seydel, "Beurteilung und Verwendung der sogen. Psychopathen und Kriegshysteriker," Munich, 10 February 1917, BayHStA, San. Amt II. A.K., Bd. 14, 1.

60. Gerz, "Bericht," 3 (emphasis in text).

61. Ibid., 5.

62. "Neurotiker-Merkblatt: Grundsätze für die Behandlung und Beurteilung der sogenannten Kriegsneurotiker," n.d., BayHStA, San. Amt II. A.K., Bd. 14, 1.

63. "Neurotiker-Merkblatt," n.d., UAT, 308/89, 5.

64. "Neurotiker-Merkblatt: Grundsätze für die Behandlung und Beurteilung der sogenannten Kriegsneurotiker," 3. This change was suggested by Gaupp in the letter to the War Ministry Medical Department, which was discussed above. See Gaupp letter to Sanitätsdepartement des K. Kriegsministeriums, Tübingen, 5 August 1918, UAT, 308/89.

65. "Im Lazarett für Kriegs-Nervenkranke. Eine Besichtigung durch Pressevertreter," no author, *Würzburger Generalanzeiger*, 31 October 1918, BayHStA, San. Amt II. A.K., Bd. 14, 1.

66. Letter from Gerz, Würzburg, 29 November 1917, BayHStA, San. Amt II. A.K., Bd. 14, 1.

67. "Im Lazarett für Kriegs-Nervenkranke."

68. Ibid.

69. R. Weiß, "Behandlung der Kriegsneurotiker."

70. "Die Kriegsneurotiker," no author, *Bayerische Landeszeitung* 33, n.d., BayHStA, San. Amt II. A.K., Bd. 14, 1.

71. Bonhoeffer, "Lebenserinnerungen von Karl Bonhoeffer," 92.

72. Ibid.

73. This refers to two tracts in particular: Sommer's *Ärztlicher Notruf* and Gaupp's "Die Revolution und das nervöse Zusammenbruch."

74. See, e.g., Heuerkamp, "Ärzte und Professionalisierung in Deutschland," 349–66.

75. Weiner, "'Le geste de Pinel': The History of a Psychiatric Myth," 232–47. J. V. Brown, "Revolution and Psychosis: The Mixing of Science and Politics in Russian Psychiatric Medicine, 1905–1913," 283–302.

76. See, e.g., Blasius, *"Einfache Seelenstörung"*; G. Mosse, "Masculinity and the Decadence"; and Klaus Dörner, *Madmen and the Bourgeoisie.*

77. Bonhoeffer, "Lebenserinnerungen," 92–93; Walter, *Psychiatrie und Gesellschaft,* 225–41.

78. Nonne, "Therapeutische Erfahrungen," 116.

79. Ibid.

80. Singer, "Was ist's mit dem Neurotiker vom Jahre 1920?" 951.

81. Loewy-Hattendorf, *Krieg, Revolution, und Unfallneurose,* 21.

82. H. Stern, "Neue Gesichtspunkte zum gegenwärtigen Neurotikerproblem," 194.

83. Wollenberg, *Erinnerungen,* 143.

84. Panse, "Das Schicksal von Renten und Kriegsneurotikern nach Erledigung ihrer Ansprüche," 61–92; Singer, "Was ist's mit dem Neurotiker vom Jahre 1920?"; Loewy-Hattendorf, *Krieg, Revolution, und Unfallneurosen.*

85. *Correspondence of Freud and Ferenczi,* 2:310.

86. Leed, *No Man's Land,* esp. 186.

87. Loewy-Hattendorf, *Krieg, Revolution, und Unfallneurosen.*

88. Pönitz, *Klinische Neuorientierung,* 36.

89. Singer, "Was ist's mit dem Neurotiker vom Jahre 1920?" 951.

90. Singer, "Das Kriegsende und die Neurosenfrage," 331.

91. Ibid., 330–31.

92. Ibid., 331.

93. Nonne, "Therapeutische Erfahrungen," 116.

94. Kretschmer, *Gestalten und Gedanken,* 94.

95. Singer, "Kriegsende," 331.

96. See Herting, "Krieg und Revolution als umittelbares Erlebnis der Irrenanstalt," 268–84. See also Eghigian, *Making Security Social,* 184–85.

97. Rittershaus, "Zur Frage der Kriegshysterie," 96.

98. Weiler, "Ein Jahr Kriegsneurotikerbehandlung," 407.

99. Ibid.

100. See, e.g., Kretschmer, *Gestalten und Gedanken,* 94.

101. Quoted in K.-H. Roth, "Die Modernisierung der Folter," 10.

102. Wollenberg, *Erinnerungen,* 143.

103. Kaufmann, "Science as Cultural Practice," 141.

104. See Eghigian, "The Politics of Victimization: Social Pensioners and the German Social State in the Inflation, 1919–1925," 383.

105. For a parallel argument, see Bessel, "The Great War in German Memory." Bessel writes: "That the public memory of the First World War came increasingly to be structured not by the experiences of the vast majority of those who fought in it or were its victims, but by the perspectives of much narrower (and politically more conservative) groups, says much about the basis upon which Weimar politics were stabilized in the mid-1920s."

106. Hildebrandt, "Forensische Begutachtung eines Spartakisten," 479–518.

107. Ibid., 518. Similarly, the Breslau psychiatrist Georg Stertz diagnosed an increase in "eccentric fanatics" (verschrobene Fanatiker), who exhibited a kind of psychopathic behavior that took on a political form. See Stertz, "Verschrobene Fanatiker," 586–88.

108. For descriptions of Munich after the war, see Kershaw, *Hitler 1889–1936: Hubris,* esp. 116–28; Martin H. Geyer, *Vekehrte Welt: Revolution, Inflation, und Moderne, München, 1914–1924,* esp. 94–129.

109. E. Kahn, "Psychopathen als revolutionäre Führer," 90.

110. Ibid., 91.

111. Ibid., 104.

112. Riedesser and Verderber, *Aufrüstung der Seelen,* 21–22; Weber, *Ernst Rüdin,* 88–90; Geyer, *Verkehrte Welt,* 98–103.

113. Quoted in Weindling, *Health, Race, and German Politics,* 313.

114. Kraepelin, "Psychiatrische Randbemerkungen," 171–83.

115. Ibid., 176.

116. Ibid.

117. Ibid., 178.

118. Ibid., 182.

119. Bonhoeffer, "Einige Schlußfolgerungen aus der psychiatrischen Krankenbewegung während des Krieges," 721–28. See also Walter, *Psychiatrie und Gesellschaft,* 213.

120. On the idea of "mass hystericization," see Lerner, "Hysterical Cures."

121. Gaupp, "Der nervöse Zusammenbruch und die Revolution," 44.

122. Oppenheim, "Seelenstörung und Volksbewegung," 1–2.

123. Bessel, *Germany after the First World War,* esp. 221–53.

124. On the history of the psychiatric reform movement and antipsychiatric sentiment, see Goldberg, "The Mellage Case: Psychiatric Reform and Wilhelmine Politics," 1–32; Engstrom, "Birth of Clinical Psychiatry," 425–43.

125. See Stelzner, "Psychopathologisches in der Revolution," 393–408.

126. See Geyer, *Verkehrte Welt,* 103. In this context Geyer quotes Hitler's well-known condemnation of Cubism and Dada as "sickly products of insane or twisted people." See also Doherty, "'See: We Are All Neurasthenics,'" 82–132.

127. Stransky, "Der seelische Wiederaufbau des deutschen Volkes und die Aufgaben der Psychiatrie," 273. See Burleigh, *Ethics and Extermination: Reflections on Nazi Genocide,* esp. 114.

128. Stransky, "Seelische," 280.

129. Ibid., 274.

130. Sommer, *Ärztlicher Notruf;* for a brief discussion of anticommunism among German doctors at this time, see Weindling, *Health, Race, and German Politics,* 307–10. On Sommer's politics, see Jakobi et al., *Aeskulap und Hakenkreuz.*

131. Sommer, *Ärztlicher Notruf.*

132. Ibid.

133. Hellpach, "Die Kriegsneurasthenie," 228; Gaupp, "Neurasthenie und Schreckneurosen," 68–101.

134. Hellpach, "Kriegsneurasthenie," 228.

135. See, e.g., Marx, "Ärztliche Gedanken zur Revolution," 279–80.

136. Kaes, *Shell Shock.*

137. Hoche, *Jahresringe,* 216–17, 223.

138. Polgar, "Faradische Ströme," 587.

139. Quoted in Eissler, *Freud As an Expert Witness,* 14–15.

140. Ibid., 15.

141. Ibid.

142. Ibid. See Shephard, *War of Nerves,* 133–42, for an interesting discussion that deals with the trial in the same context as Britain's 1922 shell-shock inquiry. See also Bogacz, "War Neurosis and Cultural Change."

143. For the public debate in France over hysteria and its treatment, see Roudebush, "Neurology in the Court of Public Opinion in France during the First World War," 29–38.

144. Gaupp, "Der Arzt als Erzieher seines Volkes," 77–80.

145. Ibid., 78.

146. See Weindling, *Health, Race, and German Politics,* 395–96; Aly, ed., *Aktion T4, 1939–45;* Burleigh, *Death and Deliverance.*

147. "Gaupp spricht über die Neurosen."

Chapter 8. Pension War

1. HUB Nervenklinik Bestand, Akte 19. In this case and all the cases that follow I am using invented names to protect the anonymity of these men, but I have used the actual initials for the benefit of future researchers.

2. Ibid.

3. Döblin, *Berlin Alexanderplatz,* 28. For a discussion of Döblin and war neurosis, see Wolfgang Schäffner, "Der Krieg ein Trauma," 31–46.

4. For an account of the war and its impact on the male mind and body, see Bourke, *Dismembering the Male.*

5. See, e.g., G. Mosse, *Fallen Soldiers.*

6. Michael Geyer, "Insurrectionary Warfare," 459–527.

7. HUB Nervenklinik Bestand, Akte 19.

8. Ibid.

9. Ibid.

10. For an important exception see Fritzsche and Confino, eds., *The Work of Memory.*

11. A good example of this approach can be found in Jay Winter's discussion of reclaiming corpses from the battlefields. See Winter, *Sites of Memory,* 13–53. See also Ulrich and Ziemann, eds., *Krieg im Frieden.* For a survey of works on memory in German and European history, see Fritzsche, "The Case of Modern Memory." See also Confino, "Collective Memory and Cultural History," 1386–1403. Important works on memory that have influenced this discussion include Halbwachs, *On Collective Memory,* and Sherman, *The Construction of Memory.*

12. Sherman, "Bodies and Names," 443–66.

13. On the impact of the war on class relations in Germany, see Kocka, *Facing Total War.*

14. Singer, "Was ist's mit dem Neurotiker?" 951.

15. On the marginalization of veterans in the Weimar state, see Kienitz, "Der Krieg der Invaliden."

16. Cohen, *War Come Home,* 150–51.

17. Anonymous, "Bekenntnisse eines Zitterkünstlers," 2–3.

18. Singer, "Was ist's mit dem Neurotiker?" 951. For a similar interpretation, see Mörchen, "Das Problem der Hysterie," 1221.

19. See, e.g., Kraft's comments in HUB Nervenklinik Bestand, Akte 20, the case of "Otto Schmied" discussed below.

20. Pönitz, *Klinische Neuorientierung,* 36. On conditions during the inflationary years, see Feldman, *The Great Disorder;* for a cultural historical account, see Widdig, *Culture and Inflation in Weimar Germany.*

21. Singer, "Kriegsende," 333.

22. Historians have estimated that at the beginning of 1920 there were some 1,537,000 disabled veterans in Germany. See Hong, *Welfare, Modernity, and the Weimar State,* 94. On demobilization and employment, see Bessel, *Germany after the First World War,* 125–65.

23. Stier, "Rentenversorgung bei nervösen und psychisch erkrankten Feldzugsteilnehmern," 186.

24. Ibid.

25. Stier, "Rentenversorgung," 171.

26. Stier, "Psychiatrie und Heer," 18.

27. Stier, "Wie kann der Entstehung," 62.

28. Pönitz, *Klinische Neuorientierung,* 37.

29. Gaupp, "Krieg und Seelenleben!" 168.

30. Nonne, "Therapeutische Erfahrungen," 117.

31. Letter from Max Nonne to Ernst Kretschmer, Hamburg, 28 October 1918, S28.4 "Briefe: Hysterie," Ernst Kretschmer Papers, private collection, Marburg.

32. Michael Geyer, "Ein Vorbote des Wohlfahrtstaates." For a discussion of the British approach to pensioning, which was done in proportion with degree of disfigurement, see Bourke, *Dismembering the Male,* esp. 65–70.

33. Whalen, *Bitter Wounds,* 89.

34. See Triebel, "Variations in Patterns of Consumption in Germany in the Period of the First World War," 161. See also Davis, *Home Fires Burning;* Bessel, *Germany after the First World War;* Cohen, *War Come Home.*

35. Cohen, *War Come Home,* 154–55.

36. Whalen, *Bitter Wounds,* esp. chap. 6.

37. "Einrichtungen der Kriegsbeschädigtenfürsorge im Reiche und in den Bundesstaaten." BA RAM, Film 36069, 8861–63.

38. Whalen, *Bitter Wounds,* 132. See also Hong, *Welfare,* esp. 92–97. More generally on the Weimar welfare system, see Crew, *Germans on Welfare.*

39. Eghigian, "Die Bürokratie und das Entstehen von Krankheit." For a contemporary view, see Panse, "Das Schicksal von Renten und Kriegsneurotikern."

40. Singer, "Was ist's mit dem Neurotiker?" 951. This does not seem to have been the case in the United States where the American Legion worked with the Veterans Administration to increase public sensitivity to war neuroses. See Cox, "Invisible Wounds."

41. Beyer made no mention of the fact that pensioning was about to become a civil matter for which the Prussian War Ministry would have no direct authority.

42. See "Pseudo-Kriegsinvaliden auf der Straße," 5 May 1919. BA RMdI, 13045, "Fürsorge für Kriegsinvaliden."

43. "Verfassungsgebende preußische Landesversammlung. 30. Sitzung am 4. Juni 1919," 2316, BA RAM, Film 36206, Akte 9338.

44. Ibid., 2324.

45. Letter from Dr. Baumann to Karl Bonhoeffer, Landsberg, 15 November 1920; HUB, Karl Bonhoeffer Papers, Akte 9.

46. Whalen, *Bitter Wounds,* 136–37.

47. Cohen, *War Come Home,* 155–57; Thomann, "'Es gibt kein Krüppeltum.'"

48. BA RMdI, Akte 12882, Kapitalabfindungsgesetz.

49. Hong, *Welfare,* 94.

50. Years later Stier bemoaned that doctors did not have ultimate authority over the pension court, which he contrasted unfavorably to the genetic health courts (Erbgesundheitsgerichte) of Nazi Germany, over which doctors did preside. Stier, "Psychiatrie und Heer," 19.

51. Whalen, *Bitter Wounds,* 142.

52. "Anhaltspunkte für die militärärztliche Beurteilung der Frage der Dientbeschädigung oder Kriegsdienstbeschädigung bei den häufigen psychischen und nervösen Erkrankungen der Heeresangehörigen. Auf Grund von Beratungen des wissenschaftlichen Senats bei der Kaiser Wilhelms-Akademie," n.d., UAT, 308/90, 1. Although this document has no date on it, references to it in the contemporary literature make clear that it was distributed after the war. For comparative perspectives on veterans, pensioning, and welfare, see Geyer, "Ein Vorbote des Wohlfahrtstaates" and Cohen, *War Come Home.*

53. "Anhaltspunkte für die militärärztliche Beurteilung der Frage der Dientbeschädigung," 1.

54. For a discussion of trauma and probability, see Wolfgang Schäffner, "Event, Series, Trauma," 81–91; Eghigian, "The German Welfare State," and *Making Security Social.*

55. "Anhaltspunkte für die militärärztliche Beurteilung der Frage der Dientbeschädigung," 2.

56. See Young, *Harmony of Illusions,* esp. 3–42.

57. See, e.g., Lerner and Micale, "Trauma, Psychiatry, and History"; Roth, "Hysterical Remembering."

58. Schäffner, "Event, Series, Trauma," 86. See also Horn, "Erlebnis und Trauma."

59. Freud, *Beyond the Pleasure Principle,* esp. 36–39. See also Leys, *Trauma: A Genealogy.*

60. For a contemporary psychiatric treatment of this distinction, see Kahn, "Unfallereignis und Unfallerlebnis," 1458–59.

61. "Anhaltspunkte für die militärärztliche Beurteilung der Frage der Dientbeschädigung," 17.

62. These examples are taken from HUB Nervenklinik Bestand: Akte 27, case of FH; Akte 38, case of FE; and Akte 30, case of AK. In a study of 142 cases of traumatic neurosis, 101 of which contained sufficient information about the subject's preneurosis life, Bonhoeffer concluded that about 50 percent were oversensitive, weak, and hypochondriachal; 25 percent overexcitable; 4 percent lacked inhibitions (*haltlos*); 10 percent were between intellectually limited and imbecilic; and a few were depressive. Among the remaining cases were those whose dispositions were acquired, such as sufferers of arteriosclerosis. Nevertheless, Bonhoeffer, maintained, under extreme circum-

stances like war even normal individuals could react hysterically. See Bonhoeffer, "Beurteilung, Begutachtung und Rechtsprechung bei den sogennanten Unfallneurosen," 180–81.

63. "Anhaltspunkte für die militärärztliche Beurteilung der Frage der Dientbeschädigung," 18.

64. Ibid., 19.

65. Ibid.

66. Kretschmer, "Entwurf zu einem einheitlichen Begutachtungsplan," 805.

67. Letter from Robert Gaupp, Tübingen, 7 August 1919, S28 "Briefe: Hysterie," no. 24, Ernst Kretschmer Papers.

68. For an elaboration of Kretschmer's critique of Freud, see Kretschmer, "Zur Kritik des Unbewußten."

69. Letter from Kretschmer (draft), 7 August 1919, S28 "Briefe: Hysterie," no. 22, Ernst Kretschmer Papers.

70. Letter from Schneider, 14 August 1919, S28 "Briefe: Hysterie," no. 18, Ernst Kretschmer Papers.

71. Letter from Schröder, 18 August 1919, S28 "Briefe: Hysterie," no. 14, Ernst Kretschmer Papers.

72. Letter from Mörchen, 5 September 1919, S28 "Briefe: Hysterie," no. 12, Ernst Kretschmer Papers.

73. Letter from A. Fischer to Reichsarbeitsminister, Hannover, 26 October 1921, BA RAM 8720, Bd. 1, Film 36027.

74. Letter from Ammon to Reichsarbeitsministerium, Berlin, Munich, 26 January 1922, BA RAM 8720, Bd. 1, Film 36027.

75. Loewy-Hattendorf, *Krieg, Revolution, und Unfallneurose,* 15–18.

76. See Bonhoeffer, His, Hildebrandt, et al., 5 February 1920, HUB Nervenklinik Bestand, Akte 1239, "Die Ausstellung von ärztlichen Attesten u. Gutachten über Kranken in der Charité (1877–1929); mit Schriftwechsel mit staatl. Dienststellen, Versicherungsämtern, und Kliniken," Blatt 342.

77. Graf, *Prisoners All,* 153–66; on Grosz and war neurosis, see Doherty, "Berlin Dada."

78. HUB Nervenklinik Bestand, Akte 23.

79. Ibid.

80. Quoted in Jolly, "Über den weiteren Verlauf," 592.

81. HUB Nervenklinik Bestand, Akte 20.

82. Ibid.

83. HUB Nervenklinik Bestand, Akte 18.

84. Ibid.

85. HUB Nervenklinik Bestand, Akte 27.

86. Whalen, *Bitter Wounds,* chap. 11.

87. HUB Nervenklinik Bestand, Akte 19.

88. Stier, "Rentenversorgung," 169.

89. Hauptmann, "Krieg der Unfalls-Hysterie!" 186–93.

90. Panse, "Das Schicksal von Renten und Kriegsneurotikern," 87. For a similar approach and the same conclusions, see His, "Beurteilung, Begutachtung und Rechtsprechung," 182–86.

91. See Eghigian, "Die Bürokratie und das Entstehen von Krankheit," 203–23.

92. Eghigian, "German Welfare State," 109.

93. Jolly, "Über den weiteren Verlauf," 593; Eghigian, "Bürokratie," 228.

94. Stier, quoted in His, "Beurteilung, Begutachtung und Rechtsprechung," 185.

95. Bonhoeffer, "Beurteilung, Begutachtung und Rechtsprechung," 182.

96. Eghigian, "German Welfare State," 109–10.

97. For a published version of the lectures, see "Die 'Unfall-(Kriegs-) Neurose,' Vorträge und Erörterungen gelegentlich eines Lehrgangs für Versorgungsärzte im Reichsarbeitsministerium vom 6.–8. März 1929," *Arbeit und Gesundheit* 13 (Berlin: Verlag von Reimar Hobbing, 1929), 9.

98. Michael Geyer, "The Place of World War II in German Memory and History." See also Bartov, *Murder in Our Midst,* esp. 33–52.

99. See also G. Mosse, *Fallen Soldiers.*

100. Michael Geyer, "Place of World War II," 12.

101. Georg Friedrich Wilhelm Schultzen, "Grundsätze für die Behandlung und Beurteilung der sogenannten Kriegsneurotiker (Neurotiker-Merkblatt)," UAT, 308/89, n.d., 9.

102. Stier, "Psychiatrie und Heer."

103. Kehrer, "Zur Frage der Behandlung," 22.

104. Ibid., 308. For the contrasts psychiatrists drew between the morale of front troops and those in the Etappe, see also Berger, *Die beratenden Psychiater des deutschen Heeres,* 59.

105. Theweleit, *Male Fantasies.*

106. See Radkau, *Zeitalter der Nervosität,* chap. 5; for the idea of war as an escape from society, see Leed, *No Man's Land.*

107. Geyer, "Place of World War II," 14.

108. On the myth of the war experience, see, e.g., Verhey, *Spirit of 1914;* Herf, *Reactionary Modernism;* Hüppauf, "Langemarck, Verdun, and the Myth of a *New Man*"; Koschorke, "Der Traumatiker als Fascist," 211–27; G. Mosse, *Fallen Soldiers;* Theweleit, *Male Fantasies,* esp. vol. 2.

109. See G. Mosse, *Fallen Soldiers,* esp. 179.

110. Kraepelin, "Psychiatrische Randbemerkungen."

111. See, e.g., Walter, *Psychiatrie und Gesellschaft;* Friedlander, *Origins of Nazi Genocide.*

112. See, e.g., Proctor, *Racial Hygiene;* Cocks, *Psychotherapy in the Third Reich.*

113. Peukert, "Genesis of the 'Final Solution,'" 242.

114. See Winter, *Sites of Memory.*

115. Mörchen, "Das Problem der Hysterie," 1221.

Bibliography

Primary Sources

Archival Sources

Bayerisches Hauptstaatsarchiv, Abteilung IV Kriegsarchiv, Munich
  Bavarian Ministry of War, Medical Department
    Deputy General Command, Bavarian I Army Corps. Sanitary Dept.
    Deputy General Command, Bavarian II Army Corps. Sanitary Dept.

Bundesarchiv, Abteilung Potsdam (now Berlin)
  Reich Ministry of Labor Collection
  Bd. 4 Versorgungsangelegenheiten
  Ministry of the Interior Collection
    Fürsorge für Kriegsinvaliden
    Kapitalabfindungsgesetz
    Pensionswesen

Columbia University, New York
  Oral History Department, Psychoanalysis Project

Eberhard-Karls-Universität, Tübingen
  Universitätsarchiv, Nervenklinik Bestand
    117/557 Allgemeines
    308/42 Gaupp
    308/43 Gaupp Briefe, 1917–1919
    308/89 Kriegsneurose
    308/90 Reservelazarett II

Geheimes Staatsarchiv Preußischer Kulturbesitz, Berlin
  Rep. 76 Kultusministerium
    4399 Medizinische und ärztliche Schriften
    4417 Miltär-Medizinal-Wesen
    VIII B Akte 1827 Schriften zur Frage des Irrenwesen
    VIII B Akten 1324, 1325 Anwendung des Hypnotismus und des Magnetismus zu
      Heilzwecken

Humboldt Universität zu Berlin
  University Archive
    Karl Bonhoeffer Papers
    Charité Nervenklinik Bestand: Akten betr. Gutachtertätigkeit
    Medizinische Fakultät

Justus-Liebig-Universität, Giessen
  University Library, Handschriftenabteilung
    Robert Sommer Papers
Leo Baeck Institute, New York
  Emil Herz Collection, AR 2538
Library of Congress, Washington, D.C.
  Sigmund Freud Collection
Militärarchiv Württemberg, Stuttgart
  Deputy General Command, XIII Army Corps.
  Württemburg Ministry of War, Medical Department
Private Collection, Marburg
  Ernst Kretschmer Papers
Sächsisches Hauptstaatsarchiv, Dresden
  Deputy General Command, XII Army Corps.
  General Command, XII Res. Corps.
  Institut für Deutsche Militärgeschichte Collection
  Saxon Ministry of War, Medical Department

Published Sources

Abraham, Hilda C., and Ernst L. Freud, eds. *A Psycho-Analytic Dialogue: The Letters of Sigmund Freud and Karl Abraham, 1907–1926.* New York: Basic Books, 1966.

Abraham, Karl. "Erstes Korreferat." *Zur Psychoanalyse der Kriegsneurosen.* 31–41. Leipzig: Internationaler Psychoanalytischer Verlag, 1919.

Alt, Konrad. "Im deutschen Heere während der Kriegszeit aufgetretene psychische Störungen. Aus dem Zyklus von Vorträgen: Über Nachbehandlung von Kriegsverletzungen und Kriegskrankheiten." *Zeitschrift für ärztliche Fortbildung* 12 (1915): 331–35, 365–70.

Anonymous. "Bekenntnisse eines Zitterkünstlers." *Hannoversche Anzeiger* 28 (August 24, 1920): 2–3.

Artwinski, Eugen von. "Uber traumatische Neurosen nach Kriegsverletzungen." *ZgNP* 45 (1919): 242–60.

Aschaffenburg, Gustav. "Winke zur Beurteilung von Nerven- und psychisch-nervösen Erkrankungen." *MMW* 62 (1915): 931–33.

Awtokratow, P. N. "Die Geisteskranken im russischen Heere im japanischen Kriege." *AZP* 64 (1907): 286–319.

Bickel, Heinrich. "Über die Kriegsneurosen, ihre Entstehung und die Erfolge ihrer Behandlung. Zur Auffassung der Hysterie als 'Affektneurose.'" *MPN* 44 (1918): 189–218.

Binswanger, Otto. "Hystero-somatische Krankheitserscheinungen bei der Kriegshysterie." *ZgNP* 38 (1915): 1–60.

——. *Die Pathologie und Therapie der Neurasthenie. Vorlesungen für Studierende und Ärzte.* Jena: Fischer, 1896.

——. *Die seelischen Wirkungen des Krieges.* Berlin: Deutsche Verlagsanstalt, 1914.

Birnbaum, Karl. "Ergebnisse der Neurologie und Psychiatrie. Kriegsneurosen und -Psychosen auf Grund der gegenwärtigen Kriegsbeobachtungen. Sammelbericht I." *ZgNP: Referate und Ergebnisse* 11 (1915): 321–69.

——. "Ergebnisse der Neurologie und Psychiatrie. Kriegsneurosen und -Psychosen auf Grund der gegenwärtigen Kriegsbeobachtungen. Sammelbericht II." *ZgNP: Referate und Ergebnisse* 12 (1915): 1–89.

——. "Ergebnisse der Neurologie und Psychiatrie. Kriegsneurosen und -Psychosen auf Grund der gegenwärtigen Kriegsbeobachtungen. Sammelbericht III." *ZgNP: Referate und Ergebnisse* 12 (1916): 317–88.

——. "Ergebnisse der Neurologie und Psychiatrie. Kriegsneurosen und -Psychosen auf Grund der gegenwärtigen Kriegsbeobachtungen. Sammelbericht IV." *ZgNP: Referate und Ergebnisse* 13 (1916): 437–533.

——. "Ergebnisse der Neurologie und Psychiatrie. Kriegsneurosen und -Psychosen auf Grund der gegenwärtigen Kriegsbeobachtungen. Sammelbericht V." *ZgNP: Referate und Ergebnisse* 14 (1917): 193–258, 313–51.

——. "Ergebnisse der Neurologie und Psychiatrie. Kriegsneurosen und -Psychosen auf Grund der gegenwärtigen Kriegsbeobachtungen. Sammelbericht VI." *ZgNP: Referate und Ergebnisse* 16 (1917): 1–79.

——. "Ergebnisse der Neurologie und Psychiatrie. Kriegsneurosen und -Psychosen auf Grund der gegenwärtigen Kriegsbeobachtungen. Sammelbericht VII." *ZgNP: Referate und Ergebnisse* 18 (1919): 1–76.

——. *Die krankhafte Willensschwäche und ihre Erscheinungsformen. Eine psychopathologische Studie für Ärzte, Pädagogen und gebildete Laien.* Wiesbaden: Bergmann, 1911.

Bloch, Iwan. "Über traumatische Impotenz." *ZfS* 4 (1918/19): 135–41.

Bonhoeffer, Karl. "Ein Beitrag zur Kenntnis des großstädtischen Bettel- und Vagabondentums. Eine psychiatrische Untersuchung." *Zeitschrift für die gesamte Strafrechtswissenschaft* 21 (1901): 1–65.

——. "Beurteilung, Begutachtung und Rechtsprechung bei den sogenannten Unfallneurosen." *DMW* 52 (1926): 179–82.

——. "Einige Schlußfolgerungen aus der psychiatrischen Krankenbewegung während des Krieges." *AfP* 60 (1919): 721–28.

——. "Granatfernwirkung und Kriegshysterie." *MPN* 42 (1917): 51–58.

——. "Lebenserinnerungen von Karl Bonhoeffer—Geschrieben für die Familie." In *Karl Bonhoeffer. Zum hundersten Geburtstag am 31. März 1968,* edited by J. Zutt et al. 8–107. Berlin: Springer, 1969.

——. "Psychiatrie und Krieg." *DMW* 40 (1914): 1777–79.

——. "Psychiatrisches zum Kriege." *MPN* 36 (1914): 435–39.

——. "Wie weit kommen psychogene Krankheitszustände und Krankheitsprozesse vor, die nicht der Hysterie zuzurechnen sind?" *AZP* 68 (1911): 371–86.

Boruttau, H. "Todesfälle durch Sinusströme." *DMW* 43 (1917): 808–9.

Bostroem, A. "Neurologische und psychologische Fronterfahrungen eines Trupenarztes." *MK* 13 (1917): 1310–14.

Böttiger, K. "Diskussion zum Vortrag Nonne, Zur therapeutischen Verwendung der Hypnose bei Fällen von Kriegshysterie." *NZ* 35 (1916): 261–62.

Bumke, Oswald. *Erinnerungen und Betrachtungen: Der Weg eines deutschen Psychiaters.* Munich: Pflaum, 1953.

——. *Kultur und Entartung.* 2d ed. Berlin: Springer, 1922.

Burchard, E. "Sexuelle Fragen zur Kriegszeit." *ZfS* 1 (1915/1916): 373–80.

Cassirer, R. "Hermann Oppenheim." *BKW* 56 (1919): 669–71.

Charcot, Jean-Martin. *Clinical Lectures on Diseases of the Nervous System,* edited and introduced by Ruth Harris. London: Routledge, 1991.

Cimbal, Walter. "Die seelischen und nervösen Erkrankungen im 9. Armeekorps seit der Mobilmachung. Vortrag im ärztlichen Verein in Hamburg am 23.II.1915." *NZ: Referate und Ergebnisse* 34 (1915): 411–15.

———. "Die Zweck- und Abwehrneurosen als sozialpsychologische Entwicklungsformen der Nervosität." *ZgNP* 37 (1917): 417–18.

Curschmann, Hans. "Zur Kriegsneurose bei Offizieren." *DMW* 43 (1917): 291–93.

Dillon, Frederick. "Treatment of Neuroses in the Field: The Advanced Psychiatric Centre." In *The Neuroses in War,* edited by E. Miller. 119–27. New York: Macmillan, 1940.

Döblin, Alfred. *Berlin Alexanderplatz.* Munich: Deutscher Taschenbuchverlag, 1965.

Donath, Julius. "Beiträge zu den Kriegsverletzungen und -erkrankungen des Nervensystems." *WKW* 28 (1915): 725–30, 763–67.

Dub, D. "Heilung funktioneller und motorischer Leiden." *DMW* 43 (1917): 293–94.

Edel, Paul, and Adolf Hoppe. "Zur Psychologie und Therapie der Kriegsneurosen." *MMW* 65 (1918): 836–40.

Engelen, Paul. *Suggestion und Hypnose.* Munich: Gmelin, 1922.

Everth, Erich. "Von der Seele des Soldaten im Felde. Bemerkungen eines Kriegsteilnehmers." *Tat-Flugschriften* no. 10 (1915).

Falzeder, Ernst, and Eva Brabant, eds. *The Correspondence of Sigmund Freud and Sándor Ferenczi, 1914–1919.* Translated by Peter T. Hofer. 2 vols. Cambridge: Harvard University Press, Belknap, 1996.

Ferenczi, Sándor. "Die Psychoanalyse der Kriegsneurosen." In *Zur Psychoanalyse der Kriegsneurosen.* 9–30. Leipzig and Vienna: International Psychoanalytischer Verlag, 1919.

———. "Über zwei Typen der Kriegsneurosen." *Internationale Zeitschrift für ärztliche Psychoanalyse* 4 (1916/1917): 131–45.

Forster, E. "Der Krieg und die traumatischen Neurosen." *MPN* 38 (1915): 72–76.

———. "Hysterische Reaktion und Simulation." *MPN* 42 (1917): 298–324.

Frank, Ludwig. "Zur Psychanalyse (Behandlung psychoneurotischer Zustände)." *ZgNP* 43 (1918): 65–75.

Fränkel, Fritz. "Über die psychopathische Konstitution bei Kriegsneurosen." *MPN* 47 (1920): 287–309.

Freimark, Hans. *Die Revolution als Massenerscheinung.* Wiesbaden: Bergmann, 1920.

Freud, Sigmund. "An Autobiographical Study." In *The Standard Edition of the Complete Psychological Works of Sigmund Freud,* edited by James Strachey. Vol. 20. 7–61. London: Hogarth Press, 1959.

———. *Beyond the Pleasure Principle.* Edited and translated by James Strachey. New York: Norton, 1961.

———. "Einleitung." In *Zur Psychoanalyse der Kriegsneurosen.* 3–7. Leipzig: Internationaler Psychoanalytischer Verlag, 1919.

———. "Introduction to Psycho-Analysis and the War Neuroses." In *The Standard Edition of the Complete Psychological Works of Sigmund Freud,* edited by James Strachey. Vol. 17. 205–10. London: Hogarth Press, 1955.

———. "Memorandum on the Electrical Treatment of War Neurotics." In *The Standard Edition of the Complete Psychological Works of Sigmund Freud,* edited by James Strachey. Vol. 17. 211–16. London: Hogarth Press, 1955.

——. "On the History of the Psychoanalytic Movement." In *The Standard Edition of the Complete Psychological Works of Sigmund Freud,* edited by James Strachey. Vol. 14. 1–66. London: Hogarth Press, 1957.

——. "Thoughts for the Times on War and Death." In *Standard Edition of the Complete Psychological Works of Sigmund Freud,* edited by James Strachey. Vol. 14. 275–300. London: Hogarth Press, 1955.

Freud, Sigmund, and Josef Breuer. *Studies on Hysteria.* Edited and translated by James Strachey. New York: Basic Books, 2000.

Fuchs, Walter. "Mobilmachungspsychosen." *Ärztliche Sachverständigenzeitung* 21 (1915): 25–29.

Gaupp, Robert. "Der Arzt als Erzieher seines Volkes." *Blätter für Volksgesundheitspflege* 19 (1919): 77–80.

——. *Die künftige Stellung des Arztes im Volke.* Tübingen: Laupp, 1919.

——. "Der nervöse Zusammenbruch und die Revolution." *Blätter für Volksgesundheitspflege* 19 (1919): 43–46.

——. *Die Nervenkranken des Krieges: Ihre Beurteilung und Behandlung. Ein Wort zur Aufklärung und Mahnung unseres Volkes.* Stuttgart: Evangelischer Presseverband für Württemberg, 1917.

——. "Die psychischen und nervösen Erkrankungen des Heeres im Weltkrieg." *Der deutsche Militärarzt* 5 (1940): 367.

——. "Hysterie und Kriegsdienst." *MMW* 62 (1915): 361–63.

——. "Krieg und Seelenleben!" *Deutsche Revue* (1918): 162–78.

——. "Kriegsneurosen." *ZgNP* 34 (1916): 357–90.

——. "Neurasthenie und Schreckneurosen." In *Geistes- und Nervenkrankheiten,* edited by Karl Bonhoeffer. 68–101. *Handbuch der ärztlichen Erfahrungen im Weltkriege, 1914–1918.* Vol. 4. Leipzig: Barth, 1922.

——. "Über den Begriff der Hysterie." *ZgNP* 5 (1911): 457–66.

——. "Zur Kritik der Verwendung des Begriffs 'Trauma' in der Ätiologie der Nervenkrankheiten." *Centralblatt für Nervenheilkunde und Psychiatrie* 21 (1898): 388–93.

Goldberg, Erich. "Die ambulante Behandlung der Kriegsneurotiker in Ambulantenstationen für Nervenkranke." *DZN* 64 (1919): 118–32.

Goldscheider, Alfred. "Über die Ursachen des günstigen Gesundheitszustandes unserer Truppen im Winterfeldzuge." *Zeitschrift für physikalische und diätetische Therapie* 19 (1915): 161–75.

——. "Zur Frage der traumatischen Neurose." *DMW* 42 (1916): 1406–11.

Goldstein, Kurt. "Über die Behandlung der Kriegshysteriker." *MK* 28 (1917): 751–58.

——. "Über die Behandlung monosymptomatischer Hysterie bei Soldaten." *NZ* 35 (1916): 842–52.

Gottstein, A. "Die Sterblichkeit in Berlin während des ersten Kriegshalbjahres." *DMW* 41 (1915): 740.

Graf, Oskar Maria. *Prisoners All.* Translated by Margaret Green. New York: Knopf, 1928.

Hargreaves, G. Ronald, Eric Wittkower, and A. T. M. Wilson. "Psychiatric Organisation in the Services." In *The Neuroses in War,* edited by E. Miller. 163–79. New York: Macmillan, 1940.

Hartmann, Fritz. "Die k.u.k. Nervenklinik Graz im Dienste des Krieges." *AfP* 59 (1918): 1162–1258.

Hauptmann, A. "Krieg der Unfalls-Hysterie!" *DZN* 88 (1925): 186–93.

——. "Kriegs-neurosen und traumatische Neurosen." *MPN* 39 (1916): 20–32.

Heinze, Robert. "Über die Behandlung und Beurteilung der Kriegsneurosen." *Therapeutische Monatshefte* 32 (1918): 192–204.

Hellpach, Willy. "Lazarettdisziplin als Heilfaktor." *MK* 11 (1915): 1207–11.

——. "Die Kriegsneurasthenie." *ZgNP* 45 (1919): 177–229.

——. *Nervenleben und Weltanschauung. Ihre Wechselbeziehung im deutschen Leben von Heute.* Wiesbaden: Bergmann, 1906.

Hermanns, Ludger M., and Ulrich Schultz-Venrath, eds. *Ernst Simmel. Psychoanalyse und Ihre Anwendungen: Ausgewählte Schriften.* Fischer: Frankfurt, 1993.

Herting, Johannes. "Krieg und Revolution als umittelbares Erlebnis der Irrenanstalt." *AZP* 92 (1929): 268–84.

Herz, Emil. *Denke ich an Deutschland in der Nacht: Die Geschichte des Hauses Steg.* Berlin: Deutscher Verlag, 1951.

Hildebrandt, Kurt. "Forensische Begutachtung eines Spartakisten." *AZP* 76 (1919): 479–518.

Hirschfeld, Magnus. *Sexual History of the World War.* New York: Cadillac Publishing Co., 1946.

Hirschfeld, R. "Aus der Praxis der sogenannten aktiven Psychotherapie." *MK* 14 (1918): 687–88.

——. "Zur Behandlung der Kriegszitterer." *MMW* 65 (1917): 824–82.

——. "Zur Behandlung im Kriege erworbener hysterischer Zustände, insbesondere von Sprachstörungen." *ZgNP* 34 (1916): 195–205.

Hirschlaff, L. *Hypnotismus und Suggestivtherapie.* 2d ed. Leipzig: Barth, 1919.

His, Wilhelm. "Beurteilung, Begutachtung und Rechtsprechung bei den sogennanten Unfallneurosen." *DMW* 52 (1926): 182–86.

Hoche, Alfred E. "Beobachtungen bei Fliegerangriffen." *AfP* 57 (1917): 570–73.

——. "Geisteskrankheit und Kultur." In *Aus der Werkstatt.* Lehmann: Munich, 1935.

——. *Jahresringe.* Munich: Lehmanns, 1935.

——. *Krieg und Seelenleben.* Freiburg: Speyer und Kaerner, 1914.

——. "Über Hysterie." *AfP* 56 (1915): 331–35.

——. "Über Wesen und Tragweite der Dienstbeschädigung bei nervös und psychisch erkrankten Feldzugsteilnehmern." *MPN* 39 (1916): 347–67.

Hoffmann, R. "Über die Behandlung der Kriegshysterie in den badischen Nervenlazaretten." *ZgNP* 55 (1920): 114–17.

Horn, Paul. "Zur Ätiologie und klinischen Stellung der Unfall- und Kriegsneurosen." *NZ* 36 (1917): 277–82.

Hübner, A. *Über Wahrsager, Weltverbesser, Nerven- und Geisteskranken im Kriege.* Bonn: Marcus and Weber, 1918.

Index-Catalogue of the Library of the Surgeon-General's Office. 3d ser. 10 vols. Washington, D.C.: Government Printing Office, 1926.

Jellinek, Stefan. "Kriegsneurose und Sinusstrom." *MK* 14 (1918): 1085–88.

Jendrássik, Ernst. "Einige Bemerkungen zur Kriegsneurose." *NZ* 35 (1916): 496–500.

Jolly, Ph. "Kriegshysterie und Beruf." *AfP* 59 (1918): 873–82.

——. "Über den weiteren Verlauf hysterischer Reaktionen bei Kriegsteilnehmern und über die Zahl der jetzigen Rentenempfänger." *NZ* 38 (1930): 589–642.

Jones, Ernest. "Die Kriegsneurosen und die Freudsche Theorie." In *Zur Psychoanalyse der Kriegsneurosen.* 61–81. Leipzig: Internationaler Psychoanalytischer Verlag, 1919.

Joseph, H., and L. Mann. "Erfolge der Rothmann'schen Narkosenmethode bei Kriegshysterie, insbesondere bei hysterischem Schütteltremor." *BKW* 54 (1917): 674–76.

Juliusberger, Otto. "Zur Kenntnis der Kriegsneurosen." *MPN* 38 (1915): 305–18.

Jünger, Ernst. *Der Kampf als inneres Erlebnis.* Berlin: Mittler, 1922.

——. "Fire." In *The Weimar Republic Sourcebook,* edited by Anton Kaes, Martin Jay, and Edward Dimendberg. 18–20. Berkeley: University of California Press, 1994.

Kahn, Eugen. "Psychopathen als revolutionäre Führer." *ZgNP* 52 (1919): 90–106.

——. "Unfallereignis und Unfallerlebnis." *MMW* 72 (1925): 1458–59.

Kaufmann, Fritz. "Die planmässige Heilung komplizierter psychogener Bewegungsstörungen bei Soldaten in einer Sitzung." *MMW* 63 (1916): 802–4.

——. "Zur Behandlung der motorischen Kriegsneurosen." *MMW* 64 (1917): 1520–23.

Kehrer, Ferdinand. "Zur Frage der Behandlung der Kriegsneurosen." *ZgNP* 36 (1917): 1–22.

——. "Behandlung und ärztliche Fürsorge bei Kriegsneurosen." *Die Kriegsbeschädigtenfürsorge* 2 (1917): 158–64.

Kraepelin, Emil. "Hundert Jahre Psychiatrie: Ein Beitrag zur Geschichte menschlicher Gesinnung." *ZgNP* 38 (1918): 161–275.

——. *Lebenserinnerungen.* Berlin: Springer, 1983.

——. *Psychiatrie: Ein Lehrbuch für Studirende und Ärzte.* 7th ed. Leipzig: Barth, 1904.

——. "Psychiatrische Randbemerkungen zur Zeitgeschichte." *Süddeutsche Monatshefte* 16 (1919): 171–83.

Kraus, Karl. *The Last Days of Humanity.* Translated by Alexander Gode and Sue Ellen Wright. New York: Ungar, 1974.

Kreisler, Fritz. *Four Weeks in the Trenches: The War Story of a Violinist.* Boston: Houghton Mifflin, 1915.

Kretschmer, Ernst. "Entwurf zu einem einheitlichen Begutachtungsplan für die Kriegs— und Unfallneurotiker." *MMW* 66 (1919): 804–5.

——. *Gestalten und Gedanken.* Stuttgart: Georg Thieme Verlag, 1963.

——. "Hysterie." *Wissen und Leben: Neue schweizer Rundschau* 17 (1923): 148–52.

——. "Hysteriebehandlung im Dunkelzimmer." *MMW* 64 (1917): 825.

——. "Hysterische Erkrankung und hysterische Gewöhnung." *ZgNP* 37 (1917): 64–91.

——. "Zur Kritik des Unbewußten." *ZgNP* 46 (1919): 368–87.

Laudenheimer, Rudolf. "Feldärztliche Beiträge über Kriegsneurosen." *MMW* 38 (1915): 1302–4.

LeBon, Gustave. *The Crowd.* Reprint, New Brunswick, N.J.: Transaction Press, 1995.

Levy-Suhl, Max. "Über Unfall- und Kriegsneurosen. Die gegenwärtige ärztliche und rechtliche Lage." *Der sozialistische Arzt* 1/2 (1927): 24–34.

Lewandowsky, Max. "Erfahrungen über die Behandlung nervenverletzter und nervenkranker Soldaten." *DMW* 41 (1915): 1565–67.

——. "Über den Tod durch Sinusströme." *DMW* 43 (1917): 1169.

——. "Was kann in der Behandlung und Beurteilung der Kriegsneurosen erreicht werden?" *MMW* 63 (1917): 989–91, 1028–31.

——. "Zur Behandlung der Zitterer." *MMW* 64 (1917): 54.

Liebermeister, Gustav. "Verhütung von Kriegsneurosen." *Medizinisches Correspondenzblatt des württembergischen ärztlichen Landesvereins* 88 (1918): 307–9.

——. *Über die Behandlung von Kriegsneurosen.* Halle: Marhold, 1917.

Liebermeister, Gustav, and Siegerist. "Über eine Neurosenepidemie im Kriegsgefangenenlager." *ZgNP* 37 (1917): 350–55.

Liebers, Max. "Zur Behandlung der Zitterneurosen nach Granatshock." *NZ* 35 (1916): 871–74.

Liepmann, H. "Über Hermann Oppenheim." *ZgNP* 50 (1919): 1–5.

——. "Zur Fragestellung zu dem Streit über die traumatische Neurose." *NZ* 35 (1916): 233–37.

Lissmann, P. "Neurosexologische Beobachtungen in der Front." *MMW* 65 (1918): 295–96.

Loewy-Hattendorf, Erwin. *Krieg, Revolution, und Unfallneurose.* Berlin: Schoetz, 1920.

Löwenfeld, Leopold. *Über den Nationalcharakter der Franzosen und dessen krankhafte Auswüchse (die Psychopathia Gallica) in ihren Beziehungen zum Weltkrieg.* Wiesbaden: Bergmann, 1914.

Lust, F. "Kriegsneurosen und Kriegsgefangene." *MMW* 63 (1916): 1829–32.

Mann, Ludwig. *Elektrodiagnostik und Elektrotherapie.* Vienna and Leipzig: A. Holder, 1904.

——. "Über Granatexplosionsstörungen." *AfP* 56 (1915): 340–45.

——. "Neue Methoden und Gesichtspunkte zur Behandlung der Kriegsneurosen." *BKW* 53 (1916): 1333–38.

Martineck, Otto. "Zur Frage der traumatischen Neurose." *DMW* 43 (1917): 44–45.

Marx, H. "Ärztliche Gedanken zur Revolution." *BKW* 56 (1919): 279–80.

Mayer-Gross, W. "Practical Psychiatry in War-Time." *The Lancet* ii (1939): 1327–30.

McCurdy, John T. *War Neuroses.* Utica, N.Y.: State Hospital Press, 1918.

Mendel, Kurt. "Die kaufmannsche Methode." *NZ* 36.5 (1917): 181–93.

——. "Psychiatrisches und Neurologisches aus dem Felde." *NZ* 34 (1915): 2–7.

Meyer, E. "Psychosen und Neurosen in der Armee während des Krieges." *DMW* 40 (1915): 2085–88.

Meyer, Max. "Behandlungsmethoden hysterischer Bewegungstörungen bei Kriegsneurosen." *Therapeutische Monatshefte* 31 (1917): 250–59.

Minor, L. "Einige statistische Angaben über die Erkrankungen des Nervensystems im russischen Heere während des russisch-japanischen Krieges (nach Beobachtungen an heimgekehrten Verwundeten und Kranken)." *NZ* 28 (1909): 854–60.

Mitchell, Silas Weir. *Fat and Blood: An Essay on the Treatment of Certain Forms of Neurasthenia and Hysteria.* 3d ed. Philadelphia: Lippincott, 1884.

Mohr, Fritz. "Aus der Praxis der Psychotherapie." *MK* 13 (1917): 1116–19.

——. "Die Behandlung der Kriegsneurosen." *Therapeutische Monatsheft* 30 (1916): 131–41.

——. "Grundsätzliches zur Kriegsneurosenfrage." *MK* 12 (1916): 90–93.

Mörchen, Friedrich. "Das Problem der Hysterie." *MMW* 68 (1921): 1220–21.

——. "Der Hysteriebegriff bei den Kriegsneurosen: Auf Grund neuerere Gefangenbeobachtungen." *BKW* 54 (1917): 1214–15.

——. "Traumatische Neurose und Kriegsgefangene." *MMW* 63 (1916): 1188–91.

Muck, Otto. *Beobachtungen und praktische Erfahrungen aus dem Gebiet der Kriegsneurosen der Stimme, der Sprache und des Gehörs.* Wiesbaden: Bergmann, 1918.

——. "Heilungen von schwerer funktioneller Aphonie." *MMW* 63 (1916): 441.

——. "Über Schnellheilungen von funktioneller Stummheit und Taubstummheit nebst einem Beitrag zur Kenntnis des Wesens des Mutismus." *MMW* 64 (1917): 165–66.

Naegli, Otto. *Unfalls- und Begehrungsneurosen.* Stuttgart: Enke, 1917.

Niessl von Maiendorf, E. "Über pathologische Tremorformen zur Kriegszeit." *MPN* 23 (1916): 221–36.

Nonne, Max. *Anfang und Ziel meines Lebens.* Hamburg: Hans Christians Verlag, 1971.
———. "In Memoriam Hermann Oppenheim und Ludwig Bruns anläßlich der Wiederkehr ihres 100. Geburtstages." In *50 Jahre deutsche Gesellschaft für Neurologie.* 24–37. Lübeck: Schmidt Römhild, 1958.
———. "Soll man wieder traumatische Neurosen diagnostizieren?" *AfP* 56 (1915): 337–39.
———. "Therapeutische Erfahrungen an den Kriegsneurosen in den Jahren 1914–1918." In *Geistes- und Nervenkrankheiten,* edited by Karl Bonhoeffer. Vol. 4. 102–21. Leipzig: Barth, 1922.
———. "Über erfolgreiche Suggestivbehandlung der hysterieformen Störungen bei Kriegsneurosen." *ZgNP* 37 (1917): 191–218.
———. "Über Psychotherapie mit Filmvorführungen und Lichtbildern." *DMW* 64 (1918): 477–78.
———. "Über Kriegsneurosen und ihre Behandlung." *MMW* 65 (1918): 358.
———. "Zum Andenken an Hermann Oppenheim." *NZ* 38 (1919): 386–90.
———. "Zur therapeutischen Verwendung der Hypnose bei Fällen von Kriegshysterie." *NZ* 35 (1916): 136–38.
Nonne, Max, and F. Wachsner. "Therapeutische Erfahrungen in der Behandlung sogenannter Neurosen." *ZgNP: Referate und Ergebnisse* 15 (1918): 271–73.
Nordau, Max. *Degeneration.* Lincoln: University of Nebraska Press, 1992.
———. *Entartung.* 2 vols. Berlin: Dunker, 1892–93.
Oehmen. "Die Heilung der hysterischen Erscheinungen in Wachsuggestion." *DMW* 43 (1917): 463–66.
Ollendorf, Kurt. "Turnen in der Behandlung der psychogen bewegungsgestörten Soldaten." *MK* 13 (1917): 765–66.
Oppenheim, Gustav. "Zur Behandlung des Zitterns." *NZ* 36 (1917): 620–24.
Oppenheim, Hermann. "Der Krieg und die traumatischen Neurosen." *BKW* 52 (1915): 257–61.
———. *Die Neurosen infolge von Kriegsverletzungen.* Berlin: Karger, 1916.
———. *Die traumatischen Neurosen nach den in der Nervenklinik der Charité in den 8 Jahren 1883–1891 gesammelten Beobachtungen.* 2d ed. Berlin: Hirschwald, 1892.
———. *Die traumatischen Neurosen nach den in der Nervenklinik der Charité in den 5 Jahren 1883–1888 gesammelten Beobachtungen.* Berlin: Hirschwald, 1889.
———. "Für und wider die traumatische Neurose." *NZ* 35 (1916): 225–33.
———. *Lehrbuch der Nervenkrankheiten für Ärzte und Studierende.* Berlin: Karger, 1894.
———. "Neurosen nach Kriegsveletzungen." *Zeitschrift für ärztliche Fortbildung* 8 (1916): 213.
———. *Psychotherapeutische Briefe.* Berlin: Karger, 1906.
———. "Seelenstörung und Volksbewegung." *Berliner Tageblatt* 48 (April 16, 1919): 1–2.
———. "Stand der Lehre von den Kriegs- und Unfallneurosen." *BKW* 54 (1917): 1169–72.
———. "Über einen sich an Kopfverletzungen und allgemeine Körpererschütterungen anschließenden cerebralen Symptomenkomplex." *BKW* 21 (1884): 725.
———. "Zur Frage der traumatischen Neurose." *DMW* 42 (1916): 1567–70.
———. "Zur Psychopathologie und Nosologie der russisch-jüdischen Bevölkerung." *Journal für Psychologie und Neurologie* 13 (1908): 1–9.
———. "Zur traumatischen Neurose im Kriege." *NZ* 34 (1915): 514–18.
Panse, Friedrich. "Das Schicksal von Renten und Kriegsneurotikern nach Erledigung ihrer Ansprüche." *AfP* 77 (1926): 61–92.
Pappenheim, Martin. "Über Psychosen bei Kriegsgefangenen." *ZgNP* 35 (1916): 518–25.

Paschen, R. "Zur Behandlung funktioneller motorischer Störungen nach Kaufmann."
  MMW 64 (1917): 169–70.
Pick, F. "Über Sexualstörungen im Krieg." *WMW* 30 (1917): 1418–20.
Pilzecker. "Der Lazarettnachweis im Reservelazarett Triberg (Schwarzwald)." *Die*
  Kriegsbeschädigtenfürsorge 2 (1917): 165–70.
Pinel, Philippe. *A Treatise on Insanity.* Translated by D. D. Davis. New York: Hafner,
  1962.
Placzek, Siegfried. *Das Geschlechtsleben des Hysterischen: Eine medizinische, soziolo-*
  gische und forensische Studie. 2d ed. Bonn: Marcus and Weber, 1922.
Polgar, Alfred. "Faradische Ströme." *Die Weltbühne* 16 (1920): 587–89.
Pönitz, Karl. *Die klinische Neuorientierung zum Hysterieproblem unter dem Einflusse*
  der Kriegserfahrungen. Berlin: Springer, 1921.
Raecke, J. "Über Aggravation und Simulation geistiger Störung." *AfP* 60 (1919): 521–
  603.
Raether, Max. "Neurosen-Heilungen nach der 'Kaufmann-Methode.'" *AfP* 57 (1917):
  489–502.
Redlich, E. "Einige allgemeine Bemerkungen über den Krieg und unser Nervensystem."
  MK 11 (1915): 467–73.
Rees, John Rawlings. *The Shaping of Psychiatry by War.* Norton: New York, 1945.
Rhein, J. H. W. "War Neuroses as Observed in Army Neurological Hospitals at the
  Front." *New York Medical Journal* 110 (1919): 177–80.
Rittershaus, Ernst. "Die psychiatrisch-neurologische Abteilung im Etappen." *ZgNP* 32
  (1916): 271–87.
——. "Zur Frage der Kriegshysterie." *ZgNP* 50 (1919): 87–97.
Rosenfeld. "Über Kriegsneurosen, ihre Prognose und Behandlung." *AfP* 57 (1917):
  221–44.
Roth, E. "Kriegsgefahr und Psyche." *Ärztliche Sachverstänidgenzeitung* 21 (1915): 1–3.
Rothmann, M. "Zur Beseitigung psychogener Bewegungsstörungen bei Soldaten in einer
  Sitzung." *MMW* 63 (1916): 1277–78.
Sänger, Alfred. "Über die durch den Krieg bedingten Folgezustände am Nervensystem.
  Vortrag im ärztlichen Verein in Hamburg am 26.I und 9.II. 1915." *MMW* 62 (1915):
  522–23, 564–67.
Sanitätsbericht über das Deutsche Heer im Weltkriege 1914/1918. Vol. 3, *Die Kranken-*
  bewegung bei dem deutschen Feld- und Besatzungsheer. Berlin: E. S. Mittler, 1934.
Sarbo, Arthur von. "Granatfernwirkungsfolgen und Kriegshysterie." *NZ* 36 (1917):
  360–74.
Sauer, W. "Zur Analyse und Behandlung der Kriegsneurosen." *ZgNP* 36 (1917): 26–45.
Schjerning, Otto von. *Die Tätigkeit und die Erfolge der deutschen Ärzte im Weltkriege.*
  Leipzig: Barth, 1920.
Schmidt, W. "Die psychischen und nervösen Folgezustände nach Granatexplosionen und
  Minenverschüttungen." *ZgNP* 29 (1915): 514–42.
Schneider, Erich. "Zur Klinik und Prognose der Kriegsneurosen." *WKW* 29 (1916):
  1295–1303.
Schneider, Kurt. "Einige psychiatrische Erfahrungen als Truppenarzt." *ZgNP* 39 (1918):
  311–12.
Schüller, Arthur. "Die Kriegsneurosen und das Publikum." *WMW* 68 (1918): 1086–94.
Schüller, L. "Heilung der Erscheinungen der Kriegshysterie in Wachsuggestion." *DMW*
  43 (1917): 652–54.

Schultze, Ernst. "Das Verbot hypnotischer Schaustellungen." *BKW* 56 (1919): 1105–8.

——. "Zur sozialen und sanitätspolizeilichen Bedeutung der Hypnose." *Ärztliche Sach-verständigen-Zeitung* 21 (1918): 260.

Schultze, Friedrich. "Bemerkungen über traumatische Neurose, Neurasthenie und Hys-terie." *NZ* 35 (1916): 610–18.

Selbach, Helmut. "Über Hermann Oppenheim." Vortrag auf der Eröffnungsfeier der Jahresversammlung der Deutschen Gesellschaft für Neurologie am 4.10.1978. AR 2538. Archive of the Leo Baeck Institute.

Simmel, Ernst. "Kriegsneurosen." In *Ernst Simmel. Psychoanalyse und ihre Anwen-dungen: Ausgewählte Schriften,* edited by Ludger M. Hermanns and Ulrich Schultz-Venrath. 204–26. Fischer: Frankfurt, 1993.

——. *Kriegs-Neurosen und "pyschisches Trauma": Ihre gegenseitige Beziehung dar-gestellt auf Grund psycho-analytischer, hypnotischer Studien.* Leipzig: Nemnich, 1918.

——. "Zweites Korreferat." In *Zur Psychoanalyse der Kriegsneurosen.* 42–60. Leipzig: Internationaler Psychoanalytischer Verlag, 1919.

Singer, Kurt. "Das Kriegsende und die Neurosenfrage." *NZ* 38 (1919): 330–34.

——. "Die zukünftige Begutachtung traumatischer Nervenkrankheiten." *Ärztliche Sach-verständigen-Zeitung* 25 (1919): 330–34, 345–49.

——. "Prinzipien und Erfolge der aktiven Therapie bei Neurosen." *Zeitschrift für physi-kalische und diätetische Therapie* 22 (1918): 275–85.

——. "Was ist's mit dem Neurotiker vom Jahre 1920?" *MK* 16 (1920): 951–53.

——. "Wesen und Bedeutung der Kriegspsychosen." *BKW* 52 (1915): 177–80.

Sombart, Werner. *Händler und Helden, patriotische Besinnungen.* Munich: Duncker and Humblot, 1915.

Sommer, Robert. *Ärztlicher Notruf.* Giessen: Brühl, 1919.

——. "Beseitigung funktioneller Taubheit, besonders bei Soldaten, durch eine experi-mental-psychologische Methode." *AfP* 57 (1917): 574–75.

——. "Beseitigung funktioneller Taubheit, besonders bei Soldaten, durch eine experi-mental-psychologische Methode." *Schmidts Jahrbücher der in- und ausländischen ge-samten Medizin* 84 (1917): 65–75.

——. *Familienforschung und Vererbungslehre.* Leipzig: Barth, 1907.

——. *Krieg und Seelenleben.* Leipzig: Nemnich, 1916.

Specht, Gustav. "Einige historische und ästhetische Nebengedanken über die Erfahrun-gen mit dem psychogenen Kriegsstörungen." *MMW* 66 (1919): 1406–7.

Stekel, Wilhelm. *The Autobiography of Wilhelm Stekel: The Life Story of a Pioneer Psy-choanalyst.* New York: Liveright, 1950.

——. *Nervöse Leute: Kleine Federzeichnungen.* Vienna: Knepler, 1911.

Stelzner, Helenfriderike. "Aktuelle Massensuggestion." *AfP* 55 (1914): 354–88.

——. "Psychopathologisches in der Revolution." *ZgNP* 49 (1919): 393–408.

Stern, Arthur. *In bewegter Zeit. Erinnerungen und Gedanken eines jüdischen Nerve-narztes. Berlin-Jerusalem.* Jerusalem: Verlag Rubin Mass, 1968.

Stern, F. "Bericht über die Kriegstagung des Deutschen Vereins für Psychiatrie in München am 21., 22, und 23. September 1916." *Ärztliche sachverständige Zeitung* 22 (1916): 236–39, 249–52.

Stern, Fritz. "Die psychoanalytische Behandlung der Hysterie im Lazarett." *Psychia-trisch-neurologische Wochenschrift* (1916/1917): 1–3.

Stern, Fritz. *Gedanken über Heeresorganisation auf arbeitswissenschaftlicher Grund-lage.* Berlin: Schmiß and Bukoszer, 1917.

Stern, Heinrich. "Neue Gesichtspunkte zum gegenwärtigen Neurotikerproblem." *ZgNP* 49 (1919): 189–97.

Stertz, Georg. "Verschrobene Fanatiker." *BKW* 56 (1919): 586–88.

Stier, Ewald. "Psychiatrie und Heer." *Der deutsche Militärarzt* 1 (1936): 15–20.

——. "Rentenversorgung bei nervösen und psychisch erkrankten Feldzugsteilnehmern." In *Geistes- und Nervenkrankheiten,* edited by Karl Bonhoeffer. 168–95. *Handbuch der ärztlichen Erfahrungen im Weltkriege, 1914–1918.* Vol. 4. Leipzig: Barth, 1922.

——. "Wie kann der Entstehung von Kriegsneurosen bei der Feldarmee vorgebeugt werden?" *Deutsche militärärztliche Zeitschrift* 47 (1918): 60–72.

Stransky, Erwin. "Einiges zur Psychiatrie und Psychologie im Kriege." *WMW* 65 (1915): 1026–30.

——. "Der seelische Wiederaufbau des deutschen Volkes und die Aufgaben der Psychiatrie." *ZgNP* 60 (1920): 271–80.

Suckau, Wilhelm. "Psychosen bei Frauen in Zusammenhang mit dem Kriege." *AZP* 72 (1916): 328–56.

Tausk, Viktor. "Zur Psychologie des Deserteurs." *Internationale Zeitschrift für ärztliche Psychoanalyse* 4 (1916/1917): 193–204, 229–40.

Trömner, Ernst. "Diskussion zum Vortrag Nonne, Zur therapeutischen Verwendung der Hypnose bei Fällen von Kriegshysterie." *NZ* 35 (1916): 21–22.

"Verhandlungen psychiatrischer Vereine: Kriegstagung des Deutschen Vereins für Psychiatrie zu München am 21. und 22. September 1916." *AZP* 71 (1916): 161–233.

Wachsner, F. "Zur Behandlung funktioneller Störungen bei Soldaten nach modifiziertem Kaufmann-Verfahren." *DMW* 43 (1917): 1104.

Wagner, F. "Arbeitstherapie und Rentenabschätzung bei Kriegsneurotikern." *ZgNP: Referate und Ergebnisse* 15 (1918): 274.

——. "Die Dienstbeschädigung bei nerven- und geisteskranken Soldaten." *ZgNP* 37 (1917): 219–244.

Weichbrodt, Rafael. "Zur Behandlung hysterischer Störungen." *AfP* 57 (1917): 519–25.

——. "Einige Bemerkungen zur Behandlung von Kriegsneurotikern." *MPN* 43 (1918): 265–69.

Weiler, Karl. "Ein Jahr Kriegsneurotikerbehandlung." *MMW* 66 (1919): 401–7.

——. "Versorgung und weitere Behandlung der psychopathischen, hysterischen, und neurotischen Kriegsteilnehmer." *MMW* 67 (1919): 531–36.

Wexberg, E. "Neurologische Erfahrungen im Felde." *WMW* 66 (1916): 1410–11.

Weygandt, W. "Versorgung der Neurosen und Psychosen im Felde." *MK* 10 (1914): 29–43.

Wilmanns, Karl. "Die Behandlung der Kranken mit funktionellen Neurosen im Bereiche des XIV A.K." *DMW* 43 (1917): 427–28.

——. "Die Wiedertüchtigung der an funktionellen Neurosen leidenden Kriegsbeschädigten." *Die Kriegsbeschädigtenfürsorge* 2 (1917): 129–50.

Wittkower, Eric, and J. P. Spillane. "A Survey of the Literature of Neuroses in War." In *The Neuroses in War,* edited by E. Miller. 1–33. New York: Macmillan, 1940.

Wollenberg, Robert. "Ein seltener Fall psychogener Kriegsschädigung." *AfP* 58 (1917): 837–51.

——. *Erinnerungen eines alten Psychiaters.* Stuttgart: Enke, 1931.

——. "Hysterie oder Simulation." *Psychiatrisch neurologische Wochenschrift* 28 (1926): 211–12.

———. "Nervöse Erkrankungen bei Kriegsteilnehmern." *MMW* 61 (1914): 2181–83.
———. "Über die Wirkung der Granaterschütterung." *AfP* 56 (1915): 335–57.

Secondary Sources

Abraham, Hilda. "Die Anfänge der Psychoanalytischen Vereinigung in Berlin (1908–1933)." In *Psychoanalyse in Berlin: Beiträge zur Geschichte, Theorie und Praxis: 50 Jahre Gedenkfeier des B.P.I.* Berlin: Hain, 1971.

Ackerknecht, Erwin H. *A Brief History of Psychiatry.* Translated by Sula Wolff. 2d ed. New York: Hafner, 1968.

Aly, Götz, ed. *Aktion T4, 1939–45: Die "Euthanasia"—Zentralle in der Tiergartenstraße 4.* Berlin: Hentrich, 1987.

Aly, Götz, Peter Chroust, and Christian Pross. *Cleansing the Fatherland: Nazi Medicine and Racial Hygiene.* Translated by Belinda Cooper. Baltimore: Johns Hopkins University Press, 1994.

Angress, Werner T. "The German Army's 'Judenzählung' of 1916: Genesis—Consequences—Significance." *Leo Baeck Institute Yearbook* 23 (1978): 117–37.

Antze, Paul, and Michael Lambek. "Introduction." In *Tense Past: Cultural Essays in Trauma and Memory,* edited by Paul Antze and Michael Lambek. xi–xxxviii. New York: Routledge, 1996.

———, eds. *Tense Past: Cultural Essays in Trauma and Memory.* New York: Routledge, 1996.

Baader, Gerhard. "Stadtentwicklung und psychiatrische Anstalten." In *Gelêrter der arzenîe, ouch apotëker: Beiträge zur Wissenschaftsgeschichte. Festschrift zum 70. Geburtstag von Willem F. Daems,* edited by Gundolf Keil. 239–53. Pattensen: Wellm, 1982.

Bartov, Omer. *Murder in Our Midst: The Holocaust, Industrial Killing, and Representation.* New York: Oxford University Press, 1996.

Berg, Manfred, and Geoffrey Cocks, eds. *Medicine and Modernity: Public Health and Medical Care in Nineteenth- and Twentieth-Century Germany.* New York: Cambridge University Press, 1997.

Berger, Georg. *Die beratenden Psychiater des deutschen Heeres 1939 bis 1945.* Frankfurt: Peter Lang, 1998.

Bessel, Richard. *Germany after the First World War.* Oxford: Clarendon Press, 1993.

———. "The Great War in German Memory: The Soldiers of the First World War, Demobilization and Weimar Political Culture." *German History* 6 (1988): 20–34.

Bianchi, Bruna. "Psychiatrists, Soldiers, and Officers in Italy during the Great War." In *Traumatic Pasts: History, Psychiatry, and Trauma in the Modern Age, 1870–1930,* edited by Mark S. Micale and Paul Lerner. 222–52. New York: Cambridge University Press, 2001.

———. "La Psychiatrie Italienne et la Guerre." In *Guerre et Cultures, 1914–1918,* edited by J. J. Becker et al. 118–31. Paris: Armand Colin, 1994.

Binneveld, Hans. *From Shellshock to Combat Stress: A Comparative History of Military Psychiatry.* Translated by John O'Kane. Amsterdam: Amsterdam University Press, 1997.

Blackbourn, David. *The Long Nineteenth Century: A History of Germany, 1780–1918.* New York: Oxford University Press, 1998.

Blasius, Dirk. *"Einfache Seelenstörung": Geschichte der deutschen Psychiatrie 1800–1945*. Frankfurt: Fischer, 1994.

———. *Umgang mit Unheilbarem: Studien zur Sozialgeschichte der Psychiatrie*. Bonn: Psychiatrie Verlag, 1986.

———. *Der verwaltete Wahnsinn: Eine Sozialgeschichte des Irrenhauses*. Frankfurt: Fischer, 1980.

Bleker, Johanna. "Medizin im Dienst des Krieges—Krieg im Dienst der Medizin. Zur Frage der Kontinuität des ärztlichen Auftrages und ärztlicher Werthaltungen in Angesicht des Krieges." In *Medizin und Krieg: Vom Dilemma der Heilberufe, 1865–1985*, edited by Johanna Bleker and H.-P. Schmiedebach. 13–28. Frankfurt: Fischer, 1987.

Bleker, Johanna, and H.-P. Schmiedebach, eds. *Medizin und Krieg: Vom Dilemma der Heilberufe, 1865–1985*. Frankfurt: Fischer, 1987.

Bock, Gisela. *Zwangsterilisation im Nationalsozialismus*. Opladen: Westdeutscher Verlag, 1986.

Boemeke, Manfred F., Roger Chickering, and Stig Förster, eds. *Anticipating Total War: The German and American Experiences*. New York: Cambridge University Press, 1999.

Bogacz, Ted. "War Neurosis and Cultural Change in England, 1914–22: The Work of the War Office Committee of Enquiry into 'Shell-shock.'" *Journal of Contemporary History* 24 (1989): 227–56.

Bourke, Joanna. *Dismembering the Male: Men's Bodies, Britain and the Great War*. London: Reaktion Books, 1996.

———. *An Intimate History of Killing: Face-to-Face Killing in Twentieth-Century Warfare*. New York: Basic Books, 1999.

Brown, Julie V. "Revolution and Psychosis: The Mixing of Science and Politics in Russian Psychiatric Medicine, 1905–1913." *The Russian Review* 46 (1987): 283–302.

Brown, Tom. "Shell Shock in the Canadian Expeditionary Force, 1914–1918: Canadian Psychiatry in the Great War." In *Health, Disease, and Medicine: Essays in Canadian History*, edited by Charles Roland. 308–32. Toronto: Hannah Institute for the History of Medicine, 1984.

Brunner, José. *Freud and the Politics of Psychoanalysis*. Oxford: Blackwell, 1995.

Burleigh, Michael. *Death and Deliverance: "Euthanasia" in Germany, ca. 1900–1945*. Cambridge: Cambridge University Press, 1994.

———. *Ethics and Extermination: Reflections on Nazi Genocide*. New York: Cambridge University Press, 1997.

Büttner, Peter. "Freud und der Erste Weltkrieg. Eine Untersuchung über die Beziehung von medizinischer Theorie und gesellschaftlicher Praxis der Psychoanalyse." Ph.D. diss., Ruprechts-Karls-Universität Heidelberg, 1975.

Campbell, Joan. *Joy in Work, German Work: The National Debate, 1800–1945*. Princeton: Princeton University Press, 1989.

Caplan, Eric. *Mind Games: American Culture and the Birth of Psychotherapy*. Berkeley: University of California Press, 1998.

———. "Trains and Trauma in the American Guilded Age." In *Traumatic Pasts: History, Psychiatry, and Trauma in the Modern Age, 1870–1930*, edited by Mark S. Micale and Paul Lerner. 57–77. New York: Cambridge University Press, 2001.

———. "Trains, Brains, and Sprains: Railway Spine and the Origins of Pyschoneuroses." *Bulletin of the History of Medicine* 69 (1995): 387–419.

Chamberlin, J. Edward, and Sander L. Gilman, eds. *Degeneration: The Dark Side of Progress.* New York: Columbia University Press, 1985.

Chickering, Roger, ed. *Imperial Germany: A Historiographic Companion.* Westport, Conn.: Greenwood Press, 1996.

——. *Imperial Germany and the Great War, 1914–1918.* Cambridge: Cambridge University Press, 1998.

——. "Total War: Use and Abuse of a Concept." In *Anticipating Total War: The German and American Experiences, 1871–1914,* edited by Manfred Boemeke, Roger Chickering, and Stig Förster. 13–28. New York: Cambridge University Press, 1998.

Chickering, Roger, and Stig Förster, eds. *Great War, Total War: Combat and Mobilization on the Western Front.* New York: Cambridge University Press, 2000.

Childers, Thomas, and Jane Caplan, eds. *Reevaluating the Third Reich.* New York: Holmes and Meier, 1993.

Cocks, Geoffrey. "The Old As New: The Nuremberg Doctors' Trial and Medicine in Modern Germany." In *Treating Mind and Body: Essays in the History of Science, Professions, and Society under Extreme Conditions.* 193–213. New Brunswick: Rutgers University Press, 1998.

——. *Psychotherapy in the Third Reich.* 2d ed. New Brunswick, N.J.: Transaction, 1997.

Cocks, Geoffrey, and Konrad Jarausch, eds. *German Professions, 1800–1950.* New York: Oxford University Press, 1990.

Cohen, Deborah. *The War Come Home: Disabled Veterans in Britain and Germany, 1914–1939.* Berkeley: University of California Press, 2001.

Confino, Alon. "Collective Memory and Cultural History: Problems of Method." *American Historical Review* 102 (1997): 1386–1403.

Cooter, Roger. "Malingering in Modernity." In *War, Medicine, and Modernity,* edited by Roger Cooter, Mark Harrison, and Steve Sturdy. 125–48. Sutton: Phoenix Mill, UK, 1998.

Cooter, Roger, and Steve Sturdy. "Of War, Medicine, and Modernity: An Introduction." In *War, Medicine, and Modernity,* edited by Roger Cooter, Mark Harrison, and Steve Sturdy. 1–21. Sutton: Phoenix Mill, UK, 1998.

Cox, Caroline. "Invisible Wounds: The American Legion, Shell-shocked Veterans, and Mental Illness, 1919–1924." In *Traumatic Pasts: History, Psychiatry, and Trauma in the Modern Age, 1870–1930,* edited by Mark S. Micale and Paul Lerner. 280–305. New York: Cambridge University Press, 2001.

Crew, David F. *Germans on Welfare: From Weimar to Hitler.* New York: Oxford University Press, 1998.

Daniel, Ute. *The War from Within: German Working-Class Women and the First World War.* New York: Berg, 1997.

——. "Women's Work in Industry and Family, Germany, 1914–1918." In *The Upheaval of War: Family, Work, and Welfare in Europe, 1914–1918,* edited by Richard Wall and Jay M. Winter. 267–96. Cambridge: Cambridge University Press, 1988.

Daum, Andreas. "Science, Politics, and Religion: Humboldtian Thinking and the Transformations of Civil Society in Germany, 1830–1870." *Osiris,* 2d ser., 17 (spring 2002): 107–40.

Davis, Belinda. *Home Fires Burning: Food, Politics, and Everyday Life in World War I Berlin.* Chapel Hill: University of North Carolina Press, 2000.

Dean, Carolyn. "The Great War, Pornography, and the Transformation of Modern Male Subjectivity." *Modernism/Modernity* 3 (1996): 59–72.

Dean, Eric T., Jr. *Shook over Hell: Post-traumatic Stress, Vietnam and the Civil War.* Cambridge, Mass: Harvard University Press, 1997.

——. "War and Psychiatry: Examining the Diffusion Theory in Light of the Insanity Defense in Post–World War I Britain." *History of Psychiatry* 4 (1993): 61–82.

Decker, Hannah S. *Freud in Germany: Revolution and Reaction in Science, 1893–1907.* New York: International Universities Press, 1977.

Doherty, Brigid. "Berlin Dada: Montage and the Embodiment of Modernity, 1916–1921." Ph.D. diss., University of California at Berkeley, 1996.

——. "'See: We Are All Neurasthenics,' or the Trauma of Dada Montage." *Critical Inquiry* 24 (1997): 82–132.

Domansky, Elisabeth. "Der Erste Weltkrieg." In *Bürgerliche Gesellschaft in Deutschland: Historische Einblicke, Fragen, Perspektiven,* edited by Lutz Niethammer et al. 285–322. Frankfurt: Fischer, 1990.

——. "Militarization and Reproduction in World War I Germany." In *Society, Culture, and the State in Germany, 1870–1930,* edited by Geoff Eley. 427–64. Ann Arbor: University of Michigan Press, 1996.

Dörner, Klaus. *Madmen and the Bourgeoisie: A Social History of Insanity and Psychiatry.* Translated by Joachim Neugroschel and Jean Steinberg. Oxford: Blackwell, 1981.

Dowbiggin, Ian. *Keeping America Sane: Psychiatry and Eugenics in the United States and Canada, 1880–1940.* Ithaca: Cornell University Press, 1997.

Drinka, George Frederick. *The Birth of Neurosis: Myth, Malady, and the Victorians.* New York: Simon and Schuster, 1984.

Easton, Laird M. *The Red Count: The Life and Times of Harry Kessler.* Berkeley: University of California Press, 2002.

Eberle, Matthias. *World War I and the Weimar Artists.* Translated by John Gabriel. New Haven: Yale University Press, 1985.

Eckart, Wolfgang U. "'The Most Extensive Experiment that the Imagination Can Conceive': War, Emotional Stress and German Medicine, 1914–1918." In *Great War, Total War: Combat and Mobilization on the Western Front,* edited by Roger Chickering and Stig Förster. 133–49. New York: Cambridge University Press, 2000.

Eckart, Wolfgang U., and Christoph Gradmann, eds. *Die Medizin und der Erste Weltkrieg.* Pfaffenweiler: Centaurus-Verlag, 1996.

Efron, John M. *Medicine and the German Jews: A History.* New Haven: Yale University Press, 2001.

Eghigian, Greg. "Die Bürokratie und das Entstehen von Krankheit. Die Politik und die Rentenneurosen, 1890–1926." In *Stadt und Gesundheit. Zum Wandel von Volksgesundheit und kommunaler Gesundheitspolitik im 19. und frühen 20. Jahrhundert,* edited by Jürgen Reulecke and Adelheit Gräfin zu Castell-Rüdenhausen. 203–23. Stuttgart: Steiner, 1991.

——. "The German Welfare State As a Discourse of Trauma." In *Traumatic Pasts: History, Psychiatry, and Trauma in the Modern Age, 1870–1930,* edited by Mark S. Micale and Paul Lerner. 92–112. New York: Cambridge University Press, 2001.

——. *Making Security Social: Disability, Insurance, and the Birth of the Social Entitlement State in Germany.* Ann Arbor: University of Michigan Press, 2000.

——. "The Politics of Victimization: Social Pensioners and the German Social State in the Inflation, 1919–1925." *Central European History* 26 (1993): 375–404.

Eissler, Kurt R. *Freud As an Expert Witness: The Discussion of War Neuroses between Freud and Wagner-Jauregg.* Translated by Christine Trollope. Madison, Wisc.: International Universities Press, 1986.

Eksteins, Modris. *Rites of Spring: The Great War and the Birth of the Modern Age.* Boston: Houghton Mifflin, 1989.

Eley, Geoff. "German History and the Contradictions of Modernity." In *Society, Culture, and the State in Germany, 1870–1930,* edited by Geoff Eley. 67–103. Ann Arbor: University of Michigan Press, 1996.

——. "Introduction: Is There a History of the *Kaiserreich*?" In *Society, Culture, and the State in Germany, 1870–1930,* edited by Geoff Eley. 1–42. Ann Arbor: University of Michigan Press, 1996.

——, ed. *Society, Culture, and the State in Germany, 1870–1930.* Ann Arbor: University of Michigan Press, 1996.

Ellenberger, Henri F. *The Discovery of the Unconscious: The History and Evolution of Dynamic Psychiatry.* New York: Basic Books, 1970.

Engstrom, Eric J. "The Birth of Clinical Psychiatry: Power, Knowledge, and Professionalization in Germany, 1867–1914." Ph.D. diss, University of North Carolina at Chapel Hill, 1997.

Eulner, H. H. *Die Entwicklung der medizinischen Spezialfächer an den Universitäten des deutschen Sprachgebietes.* Stuttgart: Enke, 1970.

Fallend, Karl, Bernhard Handlbauer, Werner Kienreich, Johannes Reichmayr, and Marion Steiner. "Psychoanalyse bis 1945." In *Geschichte der deutschen Psychologie im 20. Jahrhundert: Ein Überblick,* edited by Mitchell Ash and Ulfried Geuter. 113–46. Opladen: Westdeutscher Verlag, 1985.

Feldman, Gerald. *Army, Industry, and Labor.* Princeton: Princeton University Press, 1966.

——. *The Great Disorder: Politics, Economics, and Society in the German Inflation, 1914–1924.* New York: Oxford University Press, 1997.

Feudtner, Chris. "'Minds the Dead Have Ravished': Shell Shock, History, and the Ecology of Disease-Systems." *History of Science* 31 (1993): 377–420.

Fischer-Homburger, Esther. "Der Erste Weltkrieg und die Krise der ärztlichen Ethik." In *Medizin und Krieg: Vom Dilemma der Heilberufe 1865 bis 1985,* edited by Johanna Bleker and Heinz-Peter Schmiedebach. 122–34. Frankfurt: Fischer, 1987.

——. *Die traumatische Neurose: Vom somatischen zum sozialen Leiden.* Bern: Hans Huber, 1975.

Foucault, Michel. *Discipline and Punish: The Birth of the Prison.* Translated by Alan Sheridan. New York: Vintage, 1978.

——. *Madness and Civilization: A History of Insanity in the Age of Reason.* Translated by Richard Howard. New York: Vintage, 1965.

——. *Power/Knowledge: Selected Interviews and Other Writings, 1972–1977.* Edited and translated by Colin Gordon. New York: Pantheon, 1980.

Frevert, Ute. "Bourgeois Honor: Middle-Class Duellists in Germany from the Late Eighteenth Century to the Early Twentieth Century." In *The German Bourgeoisie: Essays on the Social History of the German Middle Class from the Late Eighteenth to the Early Twentieth Century,* edited by David Blackbourn and Richard J. Evans. 255–92. London: Routledge, 1991.

——. *Ehrenmänner: Das Duell in der bürgerlichen Gesellschaft.* Munich: Beck, 1991.

Friedlander, Henry. *The Origins of Nazi Genocide: From Euthasia to the Final Solution.* Chapel Hill: University of North Carolina Press, 1995.

Fritzsche, Peter. "The Case of Modern Memory." *Journal of Modern History* 73 (2001): 87–117.

——. *Germans into Nazis.* Cambridge: Harvard University Press, 1998.

——. *A Nation of Fliers: German Aviation and the Popular Imagination.* Cambridge: Harvard University Press, 1992.

Fritzsche, Peter, and Alon Confino, eds. *The Work of Memory: New Directions in the Study of German Society and Culture.* Urbana: University of Illinois Press, 2002.

Fussell, Paul. *The Great War and Modern Memory.* New York: Oxford University Press, 1975.

Gauld, Alan. *A History of Hypnotism.* Cambridge: Cambridge University Press, 1992.

Geuter, Ulfried. "Polemos Panton Pater—Militär und Psychologie im deutschen Reich 1914–1945." In *Geschichte der deutschen Psychologie im 20. Jahrhundert. Ein Überblick,* edited by Ulfried Geuter and Mitchell Ash. 113–146. Opladen: Westdeutscher Verlag, 1985.

——. *Die Professionalisierung der deutschen Psychologie im Nationalsozialismus.* Frankfurt: Suhrkamp, 1988.

Geyer, Martin H. *Vekehrte Welt: Revolution, Inflation und Moderne, München, 1914–1924.* Göttingen: Vandenhoeck and Ruprecht, 1998.

Geyer, Michael. *Deutsche Rüstungspolitik, 1860–1980.* Frankfurt: Suhrkamp, 1984.

——. "Ein Vorbote des Wohlfahrtstaates. Die Kriegsopferversorgung in Frankreich, Deutschland und Großbritannien nach dem Ersten Weltkrieg." *Geschichte und Gesellschaft* 9 (1983): 230–77.

——. "Insurrectionary Warfare: The German Debate about a *Levée en Masse* in October 1918." *Journal of Modern History* 73 (2001): 459–527.

——. "The Place of World War II in German Memory and History." *New German Critique* 71 (1997): 5–40.

Gilman, Sander L. *The Case of Sigmund Freud: Medicine and Identity at the Fin de Siècle.* Baltimore: Johns Hopkins University Press, 1993.

——. "The Image of the Hysteric." In *Hysteria Beyond Freud,* edited by Sander L. Gilman et al. 345–452. Berkeley: University of California Press, 1993.

——. "The Jewish Psyche: Freud, Dora, and the Idea of the Hysteric." In *The Jew's Body.* 60–104. New York: Routledge, 1991.

——. "The Struggle of Psychiatry with Psychoanalysis: Who Won?" *Critical Inquiry* 13 (1987): 293–313.

Gilman, Sander L., Helen King, Roy Porter, G. S. Rousseau, and Elaine Showalter. *Hysteria Beyond Freud.* Berkeley: University of California Press, 1993.

Goldberg, Ann. "The Mellage Case: Psychiatric Reform and Wilhelmine Politics." *Journal of Modern History* 74 (2002): 1–32.

——. "A Reinvented Public: Lunatics' Rights and Bourgeois Populism in the Kaiserreich." *German History.* Forthcoming.

——. *Sex, Religion, and the Making of Modern Madness.* New York: Oxford University Press, 1999.

Goldstein, Jan. *Console and Classify: The French Psychiatric Profession in the Nineteenth Century.* Cambridge: Cambridge University Press, 1987.

Grossmann, Atina. "*Girlkultur* or the Thoroughly Rationalized Female." In *Women in Culture and Politics,* edited by J. Friedlander. 62–80. Bloomington: University of Indiana Press, 1986.

——. "The New Woman and the Rationalization of Sexuality in Weimar Germany." In

Powers of Desire: The Politics of Sexuality, edited by Ann Snitow, Christine Stansell, and Sharon Thompson. 159–71. New York: Monthly Review Press, 1983.

——. *Reforming Sex: The German Movement for Birth Control and Abortion Reform, 1920–1950.* New York: Oxford University Press, 1995.

Hacking, Ian. *Rewriting the Soul: Multiple Personality and the Sciences of Memory.* Princeton: Princeton University Press, 1995.

Hahn, Susanne. "'Widerstandslose, minderwertige Individuen.' Der Erste Weltkrieg und das Selbstmordproblem in Deutschland." In *Die Medizin und der Erste Weltkrieg,* edited by Wolfgang Eckart and Christoph Gradmann. 273–97. Pfaffenweiler: Centaurus, 1996.

Halbwachs, Maurice. *On Collective Memory.* Translated by Lewis Coser. Chicago: University of Chicago Press, 1992.

Harrington, Anne. "Hysteria, Hypnosis, and the Lure of the Invisible: The Rise of Neomesmerism in Fin-de-Siècle French Psychiatry." In *The Anatomy of Madness,* edited by William F. Bynum, Roy Porter, and Michael Shepherd. Vol. 3. 226–46. London: Routledge, 1989.

Harris, Ruth. *Murders and Madness: Medicine, Law, and Society in the Fin de Siècle.* Oxford: Oxford University Press, 1987.

Herf, Jeffrey. *Reactionary Modernism: Technology, Culture, and Politics in Weimar and the Third Reich.* Cambridge: Cambridge University Press, 1984.

Heuerkamp, Claudia. "Ärzte und Professionalisierung in Deutschland: Überlegungen zum Wandel des Arztberufs im 19. Jahrhundert." *Geschichte und Gesellschaft* 6 (1980): 349–66.

Hirschmüller, Albrecht. *Freud's Begegnung mit der Psychiatrie: Von der Hirnmythologie zur Neurosenlehre.* Tübingen: Fuldauer Verlagsanstalt, 1991.

Hofer, Georg. "Nerven-Korrekturen: Ärzte, Soldaten, und die 'Kriegsneurosen' im Ersten Weltkrieg." *Zeitgeschichte* 27 (2000): 249–68.

Hoffmann, Louise E. "War, Revolution, and Psychoanalysis: Freudian Thought Begins to Grapple with Social Reality." *Journal of the History of the Behavioral Sciences* 17 (1981): 251–69.

Hong, Young-Sun. *Welfare, Modernity, and the Weimar State, 1919–1933.* Princeton: Princeton University Press, 1998.

Horn, Eva. "Erlebnis und Trauma: Die narrative Konstruktion des Ereignisses in Psychiatrie und Kriegsroman." In *Modernität und Trauma: Zum Zeitenbruch des Ersten Weltkrieges,* edited by Inka Mülder-Bach. 131–62. Vienna: Wiener Universitätsverlag, 2001.

Horne, John, ed. *State, Society, and Mobilization in Europe during the First World War.* Cambridge: Cambridge University Press, 1997.

Howard, Michael. *War in European History.* Oxford: Oxford University Press, 1976.

Hubenstorf, Michael. "Elektrizität und Medizin." In *Technik und Medizin,* edited by Rolf Winau. 241–57. Düsseldorf: VDI Verlag, 1993.

Hüppauf, Bernd, ed. *Ansichten vom Krieg: Vergleichende Studien zum Ersten Weltkrieg in Literatur und Gesellschaft.* Meisenheim: Hain, 1984.

——. "Experiences of Modern Warfare and the Crisis of Representation." *New German Critique* 59 (1993): 41–76.

——. "Langemarck, Verdun, and the Myth of a *New Man* in Germany after the First World War." *War and Society* 6 (1988): 70–101.

Israëls, Hans, and Morton Schatzman. "The Seduction Theory." *History of Psychiatry* 4 (1993): 23–59.

Jakobi, Helga, Peter Chroust, and Matthias Hamann. *Aeskulap und Hakenkreuz: Zur Geschichte der medizinischen Fakultät in Giessen zwischen 1933 und 1945.* Giessen: Allgemeines Studentenauschuß der Studentschaft der Justus-Liebig-Universität, 1982.

Jarausch, Konrad. *Students, Society, and Politics in Imperial Germany: The Rise of Academic Illiberalism.* Princeton: Princeton University Press, 1982.

Jens, Gerd Udo. *Die neurologisch-psychiatrischen Vorträge in der Abteilung für Neurologie und Psychiatrie der Gesellschaft deutscher Naturforscher und Ärzte von 1886 bis 1913.* Diss. med., Freie Universität Berlin, 1991.

Jeschal, Godwin. *Politik und Wissenschaft deutscher Ärzte im Ersten Weltkrieg.* Pattenson: Horst Willem Verlag, 1979.

Johnson, Jeffrey Allan. *The Kaiser's Chemists: Science and Modernization in Imperial Germany.* Chapel Hill: University of North Carolina Press, 1990.

Jones, Ernest. *Life and Work of Sigmund Freud.* 3 vols. New York: Basic Books, 1955.

Kaes, Anton. "The Cold Gaze: Mobilization and Modernity." *New German Critique* 59 (1993): 105–17.

——. *Wounded Nation: Film, Trauma, and Weimar Germany.* Princeton: Princeton University Press, forthcoming.

——. "War—Film—Trauma." In *Modernität und Trauma: Zum Zeitenbruch des Ersten Weltkrieges,* edited by Inka Mülder-Bach. 121–30. Vienna: Wiener Universitätsverlag, 2000.

Kaes, Anton, Martin Jay, and Edward Dimendberg, eds. *The Weimar Republic Sourcebook.* Berkeley: University of California Press, 1994.

Kater, Michael. *Doctors under Hitler.* Chapel Hill: University of North Carolina Press, 1989.

——. "Professionalization and Socialization of Physicians in Wilhelmine and Weimar Germany." *Journal of Contemporary History* 20 (1985): 677–701.

Kaufmann, Doris. "Science As Cultural Practice: Psychiatry in the First World War and Weimar Germany." *Journal of Contemporary History* 34 (1999): 125–44.

Kershaw, Ian. *Hitler.* Vol. 1, *1889–1936: Hubris.* New York: Norton, 1998.

Kevles, Daniel. "Testing the Army's Intelligence: Psychologists and the Military in World War I." *Journal of American History* 55 (1968): 565–81.

Kienitz, Sabine. "Der Krieg der Invaliden. Helden-Bilder und Männlichkeitskonstruktionen nach dem Ersten Weltkrieg." *Militärgeschichtliche Zeitschrift* 60 (2001): 367–402.

Kocka, Jürgen. *Facing Total War: German Society, 1914–1918.* Translated by Barbara Weinberger. Cambridge: Harvard University Press, 1984.

Komo, Günther. *"Für Volk und Vaterland": Militärpsychiatrie in den Weltkriegen.* Münster: Lit, 1992.

Koschorke, Albrecht. "Der Traumatiker als Fascist: Ernst Jünger's Essay 'Über den Schmerz.'" In *Modernität und Trauma: Beiträge zum Zeitenbruch des Ersten Weltkrieges.* 211–27. Vienna: Wiener Universitätsverlag, 2000.

Koven, Seth. "Remembering and Dismemberment." *American Historical Review* 99 (1994): 1167–1202.

Kreuter, Alma. *Deutschsprachige Neurologen und Psychiater: Ein biographisch-bibliographisches Lexikon von den Vorläufern bis zur Mitte des 20. Jahrhunderts.* 3 vols. Munich: Saur, 1996.

Kruse, W. "Die Kriegsbegeisterung im Deutschen Reich zu Beginn des Ersten Weltkrieges." In *Kriegsbegeisterung und mentale Kriegsvorbereitung*, edited by Marcel van der Linden and Gottfried Mergner. 57–89. Berlin: Duncker and Humblot, 1991.

Kühne, Thomas. *Männergeschichte, Geschlechtergeschichte: Männlichkeit im Wandel der Moderne*. Frankfurt: Campus, 1996.

Labisch, Alfons. *Homo Hygienicus: Gesundheit und Medizin in der Neuzeit*. Frankfurt: Campus Verlag, 1992.

Leed, Eric J. "Fateful Memories: Industrialized War and Traumatic Neuroses." *Journal of Contemporary History* 35 (2000): 85–100.

——. *No Man's Land: Combat and Identity in World War I*. Cambridge: Cambridge University Press, 1979.

Leese, Peter. *Shell Shock: Traumatic Neurosis and the British Soldiers of the First World War*. London: Macmillan, 2002.

Lemmens, Franz. "Funktion und Anspruchswandel der militärmedizinischen Tauglich-keitsbeurteilung in Deutschland zwischen 1914 und 1945, dargestellt am Beispiel der Psychiatrie und Neurologie." In *Ergebnisse und Perspektiven sozialhistorischer Forschung in der Medizingeschichte. Kolloquium zum 100. Geburtstag von Henry Sigerist*, edited by Susanne Hahn and Achim Thom. 164–73. Leipzig: Karl-Sudhoff-Institut, 1991.

Lerner, Paul. "From Traumatic Neurosis to Male Hysteria: The Decline and Fall of Hermann Oppenheim, 1889–1919." In *Traumatic Pasts: History, Psychiatry, and Trauma in the Modern Age, 1870–1930*, edited by Mark S. Micale and Paul Lerner. 140–71. New York: Cambridge University Press, 2001.

——. "Hysterical Cures: Hypnosis, Gender, and Performance in World War I and Weimar Germany." *History Workshop Journal* 45 (1998): 79–101.

Lerner, Paul, and Mark S. Micale. "Trauma, Psychiatry, and History: A Conceptual and Historiographical Introduction." In *Traumatic Pasts: History, Psychiatry, and Trauma in the Modern Age, 1870–1930*, edited by Mark S. Micale and Paul Lerner. 1–30. New York: Cambridge University Press, 2001.

Levin, Kenneth. "Freud's Paper 'On Male Hysteria' and the Conflict between Anatomical and Physiological Models." *Bulletin of the History of Medicine* 48 (1974): 377–97.

Leys, Ruth. *Trauma: A Genealogy*. Chicago: University of Chicago Press, 2000.

——. "Traumatic Cures: Shell Shock, Janet, and the Question of Memory." *Critical Inquiry* 20 (1994): 623–62.

Link-Heer, Ursula. "Männliche Hysterie: Eine Diskursanalyse." In *Weiblichkeit in geschichtlicher Perspektive*, edited by Ursula A. J. Becher and Jörn Rüsen. 364–96. Frankfurt: Suhrkamp, 1988.

McClelland, Charles E. *The German Experience of Professionalization: Modern Learned Professions and Their Organizations from the Early Nineteenth Century to the Hitler Era*. Cambridge: Cambridge University Press, 1991.

——. "Modern German Doctors: A Failure of Professionalization?" In *Medicine and Modernity: Public Health and Medical Care in Nineteenth- and Twentieth-Century Germany*, edited by Manfred Berg and Geoffrey Cocks. 81–98. New York: Cambridge University Press, 1997.

——. *State, Society, and University in Germany, 1700–1914*. Cambridge: Cambridge University Press, 1980.

Mendelssohn-Bartholdy, Albrecht. *The War and German Society: The Testament of a Liberal*. New Haven: Yale University Press, 1937.

Merridale, Catherine. "The Collective Mind: Trauma and Shell-shock in Twentieth-Century Russia." *Journal of Contemporary History* 35 (2000): 39–56.

Meyer zum Wischen, Michael. *"Der Seele Tiefen zu ergründen . . ." Robert Sommer und das Konzept einer ganzheitlichen, erweiterten Psychiatrie.* Giessen: Schmidt, 1988.

Micale, Mark S. *Approaching Hysteria: Disease and Its Interpretations.* Princeton: Princeton University Press, 1995.

——. "Charcot and the Idea of Hysteria in the Male: Gender, Mental Science, and Medical Diagnosis in Late Nineteenth-Century France." *Medical History* 34 (1990): 363–411.

——. "Hysteria Male/Hysteria Female: Reflections on Comparative Gender Construction in Nineteenth-Century France and Britain." In *Science and Sensibility: Gender and Scientific Enquiry, 1780–1945,* edited by Marina Benjamin. 200–42. Oxford: Oxford University Press, 1991.

——. "Jean-Martin Charcot and 'les névroses traumatiques': From Medicine to Culture in French Trauma Theory of the Late Nineteenth Century." In *Traumatic Pasts: History, Psychiatry, and Trauma in the Modern Age, 1870–1930,* edited by Mark S. Micale and Paul Lerner. 172–90. New York: Cambridge University Press, 2001.

——. "On the Disappearance of Hysteria: The Clinical Deconstruction of a Diagnosis." *Isis* 84 (1993): 496–526.

Micale, Mark S., and Paul Lerner, eds. *Traumatic Pasts: History, Psychiatry, and Trauma in the Modern Age, 1870–1930.* New York: Cambridge University Press, 2001.

Micale, Mark S., and Roy Porter, eds. *Discovering the History of Psychiatry.* New York: Oxford University Press, 1994.

Moeller, Robert. "The Kaiserreich Recast? Continuity and Change in Modern German Historiography." *Journal of Social History* 17 (1984): 655–83.

Mommsen, Wolfgang. "The Topos of Inevitable War in Germany in the Decade before 1914." In *Germany in the Age of Total War,* edited by Volker Berghahn and Martin Kitchen. 23–45. London: Croom Helm, 1981.

Moser, Gabriele. "Der Arzt im Kampf gegen 'Begehrlichkeit und Rentensucht' im deutschen Kaiserreich und in der Weimarer Republik." *Jahrbuch für kritische Medizin* 16 (1992): 161–83.

Mosse, George L. *Fallen Soldiers: Reshaping the Memory of the World Wars.* New York: Oxford University Press, 1990.

——. *The Image of Man: The Creation of Modern Masculinity.* New York: Oxford University Press, 1996.

——. "Masculinity and the Decadence." In *Sexual Knowledge, Sexual Science: The History of Attitudes to Sexuality,* edited by Roy Porter and Mikulás Teich. 134–57. Cambridge: Cambridge University Press, 1994.

Mosse, Werner E., ed. *Deutsches Judentum in Krieg und Revolution, 1916–1923.* Tübingen: Mohr, 1971.

Mülder-Bach, Inka, ed. *Modernität und Trauma: Beiträge zum Zeitenbruch des Ersten Weltkrieges.* Vienna: Wiener Universitätsverlag, 2000.

Nolan, Mary. *Visions of Modernity: American Business and the Modernization of Germany.* New York: Oxford University Press, 1994.

Nye, Robert A. *Crime, Madness, and Politics in Modern France: The Medical Concept of Decline.* Princeton: Princeton University Press, 1989.

——. *Masculinity and Male Codes of Honor in Modern France.* Berkeley: University of California Press, 1993.

Oppenheim, Janet. *The Other World: Spiritualism and Psychical Research in England.* Cambridge: Cambridge University Press, 1984.

——. *"Shattered Nerves": Doctors, Patients, and Depression in Victorian England.* New York: Oxford University Press, 1981.

Owen, Alex. *The Darkened Room: Women, Power, and Spiritualism in Late Victorian England.* Philadelphia: University of Pennsylvania Press, 1990.

Peukert, Detlev. "The Genesis of the 'Final Solution' from the Spirit of Science." In *Reevaluating the Third Reich,* edited by Thomas Childers and Jane Caplan. 234–52. New York: Holmes and Meier, 1993.

——. *The Weimar Republic: The Crisis of Classical Modernity.* Translated by Richard Deveson. New York: Hill and Wang, 1989.

Pick, Daniel. *Faces of Degeneration.* Cambridge: Cambridge University Press, 1989.

——. *Svengali's Web: The Alien Enchanter in Modern Culture.* New Haven: Yale University Press, 2000.

——. *War Machine: The Rationalisation of Slaughter in the Modern Age.* New Haven: Yale University Press, 1993.

Porter, Roy. "The Body and the Mind, the Doctor and the Patient: Negotiating Hysteria." In *Hysteria Beyond Freud,* edited by Sander Gilman et al. 225–85. Berkeley: University of California Press, 1993.

Proctor, Robert. *Racial Hygiene: Medicine under the Nazis.* Cambridge: Harvard University Press, 1987.

Pross, Christian, and Götz Aly, eds. *Der Wert des Menschen. Medizin in Deutschland, 1918–1945.* Berlin: Hentrich, 1989.

Rabinbach, Anson. *The Human Motor: Energy, Fatigue, and the Origins of Modernity.* New York: Basic Books, 1990.

Radkau, Joachim. "Die Wilhelminische Ära als nervöses Zeitalter, oder: Die Nerven als Netz zwischen Tempo- und Körpergeschichte." *Geschichte und Gesellschaft* 20 (1994): 211–41.

——. *Das Zeitalter der Nervosität. Deutschland zwischen Bismarck und Hitler.* Munich: Hanser, 2000.

Reese, Dagmar, et al., eds. *Rationale Beziehungen? Geschlechterverhältnisse im Rationalisierungsprozeß.* Frankfurt: Suhrkamp, 1993.

Reichmayr, Johannes. "Psychoanalyse im Krieg." In *Krieg und Frieden aus psychoanalytischer Sicht,* edited by P. Passet and E. Modena. 36–58. Frankfurt: Stroemfeld, 1983.

Riedesser, Peter, and Axel Verderber. *Aufrüstung der Seelen: Militärpsychiatrie und Militärpsychologie in Deutschland und Amerika.* Freiburg: Dreisam Verlag, 1985.

——. *Maschinengewehre hinter der Front: Zur Geschichte der deutschen Militärpsychiatrie.* Frankfurt: Fischer, 1996.

Ringer, Fritz. *The Decline of the German Mandarins.* Hanover, N.H.: University Press of New England, 1969.

Roth, Karl-Heinz. "Die Modernisierung der Folter in den beiden Weltkriegen." *1999: Zeitschrift für Sozialgeschichte des 20. und 21. Jahrhunderts* 2 (1987): 8–75.

Roth, Michael. "Hysterical Remembering." *Modernism/Modernity* 3 (1996): 1–30.

Roudebush, Marc. "A Battle of Nerves: Hysteria and Its Treatments in France during World War I." In *Traumatic Pasts: History, Psychiatry, and Trauma in the Modern Age, 1870–1930,* edited by Mark S. Micale and Paul Lerner. 253–79. New York: Cambridge University Press, 2001.

——. "A Battle of Nerves: Hysteria and Its Treatment in France during World War I." Ph.D. diss., University of California at Berkeley, 1995.

——. "Neurology in the Court of Public Opinion in France during the First World War." *Journal of Contemporary History* 35 (2000): 29–38.

Rowbottom, Margaret, and Charles Susskind. *Electricity and Medicine: A History of Their Interaction.* San Francisco: San Francisco Press, 1984.

Rürup, Reinhard. "Der Geist von 1914 in Deutschland. Kriegsbegeisterung und Ideologisierung des Krieges im Ersten Weltkrieg." In *Ansichten vom Krieg. Vergleichende Studien zum Ersten Weltkrieg in Literatur und Gesellschaft,* edited by Bernd Hüppauf. 1–30. Meisenheim: Hain, 1984.

Ryder, A. J. *The German Revolution of 1918: A Study of German Socialism in War and Revolt.* Cambridge: Cambridge University Press, 1967.

Samelson, Franz. "World War I Intelligence Testing and the Development of Psychology." *Journal of the History of the Behavioral Sciences* 13 (1977): 274–82.

Sauerteig, Lutz. *Krankheit, Sexualität, Gesellschaft: Geschlechtskrankheiten und Gesundheitspolitik im 19. und frühen 20. Jahrhundert.* Stuttgart: Steiner, 1999.

——. "Militär, Medizin, und Moral: Sexualität im Ersten Weltkrieg." In *Die Medizin und der Erste Weltkrieg,* edited by Wolfgang Eckart and Christoph Gradmann. 197–226. Pfaffenweiler: Centaurus, 1996.

Schäffner, Wolfgang. "Event, Series, Trauma: The Probabalistic Revolution of the Mind." In *Traumatic Pasts: History, Psychiatry, and Trauma in the Modern Age,* edited by Mark S. Micale and Paul Lerner. 81–91. New York: Cambridge University Press, 2001.

——. "Der Krieg ein Trauma: Zur Psychoanalyse der Kriegsneurose in Alfred Döblins *Hamlet.*" In *Hard War/Soft War: Krieg und Medien 1914–1945,* edited by Martin Stingelin and Wolfgang Scherer. 31–46. Munich: Fink Verlag, 1993.

——. *Die Ordnung des Wahns: Zur Poetologie psychiatrischen Wissens bei Alfred Döblin.* Munich: Fink, 1995.

Schaltenbrand, G. "Max Nonne." In *Grosse Nervenärzte,* edited by Kurt Kolle. Vol. 3. 164–73. Stuttgart: Thieme, 1963.

Schindler, Thomas-Peter. "Psychiatrie im wilhelminischen Deutschland im Spiegel der Verhandlungen des 'Vereins der deutschen Irrenärzte' (ab 1903: 'Deutscher Verein für Psychiatrie')." Diss. med., Freie Univesität Berlin, 1990.

Schivelbusch, Wolfgang. *The Railway Journey: The Industrialization of Time and Space in the Nineteenth Century.* Berkeley: University of California Press, 1977.

Schlich, Thomas. "'Welche Macht über Tod und Leben!' Die Etablierung der Bluttransfusion im Ersten Weltkrieg." In *Die Medizin und der Erste Weltkrieg,* edited by Wolfgang Eckart and Christoph Gradmann. 109–30. Pfaffenweiler: Centaurus, 1996.

Schmiedebach, Heinz-Peter. "Sozialdarwinismus, Biologismus, Pazifismus. Ärztestimmen zum Ersten Weltkrieg." In *Medizin und Krieg: Vom Dilemma der Heilberufe, 1865–1985,* edited by Johanna Bleker and Heinz-Peter Schmiedebach. 93–121. Frankfurt: Fischer, 1987.

——. "Die 'traumatische Neurose'—Soziale Versicherung und der Griff der Psychiatrie nach dem Unfallpatienten." In *Ergebnisse und Perspektiven sozialhistorischer Forschung in der Medizingeschichte. Kolloquium zum 100. Geburtstag von Henry Sigerist,* edited by Susanne Hahn and Achim Thom. 151–63. Leipzig: Karl-Sudhoff-Institut, 1991.

Schubert-Weller, Christoph. *"Kein schönrer Tod . . ." Die Militarisierung der männlichen Jugend und Ihr Einsatz im Ersten Weltkrieg.* Weinheim: Juventa, 1998.

Schultz, Ulrich, and Ludger M. Hermanns. "Die Entdeckung der Psychosomatik. Ernst Simmels psychoanalytische Klinik in Berlin-Tegel." In *Der Wert des Menschen: Medizin in Deutschland, 1918–1945,* edited by Christan Pross and Götz Aly. 50–67. Berlin: Berliner Ärztekammer, 1989.

Schwalbe, Klaus. *Wissenschaft und Kriegsmoral.* Göttingen: Musterschmidt Verlag, 1969.

Scull, Andrew. *Museums of Madness: The Social Organization of Insanity in Nineteenth-Century England.* New York: St. Martin's, 1979.

——. "Psychiatry and Its Historians." *History of Psychiatry* 1 (1990): 239–50.

——. "Psychiatry and Social Control in the Nineteenth and Twentieth Centuries." *History of Psychiatry* 2 (1991): 149–69.

——, ed. *Madhouses, Mad-doctors, and Madmen: The Social History of Insanity in the Victorian Era.* Philadelphia: University of Pennsylvania Press, 1981.

Shephard, Ben. *A War of Nerves: Soldiers and Psychiatrists, 1914–1994.* London: Cape, 2000.

Sherman, Daniel J. "Bodies and Names: The Emergence of Commemoration in Interwar France." *American Historical Review* 103 (1998): 443–66.

——. *The Construction of Memory in Interwar France.* Chicago: University of Chicago Press, 1999.

Shorter, Edward. *From Paralysis to Fatigue: A History of Psychosomatic Diseases in the Modern Era.* New York: Basic Books, 1992.

——. *A History of Psychiatry: From the Age of the Asylum to the Era of Prozac.* New York: Wiley, 1997.

——. "Mania, Hysteria, and Gender in Lower Austria, 1891–1905." *History of Psychiatry* 1 (1990): 3–31.

Showalter, Elaine. *The Female Malady: Women, Madness, and English Culture, 1830–1980.* New York: Penguin, 1985.

——. "Hysteria, Feminism, and Gender." In *Hysteria Beyond Freud,* edited by Sander L. Gilman et al. 286–344. Berkeley: University of California Press, 1993.

——. *Hystories: Hysterical Epidemics and Modern Media.* New York: Columbia University Press, 1997.

——. "Rivers and Sassoon: The Inscription of Male Gender Anxieties." In *Behind the Lines: Gender and the Two World Wars,* edited by Margaret Randolph Higonnet, Jane Jenson, Sonya Michel, and Margaret Collins Weitz, 61–69. New Haven: Yale University Press, 1987.

Siemen, Hans-Ludwig. *Das Grauen ist Vorprogrammiert: Psychiatrie zwischen Faschismus und Atomkrieg.* Giessen: Focus Verlag, 1982.

——. *Menschen Blieben auf der Strecke: Psychiatrie zwischen Reform und Nationalsozialismus.* Gütersloh: J. van Hoddis, 1987.

Slavney, Phillip R. *Perspectives on "Hysteria."* Baltimore: Johns Hopkins University Press, 1990.

Smith, Leonard. *Between Mutiny and Obedience: The Case of the French Fifth Infantry Division During World War I.* Princeton: Princeton University Press, 1994.

Smith-Rosenberg, Carroll. *Disorderly Conduct: Visions of Gender in Victorian America.* New York: Knopf, 1985.

Sombart, Nicolaus. "The Kaiser in His Epoch: Some Reflections on Wilhelmine Society, Sexuality, and Culture." In *Kaiser Wilhelm II: New Interpretations,* edited by Nicolaus Sombart and John C. G. Röhl. 287–312. Cambridge: Cambridge University Press, 1982.

Stainbrook, Edward. "The Use of Electricity in Psychiatric Treatment During the Nineteenth Century." *Bulletin of the History of Medicine* 22 (1948): 56–177.

Stone, Martin. "Shellshock and the Psychologists." In *The Anatomy of Madness,* edited by W. F. Bynum, Roy Porter, and Michael Shepard. Vol. 2. 242–71. London: Tavistock, 1985.

Tamm, Ingo. "'Ein Stand im Dienst der nationalen Sache': Positionen und Aufgaben der ärztlichen Standesorganizationen im Ersten Weltkrieg." In *Die Medizin und der Erste Weltkrieg,* edited by Wolfgang Eckart and Christoph Gradmann. 11–21. Pfaffenweiler: Centaurus, 1996.

Theweleit, Klaus. *Male Fantasies.* Vol. 1, *Women Floods Bodies History,* translated by Stephen Conway. Minneapolis: University of Minnesota Press, 1987.

———. *Male Fantasies.* Vol. 2, *Male Bodies: Psychoanalyzing the White Terror,* translated by Erica Carter and Chris Turner. Minneapolis: University of Minnesota Press, 1989.

Thomann, K.-D. "'Es gibt kein Krüppeltum, wenn der eiserne Wille vorhanden ist, es zu überwinden!' Konrad Biesalski und die Kriegsbeschädigtenfürsorge, 1914–1918." *Medizinisch orthopädische Technik* 114 (1994): 114–21.

Thomson, Mathew. *The Problem of Mental Deficiency: Eugenics, Democracy, and Social Policy in Britain, ca. 1870–1959.* New York: Oxford University Press, 1998.

———. "Status, Manpower, and Mental Fitness: Mental Deficiency in the First World War." In *War, Medicine, and Modernity,* edited by Roger Cooter, Mark Harrison, and Steve Sturdy. 149–66. Sutton: Phoenix Mill, UK, 1998.

Treitel, Corinna. "Avatars of the Soul: Cultures of Science, Medicine, and the Occult in Modern Germany." Ph.D. diss., Harvard University, 1999.

Triebel, Armin. "Variations in Patterns of Consumption in Germany in the Period of the First World War." In *The Upheaval of War: Family, Work, and Welfare in Europe, 1914–1918,* edited by Richard Wall and Jay Winter. 159–96. Cambridge: Cambridge University Press, 1988.

Trimble, Michael. *Post-Traumatic Neurosis: From Railway Spine to Whiplash.* New York: Wiley, 1981.

Tröger, Annemarie. "The Creation of a Female Assembly-Line Proletariat." In *When Biology Became Destiny: Women in Weimar and Nazi Germany,* edited by Renate Bridenthal, Atina Grossmann, and Marion Kaplan. 237–69. New York: Monthly Review Press, 1984.

Ulrich, Bernd. "Die Desillusionierung der Kriegsfreiwilligen von 1914." In *Der Krieg des kleinen Mannes: Eine Militärgeschichte von Unten,* edited by Wolfram Wette. 110–27. Munich: Piper, 1992.

———. "Krieg als Nervensache." *Die Zeit,* November 22, 1991.

———. "Nerven und Krieg: Skizzierung einer Beziehung." In *Geschichte und Psychologie: Annäherungsversuche,* edited by Bedrich Loewenstein. 163–91. Pfaffenweiler: Centaurus, 1992.

Ulrich, Bernd, and Benjamin Ziemann, eds. *Frontalltag im Ersten Weltkrieg: Wahn und Wirklichkeit.* Frankfurt: Fischer, 1994.

——, eds. *Krieg im Frieden: Die umkämpfte Erinnerung an den Ersten Weltkrieg.* Frankfurt: Fischer, 1997.

van der Hart, Onno, Paul Brown, and Bessel A. van der Kolk. "Pierre Janet's Treatment of Post-traumatic Stress." *Journal of Traumatic Stress* 2 (1989): 379–95.

van der Hart, Onno, and Barbara Friedman. "A Reader's Guide to Pierre Janet on Dissociation: A Neglected Intellectual Heritage." *Dissociation* 2 (1989): 3–16.

Veith, Ilza. *Hysteria: The History of a Disease.* Chicago: University of Chicago Press, 1965.

Verhey, Jeffrey. *The Spirit of 1914: Militarism, Myth, and Mobilization in Germany.* Cambridge: Cambridge University Press, 2000.

Walter, Bernd. *Psychiatrie und Gesellschaft in der Moderne: Geisteskrankenfürsorge in der Provinz Westfalen zwischen Kaiserreich und NS-Regime.* Paderborn: Schöningh, 1996.

Weber, Matthias M. *Ernst Rüdin: Eine klinische Biographie.* Berlin: Springer, 1994.

——. "'Ein Forschungsinstitut für Psychiatrie . . .' Die Entwicklung der deutschen Forschungsanstalt für Psychiatrie in München zwischen 1917 und 1945." *Sudhoffs Archiv für Geschichte der Medizin* 75 (1991): 74–89.

Weber, Max. "On Bureaucracy." In *From Max Weber,* edited and translated by H. Gerth and C. Wright Mills. 196–244. London: Routledge, 1948.

——. "Science As a Vocation." In *From Max Weber,* edited and translated by H. Gerth and C. Wright Mills. 129–56. London: Routledge, 1948.

Weindling, Paul J. "Bourgeois Values, Doctors, and the State: The Professionalization of Medicine in Germany, 1848–1933." In *The German Bourgeoisie: Essays on the Social History of the German Middle Class from the Late Eighteenth Century to the Early Twentieth Century,* edited by David Blackbourn and Richard J. Evans. 198–223. London: Routledge, 1991.

——. *Health, Race, and German Politics between National Unification and Nazism, 1870–1945.* Cambridge: Cambridge University Press, 1989.

——. "The Medical Profession, Social Hygiene, and the Birth Rate in Germany, 1914–1918." In *The Upheaval of War: Family, Work, and Welfare in Europe, 1914–1918,* edited by Richard Wall and Jay Winter. 417–38. Cambridge: Cambridge University Press, 1988.

Weiner, Dora B. *Comprendre et Soigner: Philippe Pinel, 1745–1826: La médecine de l'esprit.* Paris: Fayard, 1999.

——. "'Le geste de Pinel': The History of a Psychiatric Myth." In *Discovering the History of Psychiatry,* edited by Mark S. Micale and Roy Porter. 232–47. New York: Oxford University Press, 1994.

Weingart, Peter, Jürgen Kroll, and Kurt Bayertz. *Rasse, Blut, und Gene: Geschichte der Eugenik und Rassenhygiene in Deutschland.* Frankfurt: Suhrkamp, 1998.

Weiss, Sheila Faith. *Race Hygiene and National Efficiency: The Eugenics of Wilhelm Schallmeyer.* Berkeley: University of California Press, 1987.

Weitz, Eric D. *Creating German Communism, 1890–1990.* Princeton: Princeton University Press, 1997.

Wetzel, Richard F. *Inventing the Criminal: A History of German Criminology, 1880–1945.* Chapel Hill: University of North Carolina Press, 2000.

Whalen, Robert W. *Bitter Wounds: German Victims of the First World War.* Ithaca: Cornell University Press, 1984.

Widdig, Bernd. *Culture and Inflation in Weimar Germany.* Berkeley: University of California Press, 2001.

Winter, Jay. "Shell-shock and the Cultural History of the Great War." *Journal of Contemporary History* 35 (2000): 7–11.

——. *Sites of Memory, Sites of Mourning: The Great War in European Cultural History.* Cambridge: Cambridge University Press, 1995.

Winter, Jay, and Jean-Louis Robert, eds. *Capital Cities at War: London, Paris, Berlin, 1914–1919.* Cambridge: Cambridge University Press, 1997.

Young, Allan. "Bodily Memory and Traumatic Memory." In *Tense Past: Cultural Essays in Trauma and Memory,* edited by Paul Antze and Michael Lambek. 89–102. New York: Routledge, 1996.

——. *The Harmony of Illusions: Inventing Post-Traumatic Stress Disorder.* Princeton: Princeton University Press, 1995.

Zeller, G. "Die Hysterielehre." In *Karl Bonhoeffer zum Hundersten Geburtstag am 31. März 1968,* edited by J. Zutt, E. Straus, and H. Scheller. 126–29. Berlin: Springer, 1969.

Ziemann, Benjamin. *Front und Heimat: Ländliche Kriegserfahrungen im südlichen Bayern, 1914–1923.* Essen: Klarfeld, 1997.

Index

CORNELL STUDIES IN THE HISTORY OF PSYCHIATRY
  A series edited by
  Sander L. Gilman
  George J. Makari

Keeping America Sane: Psychiatry and Eugenics in the United States and Canada, 1880–1940
  by Ian Robert Dowbiggin

Dreams 1900–2000: Science, Art, and the Unconscious Mind
  edited by Lynn Gamwell

Madness in America: Cultural and Medical Perceptions of Mental Illness before 1914
  by Lynn Gamwell and Nancy Tomes

Freud and His Aphasia Book: Language and the Sources of Psychoanalysis
  by Valerie D. Greenberg

Hysterical Men: War, Psychiatry, and the Politics of Trauma in Germany, 1890–1930
  by Paul Lerner

The Mastery of Submission: Inventions of Masochism
  by John K. Noyes

Reading Psychoanalysis: Freud, Rank, Ferenczi, Groddeck
  by Peter L. Rudnytsky

Adolf Wölfli: Draftsman, Writer, Poet, Composer
  edited by Elka Spoerri

Sublime Surrender: Male Masochism at the Fin-de-Siècle
  by Suzanne R. Stewart